Contractor's Guide to the Building Code Revised

by

Jack M. Hageman

Craftsman Book Company
6058 Corte del Cedro, P. O. Box 6500, Carlsbad, CA 92008

Acknowledgements

The author expresses his thanks to the International Conference of Building Officials and to the International Association of Plumbing and Mechanical Officials for their assistance and permission to use charts, tables and quotes from their respective books, the *Uniform Building Code*, the *Uniform Plumbing Code*, and the *Uniform Mechanical Code*.

All portions of the Uniform Building Code, except where otherwise noted, are reproduced from the 1988 edition, ©1988, with permission of the publisher, the International Conference of Building Officials.

Portions of the Uniform Plumbing Code are reproduced with permission of the publisher, the International Association of Plumbing and Mechanical Officials.

Portions of the Uniform Mechanical Code are reproduced with permission of the publishers, the International Association of Plumbing and Mechanical Officials and the International Conference of Building Officials.

The interpretation and comments listed herein are solely the responsibility of the author and should bear no reflection on the publishers of the Uniform Building Code, the Uniform Plumbing Code, the Uniform Mechanical Code, or the publishers of this book.

Library of Congress Cataloging-in-Publication Data

Hageman, Jack M.

Contractor's guide to the building code.

1. Building laws—-United States.   I. Title.

KF5701.H34   1990   343.73'07869   89-71177

ISBN 0-934041-52-0   347.3037869

First edition   © 1983 Craftsman Book Company
Second edition   © 1990 Craftsman Book Company
Second printing 1990

Cartoons by John R. Hageman

Contents

This Is the Second Edition

The first edition of this manual appeared in 1983. It was intended, as the title made clear, to be a contractor's guide to the 1982 Uniform Building Code.

Nearly everyone who has tried to understand the code will agree that this guide was badly needed. The code is today (and was in 1983) a complex document written by hundreds of authors and amended, supplemented, revised, and interpreted thousands of times. Building inspectors make a career out of learning and applying the code. I know. I was one once. But contractors can't (and shouldn't have to) spend a career learning how to follow the code. Contractors have better things to do. I know. I was a construction contractor once too. So I wrote a book that I hoped would make it easy to understand what the code required.

I must have done something right, because close to fifty thousand copies of that first edition have been sold nationwide — to contractors, of course, but also to homeowners, architects, engineers, students, tradesmen, libraries and even to building inspectors.

Since the first 1983 edition of this book, the Uniform Building Code has been revised twice, once in 1985 and again in 1988. Most of these revisions were clarifications of the existing code and didn't affect the way you build. I didn't feel that these changes were important enough to make revision of this book necessary. Some changes were to design standards and didn't affect contractors directly. Other changes in the code were little more than editorial polishing. The authors of the code were trying to weave heavily amended and revised sections into a coherent whole that made sense — at least to other inspectors.

But as 1990 approached, the code had changed enough to make revision of this book essential. And as code changes were accumulating, my own thinking about the purpose of this manual was also changing. Originally I intended this book as a guide to the Uniform Building Code alone, not to any of the other building codes. But I began to see that covering the UBC wasn't enough. Most construction contractors would rather have a single guide that answered all their code questions on any residential or light commercial project. That's why I've added chapters that explain the Uniform Mechanical Code for heating, ventilation and air conditioning and the Uniform Plumbing Code for plumbing and piping. And I've also corrected an oversight brought to my attention by many readers. This revised edition has complete wood span tables from Chapter 25 of the UBC.

Since this book was first published, I've been asked many times why the code has to be so complicated. Why do the authors keep adding more sections? Isn't the code too big already? In short, how much law is too much law?

To answer that question I have to go back to a statement in the first edition, ". . . *most requirements in the UBC are the results of problems developed in the field. . . .*" Sometimes the problem was an accident that caused a loss or injury. If a change in the building code could have prevented that loss or avoided that injury, you can bet that someone will propose making a code change. I think we can all agree that public safety is the primary purpose of the code. So as long as there are losses, the code will keep growing and changing.

But the code serves another purpose. It's the tool inspectors use to promote what they consider sound construction practice. Unfortunately, the code is an imperfect tool for this purpose. Anyone with the desire and a little ingenuity can find plenty of loopholes in it. Maybe you've tried to do that yourself. And maybe it worked. Many builders, either out of ignorance or in an effort to make a few extra bucks, try to avoid complying with the *spirit* or intention of the code. Ignorance I can excuse, at least for a while. Nobody knows everything about the building code. But cutting corners to make a better profit is another matter.

Of course, I'm practical enough to realize that profit is the name of the game in construction contracting. Without profit there wouldn't be anyone in the business. If builders couldn't make a profit, we'd probably still be living in lean-tos, tents, and caves. But where profit becomes more important than safety or human life, someone's got to take charge. And inspectors have. Or at least they're trying to take charge.

Building inspectors, the people who write the code and approve the changes, are defending what they see as the public interest by closing code loopholes. Every time a contractor wins an argument because the code doesn't make something clear or doesn't quite cover the situation at hand, the inspector has a reason to get the code changed. That's one major reason why we see so many changes and additions. As long as the code isn't perfectly clear on every issue, someone is going to abuse the code and someone else is going to propose a remedy for that abuse.

Of course, there are other reasons for code changes. Construction materials and methods have changed a lot in the last 20 years. We've learned to be more conscious about public safety, more sensitive to our environment and more careful about the way we use fuels. And we've found better ways to avoid damage due to earthquakes. All these changes have been reflected in revisions to the building code.

I consider these changes to be improvements, a form of progress that we wouldn't want to see reversed. The authors of the code are just trying to keep up with progress. I hope you see it that way too. Stopping change and progress is nearly impossible. And I don't think we in the construction industry would, even if we could. My suggestion is that you welcome the changes we see in the new codes. Do your best to be a progressive builder, a construction professional who stays posted on new construction materials, methods, and the code that reflects good construction practice. It's to exactly this purpose that this book is dedicated.

Where I Come From

A lot of what's in the code is either just good sense or what good craftsmanship demands. Maybe that's why most of the building inspectors you meet consider themselves both reasonable people and good judges of craftsmanship. It's part of their job, or should be.

I took woodshop classes in high school and spent a lot of weekends working for a general contractor. To this day I enjoy laying wood shingles. I also did a lot of carpentry in the Civilian Conservation Corps. For my younger readers, the CCC was one of President Roosevelt's make-work programs. It was supposed to get us out of the Great Depression. As it turned out, the CCC didn't do it. World War II did. But the CCC taught me how to be a carpenter.

I don't consider myself a finish carpenter, mostly because I don't have enough patience for that kind of work. But I know a stud from a joist, can drive a straight nail, and enjoy the smell of a newly-framed house. That doesn't really qualify me as a carpenter. But maybe it's enough to make me a retired carpenter.

When I got out of the Army in 1946, I was older than most of the young bucks that were flooding into the construction trades. I thought I was smarter too. So I took on-the-job training as an architectural draftsman. As a draftsman and designer I had to know the code. Of course, it was a lot easier in those days. The entire building code was a slim little book then, not much thicker than my wallet. You could carry it around in your back pocket. Try doing that today.

Eventually I hung out my shingle as a construction contractor. Custom home building, spec building and remodeling can be the fastest legal way I know to get rich with only a few tools, a little capital and no special knowledge. I didn't get rich. But I made a good living and more than a few good friends in the business. And I'm proud of the product I put out: good homes where people can raise families.

No one will ever erect a monument in my memory. That's O.K. I don't need it. The homes I built in those days are monument enough. When I drive by one, I still remember having built it. I don't know the people living there and they don't know me. But I had an influence on their lives, for the better, I hope. And when I notice what these homes are selling for now, I wince. Right now I'd be one of richest people in America if I'd built those homes and never sold a one, just rented them out. That's what I should have done. But it never occurred to me at the time.

By 1965 I'd pretty well burned myself out in the contracting business. Basically, it's a young man's game, and I wasn't young any more. When the job of building inspector opened up in Kennewick, Washington in 1965, I applied. Inspecting is about the only thing I hadn't done in construction. And if knowing the code qualified me for the job, I was qualified.

1

'Cuz it says so in THE BOOK!

Why Do I Need a Permit?

One of the most common complaints I used to hear from architects, engineers and contractors was that there were too many different building codes. It seemed like every city, county and state had their own idea about what was good construction and what was bad construction.

Of course, every city, county and state has the perfect right to make up their own laws, ordinances or regulations — including laws that control building. There was a time when most did. But the result was far too many different codes. What was perfectly acceptable in one community may have been strictly prohibited in the community right next door. That's foolish.

The proliferation of codes made the task of architects, builders and inspectors far more difficult than it had to be. Fortunately, times have changed. Now most communities have adopted one of the four model codes. The Uniform Building Code is by far the most popular, followed by the BOCA (Building Officials Conference of America) Code, the Southern Building Code, and finally the National Building Code.

Some cities still write their own codes, usually because their first code was adopted before there was a national model code. Inertia keeps some of these cities from replacing their do-it-yourself code with a modern national code. But even some of these cities are switching. Eventually I expect they all will. It's to everyone's advantage to reduce the differences between building codes.

Whatever the code in your city, you're going to have building code problems. Every contractor has had an inspector hold up his job or delay a permit until some minor discrepancy is handled just the way the code requires. From your standpoint, following the code is only an annoying and expensive necessity. But the building department, and probably the owner or architect that set your project in motion, regard the code as a good defense against poor practice that might otherwise plague generations of occupants of the building you erect.

No matter what your viewpoint, the building code is a fact of life that every builder must deal with. Your objective, and mine in writing this book, is to make following the code as simple, painless and inexpensive as possible.

Every construction contract you sign assumes that you will build according to the code. You aren't going to get paid until what you build has passed inspection. It's no defense that your estimate didn't include what the inspector demands. You're assumed to know the code and build every project accordingly.

Unfortunately, knowing the code isn't easy. The building code is a complex law intended to be enforced rather than read and understood. The code book itself doesn't have a good index. Related subjects are covered in widely separated sections. Some hard-to-understand sections refer to sections that are even harder to follow. The code seems to grow larger and more complex every time it's revised. There are exceptions, within exceptions, within other exceptions. A lawyer used to handling intricate tax problems would feel right at home with the building code.

But you can't spend a career mastering the building code. At least you shouldn't. Your job is building, not nitpicking. As a builder you need to know only enough to stay out of trouble and avoid expensive mistakes. This book will help. You also need the code itself, of course. The manual you're now reading isn't the code, so don't try to quote from it to your building inspector. He may not be impressed. Instead, use it as your answer book on code problems. Go to the chapter or section in this book that addresses the problem you're having. Read enough so you have some background on what the code demands. Then go to the code itself, if necessary, to sort out the fine details. Use the index in this manual to direct you to the code sections that apply to your situation. This should save you hours of valuable time and prevent expensive mistakes.

Now a word about the code itself. The code we're talking about is the 1988 Edition of the Uniform Building Code, as published by the International Conference of Building Officials in Whittier, California. The ICBO is a non-profit organization founded in 1922. More than 1,600 city and county building departments and state agencies all across the U.S. belong to the ICBO and participate in drafting and approving the model code. Many other organizations, companies and private individuals participate in the code drafting and revising process. The ICBO also sponsors research in the field of building safety.

Every three years the code or its revisions are republished as a recommendation to the building department members of the ICBO. Each county or city then decides if it will adopt the revision as a regulation for that community. Most routinely do. The model code the ICBO publishes is a very well-researched and highly persuasive document. But many communities change some sections, delete others or add material they feel is important. So the code in force in your community may not be exactly like the most recent code published by ICBO.

Be aware that there are two other "standard" building codes in the U.S. The Building Officials Conference of America (BOCA) in Chicago and the Southern Building Code Congress also offer model codes. These have been adopted by many communities east of the Mississippi. But the ICBO code is the most widely adopted. And the differences between all three major model codes are becoming less significant. After all, what's good building practice west of the Mississippi should also be good practice east of the Mississippi.

You need a copy of the current building code in force in the communities where you do business. Some bookstores sell the UBC. If your local bookstore doesn't have a copy, buy it directly from the ICBO. The address is:

International Conference of Building Officials
5360 South Workman Mill Road
Whittier, California 90601

At the time this book went to press, the soft cover edition was $56 and the hard cover edition was $64.25. The ICBO will accept phone orders on a charge card. Their number is (213) 699-0541.

But every building department that really wants to help contractors follow the code should sell it right over the counter at every office. Only your building department has the official version enforced in your community. If the inspector can't supply one, have him refer you to a convenient source. The building department expects you to know and follow the code; expect them to furnish you a copy at reasonable cost.

No matter how carefully you build and how knowledgeable you are about the code, you're going to have an occasional dispute with an inspector. Let me offer some advice. I've stood on the inspector's side of the counter through many disputes with contractors and have heard most of the arguments. You're not going to win very many direct confrontations with a building department. But there's a lot you can do to get them to see your side of the argument.

First, understand that the building department holds all the best cards. They can make any builder's life very unpleasant and cost him a lot of money. They have the full power of government behind them and can use it effectively to compel compliance on your part. But they would usually prefer to have your voluntary cooperation.

Adopt this attitude toward the building department and inspectors you deal with: "You have a job to do. I have a job to do. Together we're going to put up a building that both you and I as professionals in the construction industry will be proud of." The more you think of building officials as implacable adversaries, the more likely they will become just that.

In a dispute with the building department, you have one big advantage. The inspector didn't make the rules and can't write the code to fit your situation. He can only enforce the code as it's written. An inspector can require anything the code demands. But that's all! He's on very shaky ground if he insists on something that isn't in the code book. That's why you need a copy of the code. If a dispute arises, have the inspector cite the specific section and words involved. Then read those words yourself in your copy of the code. If that code section doesn't support the inspector's position, you're going to win the point.

Of course, inspectors make a living by knowing the code. They probably know it much better than you ever will. But they can be wrong. So don't be afraid to request reference to a specific code section, read that section, and form your own opinion of what is required. If the inspector is wrong and can't be persuaded to change his mind, there's a perfectly good appeal process available to every contractor. More on that later in this chapter.

Inspectors know that they can't enforce what the code doesn't require. But remember that highly experienced inspectors and plans examiners wrote the code. It gives inspectors room to maneuver and negotiate where that may be in the best interest of everyone concerned.

Every experienced contractor has heard an inspector say that the code actually requires this or that, "but it will be OK if you handle it this way." No, he's not giving away the store. He's just trying to get the result the code intends while saving you some time, trouble and money.

If an inspector seems to be giving you a favorable interpretation of the code, it's probably because he (or she) wants your cooperation on some point that's not too clear in the code. You're usually better off cooperating when an inspector complains about some minor point that's vague or omitted in the code. If you demand strict interpretation of code sections, you may get *exactly* that. And the inspector can cite more sections that can be enforced strictly than you ever thought possible. The point is worth emphasizing: Cooperation is going to save you more money than confrontation.

Sometimes you're going to have a code issue so important that no easy alternative is possible. You'll have to take it up with the building department head. Before going through the appeal procedure explained in this chapter, request a meeting with one of the senior inspectors or the "Building Official." Offer to meet early in the morning before the inspectors start their field work. Be sure both the inspector involved and his supervisor can be at this meeting. Prepare your case very carefully. Show that the code doesn't really require what you are being asked to do or point out an alternative that will save money and is just as good. Above all, show that you're a conscientious, professional, cooperative contractor interested in quality construction. Invite a negotiated settlement on the issue in dispute. More than likely you'll get one if any legitimate compromise is possible.

But don't expect any inspector to waive a clear code requirement just to save you money or trouble, especially if you're asking for special treatment other contractors don't receive. Code protection is too valuable to waive on a whim. If you've traveled in other countries where no codes exist or where codes aren't enforced, you know how important building codes are. And be aware that cities and counties are liable for the mistakes their building departments make. Owners of defective buildings have recovered substantial sums from municipal governments that didn't enforce the building code they adopted. Every building official knows the importance of the code he administers.

Purpose of the Code

Several points are worth mentioning before we begin careful examination of code sections. One of these is the purpose of the code. Section 102 makes it clear that health, safety and protecting property are the primary aims of the code:

> *The purpose of this code is to provide minimum stan-*
> *dards to safeguard life or limb, health, property and*
> *public welfare by regulating and controlling the design,*
> *construction, quality of materials, use and occupancy,*
> *location and maintenance of all buildings and structures*
> *within this jurisdiction and certain equipment specific-*
> *ally regulated herein.*
>
> *The purpose of this code is not to create or otherwise*
> *establish or designate any particular class or group of*
> *persons who will or should be especially protected or*
> *benefited by the terms of this code.*

Notice the words "minimum standards" in the first sentence. You can build to higher standards. Nearly every building you put up will include far more than the code requires. But it must also include everything in the code.

There's an important point in Section 102 if you ever have to dispute some code interpretation. Argue that what you want to do protects health, safety and property as well as, or better than, what the code requires.

Can I Use That Material?

The building code doesn't demand that you use only the methods and materials it lists. Section 105 states the following:

> *The provisions of this code are not intended to prevent*
> *the use of any material or method of construction not*
> *specifically prescribed by this code, provided any alter-*
> *nate has been approved and its use authorized by the*
> *building official.*

"Building Official" is the title of the senior man in the building department office. He may require proof that the method or material conforms to the intent of the code. If you're thinking about using a new method or material, something that hasn't had much use in your area, check with the building official *beforehand.*

For example, earth-sheltered structures are being built in some areas. Many inspectors throw up their hands at inspecting earth-sheltered buildings. Why? Because they're not adequately covered in the code. This is an area where you have to look at the intent of the code and not the literal meaning.

Unfortunately, many inspectors don't have the experience or the time to do much evaluation. And there are some who feel that the only way they can prove they're doing their job is to find something wrong with every project. They forget that the purpose of the code is to make construction safe, not to impede progress.

Because it's a law, the building code is written in "legalese." To either enforce the code or comply with it, you have to first understand it. As I said, that's not always easy. And, to make matters worse, the code is written to give the inspector a chance to use good common sense. That takes both knowledge and experience. Fortunately, most inspectors have the knowledge and experience required of professionals in their field.

When an inspector sees something that isn't covered in the code, a good inspector will always start doing some homework. Some less-experienced inspectors might see the same thing, look up wide-eyed and say: "I can't find it in the book, so you can't use that material or do it that way." Fortunately, that isn't what the code says. Section 105 allows use of any material or method that is approved by the building department in your community, even if it isn't approved specifically in the code itself.

The Appeal Process

"That's fine," you say. "But how can I get approval for what I want to do?" Section 204 is titled "Board of Appeals." This section says that you have the right to appeal any inspector's decision.

> *(a) General. In order to hear and decide appeals of orders, decisions or determinations made by the building official relative to the application and interpretations of this code, there shall be and is hereby created a Board of Appeals consisting of members who are qualified by experience and training to pass upon matters pertaining to building construction and who are not employees of the jurisdiction. The building official shall be an ex-officio member and shall act as secretary to said board but shall have no vote upon any matter before the board. The Board of Appeals shall be appointed by the governing body and shall hold office at its pleasure. The board shall adopt rules of procedure for conducting its business and shall render all decisions and findings in writing to the appellant with a duplicate copy to the building official.*
>
> *(b) Limitation of Authority. The Board of Appeals shall have no authority relative to interpretation of the administrative provisions of this code nor shall the Board be empowered to waive requirements of this code.*

A key phrase here is that the board members "are qualified by experience and training . . . ." So even if the inspector lacks construction knowledge, the people you are appealing to should have it. And if what you're trying to do with your material is controversial, the inspector may want you to appeal just to get the opinion of other experts.

And notice that Subsection B clearly states that the Board can't waive any provisions of the code. That means you can't slip anything past the Board just because you asked.

When Is a Permit Needed?

Section 301(a) tells you when you'll need a permit:

> *(a) Permits Required. Except as specified in Subsection (b) of this section, no building or structure regulated by this code shall be erected, constructed, enlarged, altered, repaired, moved, improved, removed, converted or demolished unless a separate permit for each building or structure has first been obtained from the building official.*

That's pretty broad language. Almost any type of construction, no matter how minor, needs a building permit. Section 301(b) exempts certain types of work. Most important in these exemptions are small out-buildings such as playhouses, small walls and fences and finish work like painting and paperhanging. Everything else needs a permit.

Figure 1-1 shows a typical building permit. Permit fees are set by the county or city. They're calculated to pay most of the costs of the building department. (That way, tax money doesn't support your building department.) Those who use the services pay for them. Figure 1-2 shows the permit fee recommended by the Uniform Building Code. This fee schedule was probably used when the code was adopted in your community. But check with your local department to be sure.

Demolition of Buildings

You need a permit to remove or demolish a building. This usually requires a small fee which covers the cost of issuing the permit. A copy of every permit issued goes to the tax assessor. This is the assessor's cue to do some checking. Someone is about to have their tax rate changed.

BUILDING DEPARTMENT

CITY OF KENNEWICK, WASHINGTON

P. O. Box 6108
210 West 6th Avenue
Phone: (509) 586-4181, Ext. 23

1. Recorded Owner	2. Location of Property	3. Owners Address (If Different Than 2)

4. LEGAL DESCRIPTION

Lot	Block	Tract	Plat

5. Use Zone	6. Fire Zone	7. Occupancy

8. Required Inspections
Foundations
Frame
Lath and Drywall
Plumbing
Mechanical
Street or Walk
Final

BUILDING PERMIT

11. Date Issued

12 Expiration Date

8681

13. TYPE OF PERMIT

Building	☐	Street	☐
Plumbing	☐	Street Cut	☐
Sidewalk	☐	Mechanical	☐

THIS PERMIT MUST BE POSTED IN PLAIN VIEW
FOR OBSERVATION FROM THE STREET.

9. Estimated Value

10. FEES —
Building
Plumbing
Street Walk
Mechanical
Plan Check
Total

14. CLASS OF WORK:

New	☐	Alteration	☐
Addition	☐	Repair	☐
Move	☐	Demolish	☐

15. Building Size

_____ X _____

16. Lot Size

_____ X _____

17. TYPE OF CONSTRUCTION

Fire Resistive	☐
Semi-Fireproof	☐
Heavy Timber	☐
Ordinary Masonry	☐
Frame	☐
Unprotected Metal	☐

18. Plans Submitted ☐
Plot Plan Submitted ☐
Site Plan Approval ☐

20. PLUMBING

Bath Tubs	___	Grease Traps	___
Showers	___	Floor Drains	___
Lavatories	___	Urinals	___
Kitchen Sinks	___	Drink Fountain	___
Laundry Trays	___	Dental Lav.	___
Auto Washer	___	Swim Pool	___
Water Closets	___	Miscellaneous	___
Water Heaters	___	Total Units	___

21. SET BACKS	Front	Rear	Left	Right	22. Height	23. No. Stories	24. No. Families

25. MECHANICAL	Heating	Air Conditioning	Miscellaneous

26. Description of Work

27. Bldg. Cont.	29. Street & Walk Cont.
28. Plbg. Cont.	30. Mechanical Cont.

31. Bldg. Cont. State License No.   If no number please explain on attached sheet.

32. Engineering Data
Field Book No. _____
Page No. _____
Date
Sidewalk Constructed ☐
Power of Attorney ☐

I certify no work will be done except as described above or on accompanying plans. All work will be performed in compliance with all codes and ordinances of the City of Kennewick, and as summarized on back of permit.

Applicant's Signature_____

Building Inspector_____

All work must be inspected prior to concealment.

This department must have 24 hours notice for all inspections.

Figure 1-1 *Typical building permit*

TABLE NO. 3-A—BUILDING PERMIT FEES

TOTAL VALUATION	FEE
$1.00 to $500.00	$15.00
$501.00 to $2,000.00	$15.00 for the first $500.00 plus $2.00 for each additional $100.00 or fraction thereof, to and including $2,000.00
$2,001.00 to $25,000.00	$45.00 for the first $2,000.00 plus $9.00 for each additional $1,000.00 or fraction thereof, to and including $25,000.00
$25,001.00 to $50,000.00	$252.00 for the first $25,000.00 plus $6.50 for each additional $1,000.00 or fraction thereof, to and including $50,000.00
$50,001.00 to $100,000.00	$414.50 for the first $50,000.00 plus $4.50 for each additional $1,000.00 or fraction thereof, to and including $100,000.00
$100,001.00 to $500,000.00	$639.50 for the first $100,000.00 plus $3.50 for each additional $1,000.00 or fraction thereof
$500,001.00 to $1,000,000.00	$2039.50 for the first $500,000.00 plus $3.00 for each additional $1,000.00 or fraction thereof, to and including $1,000,000.00.
$1,000,001.00 and up	$3539.50 for the first $1,000,000.00 plus $2.00 for each additional $1,000.00 or fraction thereof

Other Inspections and Fees:

1. Inspections outside of normal business hours . . . .$30.00 per hour*
   (minimum charge—two hours)
2. Reinspection fees assessed under provisions of
   Section 305 (g). . . . .$30.00 per hour*
3. Inspections for which no fee is specifically
   indicated. . . . .$30.00 per hour*
   (minimum charge—one-half hour)
4. Additional plan review required by changes, additions
   or revisions to approved plans . . . .$30.00 per hour*
   (minimum charge—one-half hour)

*Or the total hourly cost to the jurisdiction, whichever is the greatest. This cost shall include supervision, overhead, equipment, hourly wages and fringe benefits of the employees involved.

From the Uniform Building Code, © 1988, ICBO

Figure 1-2   *Building permit fees*

Many cities and counties now have ordinances that control unsafe or dilapidated buildings. Even if the city requires that a building be demolished, you'll still need a demolition permit.

Posting the Permit

Always post the building permit and inspection record card on the site. In some jurisdictions, you only have to post the inspection card. There must be some place the inspector can sign that he has made a required inspection. This is your guarantee that he has been there and approved the job to that point. If your job doesn't pass the inspection, the inspector will leave a notice of non-compliance or a correction notice explaining what you have to correct before you can proceed. (See Figure 1-3.)

Many people think that work inside a building doesn't require a permit. If you're doing work exempted by the code, such as replacing kitchen cabinets, that assumption is correct. But any remodeling or renovation that isn't exempt will require a permit.

This brings up a point. I used to be a building inspector. As I traveled around my city, I would notice construction materials or rubble piled near a back door, in a driveway or under a carport. This almost always meant that work of some kind was going on inside. I usually checked with our office to see if there was a permit for work at that address. If not, I would have a little talk with the occupant. I tried not to be heavy-handed. And a little tact usually paid off. They usually wanted to know who squealed on them, never realizing that they squealed on themselves with their pile of rubble.

Right of Entry

Section 202(c) gives the building official his authority to make any necessary inspections:

> *Whenever necessary to make an inspection to enforce any of the provisions of this code, or whenever the building*

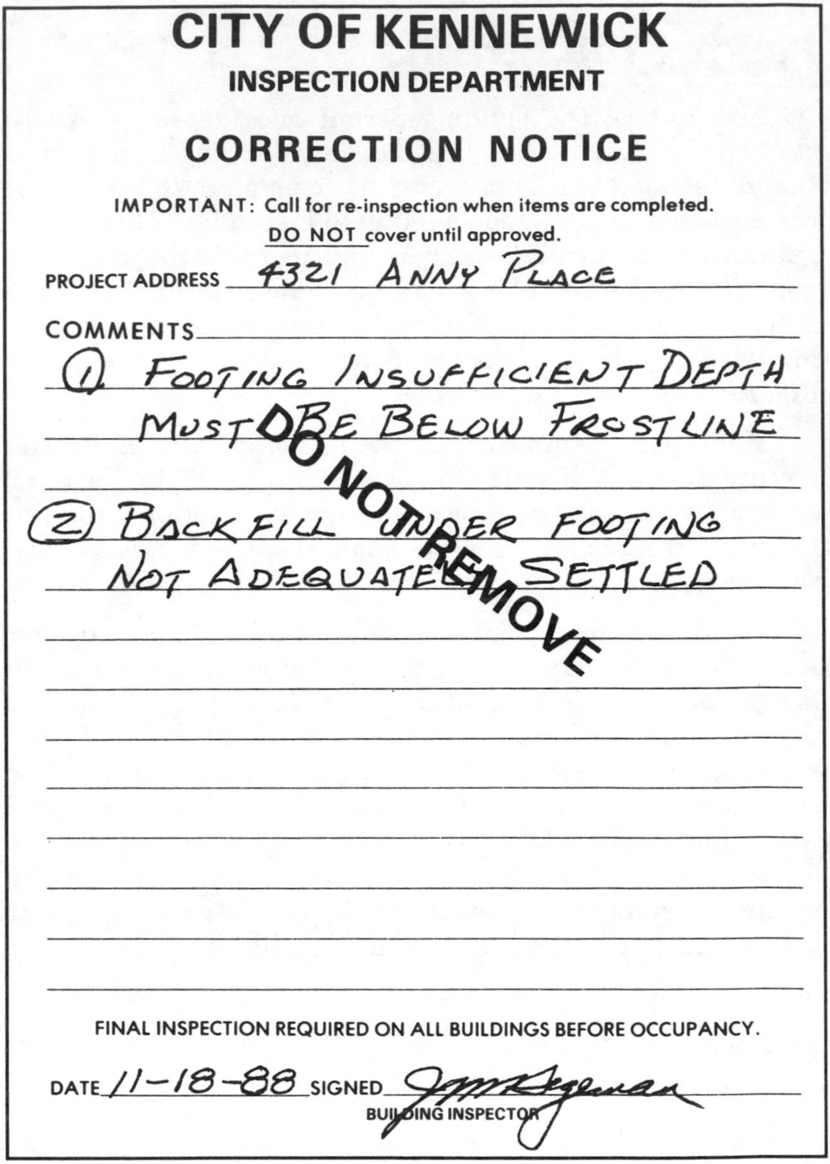

CITY OF KENNEWICK
INSPECTION DEPARTMENT

CORRECTION NOTICE

IMPORTANT: Call for re-inspection when items are completed.

DO NOT cover until approved.

PROJECT ADDRESS *4321 ANNY PLACE*

COMMENTS

① *FOOTING INSUFFICIENT DEPTH MUST BE BELOW FROSTLINE*

② *BACKFILL UNDER FOOTING NOT ADEQUATELY SETTLED*

DO NOT REMOVE

FINAL INSPECTION REQUIRED ON ALL BUILDINGS BEFORE OCCUPANCY.

DATE *11-18-88* SIGNED _____
BUILDING INSPECTOR

Figure 1-3 *Correction notice*

official or his authorized representative has reasonable cause to believe that there exists in any building or upon any premises any condition or code violation which makes such building or premises unsafe, dangerous or hazardous, the building official or his authorized representative may enter such building or premises at all reasonable times to inspect the same or to perform any duty imposed upon the building official by this code, provided that if such building or premises be occupied, he shall first present proper credentials and request entry; and if such building or premises be unoccupied, he shall first make a reasonable effort to locate the owner or other persons having charge or control of the building or premises and request entry. If such entry is refused, the building official or his authorized representative shall have recourse to every remedy provided by law to secure entry.

This right of entry is seldom needed. And it isn't nearly as ferocious as it sounds. Most people are cooperative, and most building inspectors use this right judiciously.

Required Inspections

A permit always requires some sort of inspection. The inspection depends on the scope of the job. It can be a simple drive-by to see if the obvious has been completed, in the case of a re-roof. Or there may be twelve or sixteen highly technical inspections. For most residential and small commercial work, there are five required inspections, set forth in Section 305(e).

1) *Foundation inspection:* This is made after the trenches have been excavated, the forms erected, and all the materials for the foundation delivered. Concrete supplied by the transit mix truck doesn't have to be on the site during inspection.

2) *Concrete slab or under-floor inspection:* This is made after all in-slab or under-floor building service equipment, conduit, piping accessories and their ancillary equipment items are in place, but before any concrete is poured or floor sheathing installed, including the subfloor.

3) *Frame inspection:* This is made after the roof, all framing, fire blocking and bracing are in place; chimneys and vents are complete; and after the rough electrical, plumbing and heating wires, pipes and ducts are approved.

4) *Lath or gypsum board inspection:* This is made after all lathing and gypsum board, interior and exterior are in place, but before any plastering is applied or before gypsum board joints and fasteners are taped and finished.

5) *Final inspection:* This is made after finish grading, when the building has been completed and is ready for occupancy.

In addition to these, there are a number of special inspections that may be required by the building official. The inspections required depend on the scope of the project. For example, the building official may require special inspections or tests of concrete, reinforcing steel and prestressing steel, welding, high-strength bolting, structural masonry, reinforced gypsum concrete, insulating concrete fill, spray-applied fireproofing, piling, drilled piers and caissons, special grading, excavation, or backfill. And of course, the building official can add any other tests or inspections that are felt to be needed.

If an inspection shows that the project is not acceptable, a correction notice is issued and another inspection scheduled. The project can't continue until the project passes on re-inspection. Usually there will be a fee for each re-inspection. Larger projects, such as major shopping malls and multi-storied buildings, often require a full-time inspector on the job. This inspector's salary is paid by the owner, either directly or

Figure 1-4 *This chimney is legal, but...*

through his contractor. In most cities and counties, new construction requires a Certificate of Occupancy before anyone can occupy the building and before utility companies can begin serving the building.

The Inspector Doesn't Like the Way You Did It

Occasionally, an inspector finds a job that could be done better using a different method. He may offer advice, and probably will. But his advice isn't binding unless it's supported by either the code or a local ordinance. He can stop the job for safety reasons, but only if the code backs him up. If something isn't in the code, he can't enforce it. You have the right to ask what section of the code is being invoked. And you always have the right to appeal the inspector's decision.

Building inspectors are often pretty good craftsmen themselves. It may be to your advantage to heed their advice. But an inspector isn't really inspecting the craftsmanship of your building unless craftsmanship is required by ordinance. It usually isn't. Craftsmanship is a matter of judgment, nothing more. Your opinion is just as good as mine, maybe better. But if poor craftsmanship weakens a building or makes it unsafe, the inspector will probably cite some code sections that back up his opinion. Figure 1-4 shows some questionable workmanship, but it meets the code. You decide if that's the kind of work you want to be known for.

I've often used a little charm to get shoddy work improved. I once visited a house where the trim around a split entry stairway had been butted in square, without mitering. I mentioned this to the contractor and he jumped on me about exceeding my authority. "Besides," he added, "who'll ever know?"

"Everyone will," I assured him with charm, "because I'm the biggest tattletale in town and I can hardly wait to start telling everyone you do this kind of work." When I came back later, all the corners had been neatly mitered.

Who Drew These Stupid Plans?

For many years I was a building inspector and plans examiner. What I did most was find mistakes made by architects, designers and contractors. That put me on the hot seat. No one likes to be told they made a mistake, especially a dumb mistake. But that was my job. So I tried to do it without ruffling any more feathers or crushing any more inflated egos than necessary.

Sometimes I couldn't settle a dispute without a squawk. Architects hate to admit they blew it. The truth is, though, that most architects don't have more than a basic knowledge of building codes. Architecture schools teach good design, not code compliance. Very few offer classes on the building code. And I don't know any that require a test on the code before graduating. Maybe that's a mistake.

I'd like to claim that all building inspectors and plans examiners are code experts. Like architects, they should be. But many aren't. That's too bad. Plan checking is an important part of what should happen in every building department. If both the architect and the plans examiner miss something, the owner's going to have to live (or die) with the mistake.

Since the first edition of this book was published in 1982, I've talked to lots of building inspectors. Nearly all claim to run a tight ship. But I also talk to the contractors they deal with. From them I get a different story. One contractor I talked to says his local building department sends *all* plans out to a plan checking company for review and approval. Doesn't anyone at the building department know enough about the code to approve plans? I think that adds to the cost and delays the job. But maybe I'm old fashioned. You be the judge.

So what kind of mistakes do you find on plans for a home or small commercial building? Nothing serious, usually. I do recall one time, however, when I found a room that had no door. I'm serious! No way in or out. I used to draw plans — back in the days when I was a contractor. I can guess what happened: The owner asked the designer to move a door from one wall to another. The draftsman erased the old door, filled in the wall section, took a coffee break, and then forgot to add the new opening. No one caught it.

My point is that construction is too expensive and too permanent to be careless about design and code compliance. And, unfortunately, the code is written so that only the careful and determined will understand it completely.

I recall a hospital addition I checked. According to the code, one area had to be contained by latched fire doors. Another section of the code said those doors had to be instantly operable. What would you do?

I'll drop that one like a hot potato.

2

His Nibs will see you now.

Getting Your Permit

I f you're just replacing some worn-out shingles, getting a permit is simply a matter of paying the fee down at the building department. The plans examiner can check your plan (or sketch) right at the counter and issue a permit immediately. But if you're building anything more complex, there's a lot more involved.

Usually the plans examiner will need a week or so to study your plans and find the discrepancies. He or she will then return the plans and ask you to make the changes needed. Your architect or designer then makes the revisions and you resubmit the plans for approval. If the revised set is O.K., your permit should be granted a week or so later. If more changes are needed, you'll have to make still more changes and submit the plans again.

How long will it take to get your plans approved? Of course, that depends on the size and complexity of the project, the backlog in the plans examiner's office and how good your plans are. As a rule of thumb, allow about a month for a custom home or a small store. Of course, it can go faster — and it can take much longer.

What Plans Are Needed?

The plans and specifications don't have to be drawn by an architect or engineer. Here's what UBC Section 302(b) says:

> *Plans, engineering calculations, diagrams and other data shall be submitted in one or more sets with each application for a permit. The building official may require plans, computations and specifications to be prepared and designed by an architect or engineer licensed by the state to practice as such. Submittals shall include inspection requirements as defined in Section 302(c)*

The code allows exceptions and these vary from place to place. Find out what the requirements are in your area. The code isn't too clear on plan requirements, but the policy at most building departments is something like this: Get plans for all new construction. On remodel work, the scope of the project will determine whether plans are needed. A little job may require only a simple sketch.

Not many building departments have an engineer on staff. In most cases no one in the office is qualified to judge if walls and headers and joists and supports are strong enough. But they do have many charts and tables at their disposal. And of course, everyone knows that 2 x 4's 16 inches on center will hold up the roof. No problem getting plan approval there. But if your project includes anything that might not be strong enough to support the intended load, expect the building department to require review of the plans by a licensed engineer.

The plans examiner will almost certainly accept the opinion of any state-licensed engineer you select. The engineer only has to certify that the plans meet accepted engineering standards. He or she will stamp the plans with a seal, certifying that the design meets accepted standards.

Many building departments request plans for remodeling work. Usually this is to make sure you've really thought carefully about the work that's going to be done. If you rip out a wall, is the ceiling going to collapse? Believe me, it happens. Check with your inspector to find out what plans are needed for your remodeling project.

But what about new construction? To get a permit for new construction you'll need three items:

1) Plans

2) Specifications

3) Engineering data and notes to back up items shown on the plans or the accompanying specifications.

Plans vs. Specifications

Plans (also known as *working drawings*, or *blueprints*) are a graphic representation of what's being built, and how. Specifications provide details not shown on the plans. For example, the plans may show only an exterior door and a 3'0" x 6'8" opening. The specifications may describe the door as *solid core, exterior grade, two-light, left-hand swing*. There is only room for so much detail on the drawings. What won't fit on the plans goes in the specifications. On a small job the specifications may be just one page. But I've seen specs that are several hundred pages long.

What happens when the specs and plans are in conflict? For example, suppose the specs describe a 3'6" wide door and the plans show a 3-foot wide opening. What then? I'll leave that question to the lawyers. For our purposes, we'll consider the plans and specs equally important. Whether something is in the plans or specs doesn't matter to the inspector. No part of the plans or specs takes precedence over any other part. The building code considers all documents a part of the whole.

Most plans for new construction will include the following:

1) Plot plan

2) Foundation plan

3) Floor plan

4) Roof plan

5) Elevations

6) Any sections or details needed to show what's being built and how it's being built

For larger projects, the plan sheets will usually be divided into the following categories:

1) Architectural plans

2) Structural plans

3) Electrical plans

4) Plumbing plans

5) Mechanical plans (heating, cooling and ventilation)

For smaller projects, like homes, information on structural, electrical and mechanical parts of the building may be included with the architectural drawings.

The Plot Plan

The plot plan shows a bird's eye view of the lot and where the proposed building will be on that lot. It also shows parking areas and yard improvements. The plans examiner will check the plot plan carefully to be sure the proposed building complies with any zoning ordinance in effect.

Zoning ordinances aren't building codes and I won't spend much time on them in this book. But you should know what the local zoning ordinance requires before applying for a permit. Can you build a duplex on this lot? What are the setbacks from the street and the property lines? How much of the lot area can be covered with building? Are there any height restrictions? The building department won't issue a permit until they're sure your plot plan complies with the zoning ordinance.

Zoning Laws

Zoning ordinances usually establish four broad categories of land use:

1) Residential – Where we live

2) Commercial – Stores and offices

3) Industrial – Where goods are produced

4) Agricultural – Where food is produced

Usually there are several sub-categories within each category. For example, R-1 is usually single-family residences. R-4 might be high density residential with up to twenty living units or more per acre. You should know what zones have been established in your community and what is permitted in each zone. Usually the local planning department administers zoning ordinances.

You can't always tell from looking at a neighborhood exactly how it's zoned. Just because there's a commercial building next door is no guarantee that your client can put up a store on his lot. The dividing line between R-1 and C-1 (commercial) might run right down the property line.

You can usually build "down" but you can't build "up." Residential is the highest use, followed by commercial and industrial. Agricultural is the lowest use. So you can probably build a house in a commercial zone, industrial zone or agricultural zone. But you can't put up a store in a residential zone. Check with your planning department for details.

This rule of building down but not up also applies within zones. Suppose there are three residential zones: R-1 (single-family), R-2 (duplex) and R-3 (multi-family). You can usually build a single-family home in an R-2 or R-3 zone. Just don't try putting an apartment house in an R-1 zone.

The building inspector or the planning department can tell you what's allowed and what isn't. Of course, zoning can be changed, but changing it takes time, money and effort. Usually it's easier and cheaper to buy property zoned for the use you intend than it is to change zoning for the property you have.

Other Approvals

Even if you've satisfied local zoning ordinances and have met requirements in the building code, there may be other hurdles. For example, your local fire department and health department probably regulate certain types of businesses. The building department may forward a set of your plans to these or other municipal offices to get their approval. If they find discrepancies, your permit will be held up until changes are made.

A land covenant may also affect your plans. Most communities permit land owners to agree that land will be used only for certain purposes or that only certain types of buildings will be constructed on the land. These agreements between landowners are called *covenants, conditions and restrictions*

(CC&Rs) and run with the land from one owner to the next. If you buy land in the covenant, you probably have to comply with this agreement.

Many CC&Rs require landowners to submit plans to an architectural review board before beginning construction. Your local building department won't enforce the CC&Rs, but other landowners may through the courts. Be aware of any CC&Rs that apply before you begin drawing plans. And understand that CC&Rs may conflict with the zoning. For instance, you could buy a plot in a zone that allows duplexes, but the property agreement prohibits them.

What the Inspector Looks At

Near the front of the UBC is a simple outline inspectors often use for plan checking. It's reproduced here as Figure 2-1. We'll be considering each of these points in the next few chapters. Let's start with item A-1 on the inspector's checklist, occupancy group.

Types of Occupancy

Occupancy refers to the use or type of activity intended for the proposed building. *Occupant load* refers to the number of people who will be occupying the space. We'll cover occupancy in this chapter and occupancy load in the next chapter. These two terms may look somewhat alike, but the definition is very different.

There are seven major occupancy categories: A (assembly), B (business, such as stores), E (educational), H (hazardous), I (institutional, such as hospitals), M (miscellaneous, such as garages and sheds), and R (residential). These are shown in UBC Table 5-A (Figure 2-2). Most categories are broken down into sub-categories.

EFFECTIVE USE OF THE UNIFORM
BUILDING CODE

The following procedure may be helpful in using the Uniform Building Code:

1. Classify the building:

   A. **OCCUPANCY GROUP:** Determine the occupancy group which the use of the building most nearly resembles. See the '01 sections of Chapters 6 through 12. See Section 503 for buildings with mixed occupancies.

   B. **TYPE OF CONSTRUCTION:** Determine the type of construction of the building by the building materials used and the fire resistance of the parts of the building. See Chapters 17 through 22.

   C. **LOCATION ON PROPERTY:** Determine the location of the building on the site and clearances to property lines and other buildings from the plot plan. See Table No. 5-A and '03 sections of Chapters 18 through 22 for exterior wall and wall opening requirements based on proximity to property lines. See Section 504 for buildings located on the same site.

   D. **FLOOR AREA:** Compute the floor area of the building. See Table No. 5-C for basic allowable floor area based on occupancy group and type of construction. See Section 506 for allowable increases based on location on property and installation of an approved automatic fire-sprinkler system. See Section 505 (b) for allowable floor area of multistory buildings.

   E. **HEIGHT AND NUMBER OF STORIES:** Compute the height of the building, Section 409, from grade, Section 408, and for the number of stories, Section 420. See Table No. 5-D for the allowable height and number of stories based on occupancy group and type of construction. See Section 507 for allowable story increase based on the installation of an approved automatic fire-sprinkler system.

   F. **OCCUPANT LOAD:** Compute the occupant load of the building. See Section 3302 (a) and Table No. 33-A.

2. Verify compliance of the building with detailed occupancy requirements. See Chapters 6 through 12.

3. Verify compliance of the building with detailed type of construction requirements. See Chapters 17 through 22.

4. Verify compliance of the building with exit requirements. See Chapter 33.

5. Verify compliance of the building with detailed code regulations. See Chapters 29 through 43, Chapters 47 through 54, and Appendix.

6. Verify compliance of building with engineering regulations and requirements for materials of construction. See Chapters 23 through 29.

From the Uniform Building Code, © 1988, ICBO

Figure 2-1   *Outline for simplified plan checking*

TABLE NO. 5-A—WALL AND OPENING PROTECTION OF OCCUPANCIES BASED ON LOCATION ON PROPERTY
TYPES II ONE-HOUR, II-N AND V CONSTRUCTION: For exterior wall and opening protection of Types II One-hour, II-N and V buildings, see table below and Sections 504, 709, 1903 and 2203.
This table does not apply to Types I, II-F.R., III and IV construction, see Sections 1803, 1903, 2003 and 2103.

GROUP	DESCRIPTION OF OCCUPANCY	FIRE RESISTANCE OF EXTERIOR WALLS	OPENINGS IN EXTERIOR WALLS
A See also Section 602	1—Any assembly building or portion of a building with a legitimate stage and an occupant load of 1000 or more in the building	Not applicable (See Sections 602 and 603)	
	2—Any building or portion of a building having an assembly room with an occupant load of less than 1000 and a legitimate stage	2 hours less than 10 feet, 1 hour less than 40 feet	Not permitted less than 5 feet Protected less than 10 feet
	2.1—Any building or portion of a building having an assembly room with an occupant load of 300 or more without a stage, including such buildings used for educational purposes and not classed as a Group E or Group B, Division 2 Occupancy		
	3—Any building or portion of a building having an assembly room with an occupant load of less than 300 without a legitimate stage, including such buildings used for educational purposes and not classed as a Group E or Group B, Division 2 Occupancy	2 hours less than 5 feet, 1 hour less than 40 feet	Not permitted less than 5 feet Protected less than 10 feet
	4—Stadiums, reviewing stands and amusement park structures not included within other Group A Occupancies	1 hour less than 10 feet	Protected less than 10 feet
B See also Section 702	1—Gasoline service stations, garages where no repair work is done except exchange of parts and maintenance requiring no open flame, welding, or use of Class I, II or III-A liquids		
	2—Drinking and dining establishments having an occupant load of less than 50, wholesale and retail stores, office buildings, printing plants, municipal police and fire stations, factories and workshops using material not highly flammable or combustible, storage and sales rooms for combustible goods, paint stores without bulk handling Buildings or portions of buildings having rooms used for educational purposes, beyond the 12th grade, with less than 50 occupants in any room	1 hour less than 20 feet	Not permitted less than 5 feet Protected less than 10 feet

From the Uniform Building Code, © *1988, ICBO*

Figure 2-2 *Categories of occupancy*

Getting

Cont

TABLE NO. 5-A—Continued
TYPES II ONE-HOUR, II-N AND V ONLY

GROUP	DESCRIPTION OF OCCUPANCY	FIRE RESISTANCE OF EXTERIOR WALLS	OPENINGS IN EXTERIOR WALLS
B (Cont.)	3—Aircraft hangars where no repair work is done except exchange of parts and maintenance requiring no open flame, welding, or the use of Class I or II liquids Open parking garages (For requirements, See Section 709.) Helistops	1 hour less than 20 feet	Not permitted less than 5 feet Protected less than 20 feet
	4—Ice plants, power plants, pumping plants, cold storage and creameries Factories and workshops using noncombustible and nonexplosive materials Storage and sales rooms of noncombustible and nonexplosive materials that are not packaged or crated in or supported by combustible material	1 hour less than 5 feet	Not permitted less than 5 feet
E See also Section 802	1—Any building used for educational purposes through the 12th grade by 50 or more persons for more than 12 hours per week or four hours in any one day 2—Any building used for educational purposes through the 12th grade by less than 50 persons for more than 12 hours per week or four hours in any one day 3—Any building used for day-care purposes for more than six children	2 hours less than 5 feet, 1 hour less than 10 feet[1]	Not permitted less than 5 feet Protected less than 10 feet[1]
H	See Chapter 9		

[1]Group E, Divisions 2 and 3 Occupancies having an occupant load of not more than 20 may have exterior wall and opening protection as required for Group R, Division 3 Occupancies.

From the Uniform Building Code, © 1988, ICBO

Figure 2-2 (cont'd) *Categories of occupancy*

I See also Section 1002	1—Nurseries for the full-time care of children under the age of six (each accommodating more than five persons) Hospitals, sanitariums, nursing homes with nonambulatory patients and similar buildings (each accommodating more than five persons)	2 hours less than 5 feet, 1 hour elsewhere	Not permitted less than 5 feet Protected less than 10 feet
	2—Nursing homes for ambulatory patients, homes for children six years of age or over (each accommodating more than five persons)	1 hour	Not permitted less than 5 feet, protected less than 10 feet
	3—Mental hospitals, mental sanitariums, jails, prisons, reformatories and buildings where personal liberties of inmates are similarly restrained	2 hours less than 5 feet, 1 hour elsewhere	Not permitted less than 3 feet
M[2]	1—Private garages, carports, sheds and agricultural buildings (See also Section 1101, Division 1.)	1 hour less than 3 feet (or may be protected on the exterior with materials approved for 1-hour fire-resistive construction)	
	2—Fences over 6 feet high, tanks and towers	Not regulated for fire resistance	
R See also Section 1202	1—Hotels and apartment houses Convents and monasteries (each accommodating more than 10 persons)	1 hour less than 5 feet	Not permitted less than 5 feet
	3—Dwellings and lodging houses	1 hour less than 3 feet	Not permitted less than 3 feet

[2]For agricultural buildings, see Appendix Chapter 11.

NOTES: (1) See Section 504 for types of walls affected and requirements covering percentage of openings permitted in exterior walls.
(2) For additional restrictions, see chapters under Occupancy and Types of Construction.
(3) For walls facing yards and public ways, see Part IV.
(4) Openings shall be protected by a fire assembly having a three-fourths-hour fire-protection rating.

From the Uniform Building Code, © 1988, ICBO.

Figure 2-2 (cont'd)   *Categories of occupancy*

This classification system assumes normal use of the building: The number of people and things in the building and what they're doing there is about what you would expect. That's normal occupancy. But it's also possible to have *abnormal* occupancies that create special hazards. Paint booths in a car repair shop, for example. In that case, expect the building department to impose special requirements beyond what would be required for normal occupancy.

Occupancy Is Based on Degree of Hazard

Generally, occupancies are grouped by type of hazard. For example, buildings intended for meetings (such as theaters) have special design requirements. In an emergency, everyone wants out at the same time. People will rush to the exit, fighting and climbing over each other. It takes longer to evacuate a mob of panic-stricken people than it does to evacuate an organized group the same size. Obviously, the code has to set the minimum number of exits per occupant. In addition, the building should be able to resist structural failure for a longer time.

So that you understand the thinking that went into occupancy groups, I'll review the hazards we all face in buildings.

The most important considerations in setting up occupancy groups is the hazard to human life. Property hazards are considered secondary. Let's take a look at these risks to human life.

Common hazards— People are the greatest hazard to other people. Man is his own worst enemy. He smokes, works, gathers in groups, uses flammable liquids, and fills rooms with highly combustible material. In short, man creates most of his own hazards. And, when something bad happens, he panics and creates additional hazards.

***Day and night occupancies*—** There are two broad categories, where people work and where they sleep. Where you work is usually more hazardous, depending on the type of work involved, the size of work groups, and the materials and equipment used.

Night occupancies are where you rest or sleep. These include hotels, dormitories and apartment houses, but exclude one- and two-family homes. For these, see dwelling occupancies, following. Of course, a night occupancy can be hazardous. A fire may burn out of control longer when there's no one awake to discover it.

***Dwelling occupancies*—** Dwelling occupancies are for one- and two-family homes. More deaths occur each year in one- and two-family dwellings than in any other type of occupancy. But most of these deaths are caused by fires, involve only one or two casualties and probably couldn't be prevented by changes in the building code. That may be why the code considers homes much less hazardous than other types of buildings.

***Commercial and industrial hazards*—** This is a broad category and includes many different types of uses. Generally, the hazard varies with what's happening in the building. For example, storing or using highly combustible materials creates special risks.

Hazards are lower when a building has a relatively small number of people per square foot of floor and when the occupants are familiar with potential hazards and the location of exits. For example, employees in a plant can be expected to know what to do in case of fire. Shoppers in a store might not even know where the exits are. Code requirements are based on reasonable assumptions about who will be present and what they can be expected to know.

The type of occupancy determines the minimum fire and safety precautions required, the protective devices needed, and the arrangement, area, and height of rooms. The code tries to strike a balance between safety and economy by setting requirements appropriate for each type of hazard.

Height and Area Hazards

How do height and area pose hazards? Hazards to life increase as building heights increase, especially on floors too high for fire fighters to reach from the street. And think about basement fires. Many basements don't have direct access from the street and may be hard to get out of in an emergency. Fire fighters approach basement fires with extra caution.

Area means the space on a single level which is entirely separate and enclosed by a fire-resisting barrier. If there are no fire barriers, *area* is the entire floor space on each level. The greater the area, the greater the risk of material and human loss and the harder it may be to reach the center of the fire.

Hazards in General

What are the dangers the code is trying to reduce? Let's review some of the obvious hazards found in buildings.

- Hazards based on the nature of the occupancy.

- Height and area hazards.

- Spread of fire due to air currents, dirt and lint, combustible decorations and draperies, combustible finishes, trim and the structure itself.

- Toxic and heated gases.

- Unprotected openings.

- Lack of adequate separation between areas.

- Exposure, or lack of separation between buildings.

These are the main hazards in buildings. But there's one more consideration. It's one that we've talked about before. When mixed with any of those listed above, you have the makings of a catastrophe. That hazard is large groups of people. In any decision on hazards, the building official will consider the number of people that will usually be in a building.

Occupancy Groups

Starting with the 1982 Uniform Building Code, the seven major occupancy groups were expanded into 24 sub-groups. Let's take a look at these groups and sub-groups. They're listed in order of highest hazard to lowest hazard.

A – Assembly

B – Business, including offices, factories, mercantile and storage

E – Educational

H – Hazardous

I – Institutional

M – Miscellaneous structures

R – Residential

Under the code, every building in town gets squeezed into one of these seven groups. Of course, UBC sub-groups make the classification a little easier. Let's examine these groups and sub-groups one at a time and see what the requirements are. UBC Table 5-A (Figure 2-2) describes each type of occupancy.

Group A Occupancies

Where people assemble in large numbers for entertainment, deliberation, worship, to wait for transportation or to eat, the hazards are considered to be the greatest. Assembly buildings are the first category. Group A is further broken down into five sub-groups, determined first by occupant load and second by the activity. The first sub-group is the most hazardous to human life. The last sub-group is the least hazardous. Remember, the higher the human load, the higher the hazard.

People assemble for meetings and classes in offices and schools. Why are educational and office buildings excluded from Group A? Think about what I said about familiarity with surroundings. Most Group A buildings will be occupied by people not completely familiar the building layout. Office workers and students are usually in the same building day after day. They're probably much more familiar with the buildings where they meet. They probably know what to do in case of fire or emergency.

Note in UBC Table 5-A that buildings with "legitimate" stages have the highest hazards. That's probably because so many people have been killed in theater fires. Legitimate stage, by the way, means live theater as opposed to movie theaters.

Theaters have changed a lot in the last few decades. You won't find fly galleries in drive-in theaters or most new movie theaters, nor will you find a proscenium wall. What's a fly gallery? It's a narrow platform at the side of the theater stage. Stagehands stand in the fly gallery while pulling lines that control suspended scenery. A proscenium wall is an arch that frames the stage and separates it from the rest of the auditorium.

Group A-4 covers stadiums, reviewing stands and amusement park buildings not included under Group M. Group M (miscellaneous) is used only for buildings with low human occupancy.

Group B Occupancies

Group B is referred to as the "mercantile group" because it includes most stores, offices and small factories. The downtown area of your city is mostly Group B buildings.

This group includes a few surprises. Look at UBC Table 5-A (Figure 2-2). The first surprise comes under the B-2 sub-group. The last sentence is the kicker:

> *Buildings or portions of buildings having rooms used for educational purposes, beyond the 12th grade, with less than 50 occupants in any room.*

Why put some educational buildings here when there's another, more restrictive section specifically for educational buildings? The answer is that less than 50 people will be in each room and all will be beyond the 12th grade. The group is small and the people are old enough to react rationally in an emergency.

A typical building in Group B-2 might be a beauty school. Even though these buildings are schools, they're also a lot like offices. And some may include commercial stores. For example a beauty college might include a hair dressing salon for training of beauticians. The code can't cover all the possibilities. But it does try to create categories that make sense.

There's another surprise in Group B-4. Prior to 1982 this was a catch-all category where hard-to-define uses were collected. This group now includes buildings that don't require combustible or flammable materials, have a low occupant load and very little hazard. Examples are ice plants, cold storage plants, power and pumping stations.

and very little hazard. Examples are ice plants, cold storage plants, power and pumping stations.

Group E Occupancies

Group E occupancies are day-use educational buildings. Here, the three sub-groups are concerned more with type of occupants.

Group E-3 is for day-care centers. Notice that it's based on a scale of less than six children to one adult. Fire safety isn't a major risk if one baby sitter is available to control each five children. For example, one adult can care for five or less children in a home without any extra risk.

I'll admit that a capable person could probably take care of seven or eight children, even in an emergency. The authors of the code probably didn't do much research when setting the limit at "less than six." They just needed some standard and selected what seemed like a reasonable number. That's not too uncommon. It's also the reason for the appeal process. If you think the code wasn't written with your situation in mind, the code provides a way to get special consideration.

Group H Occupancies

H stands for hazardous. Why isn't it closer to the top of the list? Remember that occupancies are based on risk to humans and on human loads. Most of the sub-groups under Group H have a relatively low human load.

H-4 is for repair garages and H-5 is for aircraft repair hangars. Why should aircraft repair be rated less hazardous than automotive repair? Think about it for a moment. Repair garages are usually smaller and have more flammable or combustible material stored closer together. Hangars are larger, with fewer people and better opportunity to control a fire.

A new sub-group appeared in the 1985 code. H-6 is used for semiconductor fabrication facilities and semiconductor research buildings. Buildings where computer chips are made didn't fit very well into any other category.

Group I Occupancies

Group I buildings usually house people under close supervision. The three sub-groups are based on the degree of supervision.

The big items here are the first two. I-1 covers children under the age of six and patients in hospitals or nursing homes who can't walk. These people couldn't respond to directions in an emergency.

But people in I-1 buildings can come and go somewhat at will. Why are prisoners in jail (Group I-3) considered less at risk? In a fire, they probably couldn't get out even if they tried. The answer is probably in the type of construction. Escape-proof buildings are naturally fire resistant. Chapter 4 has more information on these types of buildings.

Group M Occupancies

This is the least regulated occupancy group. There are only two sub-groups: Group M-1 for private garages, carports, sheds, and agricultural buildings, and Group M-2 for fences over 6 feet high, tanks, and towers.

Group R Occupancies

Group R includes hotels, motels, apartments, condominiums and private residences. There are only two sub-groups here, multi-family and single-family structures.

Notice that there isn't any R-2 category. That's space reserved for future use. If the building officials decide to create an intermediate group between R-1 and R-3, there's a place for it without re-numbering anything.

Remember the night and dwelling occupancies we talked about earlier? Typical night occupancy buildings include hotels, dormitories and large multiple dwellings. Single-family residences are under Group R-3, along with lodging houses.

But why are lodging houses listed under residences and not under hotels? It's a matter of definition. In Chapter Four of the UBC we'll find that a *hotel* is any building with six or more guest rooms. A *lodging house* can have up to five guest rooms. Again we can see that the degree of hazard is determined by the number of occupants.

Are You Confused?

Some of the occupancy classifications we've discussed in this chapter probably seem to overlap. Other types of buildings probably don't seem to be covered very well. If you're confused, don't worry. It's impossible to fit every building ever constructed into one of seven neat categories. There's lots of room for interpretation and doubt. But most buildings fit more or less into one of the seven categories. Your task is to figure out which group is most like the building you plan to construct.

If there's any doubt, get some help from the building department early in the planning process. The building department will usually favor the more restrictive classification and you'll almost certainly argue for the more permissive application. The outcome of that discussion can have a major effect on the cost of your building. And it's always more expensive to make changes later than it is to do it right the first time. Make a decision on occupancy group as early as possible.

Most disagreements on occupancy classes boil down to the way some term is defined and used in the code. Hotels and motels are a good example. In the building code there's no difference between the two. But most planners and zoning officials would insist that there *is* a difference. Motels have room access directly to the exterior. Hotels don't. But for building code purposes, a motel is always a hotel. That's just the way it is.

Now that we've determined the occupancy group for your building, let's look at occupant load and how we determine it.

Sidewalks Anyone?

Everybody knows how much kids love a good sidewalk. We know how curbs and sidewalks reduce dust and debris in a neighborhood. Well, one day about 15 years ago, the city engineer and I sat down to make life better and easier for the kids and housekeepers and homeowners in Kennewick who didn't live in neighborhoods with curbs and sidewalks. We decided to revise our public works ordinance. Anyone who built a new house or did very much remodeling had to have a sidewalk in front of their home. If they didn't already have one, they had to build one. The city council went along with us and our draft became law.

That created quite a stir. Contractors were against it. Some homeowners were against it. But the city council stood by their guns.

About a year later I had a contractor breeze into my office insisting he built the best houses around. And he also insisted that a sidewalk wasn't needed in front of the new house he was going to build. It would be the only house on the block with a sidewalk and curb. That seemed ridiculous to him. I issued him a permit for a new residence . . . and a sidewalk to go with it.

He built the house and I did the final inspection, including a check of his curb and sidewalk forms. It was a corner lot, so he had a lot of frontage. His forms checked out perfectly, so I signed off the inspection and left for the next job.

About an hour later, I had a thought: I forgot to make the final plumbing inspection for this contractor. I drove back to his job just in time to find him filling in part of the sidewalk forms with gravel. I guess he was still mad about spending those extra bucks for curb and sidewalk. Anyhow, he turned apologetic and started digging out the forms again.

"I'm curious," I said. "About how much concrete did you expect to save by filling in the forms."

"Oh, maybe ten or fifteen dollars worth."

"What do you figure your time is worth?"

He stared at me for almost a minute. Then started to grin. "Wasn't going to save much, was I?"

"Guess not," I agreed. "Let's see how long it takes you to dig out all that extra gravel. I'll sit right here and time you while you're digging. Then, when you get ready to pour, I'll be back to keep track of your time on that too." And that's exactly what I did.

I passed by that home a few months ago. Sidewalks and curbs run all the way up and down both sides of the street now. The city had to complete the last few stretches where sidewalks hadn't been installed. But my ordinance (and a little arm twisting) did the job. I'm sure the kids appreciate growing up in a neighborhood with good sidewalks. I wish I had the same advantage. And, judging by the asking prices for homes on that street, my sidewalks didn't do the homeowners any harm, either. Funny thing, I don't hear contractors complaining about my sidewalk ordinance any more. I guess people get comfortable with code changes eventually. Anyhow, they've got some newer changes to complain about now.

3

Occupancy Loads and Occupancy Groups

I talked a lot about hazards in the last chapter. But we've only scratched the surface on this important subject. *Hazard* is going to follow us through every chapter of this book. That's because the primary concern of the building code is risk to human life. If all buildings were perfectly safe, we wouldn't need building codes. Unfortunately, there's no such thing as a risk-free building. But we're a lot closer now than we were years ago before the first model codes were adopted.

In the last chapter we saw how all buildings were classified into one of seven code categories. Each category (occupancy group) has buildings with similar hazards. Later you'll see how code requirements vary for each category. But even within occupancy sub-groups the hazard can vary with the occupancy load. As the number of people in a building (the occupancy load) increases, the hazard to the people there also increases. That's why we've got to determine occupancy loads for the buildings we plan.

Computing Occupancy Loads

Figuring the occupancy load isn't a simple matter of calculating how many people can squeeze into a given area. The code is more concerned with number of people who can use the space *safely* and for its *designed purpose.*

There are two people who have a stake in this number. First, of course, is the owner, the person who will be using the property and who has to know how many people can use the restaurant, factory, shop or whatever.

The other interested party is the building inspector. How many people will occupy a site? What's their normal activity? Once we answer these questions, we can determine the type of occupancy and, in many cases, the type of construction needed for the building.

An important reference is UBC Table 33-A, *Minimum egress and access requirements,* reproduced here as Figure 3-1. Mark this spot well in your copy of the code. Of all the charts and tables in the UBC, this table will be among the most useful. It's the table the inspector normally uses to determine the number of people who will assemble in an area. Column 1 describes the use. Column 2 describes the number of occupants for which two or more exits are required. Column 3, the one we'll probably use most, lists the number of square feet assumed per person for each type of use. In this chapter we'll be dealing mainly with Columns 1 and 3.

TABLE NO. 33-A—MINIMUM EGRESS AND ACCESS REQUIREMENTS

USE[1]	MINIMUM OF TWO EXITS OTHER THAN ELEVATORS ARE REQUIRED WHERE NUMBER OF OCCUPANTS IS AT LEAST	OCCU-PANT LOAD FACTOR[2] (Sq. Ft.)	ACCESS BY MEANS OF A RAMP OR AN ELEVATOR MUST BE PROVIDED FOR THE PHYSICALLY HANDICAPPED AS INDICATED[3]
1. Aircraft Hangars (no repair)	10	500	Yes
2. Auction Rooms	30	7	Yes
3. Assembly Areas, Concentrated Use (without fixed seats) Auditoriums Churches and Chapels Dance Floors Lobby Accessory to Assembly Occupancy Lodge Rooms Reviewing Stands Stadiums	50	7	Yes[4][5]
Waiting Area	50	3	Yes[4][5]
4. Assembly Areas, Less-concentrated Use Conference Rooms Dining Rooms Drinking Establishments Exhibit Rooms Gymnasiums Lounges Stages	50	15	Yes[4][5][6]
5. Bowling Alley (assume no occupant load for bowling lanes)	50	12	Yes
6. Children's Homes and Homes for the Aged	6	80	Yes[7]
7. Classrooms	50	20	Yes[8]
8. Courtrooms	50	40	Yes
9. Dormitories	10	50	Yes[7]
10. Dwellings	10	300	No

Figure 3-1   *Minimum egress and access requirements*

USE[1]	MINIMUM OF TWO EXITS OTHER THAN ELEVATORS ARE REQUIRED WHERE NUMBER OF OCCUPANTS IS AT LEAST	OCCU-PANT LOAD FACTOR[2] (Sq. Ft.)	ACCESS BY MEANS OF A RAMP OR AN ELEVATOR MUST BE PROVIDED FOR THE PHYSICALLY HANDICAPPED AS INDICATED[3]
11. Exercising Rooms	50	50	Yes
12. Garage, Parking	30	200	Yes[9]
13. Hospitals and Sanitariums—Nursing Homes	6	80	Yes
14. Hotels and Apartments	10	200	Yes[10]
15. Kitchen—Commercial	30	200	No
16. Library Reading Room	50	50	Yes[4]
17. Locker Rooms	30	50	Yes
18. Malls (see Chapter 56)	—	—	—
19. Manufacturing Areas	30	200	Yes[7]
20. Mechanical Equipment Room	30	300	No
21. Nurseries for Children (Day care)	7	35	Yes
22. Offices	30	100	Yes[7]
23. School Shops and Vocational Rooms	50	50	Yes
24. Skating Rinks	50	50 on the skating area; 15 on the deck	Yes[4]
25. Storage and Stock Rooms	30	300	No
26. Stores—Retail Sales Rooms Basement Ground Floor Upper Floors	11 50 10	30 30 60	Yes Yes Yes
27. Swimming Pools	50	50 for the pool area; 15 on the deck	Yes[4]
28. Warehouses	30	500	No
29. All others	50	100	

Figure 3-1 (cont'd) *Minimum egress and access requirements*

FOOTNOTES FOR TABLE NO. 33-A

[1]For additional provisions on number of exits from Group H and I Occupancies and from rooms containing fuel-fired equipment or cellulose nitrate, see Sections 3320, 3321 and 3322, respectively.

[2]This table shall not be used to determine working space requirements per person.

[3]Elevators shall not be construed as providing a required exit.

[4]Access to secondary areas on balconies or mezzanines may be by stairs only, except when such secondary areas contain the only available toilet facilities.

[5]Reviewing stands, grandstands, bleachers, and folding and telescopic bleachers need not comply.

[6]Access requirements for conference rooms, dining rooms, lounges and exhibit rooms that are part of an office use shall be the same as required for the office use.

[7]Access to floors other than that closest to grade may be by stairs only, except when the only available toilet facilities are on other levels.

[8]When the floor closest to the grade offers the same programs and activities available on other floors, access to the other floors may be by stairs only, except when the only available toilet facilities are on other levels.

[9]Access to floors other than that closest to grade and to garages used in connection with apartment houses may be by stairs only.

[10]See Section 1214 for access to buildings and facilities in hotels and apartments.

[11]See Section 3303 for basement exit requirements.

[12]Occupant load based upon five persons for each alley, including 15 feet of runway.

From the Uniform Building Code, © *1988, ICBO*

Figure 3-1 (cont'd)   *Minimum egress and access requirements*

Footage Often Indicates Activity

The square footage per occupant in Column 3 varies from a minimum of 7 square feet to a maximum of 500 square feet. The assumed number of people per square foot varies with the type of activity. For example, the first item on the list is *aircraft hangars (no repair)*. Most hangars are big buildings with relatively few people per square foot of floor. The code assumes that you'll have one person in the hangar for each 500 square feet of floor. So if you have a 5,000 square foot hangar, your assumed occupant load would be 10 people.

Now compare this with *auction rooms,* the second item in the table. People usually stand shoulder to shoulder at an auction. Here, the assumed space is 7 square feet per occupant. If your auction room has 700 square feet of floor, the assumed occupant load is 100 people.

How did the authors of the code arrive at this figure of 7 *square feet* per occupant? Seven square feet is accepted as the normal amount of space a standing person needs to move and act normally. For example, if you were to stand in a closet 2 feet wide by 3-1/2 feet long (7 square feet), you probably wouldn't be too uncomfortable. You'd have room to turn around and stretch out a little. For a few hours at a time you could probably tolerate it pretty well.

Of course, there's more to the 7 square foot space standard than that. Part of that space — 2 feet by 3-1/2 feet — is usually used for aisles or hallways or furniture or machines.

Notice that there are two types of assembly areas in UBC Table 33-A. One is for *concentrated use* and the other is for *less concentrated use*. The major difference is that concentrated use refers to occupancies without fixed seats. Less concentrated use refers to areas with seating. A seated person is assumed to require 15 square feet of space.

Computing the Size of Your Building

The plans examiner will use Table 33-A to compute the assumed occupant load when you submit plans. But you can use the same space standards to design your building. If you know how many people will be using a building, let UBC Table 33-A help you compute the square footage needed. Multiply the number of occupants by the square footage per person in Figure 3-1. This will give you the total number of square feet of floor required.

The figure in the book is the *minimum size* for that occupancy. You may build larger than the minimum — as large as the owner's wallet will allow — but you may not build smaller.

Take a few minutes to study these figures. The building inspector is going to use them when computing the number of people permitted in the building — the number listed on the sign showing room capacity.

It's also important to identify the correct *use*. You may think that you're erecting a *stadium*, which requires 7 square feet of space per occupant. But if the inspector says you have a *gymnasium*, you'll have to provide twice as much floor space per occupant.

Computing Building Size for Mixed Occupancies

Many buildings house different occupancy groups. If you're designing a mixed building, go through the same steps as for a single-occupancy building — only you'll have to repeat them several times. Schools are a good example, since they have auditoriums, gymnasiums, vocational shops, libraries and administrative offices in addition to classrooms. Each has its own requirements, as shown in UBC Table 33-A.

Let's take an example. Suppose our building will house a lodge with a membership of 250 people. On dance night there may be as many as 400 people in the building. They want a dining room to accommodate 150 persons at a time and a bar that will hold another 100. They'll have a kitchen staff of four. The library, or reading room, will be open to the members and normally will serve about ten people at a time.

How much space should you provide? For the moment, let's assume that other problems such as fire resistance and type of construction have been solved. What we're after now is simply the amount of space the building will require.

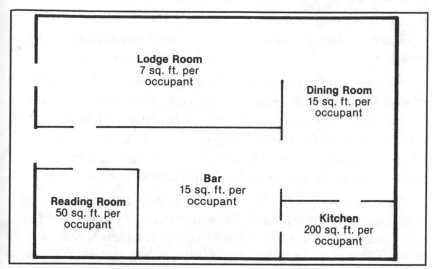

Figure 3-2 *Sketch of lodge*

Find *lodge rooms* in UBC Table 33-A (Figure 3-1). The table tells us that lodge rooms require 7 square feet per occupant. With a membership of 250 multiplied by 7, we find that the main lodge room must be no smaller than 1,750 square feet. That's a room about 35 feet wide by 50 feet long.

Look at Figure 3-2. Here's how to calculate the other areas:

Dance floor: 400 people times 7 square feet equals 2,800 square feet.

Dining room: 150 people times 15 square feet equals 2,250 square feet.

Bar: 100 people times 15 square feet equals 500 square feet.

Reading room: 10 people times 50 square feet equals 500 square feet.

Kitchen: 4 people times 200 square feet equals 800 square feet.

As you can see, the building will require at least 9,600 square feet of floor area.

So what happens if this is more space than the lodge feels they can afford? Do a little juggling. Have the design changed a bit. By making minor adjustments, you can still give your clients the space they need at the price they can afford.

You can combine the lodge hall with the dance floor, for instance. That eliminates 1,750 square feet. If you do that, the lodge couldn't hold a lodge meeting and a dance at the same time. If this is an "adults only" dining room, state liquor law may permit you to combine the bar and the dining room. You could even omit the reading room. But don't tamper with the kitchen space.

In fact, I doubt that a kitchen staff of four could operate in only 800 square feet, considering all the sophisticated kitchen equipment in use today. But I'd be inclined to go along with the recommendations of any kitchen consultants involved in designing the kitchen, so long as they provide at least 200 square feet per person.

If the membership figures are correct and the estimates of dining and dancing are also correct, the figures we've come up with should be O.K. If we need more space, a second or even a third story may be required. Of course, that will change exit requirements.

Occupancy or Occupant Load?

What we've just done was determine the occupant load for one building use. *Do not confuse this with establishing occupancy.* We did that in the last chapter. *Occupancy* is the type of business or operation being conducted. *Occupant load* is the number of people that can be expected to use the building while it's open for business.

Mixed Occupancy
and Different Ownerships

Suppose we have a building with several uses, like the lodge building, but also with several different tenants. Our approach has to be a little different. We'll begin by identifying each of the tenants and establishing them as separate uses.

Let's say the second floor is designed as a meeting hall for the Loyal Order of Hose Handlers. Part of the first floor is a ballroom to be leased by the Rompers and Stompers. The rest of the ground floor will be used by the Greasy Spoon Restaurant and Taphouse.

The lodge room would be an assembly room, probably without a stage, although it could easily have one. From the floor area, we know the occupant load will be less than 300 people. UBC Table 5-A (Chapter 2, Figure 2-2) tells us that this is either Group A-2.1 or A-3 occupancy. But beware! There's a trap here. Group A-2.1 has "an occupant load of 300 *or more* without a stage." Group A-3 can have "an occupant load of *less than* 300 without a stage." It doesn't seem like much of a difference until you consider the type of construction allowed. UBC Table 5-B (Figure 3-3) permits you to use Type II-N, III-N or V-N construction for Group A-3, but not for Group A-2.1. This difference can really add to construction costs. (We'll discuss types of construction in detail in the next chapter.)

Using the magic number of 300 as an occupant load may be the key to saving money. You may be better off reducing the floor area by a few square feet to get an occupant load of

TABLE NO. 5-B—REQUIRED SEPARATION IN BUILDINGS OF MIXED OCCUPANCY
(In Hours)

	A-1	A-2	A-2.1	A-3	A-4	B-1	B-2	B-3	B-4	E	H-1	H-2	H-3	H-4-5	H-6-7[1]	I	M[2]	R-1	R-3
A-1		N	N	N	N	4	3	3	3	N		4	4	4	4	3	1	1	1
A-2	N		N	N	N	3	1	1	1	N		4	4	4	4	3	1	1	1
A-2.1	N	N		N	N	3	1	1	1	N		4	4	4	4	3	1	1	1
A-3	N	N	N		N	3	N	1	1	N		4	4	4	3	3	1	1	1
A-4	N	N	N	N		3	1	1	N	N		4	4	4	4	3	1	1	1
B-1	4	3	3	3	3		1	1	1	3		2	1	1	1	4	1	3[3]	1
B-2	3	1	1	N	1	1		1	1	1		2	1	1	1	2	1	1	1
B-3	3	1	1	1	1	1	1		1	1		2	1	1	1	4	1	1	1
B-4	3	1	1	1	N	1	1	1		1		2	1	1	1	4	N	1	1
E	N	N	N	N	N	3	1	1	1			4	4	4	3	1	1	1	1
H-1	Not Permitted in Mixed Occupancies. See Chapter 9.																		
H-2	4	4	4	4	4	2	2	2	2	4			1	1	2	4	1	4	4
H-3	4	4	4	4	4	1	1	1	1	4		1		1	1	4	1	3	3
H-4-5	4	4	4	4	4	1	1	1	1	4		1	1		1	4	1	3	3
H-6-7[1]	4	4	4	3	4	1	1	1	1	3		2	1	1		4	3	4	4
I	3	3	3	3	3	4	2	4	4	1		4	4	4	4		1	1	1
M[2]	1	1	1	1	1	1	1	1	N	1		1	1	1	3	1		1	1
R-1	1	1	1	1	1	3[3]	1	1	1	1		4	3	3	4	1	1		N
R-3	1	1	1	1	1	1	1	1	1	1		4	3	3	4	1	1	N	

H-1: Not Permitted in Mixed Occupancies. See Chapter 9.

Note: For detailed requirements and exceptions, see Section 503.

[1] For special provisions on highly toxic materials, see Fire Code.

[2] For agricultural buildings, see also Appendix Chapter 11.

[3] For reduction in fire-resistive rating, see Section 503 (d).

From the Uniform Building Code, ©1988, ICBO

Figure 3-3. *Required separation in buildings of mixed occupancy*

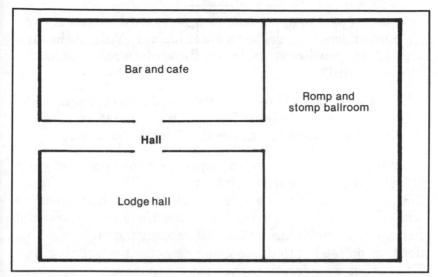

Figure 3-4 *Hall common to various occupancies*

299. On a building 30 feet wide, the reduction needed may be only a few inches.

Now, assume the dance hall has a stage. Since it will have over 300 occupants, the hall will be in an A-1 group. The bar/restaurant with less than 300 occupants is back in the A-3 grouping.

Because you have an A-1 grouping (the dance hall) in your building, you must have Type I construction throughout the entire building. This is an important consideration when mixing occupancies, If you left out the dance hall, you could go to a less expensive type of construction.

Area Separation

Area separations are like fire breaks. They help retard the spread of fire between rooms. Installing area separation lets you design part of an area for a high hazard occupancy and the remainder of an area for a lower hazard. Without the area separation, you'd have to design the entire area to meet the higher hazard.

Area separations are usually defined in terms of hours of fire protection. A one-hour fire wall means that an adjacent area will be protected from fire for at least one hour.

Will we need an area separation in our two-story lodge/ballroom/restaurant building? UBC Table 5-B (Figure 3-3) says no, but let's take a closer look. For mixed occupancies within Group A, no separation is needed except the usual partitions to divide the space and support the building. This depends on the location, area, and height of the building, and a few other considerations, but not occupancy.

Access Between Occupancies

Related to area separation is *access between occupancies*. Could you provide access from one occupancy to another without having to go out to the street and come back through another door?

You can do this by having the areas separated by a common hallway with direct outside access. See Figure 3-4. Patrons may use this hallway to go from the dining room or the bar to the dance hall. But the hall must meet some requirements. It must be short (so it won't create an additional hazard) or have enough doors to allow adequate exit to the outside. We'll discuss these code requirements later.

The idea isn't new. Enclosed shopping malls have been doing this for years. Although nearly all house the same occupancy group, most provide access to a common enclosed hallway.

Since we're on the subject of aisles, halls, and access, it's a good time to bring up *vomitories*. Vomitories have been around a long time — and they're not what you may think. You may have one in your church, theater, auditorium or gymnasium. The dictionary says it's an entrance piercing the banks of aisles of a theater or auditorium. In practice, it's an interior court into which several hallways might enter. Examples are a hallway in a shopping mall or a cluster of businesses opening into a central court.

Occupancy —
Restrictive Requirements

Now, what about some of the more restrictive requirements of the different occupancy groups we've discussed? These requirements can alter the shape, size and capacity of a proposed building. In some cases there may be trade-offs (if you do this, then you can enlarge that, for instance.)

Up to this point we've been dealing mostly in generalities. Now it's time to get a little more specific.

Buildings or parts of buildings classed in Group A-1 must be Type I or Type II-FR construction. I'll explain types of construction shortly. They can't exceed the area and height limits specified in Section 505, 506, or 507. These sections (UBC Tables 5-A, 5-B, 5-C, and 5-D) govern the gross floor area and the heights of buildings for this group. They also allow increases in the limits for safety items like automatic sprinkler systems.

Is this good or bad? That depends on what you want to do. Let's take a closer look. You'll find UBC Table 5-A in Figure 2-2 (Chapter 2). Find Table 5-B in Figure 3-3 and Tables 5-C and 5-D in Figures 3-5 and 3-6.

TABLE NO. 5-C—BASIC ALLOWABLE FLOOR AREA FOR BUILDINGS ONE STORY IN HEIGHT[1]
(In Square Feet)

OCCUPANCY	TYPES OF CONSTRUCTION										
	I F.R.	**II** F.R.	**II** ONE-HOUR	**II** N	**III** ONE-HOUR	**III** N	**IV** H.T.	**IV** ONE-HOUR	**IV** N	**V** ONE-HOUR	**V** N
A-1	Unlimited	Not Permitted									
A) 2-2.1	Unlimited	29,900	13,500	Not Permitted	13,500	Not Permitted	13,500	10,500	Not Permitted	10,500	Not Permitted
A) 3-4[2]	Unlimited	29,900	13,500	9,100	13,500	9,100	13,500	10,500	6,000	10,500	6,000
B) 1-2-3[3]	Unlimited	39,900	18,000	12,000	18,000	12,000	18,000	14,000	8,000	14,000	8,000
B-4	Unlimited	59,900	27,000	18,000	27,000	18,000	27,000	21,000	12,000	21,000	12,000
E	Unlimited	45,200	20,200	13,500	20,200	13,500	20,200	15,700	9,100	15,700	9,100
H-1	15,000	12,400	5,600	3,700	Not Permitted		5,600	4,400	2,500	4,400	2,500
H-2[4]	15,000	12,400	5,600	3,700	5,600	3,700	5,600	4,400	2,500	4,400	2,500
H-3-4-5[4]	Unlimited	24,800	11,200	7,500	11,200	7,500	11,200	8,800	5,100	8,800	5,100
H-6-7	Unlimited	39,900	18,000	12,000	18,000	12,000	18,000	14,000	8,000	14,000	8,000
I) 1-2	Unlimited	15,100	6,800	Not Permitted[8]	6,800	Not Permitted	6,800	5,200	Not Permitted	5,200	Not Permitted
I-3	Unlimited	15,100	Not Permitted[5]								
M[6]		See Chapter 11									
R-1	Unlimited	29,900	13,500	9,100[7]	13,500	9,100[7]	13,500	10,500	6,000[7]	10,500	6,000[7]
R-3	Unlimited										

[1]For multistory buildings, see Section 505 (b).
[2]For limitations and exceptions, see Section 602 (a).
[3]For open parking garages, see Section 709.
[4]See Section 903.
[5]See Section 1002 (b).
[6]For agricultural buildings, see also Appendix Chapter 11.
[7]For limitations and exceptions, see Section 1202 (b).
[8]In hospitals and nursing homes, see Section 1002 (a) for exception.

N—No requirements for fire resistance
F.R.—Fire Resistive
H.T.—Heavy Timber

From the Uniform Building Code, ©1988, ICBO

Figure 3-5 Allowable floor area for buildings one story in height

TABLE NO. 5-D—MAXIMUM HEIGHT OF BUILDINGS

OCCUPANCY	I	II			III		IV	V	
	F.R.	F.R.	ONE-HOUR	N	ONE-HOUR	N	H.T.	ONE-HOUR	N
MAXIMUM HEIGHT IN FEET	Unlimited	160	65	55	65	55	65	50	40
MAXIMUM HEIGHT IN STORIES									
A-1	Unlimited	4	Not Permitted	Not Permitted	Not Permitted	Not Permitted	Not Permitted	Not Permitted	Not Permitted
A) 2-2.1	Unlimited	4	2	Not Permitted	2	Not Permitted	2	2	Not Permitted
A) 3-4[1]	Unlimited	12	2	1	2	1	2	2	1
B) 1-2-3[2]	Unlimited	12	4	2	4	2	4	3	2
B-4	Unlimited	12	4	2	4	2	4	3	2
E[3]	Unlimited	4	2	1	2	1	2	2	1
H-1[4]	1	1	1	1	Not Permitted	Not Permitted	1	1	1
H-2[4]	Unlimited	2	1	1	Not Permitted	Not Permitted	2	1	1
H-3-4-5[4]	Unlimited	5	2	1	Not Permitted	Not Permitted	2	2	1
H-6-7	3	3	3	2	Not Permitted	Not Permitted	3	3	1
I-1[5]	Unlimited	3	1	Not Permitted	1	Not Permitted	1	1	Not Permitted
I-2	Unlimited	3	2	Not Permitted	2	Not Permitted	2	2	Not Permitted
I-3	Unlimited	2	Not Permitted[6]	Not Permitted[6]	Not Permitted[6]	Not Permitted[6]	Not Permitted[6]	Not Permitted[6]	Not Permitted[6]
M[7]	See Chapter 11								
R-1	Unlimited	12	4	2[8]	4	2[8]	4	3	2[8]
R-3	Unlimited	3	3	3	3	3	3	3	3

TYPES OF CONSTRUCTION

Figure 3-6   *Maximum height of buildings*

Water closets		Urinals	Lavatories
Males	**Females**		
4 – 401 to 600	4 – 201 to 400	4 – 401 to 600	3 – 401 to 750
Over 400, add 1 fixture for each additional 500 males and one for each 300 females.		Over 600, 1 for each additional 300 males	Over 750, 1 for each additional 500 persons

From the Uniform Plumbing Code, © 1988, IAPMO

Figure 3-7   *Plumbing requirements*

Group A-1, you'll recall, is *Any assembly building with a stage and an occupant load of 1,000 or more in the building.* Remember that we're working with gross floor area and that most of the occupants will be seated. At 15 square feet per occupant for 1,000 occupants, we'll need a gross floor area of 15,000 square feet. This isn't exceptional for a grand ballroom in some of the larger hotels. Even a skating rink could be larger than that (using nominal figures, about 100 feet times 150 feet). Type I construction is about the most fire resistive the code calls for. It's also expensive to build. Will it be worth the cost? Would a slightly smaller building (less than 15,000 square feet) be nearly as good? Of course, that's up to you, the owner, and the owner's banker.

The code also says that if the main floor slopes, the slope can't exceed one in five. Also, the building must front directly on or have access to a public street at least 20 feet wide, with the main assembly floor located at or near ground level. The code also requires you to furnish light and ventilation by windows or skylights. They must have an area at least one-eighth the total floor area, one-half of which must be openable.

(You can usually provide mechanical ventilation instead of opening windows.)

Plumbing Requirements

Plumbing requirements of the UBC aren't too restrictive for the general public, but they're more specific for the handicapped. In general, you must provide, in an approved location, at least one lavatory for each two water closets for each sex and at least one drinking fountain for each floor level. This is a rather strange requirement because the UBC doesn't cover water closets in Group A occupancies. For this you must consult your plumbing code. Figure 3-7 shows the Uniform Plumbing Code requirements.

Before anyone yells "Foul!" because of the difference in the two codes, I'll explain the discrepancies. In the first place, the Uniform Building Code and the Uniform Plumbing Code are written by different groups. If you're in an area that uses only the UBC and not the UPC, go by the requirements of the UBC. Otherwise, the more restrictive of the two would apply. Although the UBC says you need only half as many lavatories as water closets, the UPC clearly states that for 1,000 occupants you need five water closets for men and six for women. The men would also have urinals. Likewise, you would need four lavatories for each sex, even though the building code only calls for three for men and three for women.

Sprinklers and Exits

We'll take a close look at sprinklers and exits in later chapters. Section 3802 covers fire-extinguishing systems and standpipes. Chapter 33 of the UBC covers exiting.

Group A occupancies, you will remember, have five major sub-groups. You can't have Division 1, 2 and 2.1 occupancies in buildings without at least one-hour fire-resistive protection. This is spelled out in UBC Table 5-C (Figure 3-5). Let's take a look at this table and discuss how it could affect your building plans.

Type of Construction vs. Occupancy

UBC Table 5-C shows the type of construction allowed in various occupancies and the allowable square footage. The column at the left of the chart gives the occupancy. The other columns give the square footage of floor area allowed for any of these occupancies for the type of construction shown. We'll look more closely at these in the next chapter. But for now, all you need to know is that there are five main types of construction. Type I is the most fire-resistive; Type V is the least.

Building Height vs. Type of Construction

Take a look at UBC Table 5-D (Figure 3-6). This shows how the type of construction governs the height of a building. In effect, it says: If you want to build this high, this is what you have to do for this particular occupancy.

Type I construction, which is about as incombustible as you can get, has no height limitations. Type II construction may go to 160 feet with *fire-resistive (FR)* construction. All lesser types range between 40 and 65 feet high. To further confuse you, note that below the height limitation in feet is *maximum height in stories*. Also notice that in some instances there are certain occupancies that are not allowed in some types of construction regardless of height or area. This is very important to remember.

The use of "N" in these charts means there are *no requirements* for fire resistance. Unless otherwise noted, this "N" description applies to any of the UBC charts.

Allowable Area Increases

UBC Tables 5-C and 5-D may seem very restrictive. Well, maybe they are. But relief is available. For instance, there are several ways to increase the basic allowable floor area. One is to use a higher type of construction. If that's too expensive, there's another alternative. I call it *spatial separation*. It refers to allowing more space around your building as a barrier against fires that start in adjacent buildings. And conversely, it protects adjacent buildings from fires starting in *your* building.

Another good way to increase allowable floor area is to install automatic sprinkler systems. But this option is limited to certain occupancies and certain conditions. Although it's expensive, more jurisdictions are requiring it, regardless of floor area.

There are several ways to get more floor space without going to more expensive types of construction. What you do is a matter of balancing the cost against the benefit to see which alternative is best. Let's see what the UBC permits:

> **Section 506(a) General.** *The floor areas specified in Section 505 (referring to Table 5-C) may be increased by one of the following:*
>
> **1. Separation on two sides.** *Where public space, streets, or yards more than 20 feet in width extend along and adjoin two sides of the building, floor areas may be increased at a rate of one and one-quarter percent for each foot by which the minimum width exceeds 20 feet, but the increase shall not exceed 50 percent.*

2. Separation on three sides. *Where public ways, or yards more than 20 feet in width extend along and adjoin three sides of the building, floor areas may be increased at a rate of two and one-half percent for each foot by which the minimum width exceeds 20 feet, but the increase shall not exceed 100 percent.*

3. Separation on all sides. *Where public ways, or yards more than 20 feet in width, extend on all sides of a building and adjoin the entire perimeter, floor areas may be increased at a rate of five percent for each foot by which the minimum width exceeds 20 feet. Such increases shall not exceed 100 percent, except that greater increases shall be permitted for the following occupancies:*

A. Group B, Division 3 *Aircraft storage hangars not exceeding one story in height.*

B. Group B, Division 4 *Occupancies not exceeding two stories in height.*

C. Group H, Division 5 *Aircraft repair hangars not exceeding one story in height. Area increases shall not exceed 500 percent for aircraft repair hangars except as provided in Section 506(b).*

The code also states that there are no limits on any one- or two-story buildings in Group B and Group H, Division 5 occupancies if they have an approved automatic sprinkler system as specified in Chapter 38 of the code, and are entirely surrounded by public space at least 60 feet wide. And there's more. The next paragraph says that the area of Group B, Division 4 occupancies in a one-story Type II, Type III one-hour, or Type IV building can be unlimited if the building is surrounded by a public space at least 60 feet wide.

In Section 506(c) you'll find another item that might encourage you to install a sprinkler system. Both floor area and ceiling height can be increased if you install fire sprinklers.

This means that if you have a Type V one-hour building, you would normally be allowed 10,500 square feet in an R-1 occupancy (hotels and apartments). But if you installed an automatic sprinkler system, you could increase this to 31,500 square feet. This is better than you'd get if you went with Type II FR construction. But there's more to it than that. Let's take a look.

Compounding Area Computation

I explained earlier that you could increase the area in your building if it's surrounded by yards and streets — what I call *spatial separation.* Let's go back to that 10,500 square foot building. By providing sprinklers we found that you could increase that footage to 31,500, provided it was all on one story. Now let's assume that this building has a 50-foot-wide street on one side. Going back to Section 506(a) you'll find that the area can be increased again at the rate of 1-1/4 percent for each foot the minimum width exceeds 20 feet. For our 50-foot street, the excess is 30 feet. The total increase can't exceed 50 percent.

This amounts to a substantial increase in the size of your building. Let's figure it out:

10,500 x 1-1/4% x 30' x 3 (for sprinklers) = 43,311 square feet

Which should you figure first, the percent increase gained by the separation or the tripling for the sprinklers? Let's try it this way:

10,500 x 30' x 1-1/4% x 3 = 43,312 square feet

The difference is due to rounding decimals. Otherwise the answers are the same.

Let's go over this once more. This time let's assume that instead of a separation on just one side, there will be a separation on all sides. Remember, the code says that we use a 5 percent increase for each foot of sideyard by which the minimum width exceeds 20 feet. For our purposes we'll assume that the yards are all 50 feet wide.

10,500 x 30' x 5% x 3 = 96,070 square feet

This is probably more of an increase than you planned on — and it's more than you can have. You can't use all of it. You're still stuck with allowable overall increases. You must figure out which is best — more space around the building or an automatic sprinkler system — to get the space you need.

Maximum Height of Buildings and Increases

Adding sprinklers to a building increases its allowable height. The maximum height and number of stories of every building depend on its occupancy and construction. Limits are in UBC Table 5-D.

If completely sprinklered, a building may be increased in height by one story. But this increase is *not* allowed if you've already computed the increase in floor area based on the sprinklers. Sorry about that.

Towers, spires and steeples made of noncombustible material that aren't used for habitation or storage are limited in height only by structural design. If they're made of combustible material, they can't exceed 20 feet above the height limitations in UBC Table 5-D.

Elevators and High-Rise Buildings

While we're discussing building height and area, I'd like to mention several hazards posed by elevators in high-rise buildings.

In 1972, following the San Fernando, California earthquake, a study was done on elevator problems in multi-story buildings damaged by the earthquake. All that shaking caused the cables and counterweights to bang around in the elevator shafts, putting the elevators out of service even though there was little structural damage. In a five- to ten-story building this might be little more than a nuisance. But can you imagine what it would be like in a 30-story building?

If there's a fire in a high-rise building, automatic elevators can be a hazard. Most modern elevators have automatic controls. Unfortunately, the automatic controls respond to heat. The automatic control summons all elevators directly to the floor of the fire and opens the doors automatically. Any fire fighters riding in those cars would be exposed to a sudden burst of heat or flame as the door opens. And if the fire is close enough to the elevator, heat may stop the car — also an unpleasant situation for any riders. So fire fighters have to haul their equipment up many flights of stairs to get to the fire.

Most jurisdictions now require signs forbidding the use of elevators during fires.

Group B Area Requirements

Generally, Group B area requirements are quite lenient. And since most buildings outside the downtown area are surrounded by parking areas and streets, you can usually get increases. Allowable heights are also generous. UBC Table 5-A allows a B-1 occupancy in a Type V-N building (frame, with no fire-resistive construction) of 6,000 square feet. But Section 1102 limits service stations to noncombustible or one-hour fire-resistive construction. Storage garages must have floors protected against saturation.

You must separate storage areas larger than 1,000 square feet in wholesale and retail stores from the sales area with one-hour separation walls unless the building has sprinklers. Then the allowable area may be increased.

Group B, Division 2, Storage Areas

Storage areas in Group B received a lot of attention in the 1988 UBC. They require one-hour fire-resistive separation if they're connected to B-2 sales areas. There are exceptions to the 1,000 square foot limitation if the area is fully sprinklered. Fire-resistance and exiting requirements are critical if the area houses laboratories and shops used for education.

Attic Separations

This section of the code usually requires attics exceeding 3,000 square feet to be divided by area separations if they're built with combustible materials. However, if the attic will have sprinklers, the allowable area may be increased.

These separations are very important. Two serious motel fires in 1980 were aggravated by openings cut in the area separations by plumbers and electricians and not made fire-safe.

These separations must be made of gypsum wallboard (sheetrock) at least 1/2-inch-thick, 1-inch-thick tight-fitting wood, 3/8-inch-thick plywood, or other approved noncombustible material with adequate support. Protect any openings in attic separations by installing self-closing doors. And be sure to protect all wiring, plumbing and ductwork.

Exits

The code requires that all store exit doors swing in the direction of egress (the way out). These doors can't swing over the public right of way. That means all exit doors in commercial buildings built to the property line must be recessed. Many property owners are reluctant to do that because it robs them of space inside the store. On new construction this problem can be addressed in the design. But what about replacing doors in existing buildings? This is something the inspector will take a hard look at.

There's another related problem: exiting from basements in Group B occupancies. All basements in Group B occupancies need two exits, one of which must open to the outside. But many older buildings aren't designed this way. And many owners of new buildings are reluctant to meet this requirement.

It's possible to get around this by having the basement stairs end near the rear door to provide easy exit. But check with the building inspector. He'll be the one granting final approval.

Group B-4 is probably the most liberal of all the occupancies regarding building height, area, exiting and other requirements. Usually B-4 buildings have few occupants and are surrounded by open space.

How Much Remodeling Is Acceptable?

Some builders are surprised by code compliance problems when they start remodeling a home or store. One of the first questions the inspector may ask is why you intend to remodel. If you're just upgrading the property with no change in occupancy, the problems will be simpler. But if there'll be a new tenant with a different type of business, that's a different story. A changed occupancy may require basic changes in the building that weren't anticipated. You'd have to go all the way back to the basic question of occupancy group determination. For our purposes, let's assume you're only upgrading the premises.

If your city adopted the UBC without amendment, the following sections would apply:

Section 104(a) General. *Buildings and structures to which additions, alteration or repairs are made shall comply with all requirements of this code for new facilities except as specifically provided for in this section. See Section 1210 for provisions requiring installation of smoke detectors in existing Group R, Division 3 Occupancies.*

(b) Additions, Alterations or Repairs. *Additions, alterations or repairs may be made to any building or structure without requiring the existing building or structure to comply with all the requirements of this code, provided the addition, alteration or repair conforms to that required for a new building or structure. Additions, alterations or repairs shall not be made to an existing building or structure which will cause the existing building or structure to be in violation of any of the provisions of this code, nor shall such additions or alterations cause the existing building or structure to become unsafe. An unsafe condition shall be deemed to have been created if an addition or alteration will cause the existing building or structure to become structurally unsafe or overloaded; will not provide adequate egress in compliance with the provisions of this code or will obstruct existing exits; will create a fire hazard; will reduce required fire resistance or will otherwise create conditions dangerous to human life. Any building so altered, which involves a change in use or occupancy, shall not exceed the height, number of stories and area permitted for new buildings. Any build-*

ing plus new additions shall not exceed the height, number of stories and area specified for new buildings. Additions or alterations shall not be made to an existing building or structure when such existing building or structure is not in full compliance with the provisions of this code except when such addition or alteration will result in the existing building or structure being no more hazardous based on life safety, fire safety and sanitation, than before such additions or alterations are undertaken. (See also Section 911(c) for Group H, Division 6 Occupancies.)

Alteration or repairs to an existing building or structure which are nonstructural and do not adversely affect any structural member or any part of the building or structure having required fire resistance may be made with the same materials of which the building or structure is constructed. The installation or replacement of glass shall be as required for new installations.

(c) Existing Occupancy. Buildings in existence at the time of the adoption of this code may have their existing use or occupancy continued, if such use or occupancy was legal at the time of adoption of this code, provided such continued use is not dangerous to life.

Any change in the use or occupancy of any existing building or structure shall comply with the provisions of Sections 307 and 502 of this code.

For existing buildings, see Appendix Chapter 1.

If the owner is just trying to bring the building up to current code standards or making changes to qualify for more favorable insurance rates, no problem. But I suggest that you invite the building inspector to go through the place with you, pointing out all areas of non-compliance. You don't have to renovate the whole building, of course. But the inspector may require some changes that involve key hazards. It's better to find out about those early in the project.

Group E Occupancies

This group covers schools. The trend today is toward larger, consolidated schools. Usually larger contracting firms (or groups of smaller firms) get these jobs.

Normally, plans for new schools are examined very thoroughly for code compliance well before construction begins. State (and maybe federal) authorities go over the plans with a fine-tooth comb. The local building department will give them another review. All the general contractor has to do is follow the plans. But many smaller construction firms do remodeling work in public schools and build smaller private schools. In that case, some code problems may have to be worked out as you go.

Group E occupancies (the educational group) may be any type of construction. Of course, they're still governed by UBC Tables 5-C and 5-D (Figures 3-5 and 3-6). Both area and height dictate the type of construction.

Notice that all areas for kindergarten, first and second grades must be located on the first floor, not above or below. Keep this in mind when you're asked to convert a basement in an existing home into a day care center. Consult the local building inspector or fire marshal before going too far with your plans.

The building code rarely specifies a definite number of water closets, urinals and lavatories, except in Group E occupancies. Section 805 states:

> *Water closets shall be provided on the basis of the following ratio of water closets to the number of students:*
>
> *Elementary schools...Boys — 1 to 100, Girls — 1 to 35; Secondary schools...Boys — 1 to 100, Girls — 1 to 45.*

In addition, urinals shall be provided for boys on the basis of 1 to 30 in elementary and secondary schools.

There shall be provided at least one lavatory for each two water closets or urinals, and at least one drinking fountain on each floor for elementary and secondary schools.

Group E Exits and Corridors

All exit doors serving areas of more than 50 occupants must swing outward and have panic hardware. It's a good idea to have all exit doors swing outward, even where it's not required.

This is a good place to bring up the requirements for school corridors. Section 3319(e) requires that a corridor in a Group E, Division 1 occupancy must be the width required by Section 3303, plus 2 feet. Section 3303 is the section that covers the width of exits and states that a corridor may be only 44 inches wide. But in a school, no corridor may be less than 6 feet wide.

That seems like a contradiction, doesn't it? If a corridor can't be less than 6 feet wide, how can you have a 44-inch-wide corridor? It sounds as though you could have a 44-inch corridor feeding into a 6-foot exit, but that isn't so. Section 3302(b) states that the total width of exits in feet can't be less than the total occupant load served divided by 50. This raises two very important points. First, since we're talking about schools, the rule of 6-foot exits (and corridors) must apply. Second, even when you think you've found the answer, read further. Your answer may not be complete.

Can the corridor be reduced by so-called "natural" barriers? Yes, but very little. Section 3305(d) states:

> *(d) **Projections.** The required width of corridors shall be unobstructed.*

> *Exception: Handrails and doors, when fully opened, shall not reduce the required width by more than 7 inches. Doors in any position shall not reduce the required width by more than one-half. Other nonstructural projections such as trim and similar decorative features may project into required width 1-1/2 inches on each side.*

Later in this book I'll explain in detail how exit widths are determined. But there's one other requirement I'd like to mention here. The maximum distance from any point in the building to the nearest exit must not exceed 150 feet for unsprinklered buildings and 225 feet for sprinklered buildings.

Heliports and Helistops

Heliports and helistops are controlled under Group B occupancies, not Group H (hazardous) as you might think. Apparently this is because they're primarily outdoor operations, usually in a commercial area. In spite of their outdoor activities, however, requirements regarding their operation are stringent.

Even if you live in a small town, you may be called on to build a helistop or even the more sophisticated heliport. The local hospital might need one. And many crop dusters are now using helicopters in their business.

It's important to understand the difference between a heliport and a helistop, or landing pad. According to the definition section of the UBC, a heliport is any area where helicopters can be completely serviced, while a helistop is only for taking on or discharging passengers. A heliport is subject to far more restrictions because there will be flammable materials present.

The landing pad, or helistop, beside the local hospital would have very few restrictions. But if the pad were on the roof of the hospital, you'd have to include the weight of the helicopter in the anticipated roof load. However, they wouldn't be able to add fuel or do any service work up there. A simple concrete pad with adequate clearance makes the best helistop.

Groups I and H

Group I occupancies (the institutional group) must have approved fire alarm systems. Audible alarms can be used in non-patient areas, but visible alarms must be used in patient areas. The last thing a heart patient needs is a false alarm to rouse him out of a deep sleep. Smoke detectors must receive their primary power from the building wiring.

Stringent exiting, height, area, and construction requirements apply for institutions. Areas of more than 200 square feet must have two exits. In Group H, Divisions 3, 4, 5, and 6 occupancies with an area in excess of 1,000 square feet require two exits.

Group H (hazardous) occupancies include areas where highly flammable materials are stored, processed or used, or where highly combustible manufacturing is done. See UBC Table 9-A (Figure 3-8), *Exempt amounts of hazardous materials, liquids and chemicals.* Table 9-C (Figure 3-9) lists the distance from property lines and wall openings for storage of hazardous materials.

Several special provisions regulate construction in this category. The walls must be at least one-hour fire-resistive and surrounded by public space, streets, or yards at least 60 feet wide. If cars or airplanes are stored, repaired, or operated, the floor surfaces must be non-combustible.

Height is also important. If the building is over 95 feet high, the structural frame must be fire-resistive for at least

TABLE NO. 9-A—EXEMPT AMOUNTS OF HAZARDOUS MATERIALS, LIQUIDS AND CHEMICALS PRESENTING A PHYSICAL HAZARD[1]

BASIC QUANTITIES PER CONTROL AREA[1]

When two units are given, values within parentheses are in cubic feet (Cu. Ft.) or pounds (Lbs.)

CONDITION		STORAGE[2]			USE[2]—CLOSED SYSTEMS			USE[2]—OPEN SYSTEMS		
MATERIAL	CLASS	Solid Lbs. (Cu. Ft.)	Liquid Gallons (Lbs.)	Gas Cu. Ft.	Solid Lbs. (Cu. Ft.)	Liquid Gallons (Lbs.)	Gas Cu. Ft.	Solid Lbs. (Cu. Ft.)	Liquid Gallons (Lbs.)	Gas Cu. Ft.
1.1 Combustible liquid[3]	II	—	120[4 5]	—	—	120[4]	—	—	30[4]	—
	III-A	—	330[5]	—	—	330[4]	—	—	80[4]	—
	III-B	—	13,200[5 6]	—	—	13,200[6]	—	—	3,300[6]	—
1.2 Combustible dust lbs./1000 cu. ft.		1[7]	—	—	1[7]	—	—	1[7]	—	—
1.3 Combustible fiber (loose) (baled)		(100) (1,000)	—	—	(100) (1,000)	—	—	(20) (200)	—	—
1.4 Cryogenic, flammable or oxidizing			45			45			10	
2.1 Explosives		1[5 8 9]	(1)[5 8 9]	—	1/8[8]	(1/4)[8]	—	1/8[8]	(1/4)[8]	—
3.1 Flammable solid		125[4 5]	—	—	25[4]	—	—	25[4]	—	—
3.2 Flammable gas (gaseous) (liquefied)		—	15[4 5]	750[4 5]	—	15[4 5]	750[4 5]	—	—	—
3.3 Flammable liquid[3]	I-A	—	30[4 5]	—	—	30[4]	—	—	10[4]	—
	I-B	—	60[4 5]	—	—	60[4]	—	—	15[4]	—
	I-C	—	90[4 5]	—	—	90[4]	—	—	20[4]	—
Combination 1-A, I-B, I-C		—	120[4 5 10]	—	—	120[4 10]	—	—	30[4 10]	—

From the Uniform Building Code, © 1988, ICBO

Figure 3-8 *Exempt amounts of hazardous materials*

Material / Class							
4.2 Organic peroxide							
I	(5)[5]	5[5]	5[5]	(1)[4]	1[4]	1[4]	—
II	(50)[4,5]	50[5]	50[5]	(50)[4]	10[4]	10[4]	(10)[4]
III	(125)[4,5]	125[5]	125[5]	(125)[4]	25[4]	25[4]	(25)[4]
IV	(500)	500	500	(500)	100	100	(100)
V	N.L.	N.L.	N.L.	N.L.	N.L.	N.L.	N.L.
4.3 Oxidizer							
4	(1)[5,8]	1[5,8]	1[5,8]	(1/4)[8]	1/8	1/8	(1/4)[8]
3	(10)[4,5]	10[5]	10[5]	(2)[4]	2[4]	2[4]	(2)[4]
2	(250)[4,5]	250[5]	250[5]	(250)[4]	50[4]	50[4]	(50)[4]
1	(1,000)[4,5]	1,000[5]	1,000[5]	(1,000)[4]	200[4]	200[4]	(200)[4]
4.4 Oxidizer—Gas (gaseous)	1,500[5]	1,500[5]	—	1,500[5]			
(liquefied)	15[4,5]	15[4,5]	15[4,5]	—			
5.1 Pyrophoric							
4	(4)[5,8]	4[5,8]	50[5,8]	(1)[8]	1[8]	1[8]	0
6.1 Unstable (reactive)							
4	(1)[5,8]	1[5,8]	10[8]	(1/4)[8]	1/8	1/8	(1/4)[8]
3	(5)[5]	5[5]	10[5]	(1)[4]	1[4]	1[4]	(1)[4]
2	(50)[5]	50[5]	250[5]	(50)[4]	50[4]	10[4]	(10)[4]
1	(125)[5]	125[5]	750[5]	(125)[4]	125[4]	25[4]	(25)[4]
7.1 Water (reactive)							
3	(5)[5]	5[5]	—	(5)[4]	5[4]	1[4]	(1)[4]
2	(50)[5]	50[5]	—	(50)[4]	50[4]	10[4]	(10)[4]
1	(125)[5,6]	125[5,6]	—	(125)[5,6]	125[6]	25[6]	(25)[4]

N.L. = Not limited.

[1] Control area is a space bounded by not less than a one-hour fire-resistive occupancy separation within which the exempted amounts of hazardous materials may be stored, dispensed, handled or used. The number of control areas within a building used for retail and wholesale stores shall not exceed two. The number of control areas in buildings with other uses shall not exceed four.

[2] The aggregate quantity in use and storage shall not exceed the quantity listed for storage.

[3] The quantities of alcoholic beverages in retail sales uses are unlimited provided the liquids are packaged in individual containers not exceeding four liters.

The quantities of medicines, foodstuffs and cosmetics containing not more than 50 percent of volume of water-miscible liquids and with the remainder of the solutions not being flammable in retail sales or storage occupancies are unlimited when packaged in individual containers not exceeding four liters.

[4] Quantities may be increased 100 percent in sprinklered buildings. When Footnote 5 also applies, the increase for both footnotes may be applied.

[5] Quantities may be increased 100 percent when stored in approved storage cabinets or safety cans as specified in the Fire Code. When Footnote 4 also applies, the increase for both footnotes may be applied.

[6] The quantities permitted in a sprinklered building are not limited.

[7] A dust explosion potential is considered to exist if 1 pound or more of combustible dust per 1,000 cubic feet of volume is normally in suspension or could be put into suspension in all or a portion of an enclosure or inside pieces of equipment. This also includes combustible dust which accumulates on horizontal surfaces inside buildings or equipment and which could be put into suspension by an accident, sudden force or small explosion.

[8] Permitted in sprinklered buildings only. None is allowed in unsprinklered buildings.

[9] One pound of black sporting powder and 20 pounds of smokeless powder are permitted in sprinklered or unsprinklered buildings.

[10] Containing not more than the exempt amounts of Class I-A, Class I-B or Class I-C flammable liquids.

From the Uniform Building Code, © 1988, ICBO

Figure 3-8 (cont'd)   Exempt amounts of hazardous materials

TABLE NO. 9-C—DISTANCE FROM PROPERTY LINES, WALL AND OPENING PROTECTION BASED ON LOCATION ON PROPERTY

OCCUPANCY GROUP	MINIMUM DISTANCE FROM PROPERTY LINE[1]	FIRE RESISTANCE OF EXTERIOR WALLS	OPENINGS IN EXTERIOR WALLS[2]
H-1 Detached building required	75 feet See Table No. 9-D	No requirement based on location	No requirement based on location
H-2-3 Not in a detached building	30 feet when the area exceeds 1,500 sq. ft.[3]	4 hours less than 5 feet, 2 hours less than 10 feet, 1 hour less than 20 feet	Not permitted less than 5 feet, protected less than 20 feet
H-2-3 When detached building is required[4]	50 feet See Table No. 9-D	No requirement based on location	No requirement based on location
H-4[5]-6-7	No requirement	4 hours less than 5 feet, 2 hours less than 10 ft., 1 hour less than 20 feet	Not permitted less than 5 feet, protected less than 20 feet
H-5	No requirement	1 hour less than 60 feet	Protected less than 60 feet

[1]The distance specified is the distance from the walls enclosing the occupancy to all property lines including those on a public way.
[2]When protected openings are specified, the protection shall be by a fire assembly having a fire-protection rating of not less than three-fourths hour.
[3]Walls or portions of walls used for explosion venting shall be located not less than 50 feet from any property line including those on a public way.
[4]Detached buildings are required for storage of quantities of materials which exceed the amounts specified in Table No. 9-E.
[5]A Group H, Division 4 Occupancy having a floor area not exceeding 2,500 square feet may have exterior walls of not less than two-hour fire-resistive construction when less than 5 feet from a property line and of not less than one-hour fire-resistive construction when more than 5 feet but less than 20 feet from a property line.

From the Uniform Building Code © 1988, ICBO

Figure 3-9 *Distance from property lines, wall and opening protection*

four hours. In the next chapter we'll go into more detail about how to meet the fire-resistive requirements in your buildings.

If highly flammable or combustible liquids are stored, the building department may require a detailed report by an expert to identify methods of protection.

The concept of open space around a building strikes fear into the hearts of many developers. But *space* required by the UBC usually isn't a major problem. I mentioned that a street 60 feet wide would serve as part of the open space. Most buildings have a city street at least that wide on one side. Plus most zoning ordinances require a certain amount of off-street parking for commercial buildings. That usually provides plenty of space on a second side.

Exhaust Ventilation

Exhaust ventilation is strictly controlled in Group H occupancies, especially if vehicles are operating nearby. The fan system must be capable of changing the air every fifteen minutes. Exhaust ventilation must draw from points at or near floor level.

Good ventilation is just as important in your own garage if you plan to run a car engine there. But you don't need to install an exhaust system. Opening the garage door is much more effective.

Before leaving Group H occupancies, I should mention that doors which are part of an automatic ramp enclosure must be equipped with automatic closing devices.

Group M Occupancies

Group M is where the code lumps together all the miscellaneous structures that aren't considered under the other categories. These are assumed to have limited human occupancy and, therefore, relatively little impact on human safety.

About the only major restriction here is that private garages are limited to 1,000 square feet. A larger garage falls into another occupancy group and may require more restrictive construction. But don't worry. Just think how large that garage would have to be. The standard double garage is usually about 24 x 30 feet, or 720 square feet.

Group M-1 structures, the agricultural buildings, are described in Chapter 11 of the Appendix to UBC. Occupancy and type of construction are spelled out in UBC Tables A-11-A and A-11-B (Figure 3-10).

Group R - The Residential Occupancy

Most of the work you do will be either Group R (residential) or Group B (business and commercial). Group R-1 includes hotels, motels, apartment houses, convents and monasteries. Until you get into large occupant loads, the usual construction restrictions are quite liberal.

Under the UBC, hotels and motels are the same. They're both classified as hotels, maybe because hotels have been around for a long time. Motels are motor hotels and first began to appear when cars became common.

Here's the definition of a hotel under the UBC:

> *Any building containing six or more guest rooms intended or designed to be used, or which are used, rented or hired out to be occupied, or which are occupied for sleeping purposes by guests.*

A little further along in the definitions we find that the word motel means hotel in the code. There's no difference.

TABLE NO. A-11-A—BASIC ALLOWABLE AREA FOR A GROUP M, DIVISION 3 OCCUPANCY, ONE STORY IN HEIGHT AND MAXIMUM HEIGHT OF SUCH OCCUPANCY

I	II			III and IV		V	
	F-R	One-Hour	N	One-Hour or Type IV	N	One-Hour	N
ALLOWABLE AREA[1]							
Unlimited	60,000	27,100	18,000	27,100	18,000	21,100	12,000[1]
MAXIMUM HEIGHT IN STORIES[2]							
Unlimited	12	4	2	4	2	3	2

[1]See Section 1108 for unlimited area under certain conditions.
[2]For maximum height in feet, see Chapter 5, Table No. 5-D.

TABLE NO. A-11-B—REQUIRED SEPARATIONS BETWEEN GROUP M, DIVISION 3 AND OTHER OCCUPANCIES (In Hours)

Occupancy	A	E	I	H[1]	B-1	B-2	B-3	B-4	R-1	R-3	M
Rating	4	4	4	4	4	1	1	1	1	1	N

[1]See Chapter 9 for Group H, Division 1 Occupancies.

From the Uniform Building Code, © 1988, ICBO

Figure 3-10 ***Occupancy and type of construction***

In apartments, every sleeping room below the fourth floor must have an openable window or exterior door to permit emergency exit or rescue. The window must be at least 24 inches high and 20 inches wide, with a minimum of 5.7 square feet of openable area. The sill must be no more than 44 inches above the floor.

There are two main reason for this. First, floors above the fourth are excluded because that's as high as the ladders of most fire trucks can reach. Second, the code requires either Type I or Type II construction above the fourth floor. Using more fire-restrictive type of construction reduces the fire danger considerably.

A few other restrictions are noteworthy. Corridors serving 30 or more people, as determined by UBC Table 33-A (Figure 3-1), must be fire-resistive for one hour. All doors leading into this corridor must be solid core; there can be no louvers, grilles, or transoms unless they're protected by a fire shutter controlled by a 135-degree fusible link. The corridor can't have a dead-end length over 20 feet long.

Leaping from Second Stories

Fire is the major cause of death and injury in buildings. That's why the building code takes fire safety so seriously. But authors of the code can't do much about the weird things people do when there's a fire. You've probably heard about people jumping to their death from tall hotel buildings when a fire broke out many stories below. It happens. Usually you're much safer to stay in the room and keep the door closed.

Jumping from the second story isn't much of a risk compared to exiting through a burning corridor. That's why the code sets minimum window sizes and heights. But I wouldn't recommend jumping. A far better alternative is *dropping* from the second floor. Figure 3-11 makes my point. If you're stand-

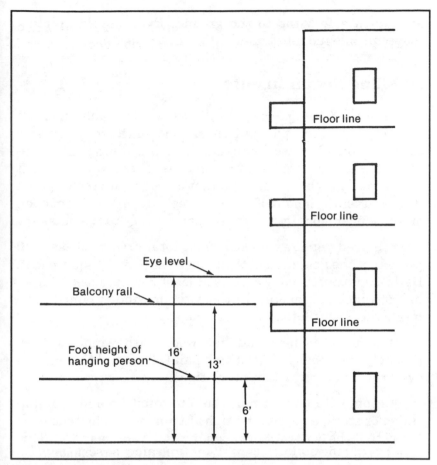

Figure 3-11 *Panic leaping from second story*

ing on a second floor balcony, your eye level is about 16 feet above the first floor (and probably the exterior grade level). The balcony railing is about 13 feet above grade. If you were hanging by your hands from the balcony railing, your feet would be only about 6 feet above grade — a relatively short and much safer drop to the ground. Even an old building inspector like me could handle that in a pinch.

Dwelling Requirements

Group R-3 occupancies (dwellings) are probably the least restricted of all occupied buildings. Most of the requirements are just common sense. For example, living, dining and sleeping rooms are required to have windows. These windows must open directly to the outside, but they can open to a roofed porch if it has a ceiling height of at least 7 feet and is 65 percent open on the longer side. It, too, must open directly to the outside.

Required windows must have a total area of at least 10 percent of the floor area of the room or at least 10 square feet. Bathrooms must have windows at least 3 square feet in area, half of which is openable. Baths without windows must have mechanical ventilation direct to the exterior.

If a house is new and has wood sash windows, they probably open easily. After being painted several times, however, the windows may be stuck tight.

A room with a toilet must be separated from food preparation or storage rooms by a tight-fitting door. The code used to say that the door couldn't open into such an area at all. This restriction has been relaxed, but I still think it's a good idea.

I grew up on a farm where the toilet was out beyond the woodshed and the bathtub was brought into the kitchen on Saturday night. It seemed fine to me. But now, under modern codes, every dwelling unit must have a water closet, lavatory, and either a bathtub or shower, and the kitchen must have a sink. These fixtures must be provided with hot and cold running water.

The code gives standard height and area requirements. Your ceiling can't be less than 7'6" for at least 50 percent of

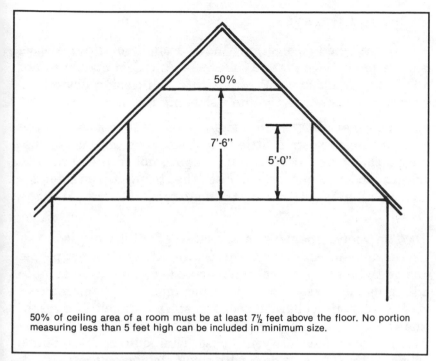

50% of ceiling area of a room must be at least 7½ feet above the floor. No portion measuring less than 5 feet high can be included in minimum size.

Figure 3-12 *Relative ceiling heights*

the area, and no part can be less than 5 feet. See Figure 3-12. One room must have at least 150 square feet of area; bedrooms must be at least 70 square feet. No room (except a kitchen) may be less than 7 feet at any dimension. A water closet compartment must be at least 30 inches wide and have a space at least 24 inches in front of the water closet.

If your building is three or more stories high, you must have either a manual or automatic approved fire alarm system.

Attached Garages

An attached garage must have a one-hour fire-resistive separation between it and the house. And door openings into the house must be solid core with a self-closing device. No garage can open directly into a sleeping room.

The separation requirement between the garage and the residence may seem a little ridiculous. A recent survey disclosed that four out of five fires began, not in the garage as often suspected, but in the house. That brings up an interesting question: What are they trying to protect — the car or the house?

The requirement for a self-closing, solid core door, deserves a comment or two. This is intended to protect people inside the house from carbon monoxide coming from an auto idling in the garage. Consider what might happen on a cold day. You open the garage door and start your car. The rest of the family is asleep and you're not aware that the wind is blowing gas fumes into your house. This could be fatal. That's why you must have a door with a self-closing device.

Don't blame the building inspector for this requirement. It's in the code and it's a good regulation. The code has many worthwhile rules. The problem is that there's no provision for follow-up. The inspector can make you install protective devices, but he can't require you to maintain them.

Smoke alarms are required by code in residential units. Many states have laws requiring them in all new residential units. But there's no law requiring regular maintenance. That's up to the occupants.

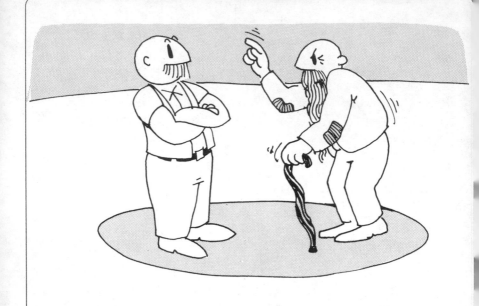

We Didn't Build Them Like That

I've been in and around construction for over 40 years. And I've seen a lot of changes in those years. Not too long ago I was talking with a retired carpenter friend about changes in the construction industry since we were apprentices. My friend complained to me about the way things are being done today. "They don't build 'em like we used to," he said.

He's right. And maybe it's a good thing. If you compare the quality of workmanship, I think today's tradesmen stand up pretty well against tradesmen 40 or 50 years ago. I've seen a lot of those houses from the good ol' days in various stages of reconstruction or remodeling. What we build today is different, and the workmanship may be better.

But we've seem more changes in materials and techniques than in workmanship. When I first got into the industry, sheathing was diagonal shiplap nailed to the studding. All of the openings were hand sawed after the walls were sheathed. Then the wall was covered with building paper and siding. We called it double-wall construction and used it on nearly every home.

That ended in the late 1940s when plywood became popular. Nothing has been the same since. "What happened to double-wall construction?" my old friend asked. "That don't look safe to me." Well, I'm always polite to the old-timers. I'm one myself, now. But I believe the plywood walls we build today are much stronger than the old diagonal shiplap. Authors of the building code seem to agree. And plywood sheathing sure goes up faster than diagonal sheathing.

There's been one more change in construction in the last 50 years. I think it's the biggest change of all. Maybe you can guess what I'm talking about. It's building codes. There weren't any in most cities and counties in the 1930s. Even the codes we had weren't very good by today's standards. And sometimes they weren't enforced.

I'm not going to claim that houses built in the 1930s aren't safe and durable. They are. Most are still in use today. But most also show their age. Plumbing, heating and electrical systems are unreliable or inadequate. They're more expensive to heat and cool. Floors squeak and sag. Windows stick. And they're drafty.

Don't misunderstand what I'm saying. To me, many older homes have a charm that newer homes can't touch. But you've got to make allowances if you like living in an antique. Most people want all the conveniences, not the inconveniences. It's for those people that building codes are written.

4

Types of Construction and Fire Resistance

I n the last two chapters we discussed occupancy groups and occupancy loads. I mentioned several times that each occupancy group requires a different type of construction. In this chapter we'll begin to look at the construction required for each of those occupancy groups.

UBC Table 17-A (Figure 4-1) shows the construction type for each occupancy group.

TABLE NO. 17-A—TYPES OF CONSTRUCTION—FIRE-RESISTIVE REQUIREMENTS
(In Hours)
For details see chapters under Occupancy and Types of Construction and for exceptions see Section 1705.

BUILDING ELEMENT	TYPE I	TYPE II NONCOMBUSTIBLE			TYPE III		TYPE IV COMBUSTIBLE	TYPE V	
	Fire-resistive	Fire-resistive	1-Hr.	N	1-Hr.	N	H.T.	1-Hr.	N
Exterior Bearing Walls	4 Sec. 1803 (a)	4 1903 (a)	1	N	4 2003 (a)	4 2003 (a)	4 2103 (a)	1	N
Interior Bearing Walls	3	2	1	N	1	N	1	1	N
Exterior Nonbearing Walls	4 Sec. 1803 (a)	4 1903 (a)	1 1903 (a)	N	4 2003 (a)	4 2003 (a)	4 2103 (a)	1	N
Structural Frame[1]	3	2	1	N	1	N	1 or H.T.	1	N
Partitions—Permanent	12	12	12	N	1	N	1 or H.T.	1	N
Shaft Enclosures	2	2	1	1	1	1	1	1 1706	1 1706
Floors-Ceilings/Floors	2	2	1	N	1	N	H.T.	1	N
Roofs-Ceilings/Roofs	2 Sec. 1806	1 1906	1 1906	N	1	N	H.T.	1	N
Exterior Doors and Windows	Sec. 1803 (b)	1903 (b)	1903 (b)	1903 (b)	2003 (b)	2003 (b)	2103 (b)	2203	2203

N—No general requirements for fire resistance.   H.T.—Heavy Timber.

[1] Structural frame elements in the exterior wall shall be protected against external fire exposure as required for exterior bearing walls or the structural frame, whichever is greater.

[2] Fire-retardant treated wood (see Section 407) may be used in the assembly, provided fire-resistance requirements are maintained. See Sections 1801 and 1901, respectively.

From the Uniform Building Code, © 1988, ICBO

Figure 4-1 *Fire-resistance requirements for types of construction*

Buildings Classified by Construction

Usually the *entire* building (or entire portion of a building within an area separation wall) must conform to the type of construction specified to meet the minimum requirements for that classification. But note that we're speaking of minimums here, not maximums. The code only requires that a building conform to the minimum requirements for occupancy, height, and area. You can always provide a higher classification of construction. For example, going to a higher classification might reduce insurance premiums enough to pay for the extra cost.

You can divide a building by fire walls so that each area is classified separately. But these area separations must be complete from the foundation to the roof, and they must meet minimum standards in the code for fire walls.

UBC Chapter 17 describes the general code restrictions that apply to all types of construction. Specific restrictions for each building type are listed in the chapters that follow:

Chapter 18 — Type I fire-resistive buildings

Chapter 19 — Type II buildings

Chapter 20 — Type III buildings

Chapter 21 — Type IV buildings

Chapter 22 — Type V buildings

In many cases, a broad rule is established for all occupancy groups and then exceptions are made for certain occupancy groups. For instance, consider Sections 1703 and 1704:

> **Section 1703.** *Usable space under the first story shall be enclosed except in Groups R, Division 3 and M Occupancies, and such enclosure when constructed of metal or wood shall be protected on the side of the usable space as*

required for one-hour fire-resistive construction. Doors shall be self-closing, of noncombustible construction or solid wood core, not less than 1-3/4 inches in thickness.

Section 1704. *Roof coverings shall be as specified in Table 32-A.*

Fire Resistance Determines Type of Construction

Notice in UBC Table 17-A (Figure 4-1) that the fire resistance of certain building elements determines the type of construction you can use. These elements are the exterior and interior bearing walls, exterior nonbearing walls, structural frame, permanent partitions, shaft enclosures, floors, roofs, exterior doors and windows.

Table 17-A is kind of sneaky. It lists everything you must do to build a certain fire resistiveness into a building and establish the type of construction. But what if you slack up on one little item? Let's say, for instance, that you're building a 15-story apartment building, Type I. Checking the UBC Table 5-D (Chapter 3, Figure 3-6) you find that a Type II building is limited to 12 stories for an apartment building. So you'll have to use Type I construction.

Maybe by reducing the roof from a two-hour fire-resistive construction to one-hour you could save a few bucks. After all, a one-hour roof is pretty safe. So you draw up your specifications and then find the building inspector shaking his head. What went wrong?

The inspector has noted that if one segment or element of Table 17-A is reduced, you've automatically reduced the whole structure one grade. Although you have a fine building, if you insist on going with the one-hour roof, you can only build a 12-story apartment building.

You have to make a choice. Are you going to build a two-hour roof, or are you going to reduce your building to 12 stories? The cost of installing that two-hour roof is very small compared to losing three floors of apartments. Evaluate all the alternatives before deciding. But remember, whenever you reduce one element of the building, the whole building must be classified in a lower grade.

It's possible to have a four-hour exterior bearing wall, three-hour structural frame, and two-hour floors — all elements of a Type I building — and still wind up with a Type V building because the rest of the elements didn't measure up to the requirements of UBC Table 17-A.

Roof Structures

This is another item that can be tricky. Generally, you'll find that skylights, penthouses, and roof structures must have the same construction as the rest of the building and be the same distance from the property lines. And any roof structure used for housing anything except mechanical equipment is counted as an additional story.

We'll cover the construction details in later chapters. But the type of construction you wish to use will always dictate the construction methods. In other words, if you're building a frame building of Type V construction, the skylight must be of at least Type V construction.

Fire-Retardant Materials

You can use fire-retardant-treated wood in nonbearing partitions — but this brings up some questions. There are two types of fire-retardant-treated wood. One is wood that has been impregnated with fire retardant under pressure. The other is wood with the retardant sprayed or painted on. Both are acceptable, and this is where the problem arises.

What does "acceptable" mean? To the inspector, it means that the material is applied according to the manufacturer's recommendations. It doesn't mean that the user applies the material the way he thinks it should be applied. There's a vast difference between the two.

For too many builders, it's a matter of economics and what they think they can get away with. If the manufacturer recommends applying a certain retardant material in four coats at eight-hour intervals, there's probably a good reason for it. It's disappointing to hear a subcontractor say that two coats applied at two-hour intervals will do just as well. "After all, the manufacturer is just trying to sell more material." Now of course, the manufacturer *is* in business for profit. He does want to sell lots of that material — but he wants his material used properly. He's put a lot of money into testing, and the reputation of his product is at stake. If he feels it takes four coats at eight-hour intervals to do the job, then I'm inclined to go along with him.

What about the subcontractor? By skimping on installation methods he can underbid his more conscientious competitor. Someone has to monitor the quality of work. It shouldn't have to be the building inspector. But the inspector will do it if no one else will.

Will Retardant-Treated Material Burn?

Yes, fire-retardant-treated material will burn, but only as long as there's an applied flame. If you throw a piece of fire-retardant wood in the fireplace, it will eventually be consumed.

Given enough time, nearly all materials are affected by flame and intense heat. What the retardant does is slow down the effects of combustion. That helps keep a structure intact and upright as long as possible. This helps fire fighters and gives the occupants a chance to escape.

Evaluation Reports

With so many building materials on the market today, how does the building inspector know if a product is acceptable? No, he doesn't have it all right off the top of his head. What he does have is the ICBO Evaluation Reports.

The International Conference of Building Officials publishes an annual report listing materials approved for construction. All members of the ICBO receive these material updates. When a manufacturer presents a material for approval it must be accompanied by a report from an acceptable testing laboratory or agency. The material and report are reviewed by the staff and members of a review committee. If the committee grants approval, ICBO publishes the Evaluation Reports.

This Report lists the product, the manufacturer's name and address, what the product is and what it does, and how it should be used. It also refers to the relevant section of the UBC. Some of these are brief, while others are quite lengthy. But they *do* give the inspector the information he needs to make a decision.

To be acceptable, you've got to use the product or material according to the manufacturer's specification as amended by the testing lab. You can't use any other method unless you're prepared to prove to the inspector that your way is superior. Proving that may be more expensive than just doing it right in the first place.

Following the Code Saves Money

You can save money by following the code. Consider non-bearing partitions, for example. In several occupancy categories, partitions don't have to meet any fire rating ("N" in UBC Table 17-A, Figure 4-1). So you could use plain wood panels in the three-quarter height partitions, since plain wood can be used in all types of construction.

But be careful. What seems to be the most economical way to build something could end up costing more in the long run. Many builders use wood panels made of thin 3/16-inch material with photoengraved grain over a shoddy backing. You can put your fist right through it. I always recommend backing it with sheetrock. True, this will add to the cost, but it also adds strength and some fire-resistance. If you can put your fist through the panel, think of what a carelessly placed piece of furniture could do.

In nearly any type of construction, wood veneer can be used over noncombustible surfaces. Wood trim and unprotected wood doors may be used where unprotected openings are permitted. But what are unprotected openings? And how do you know if they're permitted?

Unprotected Openings

Let's go back to UBC Table 5-A (Chapter 2, Figure 2-2). One of the columns is headed *Openings in Exterior Walls*. This explains how close the building can be to the property line and still have unprotected openings. This is to help prevent the spread of fire from one property to another.

What about buildings downtown that are built right to the property line, facing on a street or alley? This requires a little detective work. Let's backtrack to Section 504(a):

> *For the purpose of this section the center line of an adjoining street or alley shall be considered an adjacent property line.*

Not too much help, is it? That depends a lot on how wide the streets are in your town. Let's go to Section 506(a)1:

> *1. **Separation on two sides.** Where public ways or yards more than 20 feet in width extend along and adjoin two sides of the building. . .*

Remember this one? We mentioned it in Chapter 3 in the section about area increases. We established that a 20-foot street was the line of demarcation. But Section 1705(d) states:

> *Regardless of fire-resistive requirements for exterior walls, certain elements of the walls fronting on streets or yards having a width of 40 feet may be constructed as follows. . .*

Isn't that curious? The only difference is in our second and third definitions. One indicates 20 feet to the center line while the other refers to a street 40 feet wide. It appears to be the same thing, doesn't it? On this basis, I would have to assume that 20 feet is the magic number.

That takes care of the separation on the street side. Section 506(a)1 covers the doubtful areas. However, UBC Table 5-A is much more specific for side lot lines for the various occupancies.

Double Walls?

Construction practices are always changing, but I doubt they'll change any more in the next forty years than they have in the last forty. We still don't know for sure how energy conservation will affect the style of our houses or construction techniques. We do know, however, that many changes have taken place and more will come.

Figure 4-2   *A good example of double wall construction*

When I learned home building, most sheathing was either shiplap or plain 1-inch stock placed horizontally or diagonally on plain studs. Next came a layer of building paper and the siding. The framing was nailed together as it lay on the subfloor. Then it was erected and braced. Now, with plywood sheathing and siding, entire wall sections are assembled on the floor and lifted into place, complete (in some cases) with windows and paint. This diaphragm wall is more air-tight and may even be stronger structurally.

Old-timers wondered why I allowed single-wall construction on homes. Simple — the code permits it. Sections 1707 and 2202 allow you to put siding directly on the studding under certain conditions. But I certainly prefer double-wall construction, like that shown in Figure 4-2.

Section 1707 states that building paper must be applied over studs or sheathing of exterior walls. The paper may be omitted when the exterior wall covering consists of weather-proof panels. Exterior plywood of almost any thickness will satisfy this requirement.

According to Section 2202 (by reference to Chapter 25, UBC), three-story buildings must have the exterior walls of the first floor covered with solid wood sheathing. This implies that siding will be installed over the sheathing on the first floor of a three-story structure only. So a house of one or two stories could have bare studs covered with exterior-type plywood 3/8 inches or more, as shown below, and still satisfy the code. But will that satisfy the energy code of your area? It probably would, if your insulation includes enough R-value.

Minimum Plywood Thickness

Section 2516(g)3 covers the minimum thickness of plywood used for exterior wall covering:

> **3. Plywood.** *Where plywood is used for covering the exterior of outside walls, it shall be of the Exterior type not less than 3/8 inch thick. Plywood panel siding shall be installed in accordance with Table 25-M-1. Unless applied over 1-inch wood sheathing or 15/32-inch plywood sheathing, or 1/2-inch particle board sheathing, joints shall occur over framing members and shall be protected with a continuous wood batten, approved caulking, flashing, vertical or horizontal shiplaps; or joints shall be lapped horizontally or otherwise made waterproof.*

Table 25-M-1 is shown in Figure 4-3. In the opinion of most builders and building officials, 3/8-inch plywood isn't thick enough. But their opinion isn't worth much without the code to back it up. An inspector's opinion is only good for advice. But I'd tell you not to settle for less than 1/2-inch of thickness unless it was backed by a sheathing panel.

TABLE NO. 25-M-1—EXPOSED PLYWOOD PANEL SIDING

MINIMUM THICKNESS[1]	MINIMUM NO. OF PLIES	STUD SPACING (INCHES) PLYWOOD SIDING APPLIED DIRECT TO STUDS OR OVER SHEATHING
1. ⅜"	3	16[2]
2. ½"	4	24

[1]Thickness of grooved panels is measured at bottom of grooves.

[2]May be 24 inches if plywood siding applied with face grain perpendicular to studs or over one of the following: (a) 1-inch board sheathing, (b) ½-inch plywood sheathing, (c) ⅜-inch plywood sheathing with face grain of sheathing perpendicular to studs.

From the Uniform Building Code, © 1988, ICBO

Figure 4-3   *Exposed plywood panel siding requirements*

The 3/8-inch thickness is based on structural engineering practices. Adding a fraction of an inch to achieve the 1/2-inch thickness is just good insurance.

The 1985 edition of the code added Table 25-M-2, *Allowable Spans for Exposed Particle Board Panel Siding.* We'll talk about that a little later.

Masonry and Parapet Walls

Wood members aren't allowed to support concrete or masonry. Anything that supports concrete or masonry in buildings over one story high must either be protected with one-hour rating fire protection or meet the fire rating requirements of the wall itself, whichever is greater. You don't need to protect the underside of lintels, shelf angles, or plates that aren't part of the structural frame.

Where required, parapet walls must have the same fire-resistive rating as the walls. Parapets must be at least 30 inches above the point where the roof surface and the wall

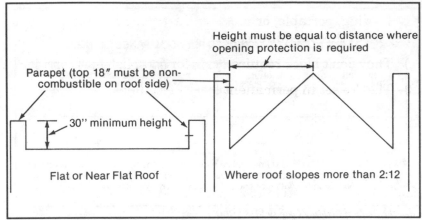

From the Uniform Building Code, © *1988, ICBO*

Figure 4-4 *Requirements for parapet walls*

meet. They can never be less than 30 inches high. If the slope of a roof toward a parapet is greater than 2 in 12, the parapet must be as high as any portion of the roof within the distance where protection of wall openings would be required. Check back to UBC Table 5-A (Figure 2-2 in Chapter 2). Figure 4-4 illustrates these requirements.

There's one further requirement. The side adjacent to a roof needs noncombustible faces for the top 18 inches, including all counterflashing and coping materials.

General Items in UBC Chapter 17

You can only use unprotected, noncombustible material for eaves, cornices and overhangs on Type I, II and III buildings. Type IV and Type V buildings may include combustible material.

Folding, portable, or movable partitions are acceptable if they meet these requirements:

1) They don't block required exits or establish exit corridors.

2) They're set in permanent tracks or guides.

3) The flame spread classification is not less than that for the rest of the room.

Except in residences, rubbish and linen chutes must terminate in rooms separated from the rest of the building by one-hour fire-resistive construction. Openings in the chutes may not open into exit corridors or stairways.

You'll find that code regulations for these shaft enclosures are strict — and rigidly enforced. That's because these shafts have a way of turning into chimneys during a fire, spreading the flames throughout the building in no time.

Water closet compartments are also closely regulated in most public and semi-public buildings, which is nearly all buildings except private dwellings. These are stringent because many of the regulations involve the handicapped.

Bathroom floors must be made of nonabsorbent materials, such as cement or ceramic tile. These materials must extend up the walls to a height of 48 inches (70 inches in shower stalls). Glass or glazing around showers and tubs, even in private residences, must be fully tempered, laminated safety glass or approved plastic.

All weather-exposed surfaces must have a weather-resistive barrier to protect the interior wall covering. Building paper and felt must be free of holes and breaks other than those created by fasteners or attachments. They must be applied weatherboard fashion, lapped at least 2 inches at horizontal joints and 6 inches at vertical joints. Balconies, landings, exterior stairways, and similar surfaces exposed to the weather and sealed underneath must be waterproofed.

All openings in floors, roofs, balconies or porches that are more than 30 inches above grade must have guardrails at least 42 inches high. The only exceptions are landing docks (none required) and private residences (36 inches is high enough).

The UBC provisions covering the use of foam plastic insulation were greatly strengthened in the 1988 edition. They must have a flame spread rating of not more than 75 and a smoke-developed rating of not more than 450.

The specific requirements in Section 1712(b) cover installation of masonry, attics or crawl spaces, cold storage, metal clad buildings, roofing, doors, and siding backer boards. This was formerly covered in Section 1717. All foam plastics must now be labeled and show the ingredients.

Chapter 17 now covers solar energy collectors as well as atriums.

Helistops

In the last chapter I suggested the main differences between heliports and helistops. The number of regulations regarding their construction is growing rapidly. Helistops may be built on buildings or other locations if constructed according to Section 710. Generally, this requires the following:

- If the helicopter weighs less than 3,500 pounds, the touchdown area must be at least 20 feet by 20 feet and surrounded on all sides by a clear area with a minimum average width at roof level of 15 feet. No width can be less than 5 feet.

- The landing area and supports on the roof of a building must be of noncombustible construction. Also, the area must be designed to confine any inflammable liquid spill-age and to drain it away from any exit or stairway.

• Exits and stairways must comply with provisions in Chapter 33 of the UBC, except that all landing areas on buildings or structures must have two or more exits. If the roof area is less than 60 feet long or less than 200 square feet, the second exit may be a fire escape or a ladder leading to the floor below.

• Approval must be obtained from the Federal Aviation Administration before operating helicopters from any helistop.

Type I Fire-Resistive Buildings

So far in this chapter I've discussed requirements that apply to nearly all buildings. Now it's time to get a little more specific, covering each building type. I'll start with the highest or most fire-resistive buildings, Type I.

The height of Type I buildings is unlimited by the code. The area is limited only in Group A occupancies. But just because a building is fire-resistant doesn't mean that it's fireproof. Some of the worst fires in history have been in so-called fireproof buildings. In fact, Type I buildings — the most fire-resistant — have been called "concrete coffins." While the building itself doesn't burn, its contents do.

Building codes can't regulate the amount of combustible goods in a building. Hospitals, for example, are usually fire-resistive buildings filled with highly combustible materials. In this country, people are seldom burned to death in building fires. Usually, smoke and toxic fumes cause the largest loss of life.

Remember the Chicago school fire a few years ago? One room contained over 30 bodies, yet papers on the desks weren't even singed. A fire-resistive building gives the occupants a better chance of escaping from the building — *if* the toxic fumes from burning material haven't done them in first.

The structural frame of a Type I building must be iron, steel, reinforced concrete, or reinforced masonry and have a three-hour fire rating. If members of the structural frame are in the outside wall, they must be protected the same as the outside wall or for four hours.

Type I buildings must have four-hour fire-resistive exterior walls. But nonbearing walls that front streets at least 50 feet wide may be of unprotected, noncombustible construction. In all occupancies except Group H, nonbearing walls may have a one-hour rating where unprotected openings are permitted, and a two-hour rating where protected openings are permitted.

UBC Table 17-A (Figure 4-1) summarizes the main requirements for all types of buildings. For miscellaneous items for each type of construction, refer to Chapters 18 through 22 of the UBC. Under Type I in Chapter 18 you'll find that a mezzanine floor can't cover more than one-third of the floor area of a room. Also, you can't have more than two mezzanine floors in any room. Mezzanine floors may be of wood or unprotected metal.

Stairs and stair platforms must be reinforced concrete, iron or steel. You can use brick, marble, tile or other noncombustible materials for the finish of treads and risers.

Group B, Division 2 office buildings and Group R, Division 1 buildings with floors used for human occupancy located more than 75 feet above the lowest level of fire department access must have an approved automatic sprinkler system.

This regulation has been in effect for some time. Newer provisions cover smoke detection systems, alarm and communication systems, smoke control, emergency power and light systems, and, above all, areas of refuge.

You must provide natural or mechanical ventilation for smoke removal. For every story, furnish ventilation at the rate of 20 square feet per 50 linear feet of wall space. There must be at least one vent for each 50 linear feet.

Providing areas of refuge is a fairly recent development. The purpose is to create smoke-free, fire-resistive compartments where people in high-rise buildings can await rescue. Since most elevators won't be working during emergencies, it takes too long and is too risky to try to evacuate a large high-rise building. Instead, the occupants should seek refuge until the danger has passed.

Type II Construction

This category is broken down into three categories. Look at UBC Table 5-C (Figure 3-5 in Chapter 3). These are Type II-FR, Type II one-hour, and Type II-N. Fire-resistive requirements are shown in UBC Table 17-A (Figure 4-1). Allowable height and area are shown in Table 5-D (Figure 3-6, Chapter 3).

Maximum height depends on the occupancy and varies from two stories for Group H-1 to 12 stories in apartment houses and most business buildings.

There's a fine line between the construction of Type II-FR and one-hour and N. The first must be of steel, iron, or concrete. In most cases where concrete is listed as a noncombustible building material, it also includes masonry (either brick or concrete block). In the last two types, one-hour and N, only the structural elements must be noncombustible.

The basic difference is in some of the lesser elements. For instance, Type II-FR requires noncombustible construction throughout. But permanent nonbearing partitions may be made of fire-retardant-treated wood. In Type II one-hour construction, all elements must be rated for only one-hour fire resistance. In Type II-N there are no fire-resistive ratings on any elements except the structural frame.

The big difference is in area and height allowance. UBC Tables 5-C and 5-D make this clear. For instance, you can have Group A-1 occupancy only in Type II-FR buildings. The area is restricted to 29,900 square feet and limited to four stories. Otherwise, Group A-1 occupancy is not allowed in anything but Type I construction. Type II-FR construction is probably the most common type of commercial and industrial construction except in tall or extra large buildings.

Type II-N Construction

Most people think of Type II-N buildings as stock steel buildings such as service stations, Butler buildings or even the little metal sheds put out by Wards and Sears. Actually, any building that is entirely noncombustible could be a Type II-N building.

You don't have to protect a Type II-N building, but it must be of noncombustible material. The area and height of a Type II-N building is limited.

I mentioned that stock steel buildings are in this category. Even though the building itself is rated as noncombustible, the skin of the building on the side opposite the fire can get red hot, and will ignite anything touching it. Therefore, allow plenty of setback room for metal buildings, both from the property line and from adjacent buildings.

What can you do to make a Type II-N building into a Type II one-hour building? Add a layer of 3/4-inch sheetrock to the wall and ceiling surfaces. If the buildings are for miscellaneous storage, install sheetrock on the outside of the frame and attach the skin directly over it. This also reduces the possibility of damage to the sheetrock. When sheetrock is broken, the one-hour fire-resistive rating vanishes.

Type III Construction

Buildings with Type III construction must have four-hour fire-resistive exterior walls. But the other elements need only have a one-hour rating (Type III one-hour) or no rating (Type III-N). We used to call this construction "masonry walls and wood guts."

One item is of special interest in the Type III category: the height is limited to 65 feet (one-hour) and 55 feet (N). Generally, the number of stories is limited to two in most occupancy groups. Have you ever seen a 65-foot-high, two-story building? I haven't.

Type IV Construction

Underfloor areas in Type IV buildings must be ventilated. That's because the floors are constructed of wood. The three higher types usually are built on slabs or over basements. Underfloor ventilation requirements will be discussed in detail in Chapter 6.

Type IV-HT (heavy timber) is the "mill type" construction found in many older industrial buildings, particularly on the west coast. Warehouses and shipping docks are usually Type

Figure 4-5 *Typical Type IV – heavy timber construction*

IV-HT construction, which uses massive beams and joists. Figure 4-5 shows a typical Type IV-HT project.

Columns must be at least 8 inches x 8 inches to be classed as heavy timber. Framed timber trusses or glued-laminated arches that support floors must be at least 6 inches x 8 inches. Glued-laminated beams on roofs must be at least 4 inches x 6 inches. Beams or girders that support floors must be at least 6 inches x 10 inches, but on roofs they need only be 6 inches x 8 inches. Framed timber trusses for roofs that do not support floors must be 4 inches thick. Roofs must be at least 2 inches thick.

These measurements are nominal lumber sizes. This means that a 4 x 8 is only about 3-1/2 x 7-1/2 inches, finished on four sides.

Why is something so combustible as a heavy timber building given a Type IV rating? Fire safety doesn't require a noncombustible frame. The issue is how long the building will stand after it begins burning. The bigger the timber, the longer it will take to burn to the point of failure or collapse. Mill buildings burn for quite a while before they collapse completely.

Type V Construction

Type V buildings are wood frame or a combination of wood frame and any other material if the exterior walls aren't required to be noncombustible. In the Type V one-hour, however, all elements must be protected for at least one hour. Type V-N buildings are usually single- and multi-family dwellings. Multi-family dwellings are restricted to two stories, while single-family dwellings may be three stories.

Most higher types of construction could easily fall to Type V if the builder hasn't fulfilled all the requirements of UBC Table 17-A.

That's the end of this summary of building types. In the next chapter, we'll take a closer look at what makes a building resist fire.

In the Line of Duty

Most cities have zoning ordinances that limit the accumulation of junk in residential zones. That's a good idea. Piles of junk are unsightly, unsanitary and hazardous. Most cities aren't very aggressive at enforcing these ordinances until someone complains. Then they have to send someone from either the building, fire, police or health department out to investigate.

In my city this chore always fell to the building department. After making a few of these calls, I began to wish that I had help from other departments. Making house calls to settle disputes between neighbors isn't my favorite way to spend an afternoon.

I even went to the city manager once with a proposal, a compromise. My department could go in rotation with the other departments. We'd handle the first call. After that the departments would go in alphabetical order: fire, health and then police. Wasn't that fair?

"Well, Jack," the city manager said, "sure, I could divide responsibility. But what will people think when a policeman, fireman or the health department pulls up to the door? They'll think there's some kind of emergency. The way I see it, your building department has exactly the low profile we need for this problem. Anyhow, nobody's better at gentle arm twisting than you are. Right, Jack? You see, it isn't really a matter of fair or unfair. It's who can get the job done best — what's best for our city. That's why we thought you'd be happy to do it."

Funny I didn't see it that way until the city manager explained it to me. I guess that's why he's the city manager and I'm the building inspector.

A little after that I had to make one of these "junk" calls. The homeowner had closed a second-hand furniture store and moved the entire inventory to his backyard. The yard was jammed with plywood shacks, every one bulging with junk. That was mistake number one. Number two was that too much of the lot area was covered with these shacks. No-no number three was that I had no permit on file for any of these buildings. It looked like an open-and-shut case to me.

Before I could knock on the door, the door was flung open and I was looking at the business end of the biggest, ugliest gun barrel I ever saw. "What do you want?" said a voice somewhere behind the gun.

"I'm the building inspector and . . ."

"I don't care if you're Jesus Christ. *Get off my property!*"

Now, if there's anything I try to avoid, it's antagonizing the citizens of our town. And what I had here was one very, very unhappy citizen. No use making things worse, I thought, as I advanced, as the Marines would say, rapidly to the rear.

Anyhow, nobody gives medals for heroism to building inspectors, even a building inspector with a wife and eight kids to support.

Obviously, there was something the city manager had overlooked. They'd sent a boy to do a man's work.

But my friend with the gun had solved the problem.

Yes sir!

This was no job for the building inspector. This was a job for the City Attorney!

5

Fire Resistance in Buildings

ost building codes aim to promote fire safety in buildings. In the last chapter we looked at how the types of construction provide fire resistance. Some materials, such as steel, concrete, glass and most mineral compounds, are noncombustible. But are they *nondestructible* as well?

Not on your life! For a long time people thought that if a material was made of iron or steel it was completely noncombustible. Basically they were right. But they didn't consider what might happen if those materials were heated beyond a certain limit.

Noncombustible
Is Not Nondestructible

The Chicago Coliseum once was considered noncombustible. But it caught fire and was a total loss. The destruction couldn't have been more complete if it had been made of matchsticks and tissue paper.

Two things happened. One, the area was filled with paper, cloth and many other combustible materials. Two, the fire gained such great headway in such a short time that fire fighters were unable to control it. What happened to the noncombustible building? Well, it didn't burn. It simply melted into a mass of twisted, warped iron and steel girders. The planners placed too much faith in the alarm system — so they didn't put enough effort in fire prevention.

This is what I try to explain when someone approaches me with a "noncombustible" tin or aluminum building. It's also why steel frame buildings need fire-resistiveness built into them.

Fire Resistiveness — How Do We Get It?

After most major fires, people look around and start thinking about fire safety. Actually, the number of people who die as the result of burns is remarkably low. And the number of people who die as the result of being trapped and burned to death is even lower.

This doesn't mean we should look the other way when it comes to fire-resistiveness. But it also doesn't mean that after a major fire we should run to our legislators demanding more laws aimed at eliminating death by fire. What we should do is to see if present laws are being enforced adequately. Often, construction budgets are the problem. Owners and contractors are always trying to find ways to cut costs. Frequently, personal safety is set aside — but only temporarily, or so they say.

Most death by fire results from asphyxiation from smoke or toxic fumes. Building fire-resistiveness into a building doesn't mean that it won't burn or that people won't die from toxic fumes. All it can hope to do is slow down the rate of combustion enough to give everyone a chance to get out.

One thing this business has taught me is that nothing is fireproof. Some building materials are noncombustible. Others are fire-resistive. But every building material I know of will fail if it gets hot enough.

Noncombustible materials transmit enough heat to maintain combustion even though the material itself won't burn. Most fire-resistive materials will burn when flame is applied. Some continue burning when the flame is removed.

Noncombustible Materials

The easiest way to understand the term *noncombustible* as used in the code is to examine the definition in Chapter 4 of the UBC:

> **Section 415.** *Noncombustible as applied to building construction material means a material which, in the form in which it is used, is either one of the following:*
>
> *1. Material of which no part will ignite and burn when subjected to fire. Any material conforming to UBC Standard 4-1 shall be considered noncombustible within the meaning of this section.*
>
> *2. Material having a structural base of noncombustible material as defined in Item No. 1 above, with a*

surfacing material not over 1/8 inch thick which has a flame-spread rating of 50 or less.

Noncombustible doesn't apply to surface finish materials. Material required to be noncombustible for reduced clearances to flues, heating appliances, or other sources of high temperature shall refer to material conforming to Item No. 1. No material shall be classed as noncombustible which is subject to increase in combustibility or flame-spread rating, beyond the limits herein established through the effects of age, moisture or other atmospheric condition.

Flame-spread rating as used herein refers to rating obtained according to tests conducted as specified in UBC. Standard No. 42-1.

What Is Flame-Spread?

Structural members in some types of buildings have to be fire-resistant. Walls and ceilings in some types of buildings have to have a fire-resistive rating. And the finish materials used in some walls and ceilings must have a flame-spread classification based on occupancy. This flame-spread classification, however, doesn't apply to the Group M occupancy.

What, exactly, does fire-resistive mean? This term appears again and again throughout this book. But to understand this term you must first understand flame-spread.

Flame-spread is classified in UBC Table 42-A (Figure 5-1) as I, II, or III, although in some codes you may find it listed as Class A, B, or C. UBC Table 42-B (Figure 5-1) shows the maximum flame-spread classification for the various occupancies. These finish requirements, however, don't apply to doors and windows or their frames and trim. Material which is less than 1/28-inch thick and cemented to the surface of walls and ceilings is also exempt if its flame-spread charac-

TABLE NO. 42-A—FLAME-SPREAD CLASSIFICATION

MATERIAL QUALIFIED BY:	
Class	Flame-spread Index
I	0-25
II	26-75
III	76-200

TABLE NO. 42-B—MAXIMUM FLAME-SPREAD CLASS[1]

OCCUPANCY GROUP	ENCLOSED VERTICAL EXITWAYS	OTHER EXITWAYS[2]	ROOMS OR AREAS
A	I	II	II[3]
E	I	II	III
I	I	I[7]	II[4]
H	I	II	III[5]
B	I	II	III
R-1	I	II	III
R-3	III	III	III[6]
M	NO RESTRICTIONS		

[1]Foam plastics shall comply with the requirements specified in Section 1712. Carpeting on ceilings and textile wall coverings shall comply with the requirements specified in Sections 4204 (b) and 4205, respectively.

[2]Finish classification is not applicable to interior walls and ceilings of exterior exit balconies.

[3]In Group A, Divisions 3 and 4 Occupancies, Class III may be used.

[4]In rooms in which personal liberties of inmates are forcibly restrained, Class I material only shall be used.

[5]Over two stories shall be of Class II.

[6]Flame-spread provisions are not applicable to kitchens and bathrooms of Group R, Division 3 Occupancies.

[7]In Group I, Divisions 2 and 3 Occupancies, Class II may be used or Class III when the Division 2 or 3 is sprinklered.

From the Uniform Building Code, ©1988, ICBO

Figure 5-1 *Flame spread classifications*

teristics are less than paper under the same circumstances. If there's an automatic fire-extinguishing system, the flame-spread classification may be reduced.

Determining flame-spread— A flame-spread rating isn't a fire-resistive rating. The flame-spread rating compares the time it takes flame to spread on the surface of the tested material with the time it takes the same flame to spread on untreated oak. Red oak has an arbitrary rating of 100 and cement asbestos board has a rating of 0.

It's easy to see why cement asbestos board is used for the 0 rating, but what's so special about red oak? Red oak was chosen because of its uniform density and uniform burning rate, not because of its resistance to flames. Also, the smoke developed by burning red oak is more uniform than that of most woods.

The actual spread of flames isn't the only item measured in the flame-spread rating. It also considers smoke density of the material and the amount of fuel it consumes. Red oak and asbestos board are also the standards by which other materials are compared.

Tunnel test— Materials are tested for flame-spread in the *tunnel test*. It was developed by the Underwriter's Laboratory. The code, however, will recognize any independent testing lab equipped to make the same test. At present, to my knowledge, only UL and one company in Texas have tunnel testing apparatus. Figure 5-2 shows the tunnel test setup.

Building Code Standard 42-1-79 describes the testing equipment and the method of testing for flame-spread. Here's how it describes the fire test chamber:

> *The fire test chamber supplied with gas fuel of uniform quality shall be employed for this test method.*
>
> *The fire test chamber is to consist of a horizontal duct having an inside width of 17-1/2 inches plus or minus*

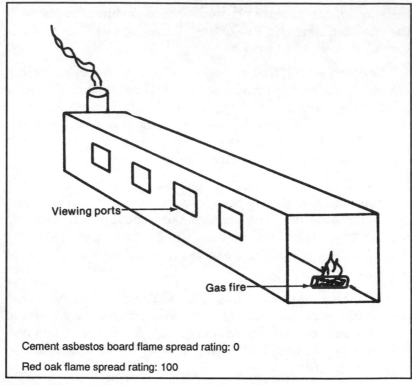

Cement asbestos board flame spread rating: 0

Red oak flame spread rating: 100

Figure 5-2 *Tunnel test for flame-spread and smoke density*

1/2 inch, a depth of 12 inches plus or minus 1/2 inch measured from the bottom of the test chamber to the ledge of the inner walls on which the specimen is supported, and a length of 25 feet. The sides and base of the duct are to be lined with insulated masonry. One side is to be provided with draft-tight observation windows so that the entire length of the test sample may be observed from outside the fire-test chamber.

The top is to consist of a removable noncombustible insulated structure of a size necessary to cover completely the fire test chamber and to accommodate the test samples. The top is to be designed so that it can be sealed against the leakage of air into the fire test chamber during the test, and it is to be designed to permit the attachment of test samples when necessary.

One end of the test chamber, designated as the "fire end," is to be provided with two gas burners delivering flames upward against the surface of the test sample, and 7-1/2 inches plus or minus 1/2 inch below the under surface of the test sample. The burners are to be positioned transversely approximately 4 inches on each side of the center line of the furnace so that the flame is evenly distributed over the cross section of the furnace.

This standard sets the type and number of controls, the amount of gas metered in, the air allowed, and other test criteria. The room in which the test is made must have a free inflow of air during the test to ensure that the room is kept at atmospheric pressure. The test chamber is calibrated so flame will spread 19-1/2 feet in 5-1/2 minutes on red oak flooring. There are photoelectric cells for determining the smoke density.

Computing flame-spread— The tester watches the progress of the flame, and notes the time it takes to travel 19-1/2 feet. This is compared to the red oak by one of the following formulas:

- If the time is 5-1/2 minutes or less, the formula is 100 times 5-1/2 divided by 19-1/2.

- When it takes more than 5-1/2 minutes, but less than 10 minutes, the formula is 100 times 5-1/2 divided by the time it took the flame to spread 19-1/2 feet plus 1/2 the difference between the result and 100.

- If it takes more than 10 minutes, the formula is 100 times the distance in feet that it traveled divided by 19-1/2.

Confusing, isn't it? This is one of those crazy tests which someone developed because no other type of equipment or measurement was available at the time. Since then, no one has bothered to make it simpler or more logical. If it works, why bother?

Table 42-A, *Flame-Spread Classification* (Figure 5-1), shows that Class I material has a flame-spread rating of 0 to 25, or about 1/4 that of red oak. Class II material has a flame-spread rating of 26 to 75, or about 3/4 that of red oak. Class III material has a flame-spread rating of 76 to 225. On that basis, red oak at 100 has a Class III rating.

UBC Table 42-B gives flame-spread requirements for finish material in various occupancies for stairs, corridors and rooms. Generally, you'll find that most wood products fall in the Class III category.

Determining Fire Resistance

The test for fire resistance of materials and assemblies is similar to the flame-spread test. A flame is applied to one side of the sample in a test chamber. Thermocouples measure the temperature on the opposite side. If the temperature doesn't exceed 250 degrees on the exposed side for the time tested, the sample is rated regardless of its condition. If the sample is a loadbearing member, it is loaded and must support the load for the time required.

When a door or window is tested for a time rating, the entire assembly must be tested including the frame, hardware, and any other items that will be a part of the assembly in actual service. If any part of the assembly fails, the assembly is rated by the time before failure. A door assembly that failed at 59 minutes would not have a one-hour rating but a 3/4-hour rating.

Wall covering materials such as sheetrock must pass the fire test and then a hose stream test. This test is made on duplicate samples after half the fire exposure time rating. Immediately after the fire is shut off, a hose stream is directed against the sample. The method of applying the stream, the size of the nozzle, the distance from the sample, and the water pressure are spelled out in the test procedures.

These test methods and procedures are found in the Building Code Standards, the book frequently referred to throughout the UBC and in this book. The Standards book is a companion to the UBC, but I doubt that you'll ever have to refer to the Standards.

Openings in Fire Assemblies

So far we've concentrated on fire-resistive assemblies and coverings. But very little has been said about openings in these assemblies. Sooner or later most fire-resistive assemblies will have to be pierced for a variety of reasons — plumbing, wiring, or doors, for example. If you have a room that requires a certain amount of fire-resistiveness, what are you going to do about the doors? What about heat ducts and lighting fixtures? And what if changes are made after a structure is completed? Will the plumber or electrician create any problems when he pierces these assemblies?

Let's lead off with ductwork. Fire dampers must be installed wherever ductwork passes through a wall, ceiling or floor that's part of a fire-resistive assembly. These dampers may be in the duct itself or in a collar fastened to the wall or ceiling. But they must be capable of operating even if the duct is damaged. Dampers must close at a temperature 50 degrees above the normal operating temperature. Dampers in ducts must be at least 16-gauge steel in ducts up to 18 inches in diameter, 12-gauge in ducts up to 36 inches in diameter, and 7-gauge in ducts over 36 inches in diameter.

Openings in area-separation walls must be protected according to the time requirements of the separation. In other words, if a four-hour separation is required, any openings would have to be protected for four hours. These assemblies must be operated by a fusible link on each side of the wall.

A smoke detection device may be required for the fire assembly. Let me add a word of caution here: Don't paint over them! It isn't unusual to find fusible links that have been completely painted over several times. Although paint isn't very thick, it may prevent the link from melting when it's supposed to. The first five minutes of a fire are the most critical.

Structural members such as beams, trusses, floor joists, and rafters may be individually protected or protected by a fire-resistive ceiling of the correct rating. Sometimes one method is more practical than another. If one-hour protection is sufficient, steel members may be painted with approved fire-retardant paint, provided they aren't exposed to the weather. If the members are protected by a ceiling, the ceiling must be noncombustible and the assembly must be rated.

Allowable Openings

You can have small openings in the wall or ceiling for pipe, duct, and electric boxes of ferrous metal. The opening can be up to 100 square inches in any 100 square feet of ceiling. You may have a client who wants to group four 100-inch openings at the center of a 400 square foot ceiling. After all, that comes

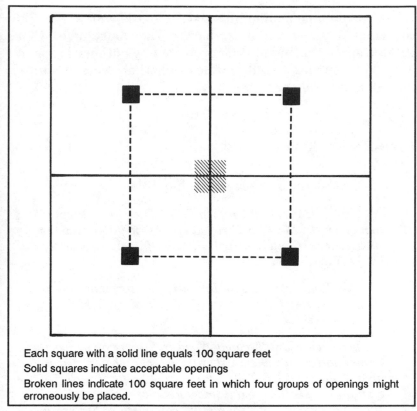

Each square with a solid line equals 100 square feet
Solid squares indicate acceptable openings
Broken lines indicate 100 square feet in which four groups of openings might erroneously be placed.

Figure 5-3   *Allowable openings*

to 100 square inches in each 100 square feet of ceiling. Is this a correct interpretation?

No. It doesn't meet the intent of the code. The code says "100 square inches in any 100 square feet." Your client better find some other way of arranging the openings. See Figure 5-3. Usually it's better to get your inspector's interpretation on questions like this before starting the work.

It has become fashionable to use textile wall and ceiling coverings, often for sound deadening. They must have a Class I flame-spread rating and be protected by automatic sprinklers. This applies to all textiles, whether napped, tufted, looped, non-woven or woven.

Fire-Rated Assemblies

The UBC defines *fire-resistive* like this:

> *Fire Code is the Uniform Fire Code promulgated jointly by the Western Fire Chiefs' Association and the International Conference of Building Officials, as adopted by this jurisdiction.*

> *Fire Resistance or Fire-Resistive Construction is construction to resist the spread of fire, details of which are specified in this code.*

> *Fire-Retardant Treated Wood is lumber or plywood impregnated with chemicals and which, when tested in accordance with UBC Standard No. 42-1 for a period of 30 minutes, shall have a flame-spread of not over 25 and show no evidence of progressive combustion. Materials which may be exposed to the weather shall maintain this fire-retardant classification when tested in accordance with the rain and weathering tests of UBC Standard No. 32-7.*

> *All materials shall bear identification showing the fire performance rating thereof and, if intended for exterior use, shall be further identified to indicate suitability for exposure to the weather. Such identification shall be issued by an approved agency having a service for inspection of materials at the factory.*

These are from the definitions section (Chapter 4) of the UBC. Section 4306(b) has the following definition:

*Fire Assembly is the assembly of a fire door, fire
windows, or fire damper, including all required hardware, anchorage, frames and sills. Fire dampers shall be
fabricated and installed in accordance with UBC Standard No. 43-7.*

How do you know what materials are fire-resistive? Many
combinations of materials qualify as fire-resistive. See more
information on this in UBC Chapter 43. UBC Tables 43-A,
43-B and 43-C are especially helpful if you need this design
data.

Fire-Resistive Construction

UBC Table 43-A, *Minimum Protection of Structural Parts
Based on Time Periods for Various Noncombustible Insulating Materials*, applies to the structural frame and the exterior
walls. A note of caution about UBC tables: Check all footnotes.
They often specify certain conditions that may apply to your
project.

Let's see how the building inspector uses Table 43-A.
Suppose the inspector notices on your plans a steel 6 inch by
6 inch column encased in Grade A concrete (not including
sandstone, granite or siliceous gravels). The concrete will be
a minimum of 2-1/2 inches thick around all portions of the
steel column. The inspector will turn to UBC Table 43-A and
find that it just happens to be the first item listed. Reading
across, you see that 2-1/2 inches of concrete provides a maximum of four-hour protection. That's good enough for a Type I
construction.

Will the concrete be able to insulate the column from fire
failure for at least four hours? The inspector consults your
specs and determines that the concrete complies. Your structural frame qualifies for Type I construction.

Of course, this shouldn't have happened by accident. Your architect knows code requirements and wrote specs that meet code requirements. If the architect made a mistake, the inspector will probably return your plans for modification. Another option would be to downgrade the type of construction. That might severely restrict what the building can be used for, as I explained in Chapter 4.

Fire Resistance for Walls and Partitions

UBC Table 43-B, *Rated Fire-Resistive Periods for Various Walls and Partitions*, will do for your walls and partitions what Table 43-A did for the structural frame. The process of determining the fire rating is exactly the same. If you're designing the building, which one would you elect to use? That depends on a number of things.

First, determine the fire-resistive rating you need. Then select the combinations of construction that will give you that rating. From there it's a matter of selecting materials that will meet code and owner requirements at the lowest cost. But remember, the code only requires the minimum rating. How far you go above that is up to you and your client.

UBC Table 43-B gives the fire-resistive rating for different wall assemblies. You can't make any substitutions in these assemblies and keep the rating unless it's shown elsewhere in the table. Only the defined construction carries that particular rating. In one-hour construction, ceilings may be omitted over unusable space, and floors may be omitted under unusable space.

Calculating the rating is the same as for Table 43-A. Select the hour rating you want, then look for the components that will give you that rating.

Fire Resistance for Floors and Roofs

UBC Table 43-C, *Minimum Protection for Floor and Roof Systems*, does for floors and roofs exactly what the other two tables did for the structural frame and the walls and ceilings. The table also works the same way as the other two.

But watch out for floor and roof penetrations. Fire-resistive floors must be continuous. All openings for mechanical and electrical equipment must be enclosed as specified in Section 1706.

There are two exceptions. First, some pipes may be installed within or through fire-resistive floors *if* they don't reduce the required fire resistance of the assembly. Second, the provisions of Section 1706 don't apply when openings comply with results of tests made under provisions of Section 4302(b). The result of these two exceptions, of course, is that you must prove your point to the inspector. It may be faster and cheaper to figure out another solution.

Protective Covering

Now that we've examined the method of determining flame-spread and some of the fire-resistive standards, let's take a look at the little things that can cause trouble.

Let's start with protective covering. The thickness of protective covering can't be less than shown in UBC Table 43-A, except as modified in Chapter 43. This pertains to all products, from fire-resistive paint to concrete. The figures shown must be the *net thickness* of the protecting materials. It doesn't include any hollow space in back of the protection.

You may be required to embed metal ties in transverse joints of unit masonry to protect steel columns. These ties must meet the requirements of UBC Table 43-A. Unit masonry, of course, is brick, block or any combination of the two.

You can't embed conduit and pipes in required fire protective coatings or in structural members. If the fire-resistive covering on columns might be damaged when the building is occupied, it must be protected.

Fire Doors

Fire doors must have automatic or self-closing hardware. Automatic closing devices must be equipped with heat-actuated devices on each side of the wall at the top of the opening. If the ceiling is more than 3 feet above the opening, the code requires a fusible link located at the ceiling on each side of the wall.

Glazed openings of 100 square inches are permitted, provided they are wire-glass or heat tempered. Doors of 3/4-hour rating may have 84 square feet of area. That means you could have a delivery door approximately 8 feet by 10.5 feet.

Windows required to have a 3/4-hour fire-resistive rating can't be larger than 84 square feet, and neither the width nor height can exceed 12 feet. The glass must be at least 1/4 inch thick and reinforced with wire mesh. Steel glazing angles must hold the glass in place except in casement windows where you can use clips.

One more note about fire doors. If the Fire Marshall inspects your plans, he'll probably insist that all fire doors be marked "Fire Door — Do Not Obstruct."

In the next chapter, we'll begin to look at the most basic step in code compliance: design and engineering.

Who Are You Going to Trust?

I think an inspector should always be willing to answer questions about the code. When a contractor asks for advice, the inspector should do his or her best to help. This isn't a guessing game we're playing: I have the answer and you have to guess what it is. It's everyone doing what they can to put up safe, practical, attractive buildings at reasonable cost.

Of course, I know inspectors who would rather hang by their thumbs than give a contractor free advice. I think that's wrong. But I can understand why they do it. They're afraid of getting sued. If you give bad advice and somebody follows it, you're at fault.

I had a city manager one time who accused me of being too friendly with contractors. Others have said that, too. But so what? I enjoy working with the contractors I know. I hope every building inspector does. And I think knowing something about the people who apply for permits is part of an inspector's job.

The code is written in black ink on white paper. But the answer to every code question isn't a matter of black and white.

Here's an example. I've had a lot of people apply for permits with little more than a rough sketch. No plans. Just an idea, a few notes and a line of chatter. What should I do? Well, first, I listened. If the project was a small carport or something simple and they knew what they were doing, I could usually send them off with a permit. That saved days or weeks of construction time and probably some money too. If an applicant obviously didn't understand the project, I'd suggest he or she prepare plans. Maybe that's discriminatory. Maybe it wouldn't work in a larger office handling hundreds of contractors and hundreds of projects a week. But it worked for me.

A lawyer once came in my office for a permit on a small office building. He had sketched the plans himself on scratch paper. I looked them over and turned him down, suggesting he hire an architect. He wasn't willing to take "no" for an answer. So I asked him a few questions: "I've got this pain in my wrist. Right here. Do you think I should give up tennis?"

"I'm a lawyer. Not a doctor. How should I know?" he answered.

"True, you're not. And you're not an architect either. I'll find a doctor for my wrist and you find an architect for your building."

Like I said, he wouldn't take "no" for an answer. He found a way to outsmart me. Back then our county hadn't adopted the UBC. Outside the city he didn't need a permit. So he built his office just outside the city limits. The basement was O.K. But then work stopped completely. I heard through the grapevine he couldn't get any subcontractors to bid from his sketches.

6

Engineering and Design Requirements

S ooner or later you'll have to confront the engineering and design sections of the code. It's not an easy subject. If you haven't studied engineering, you probably won't understand most of the formulas. But there's a lot here anyone can understand. The rest you can leave to the experts. I'll cover only the essential formulas — what you need to get a good basic understanding of engineering requirements.

Engineering is first mentioned in the UBC in Chapter 23:

> **Section 2301 Scope.** *This chapter prescribes general design requirements applicable to all structures regulated by this code.*

Loads and Loading

Section 2302 jumps right to the heart of the matter: *Loads and Loading*. This includes three items which we'll take in the order they're defined in the UBC:

> **Dead Load** *is the vertical load due to the weight of all permanent structural and nonstructural components of a building, such as walls, floors, roofs, and fixed service equipment.*

> **Live Load** *is the load superimposed by the use and occupancy of the building not including the wind load, earthquake load, or dead load.*

> **Load Duration** *is the period of continuous application of a given load, or the aggregate of periods of intermittent application of the same load.*

Another load implied by the definition of live load is the *unit live load*. Unit live loads are loads that are localized in one area. They're usually heavier than the usual loads in a building, like furniture. Loads for various uses and occupancies are shown in UBC Tables 23-A and 23-B (Figures 6-1 and 6-2).

Unit Live Loads

Designers use the unit live loads shown in UBC Table 23-A to plan floors and foundations that will hold up under both uniform (well distributed) and concentrated loads. If you're designing a factory or shop building that doesn't have isolated pieces of heavy equipment, use the column headed *Uniform Load* for the whole floor. If you have some very heavy equipment or machinery that's different from the rest of the equipment in the building, use the column headed *Concentrated Load* for those areas.

TABLE NO. 23-A—UNIFORM AND CONCENTRATED LOADS			
USE OR OCCUPANCY		UNIFORM LOAD[1]	CONCENTRATED LOAD
CATEGORY	DESCRIPTION		
1. Access floor systems	Office use	50	2000[2]
	Computer use	100	2000[2]
2. Armories		150	0
3. Assembly areas[3] and auditoriums and balconies therewith	Fixed seating areas	50	0
	Movable seating and other areas	100	0
	Stage areas and enclosed platforms	125	0
4. Cornices, marquees and residential balconies		60	0
5. Exit facilities[4]		100	0[5]
6. Garages	General storage and/or repair	100	[6]
	Private or pleasure-type motor vehicle storage	50	[6]
7. Hospitals	Wards and rooms	40	1000[2]
8. Libraries	Reading rooms	60	1000[2]
	Stack rooms	125	1500[2]
9. Manufacturing	Light	75	2000[2]
	Heavy	125	3000[2]
10. Offices		50	2000[2]
11. Printing plants	Press rooms	150	2500[2]
	Composing and linotype rooms	100	2000[2]
12. Residential[7]		40	0[5]
13. Rest rooms[8]			
14. Reviewing stands, grandstands and bleachers		100	0
15. Roof deck	Same as area served or for the type of occupancy accommodated		
16. Schools	Classrooms	40	1000[2]
17. Sidewalks and driveways	Public access	250	[6]
18. Storage	Light	125	
	Heavy	250	
19. Stores	Retail	75	2000[2]
	Wholesale	100	3000[2]

Figure 6-1 *Uniform and concentrated loads*

[1]See Section 2306 for live load reductions.
[2]See Section 2304 (c), first paragraph, for area of load application.
[3]Assembly areas include such occupancies as dance halls, drill rooms, gymnasiums, playgrounds, plazas, terraces and similar occupancies which are generally accessible to the public.
[4]Exit facilities shall include such uses as corridors serving an occupant load of 10 or more persons, exterior exit balconies, stairways, fire escapes and similar uses.
[5]Individual stair treads shall be designed to support a 300-pound concentrated load placed in a position which would cause maximum stress. Stair stringers may be designed for the uniform load set forth in the table.
[6]See Section 2304(c), second paragraph, for concentrated loads.
[7]Residential occupancies include private dwellings, apartments and hotel guest rooms.
[8]Rest room loads shall be not less than the load for the occupancy with which they are associated, but need not exceed 50 pounds per square foot.

From the Uniform Building Code, © 1988, ICBO

Figure 6-1 (cont'd) *Uniform and concentrated loads*

Table 23-B covers special situations that have to be treated individually. Here's an example. Say the floor of your building is a concrete slab 4 inches thick with wire mesh reinforcing. If heavy machinery is involved, beef up the area under your machine. Increase the floor thickness to 6 inches and add 1/2-inch rebar reinforcing, for instance.

Another example is a private garage where the load is imposed on four points — one under each wheel of a car. Because cars move into and out of a garage, these points become paths. Each path has to support 2,000 pounds without the normal live load. According to Section 2304(c), each load-bearing area must be able to carry 40 percent of the gross weight of the heaviest vehicle stored. The standard 4-inch slab will support most autos, but if you're planning to store a motor home, take another look at the thickness of the slab. This applies to your driveway as well.

When I started out in the business of building inspection, few buildings had automatic fire sprinklers. Regulations were quite lax and many exceptions were allowed. But many experts insist that fire sprinklers are more than worth the cost. In the few communities that require fire sprinklers in nearly all buildings, the fire department can almost be disbanded. That's probably why the BOCA's National Building Code requires residential sprinklers for virtually all new apartments and motels. The UBC doesn't require that. But it does recognize the load that fire sprinklers put on a building. Since 1985 the UBC has included *Fire Sprinkler Structural Support* as a special load in Table 23-B (Figure 6-2).

Roof Loads and Design

Most people are more concerned with the loading inside of a building than with the roof load. They're more worried about the floor collapsing under the weight of a piano than the weight of 2 feet of snow on the roof. Maybe that's a mistake. You can usually anticipate the load on the floor. Roofs, on the other hand, are subjected to loads that are often temporary and totally unpredictable.

Wind Loads

Two important loads affect the building exterior: wind loads and snow loads. The UBC gets pretty technical on this issue and for a very good reason — these two loads can vary from zero to very substantial forces. Builders in Los Angeles aren't particularly concerned about snow loads, but the Santa Ana winds common to Southern California can give them serious problems.

Because snow and wind loads can vary so greatly, you'll probably want to get good advice from an engineer when the issue comes up. Your building official should be able to explain the local practice to you. Of course, Chapter 23 in the UBC explains the requirements. But you need a background in engineering to understand some of the formulas. Here's some plain English from the code:

TABLE NO. 23-B—SPECIAL LOADS[1]

USE		VERTICAL LOAD	LATERAL LOAD
CATEGORY	DESCRIPTION	(Pounds per Square Foot Unless Otherwise Noted)	
1. Construction, public access at site (live load)	Walkway, see Sec. 4406	150	
	Canopy, see Sec. 4407	150	
2. Grandstands, reviewing stands and bleachers (live load)	Seats and footboards	120[2]	See Footnote 3
3. Stage accessories (live load)	Gridirons and fly galleries	75	
	Loft block wells[4]	250	250
	Head block wells and sheave beams[4]	250	250
4. Ceiling framing (live load)	Over stages	20	
	All uses except over stages	10[5]	
5. Partitions and interior walls, see Sec. 2309 (live load)			5
6. Elevators and dumbwaiters (dead and live load)		2 × Total loads[6]	
7. Mechanical and electrical equipment (dead load)		Total loads	
8. Cranes (dead and live load)	Total load including impact increase	1.25 × Total load[7]	0.10 × Total load[8]
9. Balcony railings, guard rails and handrails	Exit facilities serving an occupant load greater than 50		50[9]
	Other		20[9]
10. Storage racks	Over 8 feet high	Total loads[10]	See Table No. 23-P
11. Fire sprinkler structural support		250 pounds plus weight of water-filled pipe	See Table No. 23-P

Figure 6-2 *Special loads*

[1] The tabulated loads are minimum loads. Where other vertical loads required by this code or required by the design would cause greater stresses they shall be used.

[2] Pounds per lineal foot.

[3] Lateral sway bracing loads of 24 pounds per foot parallel and 10 pounds per foot perpendicular to seat and footboards.

[4] All loads are in pounds per lineal foot. Head block wells and sheave beams shall be designed for all loft block well loads tributary thereto. Sheave blocks shall be designed with a factor of safety of five.

[5] Does not apply to ceilings which have sufficient total access from below, such that access is not required within the space above the ceiling. Does not apply to ceilings if the attic areas above the ceiling are not provided with access. This live load need not be considered acting simultaneously with other live loads imposed upon the ceiling framing or its supporting structure.

[6] Where Appendix Chapter 51 has been adopted, see reference standard cited therein for additional design requirements.

[7] The impact factors included are for cranes with steel wheels riding on steel rails. They may be modified if substantiating technical data acceptable to the building official is submitted. Live loads on crane support girders and their connections shall be taken as the maximum crane wheel loads. For pendant-operated traveling crane support girders and their connections, the impact factors shall be 1.10.

[8] This applies in the direction parallel to the runway rails (longitudinal). The factor for forces perpendicular to the rail is 0.20 × the transverse traveling loads (trolley, cab, hooks and lifted loads). Forces shall be applied at top of rail and may be distributed among rails of multiple rail cranes and shall be distributed with due regard for lateral stiffness of the structures supporting these rails.

[9] A load per lineal foot to be applied horizontally at right angles to the top rail.

[10] Vertical members of storage racks shall be protected from impact forces of operating equipment or racks shall be designed so that failure of one vertical member will not cause collapse of more than the bay or bays directly supported by that member.

From the Uniform Building Code, © 1988, ICBO

Figure 6-2 (cont'd) *Special loads*

Section 2311(a) General. *Every building or structure and every portion thereof shall be designed and constructed to resist the wind effects determined in accordance with the requirements of this section. Wind shall be assumed to come from any horizontal direction. No reduction in wind pressure shall be taken for the shielding effect of adjacent structures.*

It then goes on to describe particular types of buildings. These sections, which apply to large buildings, will be of interest primarily to engineers and designers. The 1982 UBC refers you to ANSI 58.1. That's a standard published by the American National Standards Institute. Other standards were used in previous UBC editions. The ANSI reference makes it a bit harder for the designer and builder. You'll have to discuss this with your building official unless you happen to have a copy of the ANSI Standards.

Generally, wind and snow loads are not a problem for residences and small commercial structures. Most wood-frame and masonry buildings have the strength to withstand whatever mother nature can deliver. But in some areas special precautions are needed. You probably know if you live in an area that has unusually high snow or wind loads. Sometimes homes adjacent to natural land features have wind patterns worse than other homes nearby.

Figure 1 in the 1988 edition of the UBC (Figure 6-3 in this manual) is a wind speed map of the United States. This map, as explained in the footnotes, represents the fastest wind speeds at 33 feet above the ground for Exposure Category C. It also indicates an annual probability of 0.02, which means you might get these winds only 7.3 days per year.

The wind load formula— Even if most mathematical formulas throw you into a panic, you can handle this one. The wind load, or design wind pressure, is calculated in the following formula:

$$p = C_e\, C_q\, q_s\, I$$

Where:

p = Design wind pressure

C_e = Combined height, exposure and gust factor coefficient as given in Table 23-G (see Figure 6-4)

C_q = Pressure coefficient for the structure or portion of structure under consideration as given in Table 23-H (see Figure 6-5)

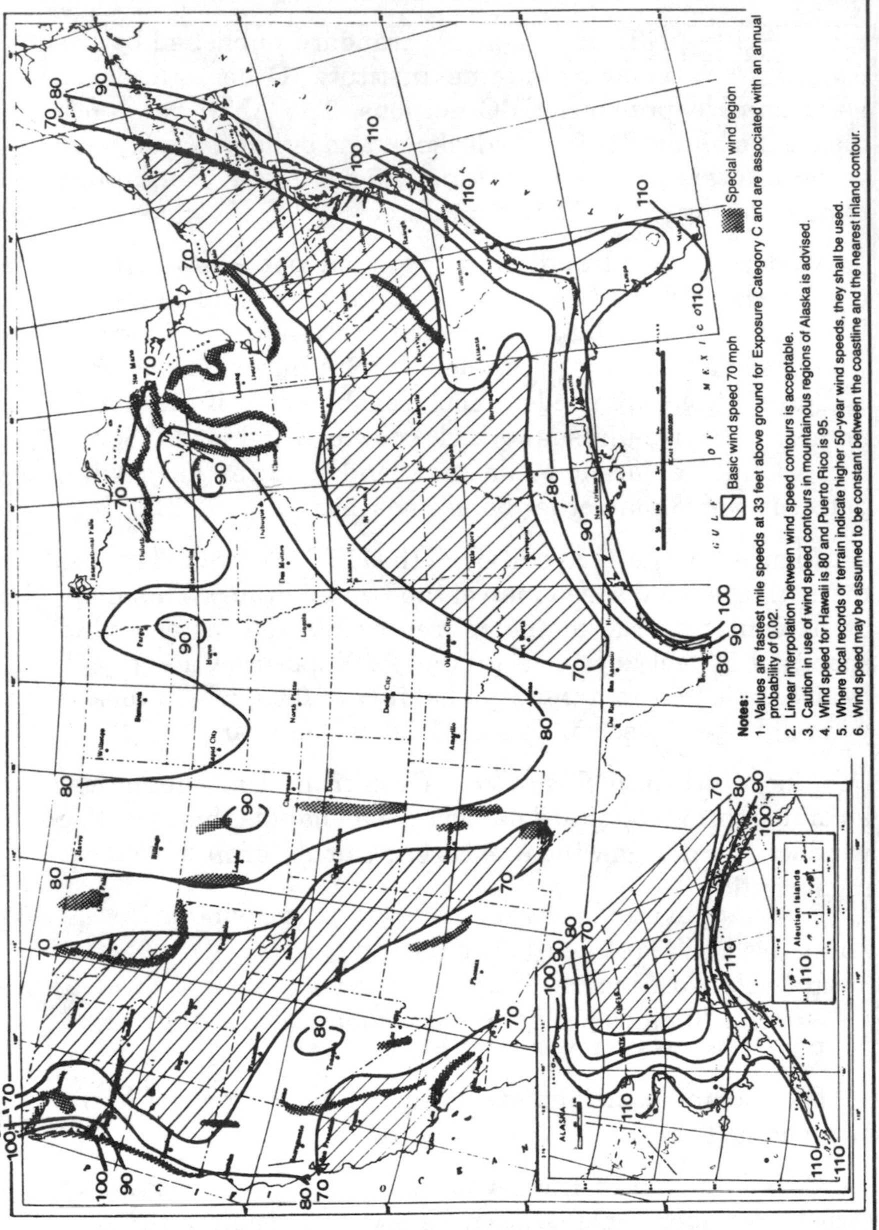

FIGURE NO. 1—BASIC WIND SPEEDS IN MILES PER HOUR

From the Uniform Building Code. © 1988. ICBO

TABLE NO. 23-G—COMBINED HEIGHT, EXPOSURE AND GUST FACTOR COEFFICIENT (C_e)		
HEIGHT ABOVE AVERAGE LEVEL OF ADJOINING GROUND, IN FEET	EXPOSURE C	EXPOSURE B
0- 20	1.2	0.7
20- 40	1.3	0.8
40- 60	1.5	1.0
60-100	1.6	1.1
100-150	1.8	1.3
150-200	1.9	1.4
200-300	2.1	1.6
300-400	2.2	1.8

From the Uniform Building Code, © 1988, ICBO

Figure 6-4   Combined height, exposure and gust factor coefficient

q_s = Wind stagnation pressure at the standard height of 30 feet as set forth in Table 23-F (see Figure 6-6)

I = Importance factor as set forth in Section 2311(h). This pertains to a factor of 1.5 if you're building a hospital, fire or police station, disaster operations or communications center, or a similar structure of an emergency station. On all other buildings a factor of 1.0 is adequate.

With that in mind, let's see what the design wind pressure would be for a residential roof with a 4 in 12 pitch in Kennewick, Washington. The wind speed map shows this area to be in the 70 miles per hour speed zone which still gives us a q_s factor of 13. Notice in UBC Table 23-H (Figure 6-5) that a roof element on an enclosed structure with a 4 in 12 pitch would have a factor of 1.1.

Now go to UBC Table 23-G (Figure 6-4). You should see the problem right away: Will our structure have Exposure B or Exposure C? A structure less than 20 feet above the average

TABLE NO. 23-H—PRESSURE COEFFICIENTS (C_q)		
STRUCTURE OR PART THEREOF	**DESCRIPTION**	C_q **FACTOR**
1. Primary frames and systems	**Method 1** (Normal force method) Walls:	
	Windward wall	0.8 inward
	Leeward wall	0.5 outward
	Roofs[1]:	
	Wind perpendicular to ridge	
	Leeward roof or flat roof	0.7 outward
	Windward roof	
	less than 2:12	0.7 outward
	Slope 2:12 to less than 9:12	0.9 outward or 0.3 inward
	Slope 9:12 to 12:12	0.4 inward
	Slope > 12:12	0.7 inward
	Wind parallel to ridge and flat roofs	0.7 outward
	Method 2 (Projected area method) On vertical projected area	
	Structures 40 feet or less in height	1.3 horizontal any direction
	Structures over 40 feet in height	1.4 horizontal any direction
	On horizontal projected area[1]	0.7 upward
2. Elements and components	Wall elements	
	All structures	1.2 inward
	Enclosed structures	1.1 outward
	Open structures	1.6 outward
	Parapets	1.3 inward or outward
	Roof elements Enclosed structures	
	Slope<9:12	1.1 outward
	Slope 9:12 to 12:12	1.1 outward or 0.8 inward
	Slope>12:12	1.1 outward or inward
	Open structures	
	Slope<9:12	1.6 outward
	Slope 9:12 to 12:12	1.6 outward or 0.8 inward
	Slope>12:12	1.6 outward or 1.1 inward

Figure 6-5 *Pressure coefficients*

STRUCTURE OR PART THEREOF	DESCRIPTION	C_q FACTOR
3. Local areas at discontinuities[2]	Wall corners	2.0 outward
	Canopies or overhangs at eaves or rakes	2.8 upward
	Roof ridges at ends of buildings or eaves and roof edges at building corners	3.0 upward
	Eaves or rakes without overhangs away from building corners and ridges away from ends of building	2.0 upward
	Cladding connections Add 0.5 to outward or upward C_q for appropriate location	
4. Chimneys, tanks and solid towers	Square or rectangular	1.4 any direction
	Hexagonal or octagonal	1.1 any direction
	Round or elliptical	0.8 any direction
5. Open-frame towers[3] [4]	Square and rectangular	
	Diagonal	4.0
	Normal	3.6
	Triangular	3.2
6. Tower Accessories (such as ladders, conduit, lights and elevators)	Cylindrical members	
	2 inches or less in diameter	1.0
	Over 2 inches in diameter	0.8
	Flat or angular members	1.3
7. Signs, flagpoles, lightpoles, minor structures[4]		1.4 any direction

[1] For one story or the top story of multistory open structures an additional outward C_q factor of 0.5 shall be used. The most critical combination shall be used for design. For definition of open structure see Section 2311 (j).

[2] Local pressures shall apply over a distance from the discontinuity of 10 feet or 0.1 times the least width of the structure, whichever is smaller.

[3] Wind pressures shall be applied to the total normal projected area of all the elements of one face. The forces shall be assumed to act parallel to wind direction.

[4] Factors for cylindrical elements are two thirds of those for flat or angular elements.

From the Uniform Building Code, © 1988, ICBO

Figure 6-5 (cont'd) *Pressure coefficients*

TABLE NO. 23-F—WIND STAGNATION PRESSURE (q_s) AT STANDARD HEIGHT OF 30 FEET							
Basic wind speed (mph)[1]	70	80	90	100	110	120	130
Pressure q_s (psf)	13	17	21	26	31	37	44

[1]Wind speed from Section 2311 (b).

From the Uniform Building Code, © 1988, ICBO

Figure 6-6   *Wind stagnation pressure*

adjoining ground carries a factor of 1.2 in Exposure C. But it's only 0.7 in Exposure B. Which is right in our case?

Section 2311(c) tells us that Exposure C represents the most severe exposure — the terrain is flat and generally open, extending one-half mile or more from the site. Exposure B has terrain with buildings, forest or surface irregularities 20 feet or more in height covering at least 20 percent of the area extending one mile or more from the site. That makes sense. You'll get the full force of the wind if your building is the only obstruction around. In this case we're in a city and can use the factor for Exposure B.

Now our formula, converted to numbers, looks like this:

Multiply 0.7 times 1.1 times 13 times 1 to get the design wind pressure of 10.01 pounds per square foot.

But don't stop here. This isn't the end. Suppose that our Exposure Coefficient comes under Exposure C, and that we're building on a knoll which extends considerably above the surrounding terrain. Do you think it would be wise to use the minimum height of 20 feet for a residential structure? I wouldn't recommend it. Instead, add the height of the knoll to the height of your building.

For example, your house will be in Exposure C (flat terrain, generally open for a half mile) but you have chosen to place it on a knoll 50 feet above the height of the surrounding countryside. This puts the roof height in the 60 to 100 bracket in Table 23-G. (The house is 20 feet high and the knoll is 50 feet high). Now our formula will look like this:

Multiply 1.6 times 1.1 times 13 times 1 to get the design wind pressure of 22.88 pounds per square foot. That difference might have some effect on the type of roof you choose and the method of installing it.

Just a minute, though. This is only a recommendation, not a requirement. It's not in the book and it's not based on engineering data. It's based on pure and simple common sense. Normally, a little added strength in your calculation won't be that expensive, especially in a home.

That's all there is to wind loads. But don't try to build that roof for a wind load of 10.01 pounds per square foot. It turns out that the expected wind loads are less than the expected live loads. UBC Table 23-C (Figure 6-7 in this book) gives the minimum roof live loads. These are the minimum figures to use, no matter what the wind load calculations suggest.

Don't stop reading the UBC when you think you have the answer. Take time to read the next paragraph.

Snow Loads

According to Section 2305(d) of the UBC:

Snow loads, full or unbalanced, shall be considered in place of loads set forth in UBC Table 23-C, where such loading will result in larger members or connections.

It seems that snow can create some unusual conditions on a roof. For instance, the shady part of a roof is the last part to thaw. Before it finally does, you can expect some strange

TABLE NO. 23-C—MINIMUM ROOF LIVE LOADS[1]

	METHOD 1			METHOD 2		
	TRIBUTARY LOADED AREA IN SQUARE FEET FOR ANY STRUCTURAL MEMBER			UNIFORM LOAD[2]	RATE OF REDUC-TION *r* (Percent)	MAXIMUM REDUC-TION *R* (Percent)
ROOF SLOPE	0 to 200	201 to 600	Over 600			
1. Flat or rise less than 4 inches per foot. Arch or dome with rise less than one eighth of span	20	16	12	20	.08	40
2. Rise 4 inches per foot to less than 12 inches per foot. Arch or dome with rise one eighth of span to less than three eighths of span	16	14	12	16	.06	25
3. Rise 12 inches per foot and greater. Arch or dome with rise three eighths of span or greater	12	12	12	12		
4. Awnings except cloth covered[3]	5	5	5	5	No Reductions Permitted	
5. Greenhouses, lath houses and agricultural buildings[4]	10	10	10	10		

[1]Where snow loads occur, the roof structure shall be designed for such loads as determined by the building official. See Section 2305 (d). For special purpose roofs, see Section 2305 (e).

[2]See Section 2306 for live load reductions. The rate of reduction *r* in Section 2306 Formula (6-1) shall be as indicated in the table. The maximum reduction *R* shall not exceed the value indicated in the table.

[3]As defined in Section 4506.

[4]See Section 2305 (e) for concentrated load requirements for greenhouse roof members.

From the Uniform Building Code, © 1988, ICBO

Figure 6-7 *Minimum roof live loads*

results. The snow melts a little and then freezes, melts a little and then freezes, causing snow and ice to pile up on the roof. While the shady side is thawing and freezing, the exposed side may be completely bare after a few days. This creates what is known as an unbalanced load. Figures A-6, A-7, A-8, A-9, A-10 from the UBC Appendix (Figure 6-8) show this very well. Figures A-13 and A-14 (Figure 6-9) indicate the increased load area in roof valleys.

Even though it's temporary, somewhat like the wind load, snow load still must be calculated into the overall roof load. This is referred to in Section 2305(d):

> *Potential accumulation of snow at valleys, parapets, roof structures and offsets in roofs of uneven configuration shall be considered. Where snow loads occur, the snow loads shall be determined by the building official.*

The pitch of a roof influences snow load. UBC Table 23-C (Figure 6-7) shows this under Method 1, indicating a gradual reduction in load as the roof pitch increases. This works well — until you get to the third column where the *Tributary Loaded Area* exceeds 600 square feet.

The snow load formula— If you don't want to use this chart, you can calculate your reduction by the following formula:

$$R_2 = \frac{S}{40} - \frac{1}{2}$$

Where: R_2 = Snow load reduction in pounds per square foot per degree of pitch over 20 degrees

S = Total snow load in pounds per square inch

Do you know what the snow loading is in your community? If you have a lot of snow, you may. But if your work is spread over a larger area, snow loading may vary considerably.

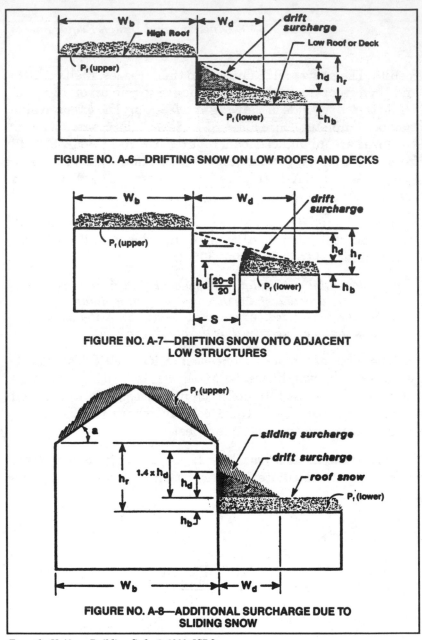

FIGURE NO. A-6—DRIFTING SNOW ON LOW ROOFS AND DECKS

FIGURE NO. A-7—DRIFTING SNOW ONTO ADJACENT LOW STRUCTURES

FIGURE NO. A-8—ADDITIONAL SURCHARGE DUE TO SLIDING SNOW

From the Uniform Building Code, © 1988, ICBO

Figure 6-8 *Drifting snow creates unbalanced loads*

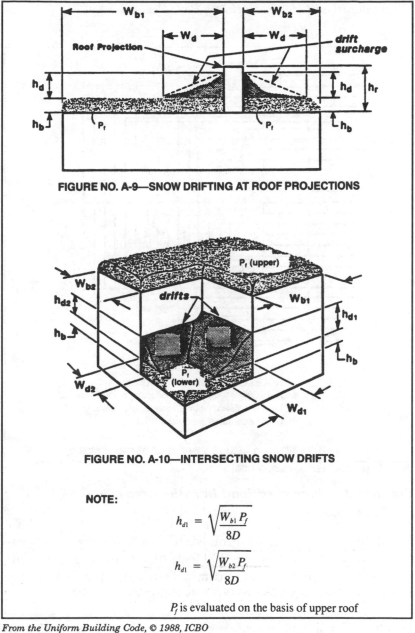

FIGURE NO. A-9—SNOW DRIFTING AT ROOF PROJECTIONS

FIGURE NO. A-10—INTERSECTING SNOW DRIFTS

NOTE:

$$h_{d1} = \sqrt{\frac{W_{b1} P_f}{8D}}$$

$$h_{d1} = \sqrt{\frac{W_{b2} P_f}{8D}}$$

P_f is evaluated on the basis of upper roof

Figure 6-8 (cont'd) *Drifting snow creates unbalanced loads*

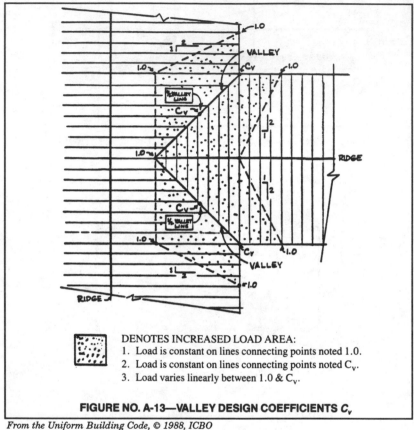

DENOTES INCREASED LOAD AREA:
1. Load is constant on lines connecting points noted 1.0.
2. Load is constant on lines connecting points noted C_v.
3. Load varies linearly between 1.0 & C_v.

FIGURE NO. A-13—VALLEY DESIGN COEFFICIENTS C_v

From the Uniform Building Code, © 1988, ICBO

Figure 6-9   *Increased load in valley areas*

My home is in Washington State. Counties vary in elevation from sea level to over 8,000 feet. At sea level the snowfall may be only a few inches and may last just a few hours or a few days, often with little or no freezing.

But I live in the mountains where snow can reach 15 feet deep or more and stay on the ground in some places from October to June. Is the entire county considered a snow area?

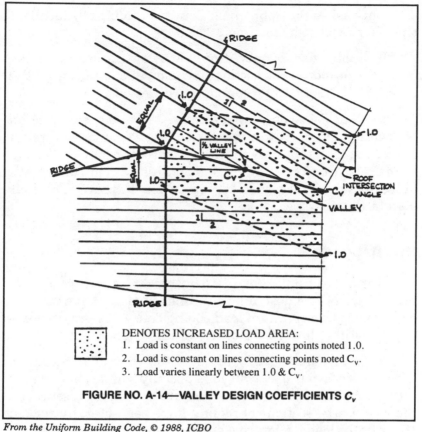

DENOTES INCREASED LOAD AREA:
1. Load is constant on lines connecting points noted 1.0.
2. Load is constant on lines connecting points noted C_v.
3. Load varies linearly between 1.0 & C_v.

FIGURE NO. A-14—VALLEY DESIGN COEFFICIENTS C_v

From the Uniform Building Code, © 1988, ICBO

Figure 6-9 (cont'd) *Increased load in valley areas*

Of course. But how do we determine snow loads for each community in the county? Where do you draw the line? At what point do you have a 30-pound load, a 40-pound load or a 50-pound load? You can't always depend on elevation because snowfall varies, even at the same elevation. So, too, will freezing and thawing conditions.

I once asked the Snohomish County building official about this. Here's what he told me:

"In Snohomish County it only snows back of the section line. On one side of the section line you get one rating, on the other side it's something completely different."

This was based on years of experience and observation in his county. Often, lacking professional assistance and reference data, that's the only route an inspector can take. He had to make a decision. If he made it on his best judgment, it's probably fair. If not, then it's up to you to prove that your standards are better.

Uplift Loads

Ever hear of uplift load? If you haven't, don't worry. It's seldom used when designing buildings. I guess that's because nearly everyone thinks of loads being caused by gravity pulling everything toward the center of the earth.

Roofs have uplift loads, just like the wing of an airplane. A roof with a parapet wall is especially vulnerable. Winds cause a vortex which creates a vacuum (negative pressure) on the roof. Large sections of roofing have been literally sucked off by uplift loads. High-rise buildings with large glass areas can have large negative loads. The only defense is a design that considers negative wind loads.

Gable roofs are also affected. Winds blowing over the roof create negative pressure on the lee side (side away from the wind) of the roof and can send shingles flying. If your chimney is too short or improperly placed, the same force can cause draft problems.

Although we understand the effect of wind, conditions vary considerably from place to place. The problem is compounded by trees and other buildings in the area. Be aware of any conditions that may create uplift loads on your building. Don't rely on trees or other buildings in the neighborhood to reduce the wind load. They may be removed in the next windstorm.

Roofs of unenclosed buildings, roof overhangs, architectural projections, eaves, canopies, cornices, marquees and the like have to be built to withstand upward pressures. In other words, when the inspector tells you to bolt your patio or carport cover to the concrete, he's just trying to keep it out of the neighbor's yard.

In the next chapter we'll discuss subterranean water. It's a problem in many areas. Besides damp basements, groundwater causes another problem. It's known officially as *hydrostatic uplift*. Section 2308(d) states that all footings, slabs and foundations subject to water pressure must be designed to resist a uniformly distributed uplift equal to the full hydrostatic pressure. If the building inspector is unsure about the hydrostatic pressure, he'll require you to test it.

Earthquake Loads

Earthquakes come under the same category as fire. In most cases they're totally unpredictable. There are now about nineteen pages of formulas and regulations in the UBC to help you protect against damage from earthquakes. The 1982 edition of the code had only six pages. But stay tuned. Our understanding of earthquake damage is changing very quickly. What's in the code today probably isn't the last word on design for earthquake safety. Check with your inspector on any special regulations.

Figure 6-10 shows an earthquake probability map. This map divides the country into seismic zones 0 through 4. Zone

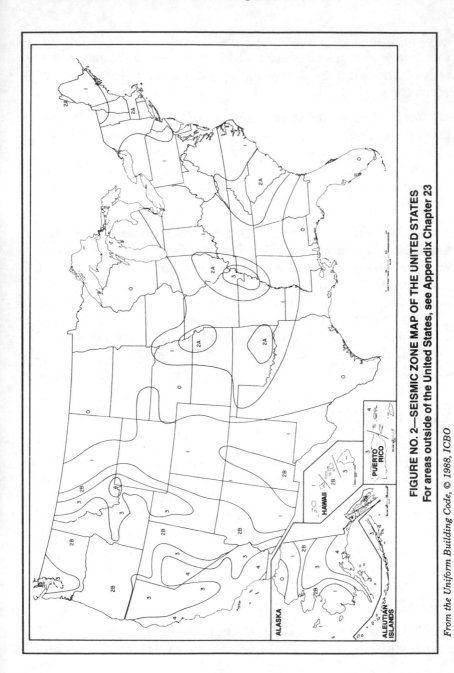

FIGURE NO. 2—SEISMIC ZONE MAP OF THE UNITED STATES
For areas outside of the United States, see Appendix Chapter 23

From the Uniform Building Code, © 1988, ICBO

Figure 6-10 Earthquake probability map

0 is where earthquakes are least likely; zone 4 is where they're most probable.

When you hear that an area is practically earthquake-free, just remember that there have been disastrous earthquakes in areas where none had occurred before. In the 16th century, Lisbon, Portugal had a severe earthquake that almost leveled the city. Loss of life was enormous. This was the only major earthquake ever to hit western Europe during recorded history. Portugal hasn't had a serious one since.

Reelfoot Lake in Tennessee was formed in the early 19th century when an earthquake caused land to settle in a large depression. There had never been an earthquake in the area before, nor has there been one since.

Use the earthquake probability map when planning any building. Many structural requirements in the UBC are based on the seismic zones shown in the earthquake map.

But there's no such thing as an earthquake-proof building, especially if you're building near a fault. Everyone knows that, including the authors of the code. They don't require the impossible, either to survive an earthquake or to overcome other possible risks. It isn't practical to design buildings to resist every conceivable force under any possible condition. If the code required that, very few projects would ever be planned. Few people could afford to build. But the code tries to strike a balance between risk to life and property and cost of construction. You're free to decide if the code is doing the job intended.

Reductions in Live Loads

Live loads are the weight of people and things that will be in the building. The code establishes live loads you have to design for in each type of building. Some reductions in live loads are permitted under certain circumstances. Formulas in the code show how and when these reductions apply. I'll spare you a discussion of those formulas. Engineers and architects usually work them out, anyway. If you're working on a large building, the designer should check his or her live load figures against the reductions permitted. This also applies to the deflection allowed in structural members. Section 2307 spells it out this way:

> *The deflection of any structural member shall not exceed the values set forth in UBC Table 23-D based upon the factors set forth in UBC Table 23-E. The deflection criteria representing the more restrictive condition shall apply. Deflection criteria for materials not specified shall be developed in a manner consistent with the provisions of this section. See Section 2305(f) for camber requirements. Span tables for light wood frame construction as specified in Sections 2518(d) and 2518(h)2, shall conform to the design criteria contained therein, except that where the dead load exceeds 50 percent of the live load, UBC Table 23-D shall govern. (For aluminum, see Section 2803.)*

Special Purpose Loads

Here are special loads which are usually grouped under the title *miscellaneous*:

- You must design greenhouse roof bars, purlins, and rafters to support a 100-pound minimum concentrated load in addition to the live load.

- Roofs must have enough slope or camber to ensure adequate drainage even if the roof sags. You must design the

roof to support maximum loads, including possible pond-
ing of water caused by deflection.

- Properly anchor the roof to walls and columns, and the
  walls and columns to the foundation to resist overturning,
  uplift and sliding.

- Fences less than 12 feet high, greenhouses, lath houses, and
  all agricultural buildings must be designed to meet the
  horizontal wind pressures in UBC Table 23-H (Figure 6-5).
  If the height of the structure is 20 feet or less, you only have
  to use two-thirds of the first line of listed values. Design the
  structures to withstand an uplift wind pressure equal to
  three-fourths the horizontal pressure.

- To determine stresses, consider that all vertical design
  loads except the roof live load and crane loads act simultaneously with the wind pressure. Snow loading is the only
  exception. You normally consider only 50 percent of the
  snow load in addition to the wind load. But the building
  official may require you to consider a greater percentage of
  snow load, depending on local conditions.

That about covers all the design and engineering you need
to know to follow the code. It's time to start looking at the
building itself. In the next chapter, we'll look at the code
requirements for concrete.

Misplaced Stake — Misplaced House

Most lots and plats have been surveyed, mapped, and staked at least once before the contractor arrives. Surveyors set stakes for streets and walks, sewers, water lines, underground power and phone lines. Stakes for these site improvements are usually uprooted, replanted, and generally kicked around while the sitework is being done. Not only that. Kids have a natural attraction for survey stakes. They make lovely swords.

By the time you get to the site, no telling where the survey stakes have wandered. That's why I always recommended a fresh survey when I issued a permit for a new building. A new survey won't cost much — usually less than $200. That's cheap insurance.

I once issued a permit with the usual warning about surveys and such. "Yeah, yeah," the contractor said. I figured he would ignore my suggestion. And he did. When I inspected the foundation, something looked wrong to me. I called the contractor and suggested he get a survey before doing any more work. He finally hired a surveyor. The foundation not only violated the setback requirements, but part of it was on the neighbor's lot!

It was a simple but costly mistake. The lot was on a curve. The contractor took the PT stake (point of tangency) for his base point (lot corner). It was the contractor's error and his loss. The contractor could have asked the owner to get a survey before starting work. I bet he did on every job after that.

7

Concrete

hen building homes, apartments or small commercial
buildings, you don't need to know very much about
concrete. After all, it arrives at the site already mixed
and ready to use. But for larger jobs, the requirements are
more demanding and there's more you have to know. The last
thing you want to have to do is break out a freshly poured
foundation.

What Is Concrete?

What's the difference between *concrete* and *cement*? Generally, cement is the powdered limestone used to make concrete. Chapter 26 of the UBC covers concrete construction —
including this definition of concrete:

Concrete. *A mixture of portland cement, fine aggregate, coarse aggregate and water.*

Section 2602 includes about 45 other definitions. Most of them only concern design, and you'll probably never need to know them. I'll just list a few of the most common items in general use.

Admixture. *A material other than portland cement, aggregate or water added to concrete to modify its property.*

Aggregate. *Inert material which is mixed with portland cement and water to produce concrete.*

Deformed Reinforcement. *Deformed reinforcing bars, bar and rod mats, deformed wire, welded plain wire fabric and welded deformed wire fabric conforming to Section 2603(f)2.*

Embedment Length. *The length of embedded reinforcement provided beyond a critical section. (That's the length of rebar you have to embed on either side of a stress point.)*

Plain Concrete. *Concrete that does not conform to the definition for reinforced concrete.*

Precast Concrete. *A plain or reinforced concrete element cast in other than its final position in the structure.*

Prestressed Concrete. *Reinforced concrete in which there have been introduced internal stresses of such magnitude and distribution that the stresses resulting from loads are counteracted to a desired degree.*

Reinforced Concrete. *Concrete containing reinforcement, including prestressing steel, and designed with the assumption that the two materials act together in resisting forces.*

> **Surface Water**. *Water carried by an aggregate except that held by absorption within the aggregate particles themselves.*

Of all construction materials, concrete is probably one of the most abused. It's mismatched, mismixed, and watered down. Products are added to slow or speed hardening. Yet in spite of all this, it's one of the most reliable building products we have.

Weather will erode it, in time, but it won't rust or rot. Even the poorest mixes will last long after the framing, wiring, and other components of a building have completely deteriorated.

Concrete block is another durable and versatile building material that's adaptable to nearly any design or building application. And it will support greater loads than most other products.

Testing Concrete

With a few exceptions, concrete is hard to inspect properly. That's why the inspector has the right to call for any tests he thinks are necessary. Many of these tests are spelled out in the job specs, so you know in advance what's expected. But if the inspector thinks the specified tests are inadequate, he can call for more sophisticated tests. Fortunately, most on-site concrete tests are easily performed. Two of the most common are the slump and the compression or compressive fracture test.

Slump Test

The slump test is probably the simplest of all concrete tests. It uses a cone-shaped device made of 16 gauge galvanized sheet metal. The cone is about 12 inches high with a base about 8 inches in diameter and a top about 4 inches in diameter. See Figure 7-1. To conduct the test, place it on a board or other flat surface and fill it with concrete. Settle the concrete by pushing a steel rod into it a prescribed number of times — in this case, 27 times. Then measure the height of the settled concrete and remove the cone. Let it settle for several minutes, then measure again. The difference between the first measurement and the second is the amount of slump in that batch.

You'll usually do three slump tests and average the results. The inspector will compare this average with the slump allowed by the specs. If they don't agree within allowed percentages, the inspector can disallow the batch of concrete.

Compressive Fracture Test

The compression test is a little more complicated. Unless a fracturing machine is taken to the job site, the test begins in the field but ends in a laboratory. A cylinder is cast in a round form that can vary from 2 inches in diameter by 4 inches long to 10 inches in diameter and 18 inches long. If the aggregate isn't more than 2 inches in diameter, the form is usually 6 inches by 12 inches. Unless required by the project specifications, don't use cylinders smaller than that.

The cylinder should be placed on a flat surface where it won't be exposed to vibrations or other disturbances, and then filled with concrete. The concrete is then rodded a prescribed number of times for even distribution. You'll find the rodding requirements in UBC Tables 26-10-A and 26-10-B (Figure 7-2.) The cylinders must be left undisturbed for the initial setup, or hardening. After that, keep movement to a minimum for the next hours. The cylinders must be protected from unusually hot or cold weather.

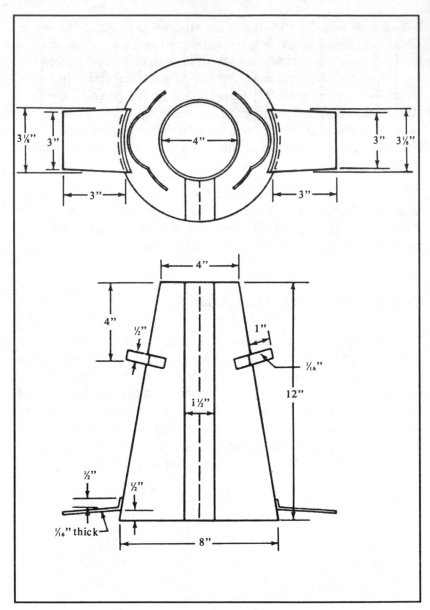

Figure 7-1   *Details of cone used for slump test*

Concrete

TABLE NO. 26-10-A—NUMBER OF LAYERS REQUIRED FOR SPECIMENS

Specimen Type and Size, as Depth, in.	Mode of Compaction	Number of layers	Approximate Depth of Layer, in.
Cylinders:			
up to 12	rodding	3 equal	
over 12	rodding	as required	4
up to 18	vibration	2 equal	
over 18	vibration	3 or more	8 as near as practicable
Prisms and horizontal creep cylinders:			
up to 8	rodding	2 equal	
over 8	rodding	3 or more	4
up to 8	vibration	1	
over 8	vibration	2 or more	8 as near as practicable

TABLE NO. 26-10-B—DIAMETER OF ROD AND NUMBER OF RODDINGS TO BE USED IN MOLDING TEST SPECIMENS

Cylinders

Diameter of Cylinder, in.	Diameter of Rod, in.	Number of Strokes/Layer
2 to <6	3/8	25
6	5/8	25
8	5/8	50
10	5/8	75

Beams and Prisms

Top Surface Area of Specimen, in.	Diameter of Rod, in.	Number of Roddings/Layer
25 or less	3/8	25
26 to 49	3/8	one for each 1 in.^{2} of surface
50 or more	5/8	one for each 2 in.^{2} of surface

Horizontal Creep Cylinders

Diameter of Cylinder, in.	Diameter of Rod, in.	Number of Roddings/Layer
6	5/8	50 total, 25 along both sides of axis

From the Uniform Building Code, © 1988, ICBO

Figure 7-2 *Number of layers and rodding requirements for concrete specimens*

The cylinders are then placed in a compression or breaking press that can apply set amounts or pressure to the cylinder. Several cylinders are tested, one at a time, at specified intervals — normally 24 hours, 7 days, and 28 days. The results are checked against the specs.

Most transit-mix companies run compressive tests on the concrete they sell. The plant may botch an occasional batch, but most problems begin after the mix arrives at the job site.

Mixing the Batch

The cement must meet the requirements and specifications for the particular job at hand. UBC Standard 26-1 lists eight types of concrete most commonly used in construction:

Type I — For use in general concrete construction when the special properties specified for Types II, III, IV, and V are not required.

Type IA — Same use as Type I where air entrainment is desired.

Type II — For use in general concrete construction exposed to moderate sulfate action, or where moderated heat of hydration is desired.

Type IIA — Same use as Type II where air entrainment is desired.

Type III — For use when high early strength is desired.

Type IIIA — Same use as Type III where air entrainment is desired.

Type IV — For use when a low heat of hydration is required.

Type V — For use when high sulfate resistance is required.

Unless your specs call for a specific concrete type, check with your supplier for recommendations. The engineer designing the job will make the final determination. Then you'll need to know the right proportions for the job at hand. This should also be spelled out in the specs, probably in three figures, such as 1-3-5. This means "1 sack cement, 3 cubic feet of sand, 5 cubic feet of stone." Finally, you'll add the amount of water necessary to get the slump required by the specs.

The aggregate must be clean and free of pollutants such as ash, dirt, grease, oil or wood chips. The nominal maximum size of the aggregate shouldn't be larger than 1/5 the narrowest dimension between the sides of the form, 1/3 the depth of the slab, or 3/4 the minimum clear spacing between reinforcing steel. Check the workability of the mix and the methods of consolidation so the finished concrete won't contain honeycombs or voids. It should still be plastic, not too runny or crumbly.

Use water free of oil, acids, alkalis, or organic materials that may affect either the concrete or the reinforcing steel. Generally speaking, if you wouldn't drink the water, you shouldn't use it for concrete.

Spacing the Reinforcement

For reinforcement, choose material that meets job specs and place it according to the plans. UBC Table 26-1 (Figure 7-3) shows the minimum bend point locations for rebar. UBC Table 26-C (Figure 7-4) shows the minimum diameters of bends.

The clear distance between parallel reinforcing bars in a layer should be at least the same as the nominal diameter of the bars, but not less than 1 inch. This code requirement doesn't apply to splices or to bundles designed as part of an

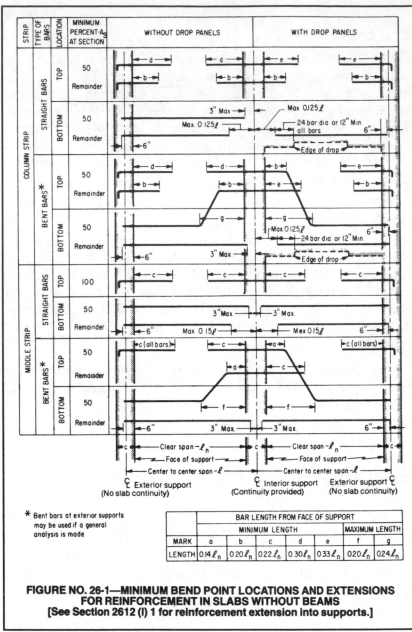

**FIGURE NO. 26-1—MINIMUM BEND POINT LOCATIONS AND EXTENSIONS
FOR REINFORCEMENT IN SLABS WITHOUT BEAMS
[See Section 2612 (I) 1 for reinforcement extension into supports.]**

Figure 7-3   *Minimum bend point locations*

TABLE NO. 26-C—MINIMUM DIAMETERS OF BEND	
BAR SIZE	MINIMUM DIAMETER
Nos. 3 through 8	$6d_b$
Nos. 9, 10 and 11	$8d_b$
Nos. 14 and 18	$10d_b$

From the Uniform Building Code, © 1988, ICBO

Figure 7-4   *Minimum diameters of bend*

overall reinforcement plan. Figure 9-2, in Chapter 9, shows how to make splices. Don't use lap splices on bars larger than No. 11 except where larger bars are used as dowels in footings.

You may use welded splices. A full welded splice has bars which are butted and welded to develop a bond of at least 125 percent of the specified yield strength of the bar.

Be sure to support all reinforcement. On vertical work, secure reinforcement so it won't touch the sides of the forms or other reinforcement, unless it's planned in the construction of the bundles or mats. In flatwork, such as slabs for floors or roofs, place reinforcement on chairs to keep it from touching the ground or form below. A chair is a metal device usually constructed of a heavy gauge wire. Figure 7-5 shows typical styles.

Some concrete workers will lay reinforcing bars or mats on the ground when they're pouring slabs. After the pour, the finisher hooks the steel and pulls it up into the concrete. This isn't acceptable. Most of the steel won't be centered in the slab. Don't let your workers or subs get by with this shortcut.

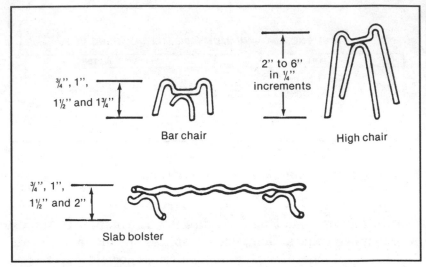

Figure 7-5 *Chairs for supporting reinforcing steel*

Placing Concrete

You can't place concrete without knowing how to build forms. Forms have to hold concrete in the shape shown on the plans until the concrete is hardened. And they have to be strong enough to hold the weight and moisture in the concrete without collapsing or leaking. I've worked on several jobs where the forms weren't braced right. I can assure you that it's a frustrating experience to see concrete seeping out where it shouldn't be.

Figure 7-6 shows a formed foundation wall with metal clips on the top of the form to keep the boards from spreading. Forms for prestressed members must allow for any movement of the member without causing damage to the form.

Figure 7-6   *Foundation wall ready for stripping the forms*

Also consider whether your forms are accessible to the ready-mix truck. If they are, the truck can pour the concrete directly into the forms. If not, you'll have to transport the concrete to the forms by wheelbarrow, pump, or even by bucket and crane.

Regardless of the method used, don't let the concrete fall more than 48 inches from the chute to the form. If this distance exceeds 48 inches, use an extension chute. Prefabricated metal chute extensions are available, but you can make your own from scrap wood at the job site. Just be careful to keep the mix from separating while you pour.

When you're ready to remove the forms, be careful not to damage the green concrete. The only loads allowed on un-shored portions during construction are the concrete itself. No construction can be supported by the new work until the concrete reaches adequate strength. This usually takes from 3 to 28 days. Generally, form removal can begin after 24 hours.

Settling or Consolidating the Concrete

The amount of settling, or consolidating, depends largely on the amount of slump in a mix. A high slump mix requires little consolidation. There are two methods of consolidating — hand spading or vibration. Mechanical vibrators do the work of settling much easier than hand-spading, and they allow for the placement of stiffer mixes. But don't use vibrators if the mix can be hand-spaded. There's always the possibility of the material separating too much. That's why you shouldn't use vibrators to move concrete horizontally.

Curing

Time is always important when you're pouring concrete. Of course, concrete additives can delay or increase the curing time, but generally it's just a matter of waiting. In about the first 24 hours, the concrete will acquire over half its strength. By the end of seven days you should have approximately 90 percent of the design strength. Concrete usually doesn't reach full strength until 28 days after pouring.

If you've just poured a basement or foundation wall for a simple structure, you can probably work around the area for a day or two while the concrete hardens. But this doesn't mean you can move a house onto a newly-poured foundation. I doubt the inspector would allow it.

To increase concrete strength, the code recommends that concrete be maintained above 50 degrees F and in a moist environment for at least the first seven days. If you were using a high early-strength concrete, this time can be reduced to about three days. But what happens in the fall and winter, when temperatures fall below 50 degrees F?

Simply covering the concrete will help. The chemical reaction in the concrete itself — the interaction of the water, cement and other chemicals in the mix — creates a great deal of heat. If it's going to be really cold, spread a layer of straw, sawdust, or even polyethylene film to keep the heat in.

Increased Temperatures and Curing Time

In Section 2605(e)3, the code provides a method that will shorten curing time a great deal.

Curing by high-pressure steam, steam at atmospheric pressure, heat and moisture, or other accepted processes, may be employed to accelerate strength gain and reduce the time of curing. Accelerated curing shall provide the compressive strength of the concrete at the load stage considered at least equal to the design strength required at that load stage. The curing process shall produce concrete with a durability at least equivalent to the curing method of Section 2605(e)1.

How do you know when the concrete has reached proper strength? Remember those test cylinders I mentioned earlier? These cylinders were from the same batch of concrete. When the samples are strong enough, the concrete used in the work should be at the right strength also.

Hot Weather

During hot weather, proper attention shall be given to ingredients, production methods, handling, placing, pro-

tection, and curing to prevent excessive concrete temperatures or water evaporation . . .

That's what Section 2605(g) of the code says about hot weather, but it doesn't say *how* hot. That varies with the humidity and wind conditions. The key is to prevent the rapid evaporation of water from the fresh concrete.

Speed of evaporation will vary with the humidity. If you're in a humid part of the country, you'll have one set of values. In an arid climate you'll have another. The Portland Cement Association reports that if the relative humidity decreases from 90 percent to 50 percent, the rate of evaporation increases five times. If the humidity falls another 10 percent, the rate of evaporation increases nine times.

When it's windy you'll find the same changes in the rate of evaporation. When the wind changes from 0 to 10 mph, the rate of evaporation increases four times; it's nine times greater when wind velocity increases to 25 mph.

Using cool materials and protecting the work from direct sunlight helps reduce evaporation. Spraying the concrete with a fine mist raises the relative humidity and helps slow evaporation.

Interrupting the Pour

Avoid interrupting the pour if you can, although the code does allow it. The requirements are in Section 2606(d):

(d) Construction Joints. Where a construction joint is to be made, the surface of the concrete shall be thoroughly cleaned and all laitance and standing water removed. Vertical joints shall be thoroughly wetted immediately before placing of new concrete.

If you've ever tried to place a thin concrete slab over an existing one — raising the height of steps or a sidewalk, for example — you're probably aware of how difficult it is to get a good seal or bond between the old concrete and the new.

The code calls for a "neat cement grout." That can be a mixture of water and cement spread over the surface. Several other products do this job very well. The point is that you just can't pour new concrete over old without preparing the existing surface first. Ask your concrete supplier about the materials you'll need and how to use them.

That UBC section requires you to remove all standing water and laitance. When standing water collects on the top of settled concrete, it brings with it a mixture of dust, impurities, small amounts of cement, and other foreign matter. When the water evaporates, it leaves a dusty, grayish-brown film on the surface of the concrete. That's laitance.

On flat slabs where the surface is worked down and smoothed as part of the finishing process, laitance is insignificant. Much of it is worked off when the slab is prefinished. The rest is worked back into the concrete. On formwork, however, laitance can be a real problem. It prevents bonding. If a pour is interrupted, the laitance must be removed before the job can proceed. This is usually done with sandblasting equipment.

Have I Got a Deal for You?

I guess I'm a little old fashioned. I get worried when I hear about some great new construction material. There are fads and fashions in construction just like in the garment industry. Comes along a new material and everyone wants to try it. Pretty soon everyone's an expert, either at applying it or selling it or both. Never underestimate the enthusiasm of America's entrepreneurs. If there's a buck to be made, someone's trying to make it.

Roof coatings are an example. A roofing truck pulls up in front of the house. Here's the spiel the homeowner gets: "Sir, I was just driving down the street and noticed that your roof isn't looking so good. I've been resurfacing roofs in this neighborhood and have enough extra time and material to resurface yours tomorrow afternoon. We use a new aerobic silicon polyester coating, the same stuff used to protect the skin of the space shuttle. It adds years to the life of your roof and costs pennies compared to a new roof."

The victim is probably a senior citizen on a limited income or someone worried about leaks in the next rain. This sales pitch is a bolt from the blue. So they sign up. Next day the roofer applies a shiny aluminized coating and it really looks good. Only the first time it rains, the coating does a meltdown. And the roof leaks the same as before. What happened?

Don't bother to look for that high-tech roofer. He's miles away by now. What he did was coat the roof with an aluminum-colored distillate. It costs about $5.00 a gallon and a gallon goes a long way. True, he charged less than the cost of a new roof. But all the homeowner got was a roof shine. Maybe if the homeowner had called the building inspector first . . . .

Remember that the next time you decide to try a new building material. Building inspectors like to be asked about new materials *before you install them* — and have good ways to identify claims that may not stand up.

8

Foundations

We've explored occupancies, types of construction related to occupancies, the fire-resistiveness of materials, and design and engineering. It's finally time to look at the building itself — beginning with the foundation. But first, let's consider the building site.

Site Consideration

Here are some of the things you'll want to check for at the site:

- Do you have a water problem (too much or too little)?

- Does the land slope excessively?

- Will you need to move dirt to place the building on the property?

- What are you going to do with any cut banks that remain?

- What about the excess dirt remaining after the backfill has been completed?

Answering each of these questions may require an understanding of the building code.

Let's say you have a high water table on site. How does that involve the building code? Probably the first thing the inspector will ask is how much water you have and what your plans are for dealing with it. Are you planning to use a sump pump or a drainage system to carry the water to a lower portion of land, or do you have some other method in mind? Perhaps you've considered dumping it into a sanitary sewer (prohibited in most cities). Or you were planning to leave it there and waterproof the basement? Maybe the building doesn't have a basement. In that case, will your building sit on piles or on a fill? Will you have a post and beam floor or a slab on grade?

These are some of the first questions you should consider. You can bet they're some of the first questions the building inspector is going to ask.

Make sure you know exactly where the property lines are, that the corners are properly staked, and that a surveyor has set the stakes for your house. Yes, this will cost a little more. But I've seen houses that encroached on the legal setback area and several that even went over the property line. I even met a contractor who built on the wrong lot!

Funny? You bet — unless you're the one caught in the net. It's not only embarrassing but awfully expensive. Hiring a surveyor is your cheapest insurance against problems like that.

Excavation and Fill

Chapter 29 of the UBC covers the quality and design of structural materials used in excavations and foundations. This chapter is backed up by Chapter 70 in the Appendix of the UBC, which regulates grading on private property. The purpose is to safeguard health, property and public welfare. It also lists the conditions for permits and permit fees. (See UBC Tables 70-A and 70-B, Figure 8-1 in this manual.)

Section 7003 of the UBC states that a permit is required for certain types of excavation and landfill. You don't need a permit, however, for these uses:

1) Grading in an isolated, self-contained area if there's no apparent danger to private or public property

2) An excavation below finished grade for basements and footings of a building, retaining wall or other structure authorized by a valid building permit

3) Cemetery graves

4) Refuse disposal sites controlled by other regulations

5) Excavations for wells, tunnels or utilities

6) Mining, quarrying, excavating, processing, stockpiling of rock, sand, gravel, aggregate or clay where established and provided for by law, if these operations don't affect the lateral support or increase the stresses on any adjacent or contiguous property

7) Exploratory excavations under the direction of soil engineers or engineering geologists

TABLE NO. 70-A—GRADING PLAN REVIEW FEES[1]

50 cubic yards or less	No fee
51 to 100 cubic yards	$15.00
101 to 1000 cubic yards	22.50
1001 to 10,000 cubic yards	30.00

10,001 to 100,000 cubic yards—$30.00 for the first 10,000 cubic yards, plus $15.00 for each additional 10,000 yards or fraction thereof.

100,001 to 200,000 cubic yards—$165.00 for the first 100,000 cubic yards, plus $9.00 for each additional 10,000 cubic yards or fraction thereof.

200,001 cubic yards or more—$255.00 for the first 200,000 cubic yards, plus $4.50 for each additional 10,000 cubic yards or fraction thereof.

Other Fees:

Additional plan review required by changes, additions or revisions to approved plans .... $30.00 per hour*
(minimum charge—one-half hour)

*Or the total hourly cost to the jurisdiction, whichever is the greatest. This cost shall include supervision, overhead, equipment, hourly wages and fringe benefits of the employees involved.

TABLE NO. 70-B—GRADING PERMIT FEES[1]

50 cubic yards or less	$15.00
51 to 100 cubic yards	22.50

101 to 1000 cubic yards—$22.50 for the first 100 cubic yards plus $10.50 for each additional 100 cubic yards or fraction thereof.

1001 to 10,000 cubic yards—$117.00 for the first 1,000 cubic yards, plus $9.00 for each additional 1,000 cubic yards or fraction thereof.

10,001 to 100,000 cubic yards—$198.00 for the first 10,000 cubic yards, plus $40.50 for each additional 10,000 cubic yards or fraction thereof.

100,001 cubic yards or more—$562.50 for the first 100,000 cubic yards, plus $22.50 for each additional 10,000 cubic yards or fraction thereof.

Other Inspections and Fees:

1. Inspections outside of normal business hours .... $30.00 per hour[2]
   (minimum charge—two hours)

2. Reinspection fees assessed under provisions of
   Section 305 (g) .... $30.00 per hour[2]

3. Inspections for which no fee is specifically indicated .... $30.00 per hour[2]
   (minimum charge—one-half hour)

[1]The fee for a grading permit authorizing additional work to that under a valid permit shall be the difference between the fee paid for the original permit and the fee shown for the entire project.

[2]Or the total hourly cost to the jurisdiction, whichever is the greatest. This cost shall include supervision, overhead, equipment, hourly wages and fringe benefits of the employees involved.

From the Uniform Building Code, © 1988, ICBO

Figure 8-1   *Grading plan review and grading permit fees*

8) An excavation which is less than 2 feet in depth, or which doesn't create a cut slope greater than 5 feet in height or steeper than one and one-half horizontal to one vertical.

9) A fill that meets these requirements: Less than 1 foot in depth placed on natural terrain with a slope flatter than five horizontal to one vertical. Or less than 3 feet in depth, not intended to support structures, which doesn't exceed 50 cubic yards on any one lot and doesn't obstruct a drainage course.

As you can see, unless you're working on steep slopes, few operations actually require a permit. So I won't spend a great deal of time on it. But we do need to spend some time on backfilling.

Backfilling and Compaction

Too few contractors know all they should about proper backfilling. This is unfortunate because sloppy backfill destroys good construction — every time.

You've probably seen homes in your area where the steps have pulled away from the house or where shrubbery around the house has sunk. Usually this is because the area around the basement backfill wasn't properly compacted. If backfilling is done without proper supervision, only a density test can determine if it was done correctly.

The UBC calls for 90 percent compaction. But in dry climates it's hard to get 90 percent. Dry soil packs loosely. When a tractor passes over soil — the usual form of compaction — only the top several inches gets compacted. Unless the backfill is placed in the trench in layers, only the top 6 to 10 inches of dirt is compacted.

Water settling is a very effective way to compact most soil. Saturate the fill, wait until it dries, add more fill and saturate again. Because this takes longer, few builders do it. So eventually, mother nature does the compaction by settling. This can happen either gradually or all at once. Either way, the home owner finds his shrubbery in a hole that wasn't there before and steps separated from the house.

For proper compaction, you have to place the fill in layers not over 12 inches deep and compact each layer. A little water will help if the soil is dry. The deeper the excavation, the more layers and the more compaction needed. Compacting a water line trench 3 feet deep won't take as long as a sewer trench 7 feet deep. For a larger job, use a hand held wacker-tamper powered by small gasoline engine.

Excavation Cut Slopes

According to the code, you can't make the cut slopes for permanent excavation steeper than two horizontal units of measure to one vertical. The same applies to slopes for permanent fill. See Figure 8-2. Whether your unit measure is feet, inches or yards, the proportion is the same.

Don't place fill next to any building or structure unless the building can withstand the additional loads caused by the fill. The usual curing time for concrete in basement walls is about seven days. That's the minimum amount of time to wait before you backfill against it, but I recommend even more time.

Cut-Slope Setbacks

In steep, hilly country you may find that your building may have to be set back from the top of a cut or the toe of a fill. Chapter 70 of the UBC has several illustrations of this. See Figure 8-3. These setbacks are minimums. In some areas the inspector, acting on the recommendations of soils engineers

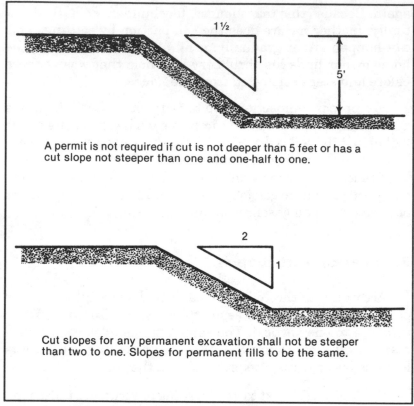

Figure 8-2 *Cut slope dimensions for excavations*

or his own knowledge of the area, will require a greater setback than shown in Figure 8-3.

A retaining wall can usually be used to reduce the setback requirement. But unless the cut or fill is shallow, you'll probably need a wall designed by a registered engineer.

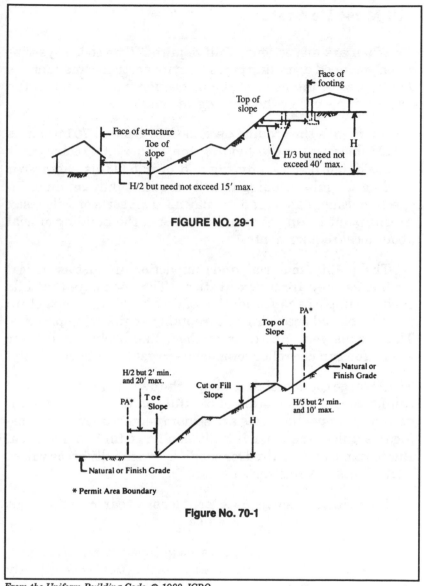

FIGURE NO. 29-1

Figure No. 70-1

* Permit Area Boundary

From the Uniform Building Code, © 1988, ICBO

Figure 8-3 *Required setbacks*

Fill Must Be Stable

When are inspections of fill required? The code says that when you need a grading permit, an inspection is mandatory. The degree or intensity of the inspection will depend on the scope of the work or the *grading designation*.

But what's the grading designation? Section 7014(b) uses 5,000 cubic yards as the dividing line. Under 5,000 cubic yards is considered *regular grading* and over 5,000 is *engineered grading*. Regular grading usually requires only minimal inspection. Engineered grading may need all sorts of soils tests. At this point it can get complicated. Ask the building official about local requirements.

The quality, material, and compaction are just as critical for fills as they are for excavations. The book says that fills used to support the foundation of any building or structure must be placed according to acceptable engineering practice. This means you have to treat them like backfill and layer them. You can use roller compactors to get the proper density.

On large commercial buildings, the owner or architect may call for compaction testing of backfills on trenches and foundations. Compaction tests are seldom required for single residences unless the home is built on a large fill in a new area. But tests may be required for subdivisions in hilly areas where a lot of cuts and fills were necessary.

If the fill has been in place for at least a year or two without any problems, it's probably stable.

Few building departments are equipped to make compaction tests. That's one reason why compaction is frequently overlooked by many inspectors. But if the inspector is on his toes and suspects there's a problem, he can order that tests be made, at the expense of the owner. This can be difficult and expensive because many communities don't have adequate testing facilities.

Soils Classification and Geology

It's not always the fill material or its placement or compaction that causes problems. Sometimes it's what's *under* the fill that creates trouble. Here's what Section 2904 in the UBC has to say about soil:

> *Section 2904(a) Soil Classification: General. For the purposes of this chapter, the definition and classification of soil materials for use in Table No. 29-B shall be according to UBC Standard No. 29-1.*
>
> *(b) Expansive Soil. When the expansive characteristics of a soil are to be determined, the procedures shall be in accordance with UBC Standard No. 29-2 and the soil shall be classified according to Table No. 29-C. Foundations for structures resting on soils with an expansion index greater than 20, as determined by UBC Standard No. 29-2, shall require special design consideration. In the event the soil expansion index varies with depth, the weighted index shall be determined according to Table No. 29-D.*

UBC Table 29-B is Figure 8-4. Figure 8-5 includes UBC Tables 29-C and 29-D. If the inspector requires you to have this information, you can only get it from a soils geologist. The geologist will take core samples or run tests on the aggregate. This is expensive. But it's seldom required except on large jobs or where the soil conditions may be questionable.

TABLE NO. 29-B—ALLOWABLE FOUNDATION AND LATERAL PRESSURE

CLASS OF MATERIALS[2]	ALLOWABLE FOUNDATION PRESSURE LBS. /SQ. FT.[3]	LATERAL BEARING LBS./SQ./FT./ FT. OF DEPTH BELOW NATURAL GRADE[4]	LATERAL SLIDING[1]	
			COEF-FICIENT[5]	RESISTANCE LBS./SQ. FT.[6]
1. Massive Crystalline Bedrock	4000	1200	.70	
2. Sedimentary and Foliated Rock	2000	400	.35	
3. Sandy Gravel and/or Gravel (GW and GP)	2000	200	.35	
4. Sand, Silty Sand, Clayey Sand, Silty Gravel and Clayey Gravel (SW, SP, SM, SC, GM and GC)	1500	150	.25	
5. Clay, Sandy Clay, Silty Clay and Clayey Silt (CL, ML, MH and CH)	1000[7]	100		130

[1]Lateral bearing and lateral sliding resistance may be combined.

[2]For soil classifications OL, OH and PT (i.e., organic clays and peat), a foundation investigation shall be required.

[3]All values of allowable foundation pressure are for footings having a minimum width of 12 inches and a minimum depth of 12 inches into natural grade. Except as in Footnote 7 below, increase of 20 percent allowed for each additional foot of width and/or depth to a maximum value of three times the designated value.

[4]May be increased the amount of the designated value for each additional foot of depth to a maximum of 15 times the designated value. Isolated poles for uses such as flagpoles or signs and poles used to support buildings which are not adversely affected by a 1/2-inch motion at ground surface due to short-term lateral loads may be designed using lateral bearing values equal to two times the tabulated values.

[5]Coefficient to be multiplied by the dead load.

[6]Lateral sliding resistance value to be multiplied by the contact area. In no case shall the lateral sliding resistance exceed one half the dead load.

[7]No increase for width is allowed.

From the Uniform Building Code, © 1988, ICBO

Figure 8-4   *Allowable foundation and lateral pressure*

Foundations and Frost Line

Now let's take a look at the foundation itself. Requirements for foundations vary considerably around the country. The code requires footings, or footers, to be placed below frost grade or as shown in UBC Table No. 29-A (Figure 8-6).

TABLE NO. 29-C—CLASSIFICATION OF EXPANSIVE SOIL

EXPANSION INDEX	POTENTIAL EXPANSION
0-20	Very low
21-50	Low
51-90	Medium
91-130	High
Above 130	Very high

TABLE NO. 29-D—WEIGHTED EXPANSION INDEX[1]

DEPTH INTERVAL[2]	WEIGHT FACTOR
0-1	0.4
1-2	0.3
2-3	0.2
3-4	0.1
Below 4	0

[1]The weighted expansion index for nonuniform soils is determined by multiplying the expansion index for each depth interval by the weight factor for that interval and summing the products.
[2]Depth in feet below the ground surface.

From the Uniform Building Code, © 1988, ICBO

Figure 8-5 *Expansive soil classification and expansion index*

Frost grade varies from city to city. There may even be variances within the counties. Here in Kennewick, Washington, the frost depth is figured for building purposes at 24 inches. All footings and water lines must be at least that deep. But the city elected to install all water lines at 36 inches. This allows the water lines to be brought in below the foundation, except for basements.

It isn't always necessary to excavate for your footings. If your lot is in a low area and you plan to fill after the house is constructed, you may place the footings on the surface, exca-

NUMBER OF FLOORS SUPPORTED BY THE FOUNDATION[3]	THICKNESS OF FOUNDATION WALL (Inches)		WIDTH OF FOOTING (Inches)	THICKNESS OF FOOTING (Inches)	DEPTH BELOW UNDISTURBED GROUND SURFACE (Inches)
	CONCRETE	UNIT MASONRY			
1	6	6	12	6	12
2	8	8	15	7	18
3	10	10	18	8	24

TABLE NO. 29-A—FOUNDATIONS FOR STUD BEARING WALLS—MINIMUM REQUIREMENTS[1] [2]

[1]Where unusual conditions or frost conditions are found, footings and foundations shall be as required in Section 2907 (a).

[2]The ground under the floor may be excavated to the elevation of the top of the footing.

[3]Foundations may support a roof in addition to the stipulated number of floors. Foundations supporting roofs only shall be as required for supporting one floor.

From the Uniform Building Code, © 1988, ICBO

Figure 8-6   *Foundations for stud bearing walls*

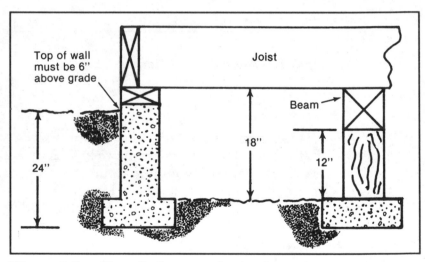

Figure 8-7   *Foundation requirements*

vating only enough so that the footing will be level. However, when the house is completed and the fill material brought in, the footings must be at or below the frost line. This, of course, is the bottom of the footing pad — not the bottom of the foundation wall. Figure 8-7 shows this measurement and other footing and foundation requirements. Typical footings and foundation walls are shown in Figure 8-8.

Excavation for the foundation must remove all stumps and roots and must go down at least 12 inches below the surface of the ground under your building. Also, when you're finished with the building, there shouldn't be any form material or wood scraps under the house or buried in the backfill. Don't provide breeding grounds for termites.

When you dig footings down to the frost line, make sure you leave 18 inches of crawl space below the joists. This is shown in Figure 8-7.

If you're going to install an underfloor furnace, you'll need to furnish some additional space, plus a crawl hole large enough to allow the heating plant to be removed or serviced without dismantling. Pipes and ducts must not interfere with access to or access within any crawl space.

All accessible underfloor space must have an entry hole at least 18 inches by 24 inches. Note the word *accessible*. That's just what it means. You can't hide it in a closet or under a rug.

Underfloor Ventilation

Whenever you have an underfloor crawl space that's not a basement or a usable space, you must provide adequate ventilation. You can cut vent holes in the foundation walls or provide mechanical ventilation such as a fan. Vent holes must have a net area of 1-1/2 square feet for each 25 linear feet of exterior foundation wall. To reduce dry rot in the foundation,

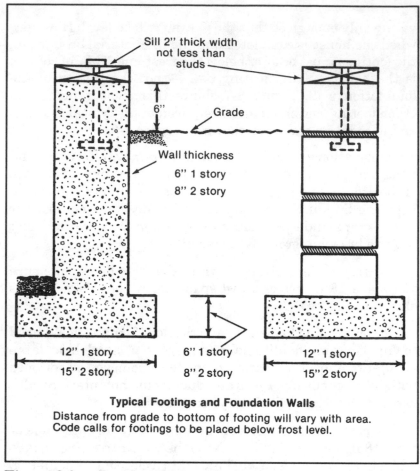

Figure 8-8 *Residential foundations*

arrange the vents to give cross-ventilation to all areas of the unused space.

Vent holes must be covered with corrosion-resistant wire mesh not less than 1/4 inch or more than 1/2 inch in any

Figure 8-9   *Prefabricated wall vent cast in wall at time of pouring*

dimension. This keeps your crawl space from becoming a maternity ward for cats.

Prefabricated vents, like those shown in Figure 8-9, are now available. They're made of plastic or galvanized metal, complete with screen, louvered cover, and a hinged flap. Many people think they have to cover their vents to have warm floors in winter. This isn't necessarily so, but hinged flaps are available and allowable. The only drawback is that the home-owners often forget to open them in the spring, which can lead to dry rot and other problems.

Foundation Plates

On the top of the foundation wall is a wooden member called a plate. This is required whether the foundation wall surrounds a crawl space or a basement. But it's not required if the rest of the structure is masonry.

Figure 8-10   *Foundation bolts cast in place*

The plate is normally a 2 x 6 laid flat and fastened to the foundation wall with bolts that were placed in the concrete when the foundation slab was laid. Plates at least 2 inches by 6 inches are customary in my area. The code doesn't specify what it has to be. Section 2517(c)3 states that all plates, sills, and sleepers must be treated wood or foundation grade redwood or cedar. This reduces the hazard of termites. If you don't have a termite problem, you can use any wood approved by the inspector.

Figures 8-10 and 8-11 and the sketch in Figure 8-8 show the proper installation of anchor bolts and plates. You'll need 1/2-inch steel bolts placed to a depth of 7 inches in concrete or masonry foundations to bolt the plate to the foundation wall. Place bolts at least every 6 feet. There must be at least two bolts in each piece of plate material and neither may be more

Figure 8-11 *Foundation plates installed*

than 12 inches from the end. That means an 8-foot plate would need two anchor bolts, but a 9-foot piece would require three.

A big problem is that these bolts are often placed incorrectly — as though there's a continuous 26-foot piece of plate material, for instance. When the framers come along to splice the plate, several anchor bolts won't conform. Some builders keep extra plate material on hand for the foundation subcontractors. But this isn't always possible and it doesn't always work, anyway.

You'll find information about foundation plates and sills in Sections 2905(d) and 2517(b). UBC Table 29-A (Figure 8-6) lists the size of the footing and foundation wall for one-, two- and three-story buildings. Notice the column called *Depth Below Undisturbed Ground Surface*. Remember, your foundation must go down to the frost line. If you're in a frost-free area, however, these are the code minimums for foundation depth.

Anchor bolts are supposed to keep the house anchored to the foundation. But I have some misgivings about their effectiveness. I have several photos of what used to be homes in earthquake and tornado zones. The anchor bolts and plates are still in place — it's the homes that are missing. But I don't know of any alternative to anchor bolts.

Post and Beam Foundation

Many houses are built of posts and beams and without concrete or masonry foundations. The code doesn't prohibit this. It simply ignores it. What it does say is in Section 2907(b):

> *Bearing Walls. Bearing walls shall be supported on masonry or concrete foundations or piles or other approved foundation system which shall be of sufficient size to support all loads. Where a design is not provided, the minimum foundation requirements for stud bearing walls shall be as set forth in Table 29-A.*
>
> *Exceptions: 1. A one-story wood or metal frame building not used for human occupancy and not over 400 square feet in floor area may be constructed with walls supported on a wood foundation plate when approved by the building official.*
>
> *2. The support of buildings by posts embedded in earth shall be designed as specified in Section 2907(f). Wood posts or poles embedded in earth shall be pressure treated with an approved preservative. Steel posts or poles shall be protected as specified in Section 2908(h).*

Confusing, isn't it? If you want to use a post and beam foundation, the building inspector will have to approve your

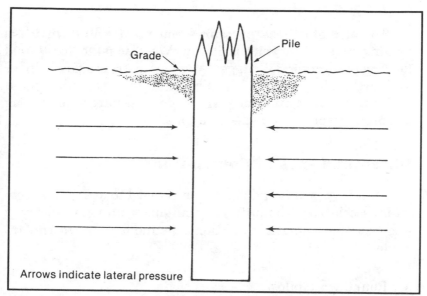

Grade

Pile

Arrows indicate lateral pressure

Figure 8-12 *Direction of lateral pressure*

plans. This means that if the inspector is inexperienced, is not an engineer, or just doesn't like post and beam construction, you may run into difficulty. In high seismic areas you might run into design problems. It's up to you to know what you're doing and to be very persuasive that what you're doing is O.K.

Pole Buildings

These are generally agricultural or light industrial buildings. They're referred to in the second exception to Section 2907(b) mentioned above.

Section 2907(f) describes how to calculate the depth of embedment to get the required lateral constraint to support your load. This lateral force is illustrated in Figure 8-12.

To calculate these pressures you must know what the loading will be on your building. We discussed loads and loading in Chapter 3. I suggest you hire a structural engineer to figure the load values. If you're constructing an engineered building, these calculations will be done as part of preparing the building plans and specifications.

Different Types of Foundations

Many types of foundations can be used to overcome problems associated with multi-story buildings, unusual soil types and extreme climatic conditions. Foundation piles can include:

- Round wood piles

- Uncased cast-in-place concrete piles

- Metal-cased concrete piles

- Precast concrete piles

- Precast, prestressed concrete piles

- Structural steel piles

- Concrete-filled steel pipe piles

These piles are usually driven or placed in the ground and covered by slabs. Complex formulas determine the size of the pile, its depth in the ground, and the number of piles required. The type of pile you use depends on lateral pressures in different types and conditions of soils, as well as on the loads to be carried. This information is listed in UBC Table 29-B,

Foundation and Allowable Lateral Pressure; Table 29-C, *Classification of Expansive Soil;* and Table 29-D, *Weighted Expansion Index.* (See Figures 8-4 and 8-5.)

Footing and Foundation Summary

Most small contractors never have to deal with the more sophisticated foundations. If you do, have a structural engineer design them. This prevents problems and can really help when you approach the building inspector for approval of your plans.

In calculating your concrete foundation wall, be sure to make the wall high enough to be at least 6 inches above grade. Here's what I mean. If the footing must go 24 inches below grade, the distance between the top of the wall and the bottom of the footing must be at least 30 inches. That 6 inches above grade helps keep wood framing out of most surface moisture.

You can use a stepped footing if the ground slopes too much for a level footing. Section 2907(c) states that the foundation must be level if your ground slopes more than 1 foot in 10. But it may be stepped so that both the top and bottom of the foundation are level. This means that if your lot slopes too much, you can step-down your foundation and use framing material to finish the walls up to the plate line of the first floor.

Remember to protect adjoining property while preparing the foundation on your lot. If leveling your lot creates a finish grade higher than that of adjoining property, protect that property from your fill. Either slope the bank or build a retaining wall. If, on the other hand, you excavate on your lot, you have to protect adjoining property with the same type of cut bank or retaining wall. If the hillside is steep, the procedure shown in Figure 8-3 may be necessary.

Retaining Walls

There isn't too much in the code about retaining walls. Section 2308(b) covers them very briefly:

> **Retaining Walls.** *Retaining walls shall be designed to resist the lateral pressure of the retained material in accordance with accepted engineering practice. Walls retaining drained earth may be designed for pressure equivalent to that exerted by a fluid weighing not less than 30 pounds per cubic foot and having a depth equal to that of the retained earth. Any surcharge shall be in addition to the equivalent fluid pressure.*

Most inspectors require the footing of a retaining wall to go at least to the frost line, the same as any footing. They're not really as concerned about the danger of frost heaving as they are about the wall tipping if the load behind it becomes too great.

My rule of thumb is that a retaining wall up to 6 feet high should be at least 8 inches thick. Walls higher than 6 feet should be engineered to determine the thickness and reinforcing steel needed. This applies only to the part of the wall subject to lateral pressure from the soil behind it. Any part of the wall above the dirt line may be reduced in thickness to suit your purposes. If the wall is engineered, include enough reinforcing steel to make up for any lack of thickness. An alternative is to use the formula in Section 2907 and then go to Chapter 27 and compute the amount of steel needed.

What's the next step, after the foundation and retaining walls? In the next chapter we'll move on to masonry walls.

A Shot in the Dark

We have high winds in my part of the country, eastern Washington. That's why I'm a stickler on roof installation. But the roofer isn't always to blame when a roof gets blown away. A contractor I know owns an apartment building that had the roof blown off twice before it was a year old. It's a flat roof with a five-layer mopped-on roof covering. There's a parapet wall three to four feet high all the way around the roof perimeter. I know the roofing subcontractor who did the job both times. He's about as professional and conscientious as they come. So why so much damage in one year?

I went out to check the building after the second storm. Roofing material was scattered a hundred yards up and down both sides of the street. Only about a third of the roof was still on top of the building. And there was something funny about what was left. Almost all roofing still there was around the roof edges. The center of the roof was almost bare. So I knew the wind hadn't found a weak spot at an edge and worked its way in.

The contractor, the roofer and I walked the entire roof and talked about it. My guess was that wind spilling over the top of the parapet wall caused a vacuum at the roof center. You know how dust swirls in the vacuum behind a big truck going down a dirt road? I guessed the same type of vacuum was lifting the roof cover. Most parapet walls have penetrations for drains. This one didn't. Roof drains went down through the exterior wall to ground level. I asked the contractor why.

"I did that to cut down on water stains on exterior walls."

"That's quality construction," I agreed, "but I think it's also turning this roof into an airplane wing in high wind. Why don't you cut a few scupper holes through each parapet wall. That might relieve the vacuum."

We decided to cut three holes along each parapet wall. It was only a shot in the dark. But it must have worked. The roof came through the next winter in perfect shape.

9

Masonry Walls

When the foundation is poured, the next step is to put up the walls. But what kind of walls? Most building walls are either masonry or wood frame. In the next chapter we'll cover the requirements for frame walls. Here we'll focus on masonry.

In the 1985 edition of the UBC, Chapter 24 was completely rewritten and shortened considerably. They added new design formulas and consolidated some of the old regulations. As usual, most of the new definitions and formulas will be of interest only to designers. But there are a few definitions you'll need to know:

Bedded area is the masonry surface in contact with mortar in the joint.

Bond adhesion describes how well mortar sticks to the masonry.

Reinforcing bond describes how well steel reinforcement sticks to the mortar or grout.

Cell is the empty space in a masonry unit. It always has a cross-section area more than 1-1/2 square inches.

Bonded walls have two or more wythes of masonry joined together to make a single wall.

Cavity walls have a continuous air space between the wythes. The minimum width of the air space is 2 inches and a maximum width is 4-1/2 inches. Wythes have to be tied together with metal ties.

Hollow unit masonry walls are made from block with empty cells set in mortar.

Wythe is a wall which is one masonry unit in thickness. A collar joint is not considered a wythe.

Masonry Usually Means Block

Concrete or cinder blocks are the most popular unit masonry today. Very few buildings have walls made entirely of brick. The brick you see in homes is nearly all veneer that covers either concrete block or wood frame walls.

With concrete block walls, there's no 2 x 6 plate on top of the foundation as I explained in Chapter 8. You can even omit the concrete foundation, building with masonry from the footing right up to the roof line.

If you use masonry block for the foundation, you'll probably have to put iron reinforcing dowels in the footing when it's poured. Space these dowels every 4 feet, as shown in Figure 9-1. When the blocks are in place, fill every cell that has a dowel with concrete grout.

Figure 9-1   *Rebar in masonry wall construction*

These reinforcing dowels don't have to run the full height of the wall. There's a practical reason for that. Masons don't like dropping blocks over reinforcing dowels 10 to 15 feet long. It takes too long and results in a lot of broken blocks. The code doesn't state that the rebar must be continuous, only that its *strength* be continuous. This can be done by splicing or welding shorter pieces together.

This is one of those areas that most inspectors can't watch very closely. They just don't have the time. As a result, few masons bother to weld their steel. Many don't even wire it. They just jam rebar into the grout in each cell. Don't let them get by with that on your jobs. Insist that spliced rebar meet code requirements.

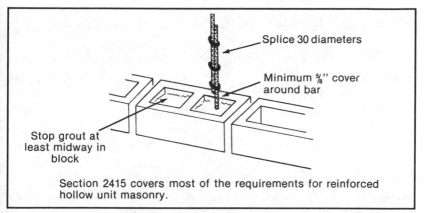

Splice 30 diameters

Minimum ⅝" cover around bar

Stop grout at least midway in block

Section 2415 covers most of the requirements for reinforced hollow unit masonry.

Figure 9-2   *Properly spliced rebar in hollow unit masonry*

Splicing and Placing Rebar

Rebar splices shouldn't be any weaker than the bar where there isn't any splice. You do that by lapping bars at least 30 diameters wherever bars join. For example, if you're using 1/2-inch bar, the lap must be 15 inches. If you are using 5/8-inch bar, lap 18-3/8 inches. For 3/4-inch bar, go to 22-1/2 inches. Figure 9-2 shows a good rebar splice.

What about the location of the bar in the cell? Do you just stick it anyplace? Hardly, although on some jobs it may look that way. Joint reinforcement must have at least 5/8-inch mortar coverage from any face that's exposed to air or the surrounding environment. All other reinforcement must have a minimum mortar coverage of the diameter of the bar, or 3/4 inch, whichever is more. If the bars are in the face exposed to the weather or soil, the minimum coverage is 1-1/2 inches in weather-exposed masonry and 2 inches in soil.

Running Pipes or Conduit Through Masonry

Let's say you're building a block basement and you want to put electrical outlets in the exterior wall. There's no problem as long as you don't reduce the structural stability of the wall itself. If the outlet has been detailed in the plans, there shouldn't be any structural problems. You can run pipe or conduit through masonry, using a sleeve large enough to pass any hub or coupling on the pipeline. If you use multiple sleeves, they must be at least 3 inches apart. That's for areas where the block must be core-filled or where rebar may be installed. Pipe or conduit placed in the unfilled cores of hollow unit masonry isn't considered embedding.

General Masonry Requirements

The first bed joint (on top of the foundation wall) must be at least 1/4 inch thick and not more than 1 inch thick. All subsequent bed joints have the same 1/4 inch minimum thickness, but the maximum is 5/8 inch. Most masonry is put up in *lifts* usually limited to 4 feet high. The code doesn't say this directly — it's just a rule of thumb. But if your wall is much higher than 4 feet, the mortar may be squeezed out of the bed joints by the weight.

Each 4-foot lift is laid, grouted and allowed to set before the next lift is started. Always use lifts when you're grouting, especially around rebar. Remember, though, that the grout should not be level with the top of the block except on the last course. It should stop at least 1-1/2 inches below the top of the block. The wall would have a weak point if the grout joint and the bed joint fell at the same level. With bond beams, however, the grout should stop 1/2 inch below the top.

Make sure that any chases or recesses you're building into the wall don't reduce the strength or fire resistance of the wall.

Occasionally you'll run across masonry walls built in the *stack bond*. This is where the blocks are placed directly over each other without the lapped joint used on most masonry work. If you use stack bond, you must include horizontal reinforcing. This reinforcing must be at least two continuous wires, with a minimum cross-sectional area of 0.017 square inch. Install these wires horizontally between courses and no more than 16 inches apart. There are stricter requirements in Seismic Zone 1.

Corbeling

If you work with masonry, you certainly know about corbeling. Webster's dictionary says that a corbel is an architectural member that projects from within a wall and supports a weight. They're usually stepped upward and outward from a vertical surface. Figure 9-3 illustrates corbeling in masonry construction.

You can only build a corbel in a solid masonry wall that's at least 12 inches thick. The projection of each course can't exceed 1 inch. It can't project more than one-third the total thickness of the wall when used to support a chimney built into the wall. The top course of all corbels must be a header course.

Be careful when building corbels in earthquake zones. The inspector may have some strict regulations. Many areas are requiring owners to remove corbels and cornices that might fall in an earthquake.

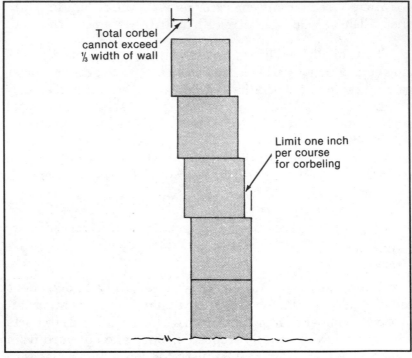

Total corbel
cannot exceed
⅓ width of wall

Limit one inch
per course
for corbeling

Figure 9-3   *Corbeling in masonry construction*

Laying Block in Cold Weather

Can you lay concrete masonry units in any kind of weather? Not according to the code, unless you take specific steps to protect the strength of the wall. Check Section 2404(c)3 of the UBC:

> *Cold Weather Construction. 1. General. All materials shall be delivered in a usable condition and stored to prevent wetting by capillary action, rain and snow ...*
>
> *3. Construction. Masonry units shall be dry. Wet or frozen masonry units shall not be laid.*

Air temperature 40 degrees F to 32 degrees F: Sand or mixing water shall be heated to produce mortar temperature between 40 degrees F and 120 degrees F.

Air temperature 32 degrees F to 25 degrees F: Sand and mixing water shall be heated to produce mortar temperatures between 40 degrees F and 120 degrees F. Maintain temperatures of mortar on boards above freezing.

The code then describes what must be done at air temperatures 25 degrees and below. As it gets colder, the code requires more precautions. Furthermore, all work must be protected and heated for 24 hours.

You may have seen buildings under construction surrounded by giant plastic cocoons. These cocoons are heated and inflated like a balloon during construction. This heat must be kept on for 24 hours after Type III portland cement is used and for 48 hours after Type I portland cement is used.

Even if the wall will be heated, don't lay brick or block that's got ice or snow clinging to it.

Thickness-to-Height Ratio

Prior to the 1985 edition, the codes carried a table of thickness-to-height ratios for both reinforced and unreinforced masonry. These were basic rules of thumb, and were sometimes misinterpreted. In 1985, that table was thrown out and this was inserted:

*Section 2407(i)2. **Ratio of height or length to thickness.** The ratio of unsupported height to thickness or the ratio of unsupported length to thickness (one or the other but not both) for solid masonry walls or bearing partitions shall not exceed 20, and shall not exceed 18 for walls of hollow masonry or cavity walls. In computing the ratio for cavity walls, the value of thickness shall be the* *sum of the nominal thicknesses or the inner and outer widths of the masonry. In walls composed of different kinds or classes of units or mortars, the ratio of height or length to thickness shall not exceed that allowed for the weakest of the combination of units and mortars of which the member is composed.*

That's what it says. I'd love to simplify it into just a few words — but I can't. It's just not practical to try to explain it all here. New earthquake regulations are making the code more complex. Now it takes an engineer to figure out how to lay up a simple wall. And I'm not sure that all building inspectors understand this section well enough to enforce it.

In a nutshell, here's what you need to know about Chapter 24: All masonry must be reinforced, with no exceptions allowed unless you have the approval of an engineer.

Use of Mass

If you make a wall thicker, you can make it higher. Builders have done this for years. It's called adding mass. As the wall gets more massive, it gets stronger. Stronger walls can be built higher. That makes perfect sense.

New York City once had a building code that stated the rule very simply. The code required brick walls for buildings to be 12 inches thick for single story buildings and an additional 4 inches thick for each additional floor. So a two-story building had to have a first floor 16 inches thick. The practical limit on the height of masonry walls was 10 stories because at that point the wall on the ground floor had to be 4 feet thick.

Types of Masonry

I'll list the various masonry types, starting with the strongest. This list is based primarily on compressive strength. But understand that these materials aren't necessarily substitutes for each other. You can usually substitute a stronger product for a lesser one, but not vice versa.

1) Brick made with sand-lime

2) Brick made of clay or shale

3) Concrete building blocks

4) Structural clay floor tile

5) Solid load-bearing concrete masonry units

6) Unburned clay

Masonry Grades

The grade of masonry units is also very important. Building bricks made of clay or shale and those made of sand-lime come in three grades: SW, MW, NW. For bricks made of clay or shale, here's what these grades mean:

SW Bricks have a high resistance to frost. Use them in areas where the brick is exposed and may freeze when wet. These are common in foundation courses and retaining walls in areas subject to frost.

MW Bricks are intended for use where temperatures go below freezing but where brick won't be exposed to water. They have only moderate and non-uniform resistance to frost. You can use them in the face of a wall above ground when not exposed to constant moisture.

NW These may be used as backup or interior masonry. You can also use them exposed in areas with no frost, or colder areas where the annual precipitation is less than 20 inches.

The three grades for the sand-lime brick are similar.

Bond Beams

A bond beam is a block cast with three sides and no ends. It's laid into a course with the open side up and filled with concrete. The lintel block, used to build lintels over doors, windows, and other openings, is a variation of the bond beam. I think lintel blocks are easier to use and look nicer than the usual cast-in-place concrete lintel.

In both bond beam and lintel blocks, the reinforcing used in the cavity depends on the strength required. Figure 9-4 shows several types of concrete block and an application of lintel block reinforcing.

Face Brick and Veneer Anchorage

The most common use of brick is as face brick veneer. Brick veneer can be used over wood frame, concrete block, or even stone buildings. These are clay building bricks, not concrete blocks. The difference is important, even though some people erroneously interchange the terms.

Most masons anchor face bricks to a concrete block wall with mortar having a high concrete ratio. This produces a tight, secure bond. But clips are also recommended. These clips are little strips of corrugated sheet metal used to attach brick veneer to the block wall. On a frame building they're nailed to the exterior sheathing and bent outward to lay between the courses.

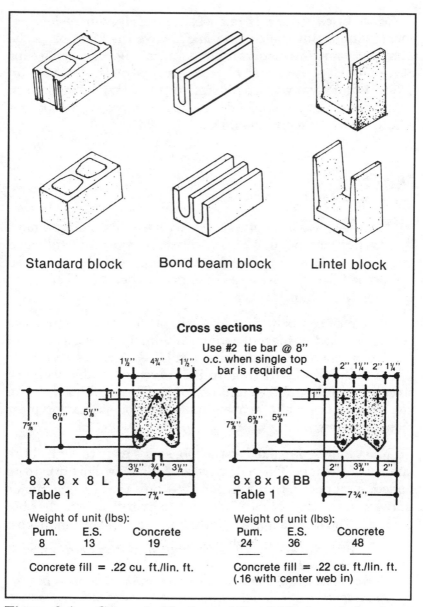

Standard block   Bond beam block   Lintel block

Cross sections

Use #2 tie bar @ 8"
o.c. when single top
bar is required

8 x 8 x 8 L
Table 1

Weight of unit (lbs):

Pum.	E.S.	Concrete
8	13	19

Concrete fill = .22 cu. ft./lin. ft.

8 x 8 x 16 BB
Table 1

Weight of unit (lbs):

Pum.	E.S.	Concrete
24	36	48

Concrete fill = .22 cu. ft./lin. ft.
(.16 with center web in)

Figure 9-4   *Concrete blocks and lintel blocks reinforcing*

Most brick veneer is anchored with clips in residential construction. But the clips aren't always installed properly. The most common mistake is not using enough or placing clips at random. If someone isn't keeping an eye on the job, you can be sure that clips won't be installed correctly. A good mason would use clips correctly and place them according to code, not wherever he feels one should go.

Mortar

Mortar has to be applied correctly if a wall is going to have the strength intended. All bricks must be laid with a full head and bed joint; all interior joints designed to be mortared should be filled. The average thickness of head and bed joints can't be more than 1/2 inch.

The mortar mix itself is also critical. There are four types of mortar used in masonry construction: Types M, S, N, and O. Mix proportions are described in UBC Table 24-A (Figure 9-5). UBC Table 24-H (Figure 9-6) gives allowable working stresses for unreinforced unit masonry. These tables will help you choose the right mortar and the proper mix for most masonry work.

Most mortar is mixed at the job, so it's easy to control the quality of the mix. The code now controls how mortar is to be mixed. I suppose that's needed — but there's one major drawback. Section 2404(b)7 applies to every job, whether big or small. You decide if the following is practical on small jobs:

Material— Handling, Storage and Preparation.
Mortar mixed at the jobsite shall be mixed for a period of time not less than 3 minutes nor more than 10 minutes in a mechanical mixer with the amount of water required to provide the desired workability. Hand mixing of small amounts of mortar is permitted. Mortar may be

TABLE NO. 24-A—MORTAR PROPORTIONS FOR UNIT MASONRY

MORTAR	TYPE	PROPORTIONS BY VOLUME (CEMENTITIOUS MATERIALS)					AGGREGATE MEASURED IN A DAMP, LOOSE CONDITION
		PORTLAND CEMENT OR BLENDED CEMENT1	MASONRY CEMENT2			HYDRATED LIME OR LIME PUTTY1	
			M	S	N		
Cement-lime	M	1	—	—	—	1/4	
	S	1	—	—	—	over 1/4 to 1/2	
	N	1	—	—	—	over 1/2 to 1 1/4	Not less than 2 1/4 and not more than 3 times the sum of the separate volumes of cementitious materials.
	O	1	—	—	—	over 1 1/4 to 2 1/2	
Masonry cement	M	1	—	—	1	—	
	M	—	1	—	—	—	
	S	1/2	—	—	1	—	
	S	—	—	1	—	—	
	N	—	—	—	1	—	
	O	—	—	—	1	—	

¹When plastic cement is used in lieu of portland cement, hydrated lime or putty may be added, but not in excess of one tenth of the volume of cement.

²Masonry cement conforming to the requirements of U.B.C. Standard No. 24-16.

From the Uniform Building Code, © 1988, ICBO

Figure 9-5 *Mortar proportions for unit masonry*

retempered. *Mortar or grout which has hardened or stiff-
ened due to hydration of the cement shall not be used, but
under no case shall mortar be used two and one-half
hours, nor grout used one and one-half hours, after the
initial mixing water has been added to the dry ingredients
at the jobsite.*

There's one more serious problem with this regulation. An inspector would have to stand there all the time masons are laying block to be sure mortar is being mixed correctly. That isn't practical.

An inspector can, of course, call for tests on the mortar. According to the UBC, if special inspectors are needed, they work at the expense of the contractor.

TABLE NO. 24-H—ALLOWABLE WORKING STRESSES IN UNREINFORCED UNIT MASONRY

MATERIAL	TYPE M Compression[1]	TYPE S Compression[1]	TYPE M OR TYPE S MORTAR Shear or Tension in Flexure[2][3]		Tension in Flexure[4]		TYPE N Compression[1]	TYPE N Shear or Tension in Flexure[2][3]	
1. Special inspection required	No	No	Yes	No	Yes	No	No	Yes	No
2. Solid brick masonry									
4500 plus psi	250	225	20	10	40	20	200	15	7.5
2500-4500 psi	175	160	20	10	40	20	140	15	7.5
1500-2500 psi	125	115	20	10	40	20	100	15	7.5
3. Solid concrete unit masonry									
Grade N	175	160	12	6	24	12	140	12	6
Grade S	125	115	12	6	24	12	100	12	6
4. Grouted masonry									
4500 plus psi	350	275	25	12.5	50	25			
2500-4500 psi	275	215	25	12.5	50	25			
1500-2500 psi	225	175	25	12.5	50	25			
5. Hollow unit masonry[5]	170	150	12	6	24	12	140	10	5
6. Cavity wall masonry solid units[5]									
Grade N or 2500 psi plus	140	130	12	6	30	15	110	10	5
Grade S or 1500-2500 psi	100	90	12	6	30	15	80	10	5
Hollow units[5]	70	60	12	6	30	15	50	10	5
7. Stone masonry									
Cast stone	400	360	8	4	—	—	320	8	4
Natural stone	140	120	8	4	—	—	100	8	4
8. Unburned clay masonry	30	30	8	4	—	—	—	—	—

[1]Allowable axial or flexural compressive stresses in pounds per square inch gross cross-sectional area (except as noted). The allowable working stresses in bearing directly under concentrated loads may be 50 percent greater than these values.

[2]This value of tension is based on tension across a bed joint, i.e., vertically in the normal masonry work.

[3]No tension allowed in stack bond across head joints.

[4]The values shown here are for tension in masonry in the direction of running bond, i.e., horizontally between supports.

[5]Net area in contact with mortar or net cross-sectional area.

Figure 9-6   *Allowable stresses in unreinforced unit masonry*

Who's Going to Header That Hole?

Every subcontractor makes mistakes. Maybe that's an understatement. I should say, everybody makes mistakes. But when it comes to mistakes by subs, framers seem to be the worst. I can say that. I was one once. Anything a framer leaves out is probably very important. I'll give an example.

Framers make their living with high production: get the foundation sill down. Install the joists. Get it plated. Tilt up the walls, and so on. The sooner framing is done, the bigger the profit, the sooner we get paid.

And framers have their excuses. But usually the real problem is lack of planning. In this case, the lumber truck dumped the load at the south side of the lot. So Mr. Framer starts setting floor joists right there, on the south side, working north at 16 inch centers. That's the quick way to do it. In a few minutes he's nailing on rim joists and almost ready for decking. This is going slick as a whistle.

Mr. Framer's finished in a few days. And no wonder. He didn't waste a minute, especially in checking the plans. But maybe he should have noticed a few things. Like where plumbing lines have to run through his precious framing. Certainly Mr. Plumber will.

Now, speaking of Mr. Plumber, here he comes. He discovers there's a joist in the way of the closet bend for his toilet. And another one goes smack through where the middle of the bathtub drain trap will come down. By this time there isn't a carpenter anywhere in sight. So he has to fall back on "Plan B." He drags out his trusty chain saw and whacks off several feet of perfectly good joist, leaving it dangling like a limb on a tree.

The writers of the Uniform Building Code, in their wisdom, decided that the ends of joists have to be supported by something solid. So here's what happens when I come along to inspect the job.

"This hole will have to be headered," I say. "What hole is that?" the foreman asks, with his most innocent expression covering his face. So I point it out. "But I didn't cut that hole. It must have been the plumber." True enough. But the code is the code, so it's got to be done.

The whole problem could have been avoided if Mr. Framer were as quick at reading plans as he is at driving nails. For this job floor joists should have been laid out from the north side of the foundation, where the plumbing fixtures are. That's probably what the architect had in mind in the first place. But I won't blame the architect. The framer should know his business. And part of that is planning for work by other trades.

10

Frame Walls

T he code has the same goal for frame walls as it did for masonry: a secure building that's warm and dry. Chapter 25 of the UBC covers wood framing. Let's start with the first section of Chapter 25:

> *Section 2501(a)* **Quality and Design**. *The quality and design of wood members and their fastenings shall conform to the provisions of this chapter, and to the applicable standards listed in Chapter 60.*

This covers just about everything involving wood and wood products. Subsections (b) and (c) govern workmanship and fabrication:

> *(b)* **Workmanship**. *All members shall be framed, anchored, tied and braced so as to develop the strength and rigidity necessary for the purposes for which they are used.*

Figure 10-1   *Grade marks clearly visible on framing members*

*(c) **Fabrication***. *Preparation, fabrication and installation of wood members and their fastenings shall conform to accepted engineering practices and to the requirements of this code.*

Lumber Grading

Because we have to rely on lumber grades as our guide to the strength of lumber, the grade marks must be clearly visible on all framing members. Figure 10-1 shows lumber with the grade marks showing. Unfortunately, grade stamps don't always indicate the strength of each individual piece.

The code accepts lumber mill grades even though they're based only on the judgement of the person grading the lumber. Nearly all framing lumber is graded by eye. Unfortunately, the human eye can't always see all the defects. That makes it your responsibility to reject any material you think isn't up to par.

Do you accept all the lumber that's delivered to your job? Just because a piece of wood has a grade mark doesn't mean that it will do the job you want it to do. If it's poor quality lumber, reject it.

If the dealer won't take it back, buy from a dealer who will. Unless you bought the lumber from a stack of bargain material, you should be able to return it. Of course, you can probably use most defective lumber for blocking or backing where strength and appearance aren't as critical.

But be careful. According to Section 2501(d), the building inspector can reject flawed lumber if he finds it on your job. He can make you replace it even if it's already installed. Here's what it says:

> *(d) Rejection. The building official may deny permission for the use of a wood member where permissible grade characteristics or defects are present in such combination that they affect the serviceability of the member.*

Suppose you have a joist with a knot that's the maximum size allowable for this particular joist. Then your plumber comes along and notches the joist near enough to this knot to weaken the entire member. This is bound to catch the inspector's eye. The inspector has four options: First, he can make you replace it. Second, he can order it cut back and headered in. Third, he can ask you to brace it, either with a post or by scabbing another piece to it. If you don't want to do any of these, the inspector can require you to hire a testing agency. At your considerable expense, they'll sandbag the floor, test it for deflections, and then certify to the inspector that the assembly has the strength required by the code.

Well, that's what the inspector can do. But it shouldn't happen. You should catch the problem and solve it by bracing before the inspector ever sees it.

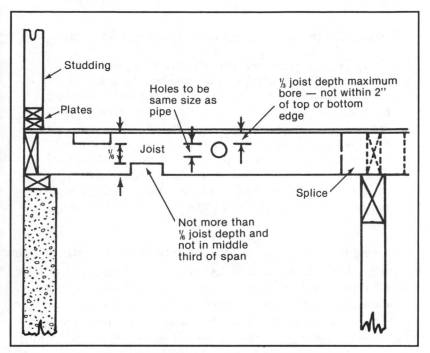

Figure 10-2 *Proper cutting and notching of joists and beams*

Notching Beams and Joists

Section 2517(d)3 of the UBC states, in part:

Notches on the ends of joists shall not exceed one-fourth the joist depth. Holes bored in joists shall not be within 2 inches of the top or bottom of the joist, and the diameter of any such hole shall not exceed one-third the depth of the joist. Notches in the top or bottom of joists shall not exceed one-sixth the depth and shall not be located in the middle third of the span.

Figure 10-2 shows joist cuts and notches that meet code requirements.

Section 315(b) of the Uniform Plumbing Code states:

> *All piping in connection with a plumbing system shall be so installed that piping or connections will not be subject to undue strain or stresses, and provisions shall be made for expansion and structural settlement in concrete or masonry walls or footings. No structural member shall be seriously weakened or impaired by cutting, notching or otherwise. Unless impractical due to structural conditions, all wood beams, girders, joists, studs and similar construction shall be bored with holes approximately the same diameter as the pipes passing through them.*

It seems that quite a few plumbers were cutting the framing members to fit their needs. This was especially true around bathrooms. A plumber would find that he needed to place a water closet bend where a joist ran. So he'd just get out his saw and make a few alterations. The next thing the general contractor knew, I'd be knocking on his door demanding that this little problem be taken care of by headering. By this time the pipes were already in place and the plumber was off on another job. Adding a header at this point isn't an easy job.

Of course, a good framer would have spotted the problem and solved it long before the plumber arrived. Simply starting the joist layout from the other side of the foundation might have solved the problem. In too many cases, however, the main problem is lack of supervision. If your framer isn't experienced, go over the layout in detail before cutting any lumber. Show him exactly where pipe chases and cutouts should be and how to header them.

The ultimate authority lies with the owner. Then it's passed through the general contractor to the other crafts and subs involved in the work. Make sure you fulfill your responsibilities in that line of command.

What Should You Do About Holes?

We've talked about cutting holes in joists for pipe, conduit, or wires — but that's not the end of it. The code clearly states that holes should be the size of the pipe or conduit going through them. But the holes are often made much larger for the convenience of the wire-puller or the person installing the pipe. The code covers this in Section 2516(f)D. It requires you to provide fire stops . . . *in openings around vents, pipes, ducts, chimneys, fireplaces, and similar places which could afford a passage for fire at ceilings and floor levels, with noncombustible materials.*

This paragraph reflects one of the code's main concerns: fire prevention. Another concern is the strength of the member. Let's take a look at 2517(g)6:

> *6. **Pipes in Walls**. Stud partitions containing plumbing, heating, or other pipes shall be so framed and the joists underneath so spaced as to give proper clearance for the piping. Where a partition containing such piping runs parallel to the floor joists, the joists underneath such partitions shall be doubled and spaced to permit the passage of such pipes and shall be bridged. Where plumbing, heating or other pipes are placed in or partly in a partition, necessitating the cutting of the soles or plates, a metal tie not less than 1/8 inch thick and 1-1/2 inches wide shall be fastened to the plate across and to each side of the opening with not less than four 16d nails.*

There's still more on pipes in the walls. Section 2517(g)9 approaches it this way:

> *9. **Bored Holes**. A hole not greater in diameter than 40 percent of the stud width may be bored in any wood stud. Bored holes not greater than 60 percent of the width of the stud are permitted in nonbearing partitions or in any wall where each bored stud is doubled, provided not more than two such successive doubled studs are so bored.*

Figure 10-3 *Pipes through stud blocking*

Figure 10-3 shows pipes running through stud blocking. Note the approximate 5/8-inch space from the edge of the block to the edge of the hole, and the galvanized plates on the edge of the blocking. The edge of the bored hole can't be less than 5/8 inch from the edge of the stud. And you can't bore holes in a section of stud that already has a cut or a notch.

What the code requires is preventative construction. The 1/8-inch plate and the 5/8-inch setback from the edge serve a single purpose — to keep sheetrock nails and screws from puncturing water lines. This is important. If a nail or screw tip punctures a water line, it might not show up immediately. But normal vibration and shrinkage after a couple of months may eventually enlarge the hole. Then you have a leak that's expensive to repair — and may do a lot of damage before it's discovered.

Determining Wood Strength

The code relies on standard formulas to determine the strength of wood, wood joints, and other wood assemblies. Since most of these formulas apply only to large structures, let's leave them for the engineers and designers. The average contractor will find nearly all the design information needed in UBC Tables 25-A-1, 25-U-J-6, and 25-U-R-1, 2, 7, 8, 10, 11, 13 and 14, and 25-V. The appendix at the back of this manual includes complete wood span tables and other tables that cover wood framing.

UBC Table 25-A-1, *Allowable Unit Stresses — Structural Lumber*, lists the more common structural lumber by name and grade and shows the allowable unit stresses in pounds per square inch. It's 43 pages long. Figure 10-4 shows just one page of Table 25-A-1 so I can give you a sample problem. The other tables in the appendix show allowable spans for floor joists, ceiling joists and high and low slope rafters.

Structural design of timber is a complex subject. But you don't have to know anything about timber engineering to frame most houses. Just follow the tables in the code. Occasionally you'll need to know more than most joist and rafter tables show. That's when some understanding of timber engineering will come in handy.

Modulus of Elasticity

This is what I call the "first line of defense." If you know the modulus of elasticity (E factor), you can find most of the other information you'll need to determine wood strength. In most cases, the modulus of elasticity should be about 1,500,000 psi.

TABLE NO. 25-A-1—ALLOWABLE UNIT STRESSES—STRUCTURAL LUMBER—(Continued)
Allowable Unit Stresses for Structural Lumber—VISUAL GRADING
(Normal loading. See also Section 2504)

SPECIES AND COMMERCIAL GRADE	SIZE CLASSIFICATION	ALLOWABLE UNIT STRESSES IN POUNDS PER SQUARE INCH							U.B.C. STDS UNDER WHICH GRADED
		EXTREME FIBER IN BENDING F_b		Tension Parallel to Grain F_t	Horizontal Shear F_v	Compression perpendicular to Grain $F_c\perp$ 21	Compression Parallel to Grain F_c	MODULUS OF ELASTICITY E 21	
		Single-member Uses	Repetitive-member Uses						
DOUGLAS FIR – LARCH (Surfaced dry or surfaced green. Used at 19% max. m.c.)									
DOUGLAS FIR – LARCH (North)									
Dense Select Structural	2" to 4" thick 2" to 4" wide	2450	2800	1400	95	730	1850	1,900,000	
Select Structural		2100	2400	1200	95	625	1600	1,800,000	
Dense No. 1		2050	2400	1200	95	730	1450	1,900,000	
No. 1		1750	2050	1050	95	625	1250	1,800,000	
Dense No. 2		1700	1950	1000	95	730	1150	1,700,000	
No. 2		1450	1650	850	95	625	1000	1,700,000	
No. 3		800	925	475	95	625	600	1,500,000	
Appearance		1750	2050	1050	95	625	1500	1,800,000	25-2 25-3 and 25-4 (See footnotes 2 through 9, 11, 13, 15 and 16)
Stud		800	925	475	95	625	600	1,500,000	
Construction	2" to 4" thick 4" wide	1050	1200	625	95	625	1150	1,500,000	
Standard		600	675	350	95	625	925	1,500,000	
Utility		275	325	175	95	625	600	1,500,000	
Dense Select Structural	2" to 4" thick 5" and wider	2100	2400	1400	95	730	1650	1,900,000	
Select Structural		1800	2050	1200	95	625	1400	1,800,000	
Dense No. 1		1800	2050	1200	95	730	1450	1,900,000	
No. 1		1500	1750	1000	95	625	1250	1,800,000	
Dense No. 2		1450	1700	775	95	730	1250	1,700,000	
No. 2		1250	1450	650	95	625	1050	1,700,000	
No. 3 and Stud		725	850	375	95	625	675	1,500,000	
Appearance		1500	1750	1000	95	625	1500	1,800,000	

From the Uniform Building Code, © 1988, ICBO

Figure 10-4 One page from Table 25-A-1

To use UBC Table 25-A-1, start with the type of material you want to use. Look at Figure 10-4. In my area most framing material is Douglas fir (North). So I'll assume that for our sample job we want to use 2 x 8 Douglas fir joists, 16 inches on center. We'll look up construction grade first since it's one of the most common types.

But can we use it? Go to the second column, *Size Classification*. This column shows that construction grade is only used in timbers 2 to 4 inches thick, 4 inches wide. Our 2 x 8 joists won't fit here. So what grade of lumber can we use? Read down the column until you come to this dimension: 2" to 4" thick, 5" and wider. Here we find that "No. 3 and Stud" has the same modulus of elasticity as construction grade. (Modulus of elasticity is given in the second column from the right.)

Before we make a firm decision, however, let's go to the column called *Extreme Fiber in Bending (Fb)*. What do we find? Although the E factor is the same, the Fb factor is not. Is this the one we should use? First, we'll have to do a little more research.

Beams are often used as single members, but joists seldom are. They're usually ganged in groups of four or more. That's what the code calls *Repetitive-Member Uses*, the second column under the *Extreme Fiber in Bending* column. In this column the Fb factor for "No. 3 and Stud" is 850, compared to 1200 for construction grade. Are we still in trouble?

Allowable Spans for Joists and Rafters

Let's go to UBC Table 25-U-J-1, (Figure 10-5) to find the joists we should use. It's called *Allowable Spans for Floor Joists*. This table might look tricky, but it's really quite simple.

Look at the first column, *Joist Size/Spacing*. It lists the common joist dimensions for light frame buildings and the

TABLE NO. 25-U-J-1—ALLOWABLE SPANS FOR FLOOR JOISTS—40 LBS. PER SQ. FT. LIVE LOAD

DESIGN CRITERIA: Deflection—For 40 lbs. per sq. ft. live load. Limited to span in inches divided by 360. Strength—Live load of 40 lbs. per sq. ft. plus dead load of 10 lbs. per sq. ft. determines the required fiber stress value.

JOIST SIZE (IN)	SPACING (IN)	Modulus of Elasticity, E, in 1,000,000 psi													
		0.8	0.9	1.0	1.1	1.2	1.3	1.4	1.5	1.6	1.7	1.8	1.9	2.0	2.2
2x6	12.0	8-6 / 720	8-10 / 780	9-2 / 830	9-6 / 890	9-9 / 940	10-0 / 990	10-3 / 1040	10-6 / 1090	10-9 / 1140	10-11 / 1190	11-2 / 1230	11-4 / 1280	11-7 / 1320	11-11 / 1410
	16.0	7-9 / 790	8-0 / 860	8-4 / 920	8-7 / 980	8-10 / 1040	9-1 / 1090	9-4 / 1150	9-6 / 1200	9-9 / 1250	9-11 / 1310	10-2 / 1360	10-4 / 1410	10-6 / 1460	10-10 / 1550
	24.0	6-9 / 900	7-0 / 980	7-3 / 1050	7-6 / 1120	7-9 / 1190	7-11 / 1250	8-2 / 1310	8-4 / 1380	8-6 / 1440	8-8 / 1500	8-10 / 1550	9-0 / 1610	9-2 / 1670	9-6 / 1780
2x8	12.0	11-3 / 720	11-8 / 780	12-1 / 830	12-6 / 890	12-10 / 940	13-2 / 990	13-6 / 1040	13-10 / 1090	14-2 / 1140	14-5 / 1190	14-8 / 1230	15-0 / 1280	15-3 / 1320	15-9 / 1410
	16.0	10-2 / 790	10-7 / 850	11-0 / 920	11-4 / 980	11-8 / 1040	12-0 / 1090	12-3 / 1150	12-7 / 1200	12-10 / 1250	13-1 / 1310	13-4 / 1360	13-7 / 1410	13-10 / 1460	14-3 / 1550
	24.0	8-11 / 900	9-3 / 980	9-7 / 1050	9-11 / 1120	10-2 / 1190	10-6 / 1250	10-9 / 1310	11-0 / 1380	11-3 / 1440	11-5 / 1500	11-8 / 1550	11-11 / 1610	12-1 / 1670	12-6 / 1780
2x10	12.0	14-4 / 720	14-11 / 780	15-5 / 830	15-11 / 890	16-5 / 940	16-10 / 990	17-3 / 1040	17-8 / 1090	18-0 / 1140	18-5 / 1190	18-9 / 1230	19-1 / 1280	19-5 / 1320	20-1 / 1410
	16.0	13-0 / 790	13-6 / 850	14-0 / 920	14-6 / 980	14-11 / 1040	15-3 / 1090	15-8 / 1150	16-0 / 1200	16-5 / 1250	16-9 / 1310	17-0 / 1360	17-4 / 1410	17-8 / 1460	18-3 / 1550
	24.0	11-4 / 900	11-10 / 980	12-3 / 1050	12-8 / 1120	13-0 / 1190	13-4 / 1250	13-8 / 1310	14-0 / 1380	14-4 / 1440	14-7 / 1500	14-11 / 1550	15-2 / 1610	15-5 / 1670	15-11 / 1780
2x12	12.0	17-5 / 720	18-1 / 780	18-9 / 830	19-4 / 890	19-11 / 940	20-6 / 990	21-0 / 1040	21-6 / 1090	21-11 / 1140	22-5 / 1190	22-10 / 1230	23-3 / 1280	23-7 / 1320	24-5 / 1410
	16.0	15-10 / 790	16-5 / 860	17-0 / 920	17-7 / 980	18-1 / 1040	18-7 / 1090	19-1 / 1150	19-6 / 1200	19-11 / 1250	20-4 / 1310	20-9 / 1360	21-1 / 1410	21-6 / 1460	22-2 / 1550
	24.0	13-10 / 900	14-4 / 980	14-11 / 1050	15-4 / 1120	15-10 / 1190	16-3 / 1250	16-8 / 1310	17-0 / 1380	17-5 / 1440	17-9 / 1500	18-1 / 1550	18-5 / 1610	18-9 / 1670	19-4 / 1780

NOTES:

(1) The required extreme fiber stress in bending (F_b) in pounds per square inch is shown below each span.

(2) Use single or repetitive member bending stress values (F_b) and modulus of elasticity values (E) from Tables Nos. 25-A-1 and 25-A-2.

(3) For more comprehensive tables covering a broader range of bending stress values (F_b) and modulus of elasticity values (E), other spacing of members and other conditions of loading, see U.B.C. Standard No. 25-21.

(4) The spans in these tables are intended for use in covered structures or where moisture content in use does not exceed 19 percent.

From the Uniform Building Code, © 1988, ICBO

common spacing (12, 16, and 24 inches). The columns to the right give the E factors, beginning at 800,000 psi and ranging up to 2.2 million psi. Look at the first line of the column headed 0.8. That's 2 x 6 joists, 12 inches on center, with an E factor of 0.8 psi. You'll find a set of numbers that looks like this: 8-6/720. Translated, that means that a 2 x 6 joist, 12 inches o.c. with a Fb factor of 720 will span 8'6".

The hyphenated number is the span in feet and inches for a 2 x 6 joist with an Fb factor of 720 when it's placed 12 inches o.c. If we were to space that same timber 16 inches o.c., the span would be reduced to 7'9", but the Fb factor would be increased to 790.

So what about our problem? Let's say that the house we're building is 25 feet wide with a beam down the middle. That makes the span 12'6". Look at Figure 10-5, on the line for a 2 x 8 joist spaced 16 inches o.c. Follow it to the right until you come to the figure closest to the span. That's 12'7", which requires an Fb factor of 1200. That's more than the Fb factor of 800 we found in UBC Table 25-A-1. We can't use it.

What if we lay them 12 inches on center? On the 12-inch o.c. line, we find that the Fb factor is 890 for a span of 12'6". Should we do that?

It might depend on how strict the inspector is. I think it would do the job, but it might give you some pretty springy floors. You may be able to push the lighter material past the inspector. But remember that he'll be looking at the same charts we've just been reviewing. And your reputation is on the line. Is a springy floor worth the few dollars you'll save? I recommend going to a larger timber, a 2 x 10, 16 inches o.c.

If you're using a plan prepared by an engineer, the drawings will probably indicate the size of the joists, the spacing, and the direction of run. They should also include the species and the grade.

Diaphragms and Framing

A wood diaphragm is an assembly of lumber and plywood designed to resist horizontal and vertical pressures and loads. Certain deflections are allowed, as long as the diaphragm can still support the assumed loads without danger to the structure or its occupants.

A roof, floor, or wall can be a diaphragm. UBC Table 25-J-1 (Figure 10-6) is called *Allowable Shear in Pounds per Foot for Horizontal Plywood Diaphragms.* It shows some typical diaphragms.

Particleboard is accepted more and more in place of plywood. At first its primary function was only as underlayment for floors. But now there's even one type that's occasionally used in finish work.

Joists and Joist Problems

Now we know how to determine joist sizes and loading. But there's more involved than just laying them out on top of the foundation plate. Joists must be supported laterally by solid blocking at the ends and at support points unless the joist ends are nailed to a header, band, rim joist, or an adjoining stud. Solid blocking must be at least 2 inches thick and the full depth of the joist. That information comes from Chapter 25 of the UBC.

No cross-bridging or blocking is required between the ends of the joists except as noted in Section 2506 below. Notice that I said between the ends of joists; the ends themselves must still be solid blocked. Here's what Section 2506(h) says about blocking:

TABLE NO. 25-J-1—ALLOWABLE SHEAR IN POUNDS PER FOOT FOR HORIZONTAL PLYWOOD DIAPHRAGMS WITH FRAMING OF DOUGLAS FIR-LARCH OR SOUTHERN PINE[1]

| PLYWOOD GRADE | Common Nail Size | Minimum Nominal Penetration in Framing (In Inches) | Minimum Nominal Plywood Thickness (In Inches) | Minimum Nominal Width of Framing Member (In Inches) | BLOCKED DIAPHRAGMS — Nail spacing at diaphragm boundaries (all cases), at continuous panel edges parallel to load (Cases 3 and 4) and at all panel edges (Cases 5 and 6) / Nail spacing at other plywood panel edges | | | | UNBLOCKED DIAPHRAGM — Nails spaced 6" max. at supported end | |
					6 / 6	4 / 6	2½ / 4	2 / 3	Load perpendicular to unblocked edges and continuous panel joints (Case 1)	Other configurations (Cases 2, 3 and 4)
STRUCTURAL I	6d	1¼	5/16	2 / 3	185 / 210	250 / 280	375 / 420	420 / 475	165 / 185	125 / 140
	8d	1½	3/8	2 / 3	270 / 300	360 / 400	530 / 600	600 / 675	240 / 265	180 / 200
	10d[3]	1⅝	15/32	2 / 3	320 / 360	425 / 480	640 / 720	730 / 820	285 / 320	215 / 240
C-D, C-C, STRUCTURAL II and other grades covered in U.B.C. Standard No. 25-9	6d	1¼	5/16	2 / 3	170 / 190	225 / 250	335 / 380	380 / 430	150 / 170	110 / 125
			3/8	2 / 3	185 / 210	250 / 280	375 / 420	420 / 475	165 / 185	125 / 140
	8d	1½	3/8	2 / 3	240 / 270	320 / 360	480 / 540	545 / 610	215 / 240	160 / 180
			15/32	2 / 3	270 / 300	360 / 400	530 / 600	600 / 675	240 / 265	180 / 200
	10d[3]	1⅝	15/32	2 / 3	290 / 325	385 / 430	575 / 650	655 / 735	255 / 290	190 / 215
			19/32	2 / 3	320 / 360	425 / 480	640 / 720	730 / 820	285 / 320	215 / 240

Figure 10-6   *Allowable shear for horizontal plywood diaphragms*

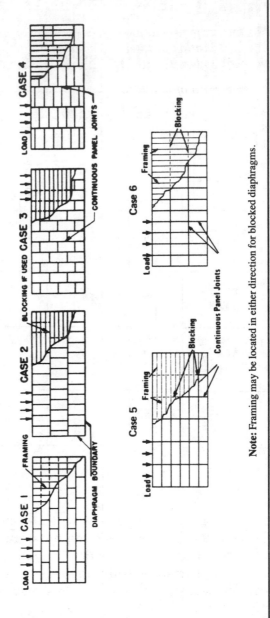

¹These values are for short-time loads due to wind or earthquake and must be reduced 25 percent for normal loading. Space nails 10 inches on center for floors and 12 inches on center for roofs along intermediate framing members.

Allowable shear values for nails in framing members of other species set forth in Table No. 25-17-J of U.B.C. Standards shall be calculated for all grades by multiplying the values for nails in STRUCTURAL I by the following factors: Group III, 0.82 and Group IV, 0.65.

²Framing at adjoining panel edges shall be 3-inch nominal or wider and nails shall be staggered where nails are spaced 2 inches or 2¹/₂ inches on center.

³Framing at adjoining panel edges shall be 3-inch nominal or wider and nails shall be staggered where 10d nails having penetration into framing of more than 1⁵/₈ inches are spaced 3 inches or less on center.

Note: Framing may be located in either direction for blocked diaphragms.

From the Uniform Building Code, © 1988, ICBO

Figure 10-6 (cont'd) *Allowable shear for horizontal plywood diaphragms*

*(h) **Lateral Support**. Solid-sawn rectangular lumber beams, rafters and joists shall be supported laterally to prevent rotation or lateral displacement in accordance with the following:*

If the ratio of depth to thickness, based on nominal dimensions, is:

1. Two to 1, no lateral support is required. (Note: 2 x 4, 3 x 6 or 4 x 8.)

2. Three to 1 or 4 to 1, the ends shall be held in position, as by full-depth solid blocking, bridging, nailing or bolting to other framing members, approved hangers or other acceptable means. (Note: 2 x 6, 2 x 8, etc.)

3. Five to 1, one edge shall be held in line for its entire length. (Note: Floor or roof sheathing should suffice for this on 2 x 10s)

4. Six to 1, bridging, full-depth solid blocking or cross bracing shall be installed at intervals not exceeding 8 feet unless both edges are held in line.

5. Seven to 1, both edges shall be held in line for their entire length.

Joists joining from opposite sides of a beam, girder, or partition should be lapped by at least 3 inches on the opposing joists or fastened together in an approved manner. You must double joists running parallel under bearing partitions.

When the span of the header exceeds 4 feet, double the header joists or use lumber that's the same cross section as a doubled header. The ends of header joists more than 6 feet long must be supported by framing anchors or joist hangers unless they're bearing on a beam. This means that if your opening is less than 4 feet, a single header will do. In any case it must be as wide as the joist it supports.

Framing Floors

Let's first look at subflooring. This is where the trouble usually begins. Usually squeaky, noisy floors begin with a bad subfloor.

I once owned a house with a squeaking floor in the hall and bathroom. Tiles kept popping up. Finally I tore up the floor to see what the trouble was. The subfloor was nothing but scrap lumber laid (not nailed) on the joists. It wasn't even laid tight. I had to replace the entire floor from the joists up.

Laying Subfloor

Joints in subflooring should all be made over joists unless you're using endmatched lumber. When properly installed, endmatched lumber acts as one continuous piece. Each piece must rest on at least two joists. If you're using plywood for subflooring, as nearly everyone does now, you'll have to meet the requirements shown in Tables 25-S-1 or 25-S-2 (Figure 10-7).

Figure 10-8 (Table 25-R-1) gives allowable spans for lumber floor and roof sheathing. The second table in Figure 10-8, 25-S-2, lists the types and grades of lumber you can use in floor and roof sheathing. The UBC Standard numbers tell you where these grades are defined in the Standards. But all you usually have to do is check the grade markings on the timber.

A companion table that goes with UBC Table 25-R-1 is UBC Table 25-T-1 (Figure 10-9). This one has a sneaky little number in it that might surprise you. Do you see the column called *Species Groups*? You have to refer to Table 25-9-A from the UBC Standards (Figure 10-10) to find out what the groups are.

TABLE NO. 25-S-1—ALLOWABLE SPANS FOR PLYWOOD SUBFLOOR AND ROOF SHEATHING CONTINUOUS OVER TWO OR MORE SPANS AND FACE GRAIN PERPENDICULAR TO SUPPORTS[1] [8]

| PANEL SPAN RATING[3] | PLYWOOD THICKNESS (inch) | ROOF[2] | | | | FLOOR MAXIMUM SPAN[4] (In Inches) |
| | | Maximum Span (In Inches) | | Load (In Pounds per Square Foot) | | |
		Edges Blocked	Edges Unblocked	Total Load	Live Load	
1. 12/0	$5/16$	12		135	130	0
2. 16/0	$5/16$, $3/8$	16		80	65	0
3. 20/0	$5/16$, $3/8$	20		70	55	0
4. 24/0	$3/8$	24	16	60	45	0
5. 24/0	$15/32$, $1/2$	24	24	60	45	0
6. 32/16	$15/32$, $1/2$, $19/32$, $5/8$	32	28	55	35[5]	16[6]
7. 40/20	$19/32$, $5/8$, $23/32$, $3/4$, $7/8$	40	32	40[5]	35[5]	20[6] [7]
8. 48/24	$23/32$, $3/4$, $7/8$	48	36	40[5]	35[5]	24

[1]These values apply for C-C, C-D, Structural I and II grades only. Spans shall be limited to values shown because of possible effect of concentrated loads.

[2]Uniform load deflection limitations $1/180$ of the span under live load plus dead load, $1/240$ under live load only. Edges may be blocked with lumber or other approved type of edge support.

[3]Span rating appears on all panels in the construction grades listed in Footnote No. 1.

[4]Plywood edges shall have approved tongue-and-groove joints or shall be supported with blocking unless $1/4$-inch minimum thickness underlayment, or $1\,1/2$ inches of approved cellular or lightweight concrete is placed over the subfloor, or finish floor is $25/32$-inch wood strip. Allowable uniform load based on deflection of $1/360$ of span is 165 pounds per square foot.

[5]For roof live load of 40 pounds per square foot or total load of 55 pounds per square foot, decrease spans by 13 percent or use panel with next greater span rating.

[6]May be 24 inches if $25/32$-inch wood strip flooring is installed at right angles to joists.

[7]May be 24 inches where a minimum of $1\,1/2$ inches of approved cellular or lightweight concrete is placed over the subfloor and the plywood sheathing is manufactured with exterior glue.

[8]Floor or roof sheathing conforming with this table shall be deemed to meet the design criteria of Section 2516.

Figure 10-7   *Allowable spans for plywood subfloor and roof sheathing*

| | | NO. OF | | TOTAL | LIVE |
| | THICKNESS | PLIES | SPAN | LOAD | LOAD |

TABLE NO. 25-S-2—ALLOWABLE LOADS FOR PLYWOOD ROOF SHEATHING CONTINUOUS OVER TWO OR MORE SPANS AND FACE GRAIN PARALLEL TO SUPPORTS[1] [2]

	THICKNESS	NO. OF PLIES	SPAN	TOTAL LOAD	LIVE LOAD
STRUCTURAL I	$^{15}/_{32}$	4	24	30	20
		5	24	45	35
	$^{1}/_{2}$	4	24	35	25
		5	24	55	40
Other grades covered in U.B.C. Standard No. 25-9	$^{15}/_{32}$	5	24	25	20
	$^{1}/_{2}$	5	24	30	25
	$^{19}/_{32}$	4	24	35	25
		5	24	50	40
	$^{5}/_{8}$	4	24	40	30
		5	24	55	45

[1]Uniform load deflection limitations: $^{1}/_{180}$ of span under live load plus dead load, $^{1}/_{240}$ under live load only. Edges shall be blocked with lumber or other approved type of edge supports.

[2]Roof sheathing conforming with this table shall be deemed to meet the design criteria of Section 2516.

From the Uniform Building Code, © 1988, ICBO

Figure 10-7 (cont'd) *Allowable spans for plywood subfloor and roof sheathing*

Post and Beam — Plank and Beam

The two names are often used interchangeably although they're not actually the same. Figure 10-11 shows a post and beam floor system. A plank and beam system has planks covering the beams, although today we usually use 5 quarter plywood instead of planks.

Post and beam floors must meet the same general requirements as other types of floors. But where you were using 2-inch-thick joists on edge and 5/8-inch or 3/4-inch subflooring, now you'd use 2-inch-thick planks or decking, then heavier beams and greater spans. Requirements for endmatched lumber are also the same. You don't have to rest the joints on the joists as you would if you used plain unmatched planks.

TABLE NO. 25-R-1—ALLOWABLE SPANS FOR LUMBER FLOOR AND ROOF SHEATHING[1] [3]

SPAN (Inches)	MINIMUM NET THICKNESS (Inches) OF LUMBER PLACED			
	PERPENDICULAR TO SUPPORTS		DIAGONALLY TO SUPPORTS	
	Surfaced Dry[2]	Surfaced Unseasoned	Surfaced Dry[2]	Surfaced Unseasoned
FLOORS				
1. 24	$3/4$	$25/32$	$3/4$	$25/32$
2. 16	$5/8$	$11/16$	$5/8$	$11/16$
ROOFS				
3. 24	$5/8$	$11/16$	$3/4$	$25/32$

[1]Installation details shall conform to Sections 2517 (e) 1 and 2517 (h) 7 for floor and roof sheathing, respectively.

[2]Maximum 19 percent moisture content.

[3]Floor or roof sheathing conforming with this table shall be deemed to meet the design criteria of Section 2516.

TABLE NO. 25-R-2—SHEATHING LUMBER SHALL MEET THE FOLLOWING MINIMUM GRADE REQUIREMENTS: BOARD GRADE

SOLID FLOOR OR ROOF SHEATHING	SPACED ROOF SHEATHING	U.B.C. STANDARD NUMBER
1. Utility	Standard	25-2, 25-3 or 25-4
2. 4 Common or Utility	3 Common or Standard	25-2, 25-3, 25-4 25-5 or 25-8
3. No. 3	No. 2	25-6
4. Merchantable	Construction Common	25-7

From the Uniform Building Code, © 1988, ICBO

Figure 10-8 *Allowable spans for lumber floor and roof sheathing*

TABLE NO. 25-T-1—ALLOWABLE SPAN FOR PLYWOOD COMBINATION SUBFLOOR-UNDERLAYMENT[1][2]
Plywood Continuous over Two or More Spans and Face Grain Perpendicular to Supports

IDENTIFICATION	SPACING OF JOISTS (inches)			
	16	20	24	48
Species Group[3]	Thickness in inches			
1	1/2	5/8	3/4	—
2, 3	5/8	3/4	7/8	—
4	3/4	7/8	1	—
Span Rating[4]	16 o.c.	20 o.c.	24 o.c.	48 o.c.

[1]Spans limited to value shown because of possible effect of concentrated loads. Allowable uniform load based on deflection of 1/360 of span is 125 pounds per square foot, except allowable total uniform load for 1 1/8-inch plywood over joists spaced 48 inches on center is 65 pounds per square foot. Plywood edges shall have approved tongue-and-groove joints or shall be supported with blocking, unless 1/4-inch minimum thickness underlayment is installed, or finish floor is 25/32-inch wood strip.

If wood strips are perpendicular to supports, thicknesses shown for 16-inch and 20-inch spans may be used on 24-inch span.

[2]Floor panels conforming with this table shall be deemed to meet the design criteria of Section 2516.

[3]Applicable to all grades of sanded exterior-type plywood. See U.B.C. Standard No. 25-9 for plywood species groups.

[4]Applicable to underlayment grade and C-C (plugged).

From the Uniform Building Code, © 1988, ICBO

Figure 10-9 *Allowable span for plywood subfloor underlayment*

If you use the usual "5-quarter" or "4-for-1" plywood, check UBC Table 25-S-1. If you lay these panels with the long edges across the joists, unsupported spans of 48 inches may be permitted. But I've found that this creates a spongy floor if it has to support loads like a water bed or piano. Most builders now use 32-inch spacing in their floor beams. The extra cost is very small.

TABLE NO. 25-9-A—CLASSIFICATION OF SPECIES

Group 1	Group 2	Group 3	Group 4
Apitong(a) (b)	Cedar, Port Orford	Alder, Red	Aspen
Beech, American	Cypress	Birch, Paper	Bigtooth
Birch	Douglas Fir 2(c)	Cedar, Alaska	Quaking
Sweet	Fir	Fir, Subalpine	Cativo
Yellow	California Red	Hemlock, Eastern	Cedar
Douglas Fir(c)	Grand	Maple, Bigleaf	Incense
Kapur(a)	Noble	Pine	Western Red
Keruing(a) (b)	Pacific Silver	Jack	Cottonwood
Larch, Western	White	Lodgepole	Eastern
Maple, Sugar	Hemlock, Western	Ponderosa	Black (Western Poplar)
Pine	Lauan	Spruce	Pine
Caribbean	Almon	Redwood	Eastern White
Ocote	Bagtikan	Spruce	Sugar
Pine, Southern	Mayapis	Black	
Loblolly	Red Lauan	Englemann	
Longleaf	Tangile	White	
Shortleaf	White Lauan		
Slash	Maple, Black		
Tanoak	Mengkulang(a)		
	Meranti, Red(a) (d)		
	Mersawa(a)		
	Pine		
	Pond		
	Red		
	Virginia		
	Western White		
	Spruce		
	Red		
	Sitka		
	Sweetgum		
	Tamarack		
	Yellow-poplar		

(a) Each of these names represents a trade group of woods consisting of a number of closely related species.

(b) Species from the genus Dipterocarpus are marketed collectively: Apitong if originating in the Philippines; Keruing if originating in Malaysia or Indonesia.

(c) Douglas fir from trees grown in the states of Washington, Oregon, California, Idaho, Montana, Wyoming, and the Canadian Provinces of Alberta and British Columbia shall be classed as Douglas fir No. 1. Douglas fir from trees grown in the states of Nevada, Utah, Colorado, Arizona and New Mexico shall be classed as Douglas fir No. 2.

(d) Red Meranti shall be limited to species having a specific gravity of 0.41 or more based on green volume and oven dry weight.

From the Uniform Building Code, © 1988, ICBO

Figure 10-10   Classification of species

Figure 10-11 *Post and beam floor system*

Framing Walls

When the subfloor is down, the next step is to get the studding up. When I was an apprentice, all studs were called scantlings. I haven't heard the term for many years — it probably disappeared along with the old-timers who taught me the trade.

Studs (usually 2 x 4s or 2 x 6s) form the building walls. Siding and wallboard hang from the studs and the second floor and roof are supported by wall studs. Whether you call them studding or scantling, they're an important part of every wood-frame building.

TABLE NO. 25-R-3—SIZE, HEIGHT AND SPACING OF WOOD STUDS[1]

STUD SIZE (Inches)	BEARING WALLS				NONBEARING WALLS	
	LATERALLY UNSUPPORTED STUD HEIGHT[3] (Feet)	SUPPORTING ROOF AND CEILING ONLY	SUPPORTING ONE FLOOR, ROOF AND CEILING	SUPPORTING TWO FLOORS, ROOF AND CEILING	LATERALLY UNSUPPORTED STUD HEIGHT[3] (Feet)	SPACING (Inches)
		SPACING (Inches)				
1. 2 x 3[2]	—	—	—	—	10	16
2. 2 x 4	10	24	16	—	14	24
3. 3 x 4	10	24	24	16	14	24
4. 2 x 5	10	24	24	—	16	24
5. 2 x 6	10	24	24	16	20	24

[1]Utility grade studs shall not be spaced more than 16 inches on center, nor support more than a roof and ceiling, nor exceed 8 feet in height for exterior walls and load bearing or 10 feet for interior nonload-bearing walls.

[2]Shall not be used in exterior walls.

[3]Listed heights are distances between points of lateral support placed perpendicular to the plane of the wall. Increases in supported height are permitted where justified by an analysis.

From the Uniform Building Code, © 1988, ICBO

Figure 10-12 *Floor stud sizes*

Stud Spacing

If studs are supporting floors above, space them not more than 16 inches o.c. But 2 x 4 studs that support only a ceiling and a roof may be spaced up to 24 inches o.c. You can also use 24-inch spacing for nonbearing interior walls. With 24-inch spacing, center the roof trusses directly over the studding. This transfers the vertical roof load directly through the studding to the foundation. Studding sizes and heights are given in Figure 10-12.

Make sure your carpenters place the studs with the wide dimension of the timber at right angles to the wall.

The code doesn't require double wall plates on nonbearing interior partitions. But since studs are sold in bundles precut to length, many contractors prefer to use double plates even on interior partitions. That saves ordering two different sizes of studs for the job.

Offset joints in double top plates at least 48 inches. Joining partitions must be overlapped on the top plate. Make sure studs bear on a plate or sill not less than 2 inches thick. The bottom plate must be at least as wide as the wall stud.

I once inspected a job where exterior stud spacing varied from 10 to 16 inches on center. The interior walls were even worse — the spacing varied up to 24 inches o.c. I'd never seen anything like it. But checking my code book, I found that I had to pass it. After all, the spacing didn't exceed the code maximums, 16 inches on exterior and 24 inches on interior walls. The code doesn't require even stud spacing. Of course, a magician was needed to hang drywall on that job. Finding studs to nail to under the drywall was sure to be a nightmare.

Corner Bracing

All exterior walls must be braced. The most common method is placing plywood panels at each corner. Another method uses a 1 x 4 brace inset at an angle into the studs. This angle brace runs from the floor to the upper plate at an angle not over 60 degrees.

You can use manufactured wallboard of structural quality instead of angle bracing or plywood. But before you buy, check with the inspector. Verify that your brand has been approved and find out how it must be installed. Yes, the code even specifies the number of nails. Figure 10-13 shows plywood siding being attached over aluminized sheathing. This particular brand has qualified as structural grade.

Figure 10-13 *Plywood siding installed over aluminized sheathing*

Header All Openings

In Section 2517 of the UBC, there's an interesting note about the framing of headers. Headers and lintels over openings 4 feet wide or less can be made of double 2 x 4s on edge. Here's the rule of thumb: For each 2 feet of opening over 4 feet, increase the lumber size 2 inches. In other words, you would use 2 x 4s on edge over a 4-foot opening, 2 x 6s over a 6-foot opening, 2 x 8s over 8 feet, and so on. And you don't have to use doubled 2-inch stock. Solid or 4-inch-thick material will do as well. There's no reason why you can't substitute a 4 x 6 for two 2 x 6s.

All headers and lintels must have at least 2-inch solid bearing at each end to the floor or bottom plate, unless you use other approved framing methods or joint brackets. There are a number of these brackets on the market now. Some are made of plastic but most are galvanized steel.

Some contractors prefer to use solid headers over window and door openings. If you use a narrower size, you need a certain amount of blocking between them and the top plate. Some even extend this header to each side of the window opening instead of using curtain blocking. But it's not required.

Cripples and Cripple Walls

I haven't covered all the framing details needed to frame a house. For instance, in framing window openings it's customary to put cripples under the lower side of the opening. (Cripples are short pieces of stud material.) They double up the stud where the lower framing cross member touches the studs at the sides of the opening. This gives additional support to that member. Although it's not always required by the code, I recommend using a cripple because it increases the strength of the wall.

Section 2517(g)4 of the code gives requirements for a cripple wall. It states that foundation walls must be framed of studs at least the size of the studding above with a minimum length of 14 inches. If the cripple wall exceeds 4 feet in height, the studs must be the size required for an additional story.

Miscellaneous Requirements

Earlier in this book I mentioned crawl spaces and crawl holes. You may remember that crawl holes have to be at least 18 inches by 24 inches. Even if you have a partial basement, you still must have a crawl hole or access to the unexcavated portion.

Plans often call for beams set in pockets constructed in the foundation wall. Just remember to leave at least 1/2 inch of clearance at the tops, sides and ends of the beams unless you're using either an approved wood that resists decay, or treated wood. The only woods that I know of with a natural resistance to decay are redwood and cypress.

We've discussed foundation ventilation, so you know the framing material must be 6 inches from any earth unless separated by at least 3 inches of concrete. But what about the planter boxes installed adjacent to wood framing? These are usually masonry boxes built on the ground, often adjacent to the entry. The planter box must have at least 2 inches of space between it and the adjacent wall. And the adjacent wall must have flashing if it's within 6 inches of the planter.

Firestops

Firestops are installed between studs to form a barrier to air movement in the framing and between floors. Most framing provides enough fire stops without adding any extra blocks. There are a few areas, however, that may require additional firestops. According to Section 2516(f), firestopping should be used in the following places:

A. In concealed spaces of stud walls and partitions, including furred spaces, at the ceiling and flooring levels and at 10-foot intervals along the length of the wall. Exception: Firestops may be omitted at floor and ceiling levels when approved smoke-actuated fire dampers are installed at these levels.

B. At all interconnections between concealed vertical and horizontal spaces such as occur at soffits, drop ceilings and cove ceilings.

C. In concealed spaces between stair stringers at the top and bottom of the run and between studs along and in line with the run of the stairs if the walls under the stairs are unfinished.

D. *In openings around vents, pipes, ducts, chimneys, fireplaces and similar openings which afford a passage for fire at ceiling and floor levels, with non-combustible materials.*

Firestops must be nominal 2-inch-thick wood, gypsum board, cement asbestos-board, mineral wool, or other approved noncombustible materials securely fastened in place.

Siding

Rustic, drop siding or shiplap siding should be at least 3/8 inch thick unless you're putting it over sheathing permitted by the code. This thickness is based on a maximum stud spacing of 16 inches on center. There's a movement afoot to get the maximum spacing increased to 24 inches for studding in the exterior walls. In that case you would have to use thicker plywood or use sheathing underneath the siding.

Bevel siding must be at least 7/16-inch on the butt and 3/16-inch tip thickness. You may be able to use thinner siding. But first check with your local inspector.

All weatherboarding or siding must be nailed securely to each stud. Use at least one nail every 6 inches on the edges and every 12 inches on the field. For conventional siding, there should be at least one nail per stud. Conventional siding installed over 1-inch nominal sheathing or 1/2-inch plywood sheathing must be fastened with nails spaced not more than 24 inches on center in each piece of weatherboarding or siding.

Unless you've applied the siding over sheathing, joints must be over the framing members and covered with a continuous wood batt, lapped horizontally, or otherwise made waterproof to the satisfaction of the inspector. This may be done with caulking or flashing.

TABLE NO. 25-L—WOOD SHINGLE AND SHAKE SIDEWALL EXPOSURES

| SHINGLE OR SHAKE | MAXIMUM WEATHER EXPOSURES | | | |
| | Single-Coursing | | Double-Coursing | |
Length and Type	No. 1	No. 2	No. 1	No. 2
1. 16-inch Shingles	7½"	7½"	12"	10"
2. 18-inch Shingles	8½"	8½"	14"	11"
3. 24-inch Shingles	11½"	11½"	16"	14"
4. 18-inch Resawn Shakes	8½"	—	14"	—
5. 18-inch Straight-Split Shakes	8½"	—	16"	—
6. 24-inch Resawn Shakes	11½"	—	20"	—

From the *Uniform Building Code*, © 1988, ICBO

Figure 10-14 *Exposure allowed for wood shingles and shakes*

Shingles or shakes, whether of wood, asbestos cement or other approved materials, have different rules. They may be applied over furring strips, wood sheathing or approved fiberboard shingle backer. But they must be placed over building paper unless they're applied over solid sheathing. If fiberboard backing is used, they must be attached with corrosion-resistant annular grooved nails.

The weather exposure of wood shingles or shake siding can't exceed the maximums in UBC Table 25-L (Figure 10-14).

Nails

UBC Table 25-Q (Figure 10-15) gives nailing requirements for most carpentry joints used in residential construction. UBC Table 25-G (Figure 10-16) lists the required penetration for both box and common nails when they're

TABLE NO. 25-Q—NAILING SCHEDULE

CONNECTION	NAILING[1]
1. Joist to sill or girder, toenail	3-8d
2. Bridging to joist, toenail each end	2-8d
3. 1" x 6" subfloor or less to each joist, face nail	2-8d
4. Wider than 1" x 6" subfloor to each joist, face nail	3-8d
5. 2" subfloor to joist or girder, blind and face nail	2-16d
6. Sole plate to joist or blocking, face nail	16d at 16" o.c.
7. Top plate to stud, end nail	2-16d
8. Stud to sole plate	4-8, toenail or 2-16d, end nail
9. Double studs, face nail	16d at 24" o.c.
10. Doubled top plates, face nail	16d at 16" o.c.
11. Top plates, laps and intersections, face nail	2-16d
12. Continuous header, two pieces	16d at 16" o.c. along each edge
13. Ceiling joists to plate, toenail	3-8d
14. Continuous header to stud, toenail	4-8d
15. Ceiling joists, laps over partitions, face nail	3-16d
16. Ceiling joists to parallel rafters, face nail	3-16d
17. Rafter to plate, toenail	3-8d
18. 1" brace to each stud and plate, face nail	2-8d
19. 1" x 8" sheathing or less to each bearing, face nail	2-8d
20. Wider than 1" x 8" sheathing to each bearing, face nail	3-8d
21. Built-up corner studs	16d at 24" o.c.
22. Built-up girder and beams	20d at 32" o.c. at top and bottom and staggered 2-20d at ends and at each splice

(Continued)

Figure 10-15 *Nailing schedule*

CONNECTION	NAILING[1]
23. 2″ planks	2-16d at each bearing
24. **Plywood and particleboard:**[5] **Subfloor, roof and wall sheathing (to framing):** 1/2″ and less	6d[2]
19/32″-3/4″	8d[3] or 6d[4]
7/8″-1″	8d[2]
1 1/8″-1 1/4″	10d[3] or 8d[4]
Combination Subfloor-underlayment (to framing): 3/4″ and less	6d[4]
7/8″-1″	8d[4]
1 1/8″-1 1/4″	10d[3] or 8d[4]
25. **Panel Siding (to framing):** 1/2″ or less	6d[6]
5/8″	8d[6]
26. **Fiberboard Sheathing:**[7] 1/2″	No. 11 ga.[8] 6d[3] No. 16 ga.[9]
25/32″	No. 11 ga.[8] 8d[3] No. 16 ga.[9]

[1]Common or box nails may be used except where otherwise stated.

[2]Common or deformed shank.

[3]Common.

[4]Deformed shank.

[5]Nails spaced at 6 inches on center at edges, 12 inches at intermediate supports (10 inches at intermediate supports for floors), except 6 inches at all supports where spans are 48 inches or more. For nailing of plywood and particleboard diaphragms and shear walls, refer to Section 2513 (c). Nails for wall sheathing may be common, box or casing.

[6]Corrosion-resistant siding or casing nails conforming to the requirements of Section 2516 (j) 1.

[7]Fasteners spaced 3 inches on center at exterior edges and 6 inches on center at intermediate supports.

[8]Corrosion-resistant roofing nails with 7/16-inch-diameter head and 1 1/2-inch length for 1/2-inch sheathing and 1 3/4-inch length for 25/32-inch sheathing conforming to the requirements of Section 2516 (j) 1.

[9]Corrosion-resistant staples with nominal 7/16-inch crown and 1 1/8-inch length for 1/2-inch sheathing and 1 1/2-inch length for 25/32-inch sheathing conforming to the requirements of Section 2516 (j) 1.

From the Uniform Building Code, © 1988, ICBO

Figure 10-15 (cont'd) *Nailing schedule*

TABLE NO. 25-G—SAFE LATERAL STRENGTH AND REQUIRED PENETRATION OF BOX AND COMMON WIRE NAILS DRIVEN PERPENDICULAR TO GRAIN OF WOOD

SIZE OF NAIL	STANDARD LENGTH (Inches)	WIRE GAUGE	PENETRA-TION REQUIRED (Inches)	LOADS (Pounds)[1][2][3]	
				Douglas Fir Larch or Southern Pine	Other Species
BOX NAILS					
6d	2	12½	1⅛	51	
8d	2½	11½	1¼	63	
10d	3	10½	1½	76	See U.B.C. Standard No. 25-17
12d	3¼	10½	1½	76	
16d	3½	10	1½	82	
20d	4	9	1⅝	94	
30d	4½	9	1⅝	94	
40d	5	8	1¾	108	
COMMON NAILS					
6d	2	11½	1¼	63	
8d	2½	10¼	1½	78	
10d	3	9	1⅝	94	See U.B.C. Standard No. 25-17
12d	3¼	9	1⅝	94	
16d	3½	8	1¾	108	
20d	4	6	2⅛	139	
30d	4½	5	2¼	155	
40d	5	4	2½	176	
50d	5½	3	2¾	199	
60d	6	2	2⅞	223	

[1]The safe lateral strength values may be increased 25 percent where metal side plates are used.

[2]For wood diaphragm calculations these values may be increased 30 percent. (See U.B.C. Standard No. 25-17.)

[3]Tabulated values are on a normal load-duration basis and apply to joints made of seasoned lumber used in dry locations. See U.B.C. Standard No. 25-17 for other service conditions.

From the Uniform Building Code, © 1988, ICBO

Figure 10-16 *Nail specifications*

driven perpendicular to the grain of the wood. It also gives the length and wire gauge for both kinds of nails. Nails and spikes have a required penetration of at least 11 diameters. You can interpolate allowable loads for sizes that aren't given in the table.

The code also spells out the spacing for nailing. For wood-to-wood joints, use a center-to-center spacing that's not less than the required penetration. Edge distances may not be less than one-half the required penetration. If you have to bore holes for nails to prevent splitting, make the hole smaller in diameter than the nail you'll use.

Staples

Staples are popular with many tradesmen because they make the work easier and save time. Staples and staplers can be very effective. When there's a problem, it's usually the fault of the operator. No matter how well a tool is designed and built, there's always someone who can foul it up.

Staples are an acceptable replacement for nails in most cases, if the end result is as strong as nailing. But it won't be unless you use the right staple for the particular job at hand. You wouldn't staple down a roof with an ordinary office stapler. Well, using the wrong staple, even in the right gun, can have the same effect. And once the job is finished and the paint is on, it's hard to tell the difference. But the owner will know the difference after the first storm.

Trusses

Manufactured roof trusses are assembled at the factory with metal connectors or gussets instead of nails. They're made of galvanized metal, engineered for a particular application with specific loadings. The strength of the truss depends on both the size and grade of the timber and the size of the connector and the number of spikes it has.

One problem with these trusses is that some manufacturers don't follow the engineered design. They may cheat on the material grades or on the size of the metal connectors. It's a good idea to get your hands on the engineer's specs and make sure the manufacturer is following them. If he isn't, return the trusses.

True, this may delay your job. But if you use faulty materials and the inspector finds out, it can cost you a lot more than just a short delay. I suggest you use the inspector's Evaluation Reports to check the various types and manufacturers.

The Traveling Solid Core Door

I suppose there are more ways to fool building inspectors than there are building inspectors to fool. I've learned to never underestimate the ingenuity of an entrepreneur who's determined to save a buck, even if it costs two dollars to do it. Here's a case in point.

Once I issued permits to a local contractor for three single-family residences on three adjoining lots. His practice was to begin one home, get it well along, then start with the next. Most of the time during construction he had three houses at different stages of completion. As he finished each part of the job, he called for the usual inspections.

On the final inspection for the first house, I entered the residence through the door that separated the garage from the entry to the kitchen. The code says any door separating a garage from living space has to be solid core, and for good reason. A solid core door is designed to take heavy use and abuse. It's much more likely to keep garage fumes out of the living area for the life of the home. Spending an extra $20 on a solid core door is worth the money.

As I came in, I gave the door a couple of raps with my knuckles. The dull thud told me it was solid core, just like the code required. Later I made the same final inspection on each of the other houses. Eventually all three houses passed inspection and were sold.

Several years later the FHA foreclosed on the second of those three houses. They called me in to certify code compliance so the house could be sold under an FHA program. That probably wasn't necessary. After all, I had inspected those houses myself only a few years earlier. Anyhow, I checked the plumbing, made sure kitchen and bath fans exhausted to the outside, counted the foundation vents — all the usual stuff. Everything checked out.

I started back into the house to write up my report for the FHA. As I went through the opening between the garage and the kitchen, I gave the door a rap with my knuckles. It sounded hollow, not solid. Funny, why would anyone remove a solid core door and replace it with a hollow core door? While I was mulling this over, I got another thought.

I went over to the first of the three houses, introduced myself, and asked to check the kitchen door. Sure enough, it was hollow core too. So I went down to the third house in the line and checked the same door. This door was a solid core door. Then it dawned on me — I had inspected the same door when I'd made the final inspection on all three houses.

11

Exits and Clearances

his chapter is about something we all take for granted — getting in and out of buildings. Obviously, having the right kind of door where and when you need it can be very important. In a fire, exiting can be a life or death matter. That's why the code is so particular about doorways and clearances.

I once plan-checked a building that had a room with no door at all. Perfect! Nobody could get in the room so nobody could get trapped inside. I can guess how an oversight like that happened. The owner decided that the original door wasn't in the right place. The draftsman rubbed the door off the plan and was interrupted before drawing the new door. He never got back to it, and the reviewer never caught the mistake. But I did.

What Are Exits?

Every room in every building needs a way in and out, so let's take a closer look at exiting. Chapter 33 in the UBC covers exiting — including the definition of *exit*.

> *Exit* is a continuous and unobstructed means of egress to a public way and shall include intervening aisle, doors, doorways, corridors, exterior exit balconies, ramps, stairways, smokeproof enclosures, horizontal exits, exit passageways, exit courts and yards.

> *Exit court* is a yard or court providing access to a public way for one or more required exits.

> *Exit passageway* is an enclosed exit connecting a required exit or exit court with a public way.

> *Horizontal exit* is an exit from one building into another building on approximately the same level, or through or around a wall constructed as required for a two-hour occupancy separation and which completely divides a floor into two or more separate areas so as to establish an area of refuge affording safety from fire or smoke coming from the area from which escape is made.

In other words, an exit is all the ways out of a building. But there's more to it than that. The inspector and the fire marshal need to know how many people can get out quickly from any given point. And there's more to that access business than meets the eye. For example, you could have a hangar with a door 40 feet wide, but if one person can't easily get out of the building in an emergency, then you don't have adequate exits.

Exit Standards Promote Safety

The definitions of *exit* imply that eventually, all exits lead outdoors and to safety. To be more precise, when you leave a building through an exit, it will eventually lead to a *public way*. What's a public way? The code defines it this way:

> **Public way** *is any street, alley or similar parcel of land essentially unobstructed from the ground to the sky which is deeded, dedicated or otherwise permanently appropriated to the public for public use and having a clear width of not less than 10 feet.*

To determine the size and number of exits for a building, you must know how many people will normally occupy a given space. In Chapter 3 we learned how to determine the occupant load. For this you must use UBC Table 33-A, *Minimum Egress and Access Requirements* (Figure 3-1 in Chapter 3).

The issue of occupant load is at the root of many arguments over the building code. The owner of a store may try to bargain with the inspector, saying, "You know I probably won't have that many customers in my store on even the busiest day. Why can't we figure it on what I think I'll have?"

There's only one good answer to that question: "Because it says so in The Book!" After all, codes are written to establish safe building standards. Of course, there'll always be those who question these standards. Usually they'll complain that the standards are too strict. But often the regulations are too generous. Most were designed to set minimum standards, leaving the inspector some room for interpretation. That's certainly true of occupant loads.

To find the occupant load permitted in any building or part of a building, divide the floor area by the square feet per occupant required in UBC Table 33-A. If the table doesn't cover a particular occupancy, the building official will decide, based on the occupancy it most nearly resembles. And that can lead to legitimate arguments.

You can increase the occupant load by providing extra exits. But most inspectors are skeptics. You'll need an approved aisle or seating diagram to prove your point.

Determining Occupant Load for Exits

In determining the occupant load, the code assumes that all areas of a building will be occupied at the same time. That means that if you have a building of mixed occupancy with most of the occupants using the same exits, the building must be calculated as though each occupancy was used to the maximum all the time. But that doesn't mean that the most restrictive provisions apply to the entire building. Each separate occupancy is rated on its own usage. But it's assumed that all areas are used simultaneously. Let's look at an example.

Remember the lodge building we discussed back in Chapter 3? It had a dance floor, dining room, reading room, bar and kitchen. We used the figure of 7 square feet per occupant for the dance floor and 15 square feet per occupant for the dining room and the bar. The reading room needed 50 square feet per occupant and the kitchen a whopping 200 square feet per occupant. Let's look at that lodge building again. You'll find it in Figure 11-1.

We decided, back in Chapter 3, that the lodge building could be 9,000 square feet and accommodate 664 people. But the lodge only meets once a week. The dining room is open only from 3 p.m. to midnight and the reading room from 10 a.m. until 5 p.m. They hold a dance once a week.

Do they need an exit designed to handle the whole crowd of 664? Or could they get by with exits to handle the crowd they actually expect to be in the building at any one time? You

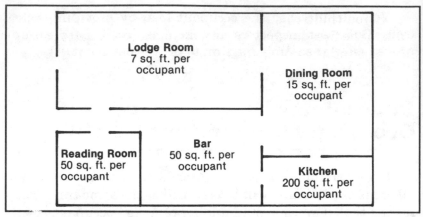

Figure 11-1   *Sketch of lodge*

guessed it. Under the code, exits have to be designed to handle all 664 people.

Overloading an Occupancy

There's one more situation to consider. We originally designed the bar to hold 100 people. But during an intermission at the dance, there might be more than 100 people in there. If the owner hadn't thought of it, the builder should suggest a way to deal with this overflow.

Section 3302(c) warns that the number of occupants of any building or room can't exceed the posted capacity. The building owner or manager must enforce this rule. If he doesn't, the fire marshal has the authority to shut them down until the crowd is thinned out. Subsection (c) also says that any room with fixed seats with an occupant load of more than 50 must have the capacity clearly posted.

If you think this might present an enforcement problem, talk to the fire marshal. Try to work out a better ratio between the bar and the dance floor. This usually isn't a big problem because most dance floors are located in or next to the bar.

Establishing Exit Size

The first point to make here is that every building or usable portion of a building must have at least one exit. There's a column in UBC Table 33-A headed *Minimum of Two Exits Required Where Number of Occupants Is Over . . . .* Suppose your dance floor is 900 square feet. Table 33-A requires 7 square feet per occupant. Divide 900 by 7 to find an occupant load of 128. The table also shows that we need at least two exits. But we still haven't established how big they'll be.

Exit width is discussed in Section 3303(b) of the UBC:

> *The total width of exits in feet shall not be less than the total occupant load served divided by 50. Such width of exits shall be divided approximately equally among the separate exits.*

Looks easy, doesn't it? Seems like you'll need only 3 feet of exit width. But the book says you must have two exits. What happens now? Do you put in two 18-inch doors? Of course not. Section 3304(f) states that every required exit doorway must allow the installation of a door at least 3 feet wide. In other words, what you thought was going to be 3 feet of exit has now become 6 feet.

Not only is there a minimum size for a door, there's also a maximum size. No leaf of an exit door may be more than 4 feet wide. In other words, if you have a double door, the width of the opening would have to be at least 6 feet and not more than

8 feet. Here's another way to look at it. If you need 5 feet of exit width, you'll have to install two 3-foot doors, because no door may be 5 feet wide.

All exit doors must be clearly marked. We don't want strangers in the building winding up in a broom closet in an emergency. And the hardware for these doors must be designed so that it doesn't require any unusual skill or strength to open the door.

Establishing Exit Position

So you'll need two 3-foot doors where you originally thought that 3 feet of total doorway area would be enough. Why not just put in a double door? Because if you do, you'll have the inspector breathing down your neck. The code says that if two or more doors are required, they must be positioned apart from each other. Here's a quote from Section 3303(c):

> *(c) Arrangement of Exits. If only two exits are required they shall be placed a distance apart equal to not less than one-half of the length of the maximum overall diagonal dimension of the building or area to be served measured in a straight line between exits . . .*

Where three or more exits are required, at least two exits shall be placed a distance apart equal to not less than one half of the length of the maximum overall diagonal dimension of the building or area to be served measured in a straight line between exits, and the additional exits shall be arranged a reasonable distance apart so that if one becomes blocked the others will be available.

Let's look at a sketch of a dance floor (Figure 11-2). It's 30 feet wide by 30 feet long, or 900 square feet. The longest diagonal measurement of this square dance floor will be about

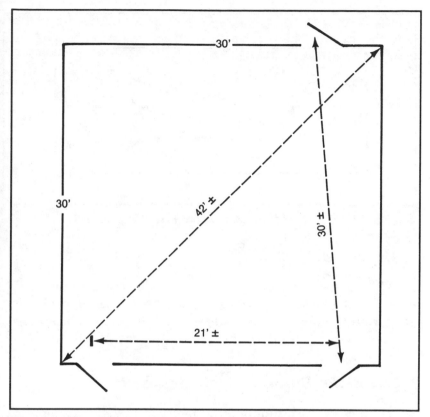

Figure 11-2 *Placing exits on dance floor*

42 feet. To find this, find the square of the length of the two sides, add them, then find the square root of the total.

The doors must be separated by half the diagonal, or 21 feet. That means you could put both exits on one wall, as shown in Figure 11-2. But wouldn't it be better to have a door at the front and one at the rear? Yes — if both would have access to a public way. In fact, I highly recommend it.

281

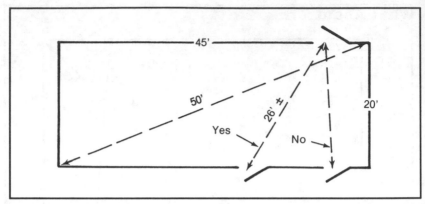

Figure 11-3   *Exits on long narrow building*

Check the code first, though. Is it allowed? The code only specifies the distance. So one door at the front and one at the rear would conform to the code because they would be at least 30 feet apart. Our minimum separation was 21 feet.

What If the Building Isn't Square?

Suppose your building is 20 feet wide by 45 feet long, as shown in Figure 11-3. It's still 900 square feet. Could you put two doors directly opposite each other on the long sides? Probably not. Because the building has different dimensions, we have to recalculate the diagonal.

Take the new length and width and do some squaring. Twenty squared is 400; 45 squared is 2025. Together they add up to 2425. The square root of 2425 is almost 50 feet. Remember, we have to use at least one-half of that distance as a minimum distance between two exits. So our two exits would have to be at least 25 feet apart. Figure 11-3 shows one possible arrangement of exits. Or you could put them at each end of the building.

What About Three Exits?

If you were to put three exits in that building, you could have two exits directly opposite or even on the same wall at opposite corners. If three or more exits are required, at least two have to conform to the diagonal formula. The third may be a reasonable distance away, so that if one is blocked, the others will be available. If the building doesn't have sprinklers, no part of it may be more than 150 feet from an exterior exit door, a horizontal exit, an exit passageway, or an enclosed stairway. This distance has to be measured along the line of travel. If you have to go around objects such as desks, files, machinery, or any permanent or semi-permanent fixtures, the 150 feet has to include that detour.

On the other hand, if your building has sprinklers (and I hope it has), this distance may be increased to 200 feet.

Exits may lead into adjoining or intervening rooms or areas if they're easily accessible and provide a direct route to an outside exit. Exits cannot pass through kitchens, store-rooms, rest rooms, closets, or spaces used for similar purposes.

Landings Required

Most exit requirements are based on an occupancy of more than ten. Section 3304(i) covers these. But notice the difference between occupancy and occupant load. Landings are required, regardless of occupant load.

(i) Change in Floor Level at Doors. Regardless of the occupant load, there shall be a floor or landing on each side of a door. When access for the physically handicapped is required by Section 3301(e) the floor or landing shall be not more than 1/2 inch lower than the threshold of the doorway. When such access is not required such dimen-

*n shall not exceed 1 inch. Landings shall be level except
exterior landings, which may have a slope not to exceed
1 / 4 inch per foot.*

Section 3304(j) says that landings must be at least as wide
as the stairway or door, and that the door can't reduce that
dimension by more than 7 inches when it's fully opened. If you
have an occupant load of 50 or more, then doors in any position
can't reduce the width of the landing more than 50 percent.
The landing length in the direction of travel must be at least
44 inches. But before you panic, there is an exception:

> **Exception:** *In Groups R, Division 3, and M Occupan-
> cies and within individual units of Group R, Division 1
> Occupancies, such length need not exceed 36 inches.*

Figure 11-4 shows an approved landing. The code lists four
exceptions that cover private residences. A stair opening is
excepted if it doesn't open over the top step or a landing and
the first step or landing is not more than 7-1/2 inches below
floor level. Other landings in homes need not be wider than
the door. Screen or storm doors don't require a landing.

Requirements for Exterior Exit Doors

The code has some rigid requirements for exit doors. It
says you can't use revolving, sliding and overhead doors as a
required exit, even though you see them all over town. You've
probably seen pneumatically-operated doors, overhead doors
and various forms of sliding doors. But take a good look at
those sliding and pneumatically-operated doors. You'll find a
little note, probably in one of the upper corners, that says
something like: "In case of emergency, push on door panel."

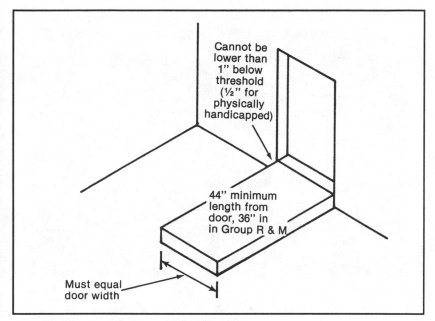

Figure 11-4   *Approved landings*

That means that in case of a power outage or equipment failure, the door panel will either push out or swivel out so that people inside can get out. Occasionally you'll run across an older model that doesn't operate this way. Doors like that met the regulations in force at the time, and were grandfathered in when the code changed. If they're ever replaced, it must be with the newer style doors with warnings and armor plate glass.

Rolling Overhead Doors

You've probably been to a modern shopping mall where the shops are secured at night by overhead rolling doors or

Figure 11-5 *Rolling overhead door*

sliding doors. They're legal because they're not used during the day when the business is open. They're only closed at night for security reasons. Figure 11-5 shows a rolling overhead door typical of what you find at shopping malls.

But what about power-operated doors? Here's what Section 3304(h) says:

> *(h) Special Doors. Revolving, sliding and overhead doors shall not be used as required exits.*
>
> *Power-operated doors complying with UBC Standards No. 33-1 may be used for exit purposes. Such doors when swinging shall have two guide rails installed on the swing side projecting out from the face of the door jambs for a distance not less than the widest door leaf. Guide rails shall be not less than 30 inches in height with solid*

*or mesh panels to prevent penetration into door swing and
shall be capable of resisting a horizontal load at top of rail
of not less than 50 pounds per lineal foot.*

The guide rails are designed to keep people from walking
into swinging doors.

Exit Width into an Exit Court

If your exit doesn't have access to a public way, it can open
onto an *exit court*. The size of the exit court depends on the
number of occupancies it must serve and the number of
occupants. Section 3303 is your guide:

>   *. . . The total exit width required from any story of a
> building shall be determined by using the occupant load
> of that story plus the percentages of the occupant loads of
> floors which exit through the level under consideration, as
> follows:*
>
>   *1. Fifty percent of the occupant load in the first adja-
> cent story above and the first adjacent story below, when
> a story below exits through the level under consideration.*
>
>   *2. Twenty-five percent of the occupant load in the story
> immediately beyond the first adjacent story.*

The maximum exit width required from any story of a
building shall be maintained.

How would this affect our exit court? Let's assume that we
have three buildings that form a central court. Each of the
three buildings has an occupant load of 300. Section 3303(b)
also says:

>   *The total width of exits in feet shall be not less than
> the total occupant load divided by 50.*

If there are 300 people in each of three buildings, that
totals 900 people who might want out. Nine hundred divided

by 50 equals an exit 18 feet wide. This can be a single exit or a total of 18 feet spread among several exits.

That's assuming that all the occupants will be coming out at once and reaching the exit at the same time. We know they can't all move like that. But for a single-story building, you've got to plan for all of them exiting at the same time. Let's see what's required for a three-story building.

We'll assume that the occupants are divided equally throughout the buildings, 100 to each floor. In that case, your figures might look something like this, according to Section 3303(b):

First floor: Full count — 100 people

Second floor: 50 percent of count — 50 people

Third floor: 25 percent of count — 25 people

This is the estimated number of people who could be passing through the exit within a very short time. That totals 175 people; divide that by 50 and you get 3.75 feet of exit width. So each building needs an exit at least 4 feet wide. So for the three multi-story buildings, you need a total exit width of 12 feet.

Exit Enclosures

When does an exit have to be enclosed? Section 3309(a) says you *don't* have to enclose interior stairways, ramps, or escalators that serve only one adjacent floor and aren't connected with corridors or stairways serving other floors. All others must be enclosed.

An exit enclosure, which is a fire-safe exit way, usually means an emergency exit. Though they may never be needed for an emergency, they must be ready. That's the reason for the strict requirements. Consequently, you can't have any openings into exit enclosures, except for exit doorways and at landings and parts of floors connecting stairway flights. Also there must be a corridor on the ground floor leading outside from the stairway. All exits must be one-hour fire protection assemblies with self-closing or automatic closing devices.

Smokeproof Enclosures

If a floor is more than 75 feet above the highest grade, one of the required exits must be a smokeproof enclosure. This must have a vestibule at least 44 inches by 72 inches. Both the vestibule and the adjacent stairway must be enclosed by walls that are fire-resistive for at least two hours. The ceiling of the vestibule serves as a smoke and heat trap.

The smokeproof enclosure must have mechanical ventilation unless the building is completely air-conditioned. Emergency lights are also required.

Exit Lights and Signs

For occupancies other than Group R-3, you've got to provide exit lights and signs. Any time the building is occupied, the exits must be illuminated by at least one foot-candle of light at floor level. The light must have separate circuits or separate power sources, so the exits will be lit in an emergency.

Groups A-1 through A-4, Group I, and Group R-1 (motels and apartments) with an occupant load of 50 or more must also have exit signs at each doorway and anywhere the direction of the exit may be in question. The lettering has to be at least 6 inches high. When the occupant load is over 100 for any occupancy, signs are required.

Most of the occupancies of 100 or more must have illuminated signs. Illuminated signs must have at least two 15-watt lamps. Why two lamps? It's a safety precaution. You never know when these lamps are going to burn out. It's unlikely both will burn out at the same time.

There used to be a lot of arguing about whether exit signs should be red or green. Some said that red would be easy to spot. Others pointed out that in a dark, smoked-filled room, fire fighters had occasionally wasted time and water on a red glow that turned out to be an exit sign. Both sides must have compromised because the code doesn't specify which color to use. It can be either red or green.

The code does say, however, that all graphics, whether arrows, letters, or other symbols, must be high contrast and letters must be at least 6 inches high with a stroke not less than 3/4-inch wide.

Certain high-density occupancies are required to have two separate power sources for the exit lights and signs. These are *sources*, not circuits. The second source is usually a battery system. If the emergency and sign lighting are on a separate circuit, they can be attached to a generator.

Corridors

A corridor in a public building, according to Section 3305, must be at least 44 inches wide and must be unobstructed. In private residences, or for occupant loads of 10 or less, 36 inches is the minimum width. There are a few special conditions relating to trim, handrails, and some forms of hardware. Nonstructural trim and similar decorative features can't reduce the width more than 1-1/2 inches on each side.

Doors opening into corridors may not reduce the required width of the corridor by more than 7 inches when fully opened. Doors in any position may not obstruct more than half of the corridor. That means that if you have a 3-foot-wide door and a 44-inch-wide hallway, you'll either have to reverse the swing of your door, or the doorway itself will have to be inset into the room.

If you decide to reverse the swing of your door, check your occupant load. Remember? Occupant loads over 50 require that the door swing in the direction of exit travel.

Partitions, rails, counters and similar space dividers that aren't over 5'9" don't form corridors. And here's one final word about corridors: A dead-end corridor may not be more than 20 feet long.

Stairways and Ramps

The rise of each step must not be less than 4 inches or more than 7 inches. The tread can't be less than 10 inches deep. There are, of course, exceptions. Stairs or ladders used only for equipment are exempt. Stairs in private residences have a whole new set of rules — the maximum rise is 8 inches and the minimum tread only 9 inches.

Stairs, generally, may not rise more than 12 feet without a landing at least as wide as the stairs. But the run of the landing doesn't have to be more than 4 feet. You need a minimum of 6'8" of headroom between a line drawn over the nose of the treads and any ceiling or projection in the ceiling above. This is shown in Figure 11-6.

Private stairways may be as narrow as 30 inches. Public stairways serving an occupant load of up to 50 must be at least

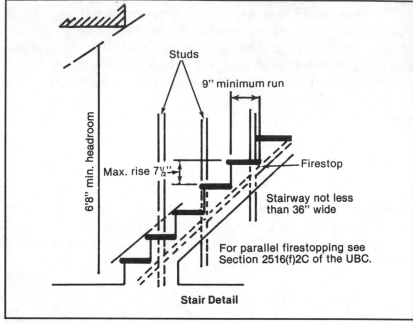

Stair Detail

From the Uniform Building Code, © 1988, ICBO

Figure 11-6 *ICBO's stair detail*

36 inches wide. If the occupant load is greater than 50, you must go to a 44-inch stairway.

Section 3306(q) requires that all stairways in buildings four or more stories in height have stairway identification signs at each floor stating the floor number, whether there is roof access, and the upper and lower terminus of the stairway. The sign must be readily visible and approximately 5 feet above the floor landing.

Spiral and Circular Stairs

There are two differences between a spiral and a circular stairway: the radius, and where you can use them. You can

use a circular stairway as a public stairway if the m.
width of the run is at least 10 inches and the smallest
is not less than twice the width of the stair. For exam
you had a 5-foot-wide circular stairway in a commercial building, it couldn't curve any faster than it would take to circle a
10-foot column or circular space.

The spiral stairway, on the other hand, may only be used
in Group R, Division 1 and 3 occupancies. The steps must be
at least 7-1/2 inches wide at a point 12 inches from the side of
the stairs where the tread is narrowest. The rise can't exceed
9-1/2 inches, and you need at least 6'6" headroom.

Spiral stairs are used in many homes and for access to
mechanical rooms (rooms where heating and air conditioning
equipment are located). But you can't use them for a public
exit.

That's the code's stair requirements in a nutshell. There's
just one more thing. On public stairs the floor number, the
terminus of the top and bottom levels, and the identification
of the stairs must appear at each floor in buildings over four
stories high.

Understair Space

If the stairs in your building go down to the basement or
any area below grade level, you need an approved barrier at
grade level. That's to prevent anyone from accidentally winding up in the basement during an emergency. Also, any usable
space under the stairways in an exit enclosure must be open
and unused. That's to prevent the storage of anything under
the stairs that could cause a fire and block the exit.

But what about closets under the stairs in private homes?
Are they legal? Remember that most exit requirements only

Figure 11-7   *Ramp providing access for the handicapped*

apply to occupancies of 10 or more. That makes most single-family residences exempt.

Get to know Chapter 33 of the UBC. Many of the items I've discussed are exempt in Group R and M occupancies. So go ahead and store your Christmas ornaments under the stairs at home. But don't do it in your office!

Ramps

You have to build a ramp for any change in elevation in a corridor if the change is less than 10 inches vertically. The width and clearance requirements for corridors also apply to ramps. But there's one additional requirement in UBC Table 33-A:

Access by means of a ramp or an elevator must be provided for the physically handicapped as indicated.

Figure 11-7 shows a typical ramp. Whenever Table 33-A calls for a ramp or elevator, the slope of the ramp must not exceed 1 vertical inch to 12 horizontal inches. Ramps that aren't specifically for the handicapped can have a slightly steeper slope, 1 inch vertically to 8 inches horizontally.

If your ramp exceeds 1 vertical to 15 horizontal, you must install a handrail. Also, the surface must be roughened or covered with a non-slip material.

Aisles and Aisleways

Aisles between furniture, equipment, merchandise, or other obstructions must be at least 3 feet wide if they serve one side of the aisle, or 3-1/2 feet wide if they serve both sides of the aisle. Regardless of the width of the aisle, the distance to the nearest exit can't be more than 150 feet on the line of travel. If the building has fire sprinklers, you can increase the travel distance to 200 feet. Where there's permanent standard seating, there can't be more than six intervening seats between any seat and the nearest aisle.

Aisles must terminate in a cross aisle, foyer, exit or vomitory. There's a formula for finding the required width of the cross aisle or vomitory. Begin with the required width of the widest aisle and add 50 percent of the total width of the remaining aisles leading into it. Look at Figure 11-8. Both middle aisles are 42 inches wide, as required. The side aisles are 36 inches wide. Begin with a middle aisle (42 inches) and add half of the sum of the other aisles (57 inches). So the cross aisle must be at least 99 inches, or 8'3" wide.

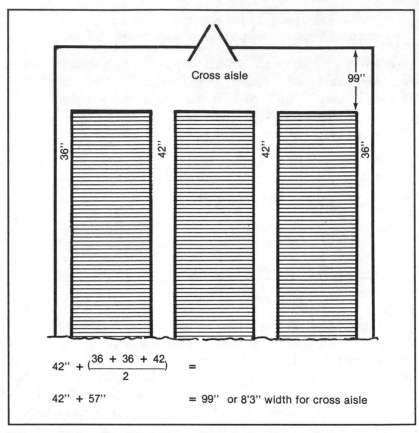

Figure 11-8   *Finding the width of the cross aisle*

Fixed Seating

For rooms with fixed seating, such as pews, booths and benches, it's pretty easy to determine occupancy loads. Just count the seats and multiply by 18 inches. For benches or pews, you're allowed so many people for so many feet of bench or pew. For booths in dining areas, you can figure one person for each 24 inches of the length of the booth.

Basically, there are two types of fixed seating, standard and continental. *Standard seating* consists of individual chairs. *Continental seating* is row seats.

Here's what the code says about standard seating in Section 3316:

> **Section 3316(a) Standard Seating.** *With standard seating, the spacing of chairs shall provide a space of not less than 12 inches from the back of one chair to the front of the most forward projection of the chair immediately behind. The rows of chairs shall be spaced not less than 33 inches back-to-back. Horizontal measurements shall be made between vertical planes. When all chairs in a row have automatic- or self-rising seats, the measurement may be made with the seats in the up position. When any chair in the row does not have an automatic- or self-rising seat, then the measurement shall be made with the seat in the down position.*

That's pretty clear. If the seats rise automatically, like theater seats, measure with the seats up. If they're not automatic, measure with the seat down.

The minimum clear distance for continental seating ranges from 18 to 24 inches:

- 18 inches clear between rows for 1-18 seats

- 20 inches clear between rows for 19-35 seats

- 21 inches clear between rows for 36-45 seats

- 22 inches clear between rows for 46-59 seats

- 24 inches clear between rows for 60 seats or more

This whole section on fixed seating applies only to seats inside a building. Outdoor grandstands and bleachers are a whole new ball game.

Grandstands and Bleachers

Let's begin with the code definitions of bleachers and grandstands.

Bleachers are tiered or stepped seating facilities without backrests in which an area of 3 square feet or less is assigned per person for computing the occupant load.

Grandstands are tiered or stepped seating facilities wherein an area of more than 3 square feet is provided for each person.

Figure 11-9 shows typical outdoor seating. The code considers bleachers temporary if they won't be used in one location for more than 90 days. But most rules for outdoor seating are the same whether the grandstands or bleachers are temporary or permanent.

Exit requirements are based on the number of occupants, which is based on the number of seats. For chairs, just count the chair backs, For benches, assume each person will occupy 18 inches of bench.

Stairs and ramps must conform to Section 3305 and Section 3306. Regulations on aisles are the same as for interior auditoriums. But there's one thing that's different. You need guardrails on all portions of elevated seating more than 30 inches above grade. The guardrails must be at least 42 inches high. You also need a 4-inch-high barrier below the guardrail on the edge of all walking platforms. Cross aisles and vomitories must be at least 54 inches wide and terminate at an exit, enclosed stairway, or exterior perimeter ramp.

Figure 11-9 *Grandstands and bleachers*

Row Spacing

The spacing for rows of outdoor seating differs from that of indoor seating. Section 3323(e) covers the subject. You need clear space of 12 inches or more between the front of the seat and the back or backrest of the seat in front of it. And measuring from back to back, the minimum distances are:

- 22 inches for seats without backrests

- 30 inches for seats with backrests

- 33 inches for chair spacing

Barrier-Free Design

State and federal authorities haven't settled on uniform requirements for handicapped access to buildings. They all agree that you must provide access. But the details depend on who's making the rules. Contact your local inspector to find out what they're requiring. Here are the UBC sections that address the problem:

Access to buildings — 3301(e), 3304(i)

Access to building uses — 1214, Table 33-A

Access to toilet facilities — 511(a) and (b)

Some rules on access by the handicapped are in the Uniform Plumbing Code. My home state, Washington, offers contractors a booklet titled *An Illustrated Handbook for Barrier-Free Design*. Ask your local building department if there's a similar publication you can use.

Who'll Cast the First Stone?

In 1972 I bought a house that had been built in 1955. The last few years hadn't been kind to it. Part of my deal with the VA was that I would "earn" part of my down payment. I agreed to paint the house inside and out and reroof it. My real estate agent furnished the shingles and I went to work on it. My wife and the youngest of my eight kids did most of the painting. I led the roofing crew (my oldest kids).

Believe it or not, I'd never laid T-lock asphalt shingles before. When one of my kids asked a question I couldn't answer, I went looking for the product information slip that has to be included in every package of roofing. Boy, was I in for a surprise.

The code makes it clear, all roofing must come with the name of the manufacturer, the type of roofing, fire rating, and weight per square, among other things. The slips I found had none of this information. Nothing was printed on the cartons either. So there I was, roof half done with non-code materials.

And I was the building inspector! You know what I'd have to do if I caught a roofer doing that.

I traced the roofing supplier through the real estate agent. He couldn't remember who his dealer was but insisted the manufacturer was a reputable firm. It's just that he couldn't remember the name. I found more of the material in his yard and advised him to get rid of it. But not in my town, because if I found any on a job, I'd make him pick it up.

I shouldn't have, but I finished my roof with the materials we had. As it turned out, the T-locks must have been O.K. I still own the house and we haven't seen a leak yet. I'll say this, though. The experience makes me feel a little more humble when I see non-code materials on a job. It can happen to anyone, even the building inspector!

12

Keeping Your Building Warm and Dry

 o far we've covered foundations, walls, exits and occupancies — which gives us a box without a lid. Before we go much farther, we need a roof.

Roof Construction

Chapter 32 of the UBC deals with roof construction and covering. The chapter was revised in the 1988 edition to reflect new materials, standards and methods of installation. Related areas are covered in other chapters: skylights (Chapter

34), penthouses (Chapter 36), use of plastics (Chapter 52) and solar energy collectors (Section 1714).

Section 3201 describes what a roof is supposed to do:

> *Roof coverings shall be securely fastened to the supporting roof construction and shall provide weather protection for the building at the roof.*

Subject to the requirements of this chapter, combustible roof coverings and roof insulation may be used in any type of construction.

The first part sounds pretty simple, but watch out for that second paragraph. It can be misleading. Remember, Chapter 17 of the UBC states that an entire building will be reduced to a lower grade if even one part of the building doesn't meet the requirements. So if your building type calls for a one-hour fire resistiveness, your roof must be one-hour rated. If you use a combustible or a non-rated roofing, your building will be reduced to a lower type classification.

Each package of roofing material must be labeled to show the type of material and the name and address of the manufacturer. This applies to all shakes, shingles, or manufactured roofing. The label should also include the grade, and, in the case of manufactured roofing, the weight per roofing square.

Definitions

I won't quote all the definitions here — just the key ones you'll need most often:

Base ply is one layer of felt secured to the deck over which a built-up roof is applied.

Base sheet is a product used as the base ply in a built-up roofing membrane.

Built-up roof covering is two or more layers of felt cemented together and surfaced with cap sheet, mineral aggregate, smooth coating or similar surfacing material.

Cap sheet is roofing made of organic or inorganic fibers, saturated and coated on both sides with a bituminous compound, surfaced with mineral granules, mica, talc, ilmenite, inorganic fibers or similar material.

Fire-retardant shakes and shingles are wood shakes and shingles that comply with UBC Standard 32-8 or 32-11. They're impregnated by the full-cell vacuum-pressure process with fire-retardant chemicals, and have been qualified for use on Class A, B or C roofs. Each bundle of treated wood shakes and shingles must have a label identifying their roof-covering classification and approved quality-control agency.

Modified bitumen membrane roof covering is one or more layers of polymer modified asphalt sheet membranes. The sheet materials may be attached with adhesives or mechanically, or held in place with an appropriate ballast layer.

Roofing ply is a layer of felt in a built-up roofing membrane.

Thermoplastic membrane roof covering has plastic layers welded together either by either heat or solvent.

Thermoset membrane roof covering has a vulcanized or crosslinked sheet membrane.

Vapor retarder is a layer of material that reduces the flow of water vapor into a roof.

Roof Covering Classifications

The 1988 UBC had another major revision that's important to note. In previous editions, there were just two types of roofing material: fire retardant and ordinary. Now they're broken down into five different classifications to fit different types of construction. There's no longer any "ordinary" roofing. Look at Table 32-A (Figure 12-1).

Class A Roof Covering shall be one of the following roofings: (1) any Class A roofing assembly. (2) Asbestos-cement shingles or sheets. (3) Exposed concrete slab roof. (4) Sheet ferrous or copper roof covering. (5) Slate shingles. (6) Clay or concrete roof tile.

Class B Roof Covering shall be any Class B roofing assembly.

Class C Roof Covering shall be any Class C roofing assembly.

Nonrated Roof Covering shall be one of the following: (1) Any mineral aggregate surface built-up roof having a slope of not more than 3 inches in 12 inches, consisting of not less than the following: Three layers of felt; 300 pounds per roofing square of gravel or other approved material or 250 pounds per square of crushed slag. (2) Wood shingles. (3) Wood shakes.

Special Purpose Roofs. (1) Wood shakes and shingles with nonbituminous saturated felt. (2) Wood shakes or shingles with gypsum board underlayment.

Classes of Roofing

These are fire-retardancy ratings, as set forth in the UBC Standard 32-7:

Class A roof coverings are effective against severe fire exposure. Under such exposures, roof coverings of this class are not readily flammable, afford a fairly high degree of fire protection to the roof deck, do not slip from position and pose no flying-brand threat.

TABLE NO. 32-A—MINIMUM ROOF CLASSES

	TYPES OF CONSTRUCTION								
	I	II			III		IV	V	
OCCUPANCY	F.R.	F.R.	1-HR	N	1-HR	N	H.T.	1-HR	N
A-1	B	B	—	—	—	—	—	—	—
A) 2-2.1	B	B	B	—	B	—	B	B	—
A-3	B	B	B	B	B[3]	B[3]	B[3]	B[3]	B[3]
A-4	B	B	B	B	B	B	B	B	B[3]
B) 1-2	B	B	B	B	B[3]	B[3]	B[3]	B[3]	B[3]
B) 3-4	B	B	B	B	B	B	B	B	B[3]
E	B	B	B	B	B	B	B	B	B[3]
H-1	A	A	A	A	B	B	B	B	B
H) 2-3-4-5-6	A	B	B	B	B	B	B	B	B
I) 1-2	A	B	B	—	B	—	B	B	—
I-3	A	B	B[1]	—	B[1]	—	—	B[2]	—
M	B	B	B	B	NR[4]	NR[4]	NR[4]	NR[4]	NR[4]
R-1	B	B	B	B	B[2 3]	B[2 3]	B[2 3]	B[2 3]	B[2 3]
R-3	B	B	B	B	NR	NR	NR	NR	NR

From the Uniform Building Code, © 1988, ICBO

Figure 12-1 ***Minimum roof classes***

[1]See Section 1002 (b)

[2]Nonrated roof coverings may be used on buildings which are not more than two stories in height and have not more than 3000 square feet of projected roof area and there is a minimum of 10 feet from the extremity of the roof to the property line on all sides except for street fronts.

[3]Buildings which are not more than two stories in height and have not more than 6000 square feet of projected roof area and there is a minimum of 10 feet from the extremity of the roof to the property line or assumed property line on all sides except for street fronts may have Class C roof coverings which comply with U.B.C. Standard No. 32-7 and roofs of cedar or redwood shakes and No. 1 shingles constructed in accordance with Section 3204 (e), Special Purpose Roofs.

[4]Unless otherwise required because of location as specified in Parts IV and V of this code, Group M, Division 1 roof coverings shall consist of not less than one layer of cap sheet, or built-up roofing consisting of two layers of felt and a surfacing material as specified in Section 3204 (d) 1.

A—Class A roofing
B—Class B roofing
C—Class C roofing
NR—Nonrated roof coverings
N—No requirements for fire resistance
F.R.—Fire Resistive
H.T.—Heavy Timber

From the Uniform Building Code, © 1988, ICBO

Figure 12-1 (cont'd) *Minimum roof classes*

Class B roof coverings are effective against moderate fire exposure. Under such exposures, roof coverings of this class are not readily flammable, afford a moderate degree of fire protection to the roof deck, do not slip from position and pose no flying-brand hazard.

Class C roof coverings are effective against light fire exposure. Under such exposures, roof coverings of this class are not readily flammable, afford a measurable degree of fire protection to the roof deck, do not slip from position and pose no flying-brand hazard.

Testing Methods

These are the tests used to determine the classification of the materials:

1) Intermittent-flame test

2) Spread-of-flame test

3) Burning-brand test

4) Flying-brand test

5) Rain test

6) Weathering test

For the burning-brand and intermittent-flame tests, the material is applied to a test deck just as it would be installed on the job. The only difference is that the edges of the deck are mortared with a mixture of asbestos-gypsum and water. This keeps heated gases produced by the test from getting to both sides of the material at once. The test deck is 3-1/3 feet wide by 4-1/3 feet long. The roofing material used is all store-grade as defined in Section 32.703, UBC Standards. The exact construction of the deck is also outlined so tests can be done the same way.

Air is directed over the sample in a prescribed direction at 12 miles per hour. For shingle roofs the deck is inclined at least 5 inches per horizontal foot; for built-up roofs the maximum slope is 5 inches per horizontal foot. The test applies a luminous gas flame over the width of the deck at the bottom edge. It must heat the sample uniformly, except for the two upper corners.

The flame develops a temperature of 1400 degrees for Class A and B roofing and 1300 degrees for Class C roofing. It's applied to the test sample for a specified time and then shut off for a specified time. This cycle is repeated throughout the test.

The spread-of-flame test is similar. The amount of combustion is measured against flame spread, production of flaming or glowing brands, and the displacement of portions of the test sample.

The last three tests are used only on treated wood shingles and shakes. Of all the tests, the weathering test takes the most time.

Marquees and Mansards

What about architectural appendages such as marquees and pseudo-mansard designs, the ones with shakes and shingles? Well, the code sections I'm describing here apply only to roofs. Even though a mansard might look like a roof, it's actually more of a decoration. Chapter 17 of the UBC allows mansards attached to the side of a building facing a street or adequate adjoining space (like a parking lot) — *if* the building is noncombustible.

How do marquees and mansards affect the fire resistance of a building? Except for the electrical wiring in a marquee, there's little in a marquee or mansard that can cause a fire. A marquee or mansard attached to a noncombustible surface wouldn't damage the rest of the building even if it burned for a considerable time.

The inspector may require a layer of weather-resistant sheetrock between the roofing material and the sheathing. It's a good idea to check with the inspector before you begin.

Roof Application Methods

UBC Chapter 32 also covers the approved ways to apply the roofing materials. First, let's look at built-up roofing.

Built-up Roofing

Built-up roofing is appropriate only on flat or near-flat roofs — and flat roofs always bother me. Yes, the code allows them. But buildings settle in time, and materials don't always shrink evenly. That means the roof will eventually develop low spots that trap water unless the installation is first class. Let's look at the code requirements, which depend on whether the roof deck is nailable (such as wood) or non-nailable (such as metal)

On *nailable* roofs, nail the base sheet with at least one nail for each 1-1/2 square feet, using nails specified by the roofing material manufacturer. Then cement the following layers to the base sheets, using the specified type and amount of cementing material.

For a *non-nailable* roof, you must mop the base sheet with at least 20 pounds of hot asphalt per roofing square for solid roofing, or at least 30 pounds of coal tar pitch per roofing square.

On mineral-aggregate surfaced roofs, apply at least 50 pounds of hot asphalt or other cementing material per roofing square. Then embed at least 300 pounds of gravel or 250 pounds of crushed slag. Cement cap sheets to the base sheets with the same amount of cementing material used on other layers.

Hot asphalt must be between 375 degrees and 450 degrees F. Never heat it over 475 degrees F. Coal tar must be between 350 degrees and 400 degrees F.

Applying heat to asphalt can be like putting a match to a dynamite fuse: it's safe if it doesn't go too far. Heating the material beyond its *flash point* — the point at which it will ignite — creates a dangerous fire hazard. The flash point should be clearly printed on the label.

What Is a Roofing Square?

Roofing materials are sold by the *square*, the quantity needed to cover 100 square feet of roof surface when laid to the manufacturer's specs. It usually takes three bundles of composition shingles to cover one square.

Figure 12-2 shows how to determine roof coverage. To calculate the quantity of material needed, divide the roof area by 100. This gives the number of squares required to cover the roof. If there are many ridges and valleys, as much as 15 percent more material may be required.

Applying Composition Shingles

Apply composition shingles only to solidly sheathed roofs with a slope of more than 2 inches to 12 inches in temperate climates. Use only approved self-sealing shingles as indicated in UBC Table 32-B-1 (Figure 12-3).

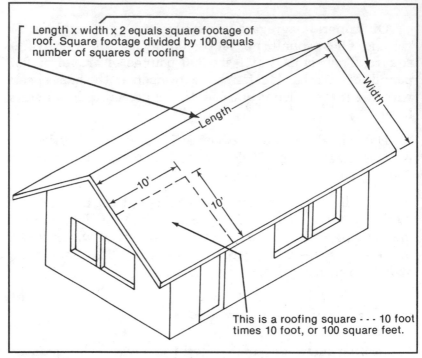

Length x width x 2 equals square footage of roof. Square footage divided by 100 equals number of squares of roofing

This is a roofing square - - - 10 foot times 10 foot, or 100 square feet.

Figure 12-2 *Calculating roof coverage*

Fasten composition shingles according to the manufacturer's instructions, using at least four nails for each strip shingle 36 to 40 inches wide and two nails for each shingle 9 to 18 inches wide. You must have an underlayment of at least two layers of 15-pound felt for a roof pitch of 7 inches to 12 inches. For a steeper roof, you can use just one layer of 15-pound felt.

Applying Wood Shingles or Shakes

You can apply wood shingles on a roof with either solid sheathing or spaced sheathing. For spaced sheathing on wood

TABLE NO. 32-B-1—SHINGLE APPLICATION

ROOF SLOPE	ASPHALT SHINGLES	
	NOT PERMITTED BELOW 2:12	
	2:12 to less than 4:12	4:12 and over
DECK REQUIREMENT	Asphalt shingles shall be fastened to solidly sheathed roofs. Sheathing shall conform to Sections 2516 (i) and 2517 (h) 7.	
UNDERLAYMENT Temperate climate	Asphalt strip shingles may be installed on slopes as low as 2 inches in 12 inches, provided the shingles are approved self-sealing or are hand-sealed and are installed with an underlayment consisting of two layers of nonperforated Type 15 felt applied shingle fashion. Starting with an 18-inch-wide sheet and a 36-inch-wide sheet over it at the eaves, each subsequent sheet shall be lapped 19 inches horizontally.	One layer nonperforated Type 15 felt lapped 2 inches horizontally and 4 inches vertically to shed water.
Severe climate: In areas subject to wind-driven snow or roof ice buildup.	Same as for temperate climate, and additionally the two layers shall be solid cemented together with approved cementing material between the plies extending from the eave up the roof to a line 24 inches inside the exterior wall line of the building.	Same as for temperate climate, except that one layer No. 40 coated roofing or coated glass base sheet shall be applied from the eaves to a line 12 inches inside the exterior wall line with all laps cemented together.

From the Uniform Building Code, © 1988, ICBO

Figure 12-3   Shingle application

ATTACHMENT Type of fasteners	Corrosion-resistant nails, minimum 12-gauge $^3/_8$-inch head, or approved corrosion-resistant staples, minimum 16-gauge $^{15}/_{16}$-inch crown width. Fasteners shall comply with the requirements of U.B.C. Standard No. 25-17. Fasteners shall be long enough to penetrate into the sheathing $^3/_4$ inch or through the thickness of the sheathing, whichever is less.
No. of fasteners[1]	4 per 36-40-inch strip 2 per 9-18-inch shingle
Exposure Field of roof Hips and ridges	Per manufacturer's instructions included with packages of shingles. Hip and ridge weather exposures shall not exceed those permitted for the field of the roof.
Method	Per manufacturer's instructions included with packages of shingles.
FLASHING Valleys Other flashing	Per Section 3208 (c) 1 A Per Section 3208 (c) 2

[1]Figures shown are for normal application. For special conditions such as mansard application and where roofs are in special wind regions, shingles shall be attached per manufacturer's instructions.

From the Uniform Building Code, © *1988, ICBO*

Figure 12-3 (cont'd) *Shingle application*

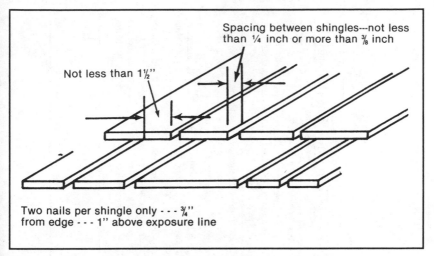

Figure 12-4   *Shingle laying diagram*

roofs, limit the spaces to 6 inches or the nominal width of the sheathing board, whichever is less. In any case, the sheathing board must be at least 1 x 4 nominal dimensions. Figure 12-4 shows the technique for laying and nailing wood shingle roofs.

Wood shingles vary from 3 inches to 14 inches wide and from 16 inches to 24 inches long. UBC Tables 25-R-1 and 25-R-2 (Figure 10-8 in Chapter 10) show sheathing sizes and spans. For laying wood shingles, refer to UBC Tables 32-B-1 and 32-B-2 (Figures 12-3 and 12-5). Table 32-C (Figure 12-6) shows the maximum exposure to the weather for each shingle length and roof slope. And don't forget you have to double the beginning course of shingles.

The requirements for shakes are similar, except that the spacing between shakes can't be less than 3/8 inch. Because most shakes are split instead of sawed, they don't always have straight edges. The code just requires them to be parallel

TABLE NO. 32-B-2—SHINGLE OR SHAKE APPLICATION

	WOOD SHINGLES	WOOD SHAKES
ROOF SLOPE	NOT PERMITTED BELOW 3:12 See Table No. 32-C	NOT PERMITTED BELOW 4:121 See Table No. 32-C
DECK REQUIREMENT	Shingles and shakes shall be applied to roofs with solid or spaced sheathing. Spaced sheathing for wood roofs shall be spaced not to exceed 6 inches clear nor more than the nominal width of the sheathing board. Sheathing boards shall be not less than 1 inch by 4 inches nominal dimensions. Sheathing shall conform to Sections 2516 (i) and 2517 (h) 7.	
UNDERLAYMENT Temperate climate	No Requirements	One 18-inch-wide interlayment of Type 30 felt shingled between each course in such a manner that no felt is exposed to the weather below the shake butts.
Severe climate: In areas subject to wind-driven snow or roof ice buildup.	Two layers of nonperforated Type 15 felt applied shingle fashion shall be installed and solid cemented together with approved cementing material between the plies extending from the eave up the roof to a line 36 inches inside the exterior wall line of the building.	Sheathing shall be solid and the shakes shall be applied over a layer of nonperforated Type 15 felt applied shingle fashion. Two layers of nonperforated Type 15 felt applied shingle fashion shall be installed and solid cemented together with approved cementing material between the plies extending from the eave up the roof to a line 36 inches inside the exterior wall line of the building.

From the Uniform Building Code, © 1988, ICBO

Figure 12-5 *Shingle or shake application*

ATTACHMENT Type of fasteners	Corrosion-resistant nails, minimum No. 14½-gauge 7/32-inch head, or corrosion-resistant staples, when approved by the building official.	Corrosion-resistant nails, minimum No. 13-gauge 7/32-inch head, or corrosion-resistant staples, when approved by the building official.
	Fasteners shall comply with the requirements of U.B.C. Standard No. 25-17. Fasteners shall be long enough to penetrate into the sheathing ¾ inch or through the thickness of the sheathing, whichever is less.	
No. of fasteners	2 per shingle	2 per shake
Exposure Field of roof	Weather exposures shall not exceed those set forth in Table No. 32-C.	
Hips and ridges	Hip and ridge weather exposures shall not exceed those permitted for the field of the roof.	
Method	Shingles shall be laid with a side lap of not less than 1½ inches between joints in adjacent courses, and not in direct alignment in alternate courses. Spacing between shingles shall be approximately ¼ inch. Each shingle shall be fastened with two nails only, positioned approximately ¾ inch from each edge and approximately 1 inch above the exposure line. Starter course at the eaves shall be doubled.	Shakes shall be laid with a side lap of not less than 1½ inches between joints in adjacent courses. Spacing between shakes shall be not less than 3/8 inch nor more than 5/8 inch except for preservative-treated wood shakes which shall have a spacing not less than ¼ inch nor more than 3/8 inch. Shakes shall be fastened to the sheathing with two nails only, positioned approximately 1 inch from each edge and approximately 2 inches above the exposure line. The starter course at the eaves shall be doubled. The bottom or first layer may be either shakes or shingles. Fifteen-inch or 18-inch shakes may be used for the starter course at the eaves and final course at the ridge.
FLASHING Valleys Other flashing	Per Section 3208 (c) 1 D Per Section 3208 (c) 2	

¹When approved by the building official, wood shakes may be installed on a slope of not less than 3 inches in 12 inches when an underlayment of not less than nonperforated Type 15 felt in installed.

From the Uniform Building Code, © 1988, ICBO

Figure 12-5 (cont'd) *Shingle or shake application*

TABLE NO. 32-C—MAXIMUM WEATHER EXPOSURE		
GRADE LENGTH	3" TO LESS THAN 4" IN 12" Inches	4" IN 12" AND STEEPER Inches
WOOD SHINGLES		
No. 1 16-inch	3³/₄	5
No. 2¹ 16-inch	3¹/₂	4
No. 3¹ 16-inch	3	3¹/₂
No. 1 18-inch	4¹/₄	5¹/₂
No. 2¹ 18-inch	4	4¹/₂
No. 3¹ 18-inch	3¹/₂	4
No. 1 24-inch	5³/₄	7¹/₂
No. 2¹ 24-inch	5¹/₂	6¹/₂
No. 3¹ 24-inch	5	5¹/₂
WOOD SHAKES²		
18-inch	7¹/₂	7¹/₂
24-inch	10	10

¹To be used only when specifically permitted by the building official.
²Exposure of 24-inch by ³/₈-inch resawn handsplit shakes shall not exceed 5 inches regardless of the roof slope.

From the Uniform Building Code, © 1988, ICBO

Figure 12-6 *Maximum weather exposure*

within 1 inch. Nail shakes within 1 inch of the edge of the shake and approximately 2 inches above the exposure line.

You have to double the beginning course of shakes, also, but the bottom course can be shingles. Shakes must have a layer of Type 30 felt between each course, with no felt exposed below the butts.

Snow is a special problem for shake roofs. In more severe climates, there are additional requirements, including solid sheathing and two layers of felt from the eave to 36 inches inside the exterior wall line. See UBC Table 32-B-2 (Figure 12-5).

Applying Tile Roofing

Tile roofs, either slate, ceramic or concrete, must be applied according to UBC Table 32-D-1 or 32-D-2 (Figure 12-7). The requirements are clear and straightforward.

Valley Flashing

Complex roofs, with many ridges and valleys, mean extra work — including the valley flashing. Flashing requirements for most roofs are about the same. It has to be underlaid with Type 15 felt, and the valley iron must be 28-gauge galvanized sheet metal. Application details are in Tables 32-B-1 and 32-B-2 (Figures 12-3 and 12-5) and Tables 32-D-1 and D-2 (Figure 12-7).

There are, however, some variations:

Wood shingles and shakes: Sections of flashing must overlap at least 4 inches and extend 8 inches from the centerline each way for shingles and 11 inches for shakes.

Asphalt shingles: Use metal flashing and either laced asphalt shingles or a 90-pound mineral cap sheet if they are cemented together. The bottom layer should be 12 inches wide and laid face down, the top layer 24 inches wide and laid face up.

Metal shingles: Extend metal flashing 8 inches from the centerline, with a splash diverter as part of the flashing. The splash diverter must be at least 3/4 inch high at the flow line.

Asbestos-cement shingles, slate shingles, clay and concrete tile: Extend metal flashing 11 inches from the centerline, with a splash diverter rib at the flow line at least 1 inch high formed as part of the flashing.

**TABLE NO. 32-D-1—ROOFING TILE APPLICATION[1]
FOR ALL TILES**

ROOF SLOPE	2½:12 to less than 3:12	3:12 and over
DECK REQUIREMENTS	Solid sheathing per Sections 2516 (i) and 2517 (h) 7	
UNDERLAYMENT In climate areas subject to wind-driven snow, roof ice damming or special wind regions as shown in Figure No. 4 of Chapter 23.	Built-up roofing membrane, three plies minimum, applied per Section 3208 (b) 4. Surfacing not required.	Same as for other climate areas, except that extending from the eaves up the roof to a line 24 inches inside the exterior wall line of the building, two layers of underlayment shall be applied shingle fashion and solidly cemented together with an approved cementing material.
Other climate areas		One layer heavy-duty felt or Type 30 felt side lapped 2 inches and end lapped 6 inches.
ATTACHMENT[2] Type of fasteners	Corrosion-resistant nails not less than No. 11 gauge, 5/16-inch head. Fasteners shall comply with the requirements of U.B.C. Standard No. 25-17. Fasteners shall be long enough to penetrate into the sheathing 3/4 inch or through the thickness of the sheathing, whichever is less. Attaching wire for clay or concrete tile shall not be smaller than No. 14-gauge, and shall comply with U.B.C. Standards Nos. 32-6 and 32-13.	
No. of fasteners[2,3]	One fastener per tile. Flat tile without vertical laps, two fasteners per tile.	Two fasteners per tile. Only one fastener on slopes of 7:12 and less for tiles with installed weight exceeding 7.5 pounds per square foot having a width no greater than 16 inches.[4]
Tile headlap	3 inches minimum	
FLASHING	Per Sections 3208 (c) 1 C and 3208 (c) 2	

[1]In snow areas a minimum of two fasteners per tile are required.
[2]In areas designated by the building official as being subject to repeated wind velocities to excess of 80 mph or where the roof height exceeds 40 feet above grade, all tiles shall be attached as follows:
(a) The heads of all tiles shall be nailed.

From the Uniform Building Code, © 1988, ICBO

Figure 12-7   Roofing tile application

FOOTNOTES FOR TABLE NO. 32-D-1—(Continued)

(b) The noses of all eave course tiles shall be fastened with approved clips.

(c) All rake tiles shall be nailed with two nails.

(d) The noses of all ridge, hip and rake tiles shall be set in a bead of approved roofer's mastic.

[3] In snow areas a minimum of two fasteners per tile are required, or battens and one fastener.

[4] On slopes over 24:12, the nose end of all tiles shall be securely fastened.

TABLE NO. 32-D-2—CLAY OR CONCRETE ROOFING TILE APPLICATION INTERLOCKING TILE WITH PROJECTING ANCHOR LUGS

ROOF SLOPE	4:12 and over
DECK REQUIREMENTS	Spaced structural sheathing boards or solid roof sheathing.
UNDERLAYMENT In climate areas subject to wind-driven snow, roof ice or special wind regions as shown in Figure No. 23-4.	Solid sheathing one layer of Type 30 felt lapped 2 inches horizontally and 6 inches vertically, except that extending from the eaves up the roof to line 24 inches inside the exterior wall line of the building, two layers of the underlayment shall be applied shingle fashion and solid cemented together with approved cementing material.
Other climates	For spaced sheathing, approved reinforced membrane. For solid sheathing, one layer heavy-duty felt or Type 30 felt lapped 2 inches horizontally and 6 inches vertically.
ATTACHMENT[1] Type of fasteners	Corrosion-resistant nails not less than No. 11 gauge, 5/16-inch head. Fasteners shall comply with the requirements of U.B.C. Standard No. 25-17. Fasteners shall be long enough to penetrate into the battens[2] or sheathing 3/4 inch or through the thickness of the sheathing, whichever is less. Attaching wire for clay or concrete tile shall not be smaller than 14 gauge and shall comply with U.B.C. Standards Nos. 32-6 and 32-13. Horizontal battens are required on solid sheathing for slopes 7:12 and over.[1] Horizontal battens are required for slopes over 7:12.[2]

From the Uniform Building Code, © 1988, ICBO

Figure 12-7 (cont'd) *Roofing tile application*

No. of fasteners[3]	Below 5:12, fasteners not required. 5:12 to less than 12:12, one fastener every other row. 12:12 to 24:12, one fastener every tile.[4] All perimeter tiles require one fastener.[5] Solid sheathing without battens, one fastener per tile required. Tiles with installed weight less than 9 pounds per square foot require a minimum of one fastener per tile.[3]
With battens	
Without battens	One fastener every tile.
Tile headlap	3-inch minimum
FLASHING	Per Section 3208 (c) 1 C and 3208 (c) 2

[1]In areas designated by the building official as being subject to repeated wind velocities to excess of 80 mph, or where the roof height exceeds 40 feet above grade, all tiles shall be attached as set forth below:
(a) The heads of all tiles shall be nailed.
(b) The noses of all eave course tiles shall be fastened with a special clip.
(c) All rake tiles shall be nailed with two nails.
(d) The noses of all ridge, hip and rake tiles shall be set in a bead of approved roofer's mastic.

[2]Battens shall be not less than 1-inch by 2-inch nominal. Provisions shall be made for drainage beneath battens by a minimum of 1/8-inch risers at each nail or by 4-foot long battens with at least 1/2-inch separation between battens. Battens shall be fastened with approved fasteners spaced at not more than 24 inches on center.

[3]In snow areas a minimum of two fasteners per tile are required, or battens and one fastener.

[4]Slopes over 24:12, nose ends of all tiles must be securely fastened.

[5]Perimeter fastening areas include three tile courses but not less than 36 inches from either side of hips or ridges and edges of eaves and gable rakes.

From the Uniform Building Code, © *1988, ICBO*

Figure 12-7 (cont'd) *Roofing tile application*

Attics

Any house with an attic that has more than 30 inches in vertical clear height (from the top of the joist to the underside of the rafter) must have an attic opening. This opening must be at least 22 inches by 30 inches, with at least 30 inches of clear headroom above the access opening. Section 3205 (a) describes the location this way:

> **Access.** *An attic access opening shall be provided in the ceiling of the top floor of buildings with combustible ceilings or roof construction. The opening shall be located in a corridor or hallway of buildings of three or more stories in height and readily accessible in buildings of any height.*

How would you define "readily accessible?" Many contractors put these openings in a closet to keep them out of sight. Is this readily accessible? The building inspector and the fire marshal probably wouldn't think so. But your choice may be limited where headroom is only 30 inches.

Roof Insulation, Draft Stops and Ventilation

Every roof needs insulation, either under or over the sheathing. In most houses, it's installed between the rafters where it doesn't interfere with the roofing. But when you use rigid insulation as a base for roof covering, there's a whole new set of rules. Section 3208 (d) covers it this way:

> **Roof Insulation.** *Roof insulation shall be of a rigid type suitable as a base for application of a roof covering. Foam plastic roof insulation shall conform to the requirements of Section 1712. The use of insulation in fire-restrictive construction shall comply with Section 4305 (a).*

The roof insulation, deck material and roof covering shall meet the fire retardancy requirements of Section 3204 and Table 32-A.

Insulation for built-up roofs shall be applied in accordance with Table No. 32-E. For other roofing materials such as shingles or tile, the insulation shall be covered with a suitable nailing base secured to the structure.

Figure 12-8 shows Tables 32-E, F, and G, which cover built-up roof application. You'll have to read and follow these sections carefully. Each step is critical. And there's also some room for interpretation. For instance, when do you need a vapor retarder over an insulated deck? When the average January temperature is under 45 degrees *or* you anticipate excessive moisture conditions inside the building. It's up to you and the building inspector to define "excessive moisture."

Draft Stops

Any enclosed attic with more than 3,000 square feet must be divided by partitions extending from the ceiling to the roof. The partitions must be at least 1/2-inch-thick gypsum wallboard, 1-inch nominal tight-fitting wood, or 3/8-inch-thick plywood. There are other materials you can use, if you check with the inspector first. If you have to install doors to provide access from one section of the attic to another, they must be self-closing and have the same fire resistance as the partition.

Ventilation

You can provide air through vents in the eaves or cornice, but these areas may be plugged if insulation is blown in. A blocking strip between the rafters prevents this and helps move the air over the insulation.

TABLE NO. 32-E—BUILT-UP ROOF COVERING APPLICATION

	MECHANICALLY FASTENED SYSTEMS	ADHESIVELY FASTENED SYSTEMS
DECK CONDITIONS	Decks shall be firm, broom-clean, smooth and dry. Insulated decks shall have wood insulation stops at all edges of the deck, unless an alternative suitable curbing is provided. Insulated decks with slopes greater than 2:12 shall have wood insulation stops at not more than 8-feet face-to-face. Wood nailers shall be provided where nailing is required for roofing plies.	
	Solid wood sheathing shall conform to Sections 2516 (i) and 2517 (h) 7.	Provide wood nailers where nailing is required for roofing plies (see below).
UNDERLAYMENT	One layer of sheathing paper, Type 15 felt or other approved underlayment nailed sufficiently to hold in place, is required over board decks where openings between boards would allow bitumen to drip through. No underlayment requirements for plywood decks. Underlayment on other decks shall be in accordance with deck manufacturer's recommendations.	Not required
BASE PLY REQUIREMENTS Over non-insulated decks	Over approved decks, the base ply shall be nailed using not less than one fastener for each 1 1/3 square feet.	Decks shall be primed in accordance with the roofing manufacturer's instructions. The base ply shall be solidly cemented or spot mopped as required by the type of deck material using adhesive application rates shown in Table No. 32-F.
MECHANICAL FASTENERS	Fasteners shall be long enough to penetrate 3/4 inch into the sheathing or through the thickness of the sheathing, whichever is less. Built-up roofing nails for wood board decks shall be minimum No. 12 gauge 7/16-inch head driven through tin caps or approved nails with integral caps. For plywood, No. 11 gauge ring-shank nails driven through tin caps or approved nails with integral caps shall be used. For gypsum, insulating concrete, cementitious wood-fiber and other decks, fasteners recommended by the manufacturer shall be used.	When mechanical fasteners are required for attachment of roofing plies to wood nailers or insulation stops, (see below), they shall be as required for wood board decks.

From the Uniform Building Code, © 1988, ICBO

Figure 12-8 Built-up roofing

VAPOR RETARDER Over insulated decks	A vapor retarder shall be installed where the average January temperature is below 45°F., or where excessive moisture conditions are anticipated within the building. It shall be applied as for a base ply.	
INSULATION	When no vapor retarder is required, roof insulation shall be fastened in an approved manner. When a vapor retarder is required, roof insulation is to be solidly mopped to the vapor retarder using the adhesive application rate specified in Table No. 32-F. See manufacturer's instructions for the attachment of insulation over steel decks.	When no vapor retarder is required, roof insulation shall be solid mopped to the deck using the adhesive application rate specified in Table No. 32-F. When a vapor retarder is required, roof insulation is to be solidly mopped to the vapor retarder, using the adhesive application rate specified in Table No. 32-F. See manufacturer's installation instructions for attachment of insulation over steel decks.
ROOFING PLIES	Successive layers shall be solidly cemented together and to the base ply or the insulation using the adhesive rates shown in Table No. 32-F. On slopes greater than 1:12 for aggregate-surfaced, or 2:12 for smooth-surfaced or cap sheet surfaced roofs, mechanical fasteners are required. Roofing plies shall be blind-nailed to the deck, wood nailers or wood insulation stops in accordance with the roofing manufacturer's recommendations. On slopes exceeding 3:12, plies shall be laid parallel to the slope of the deck (strapping method).	
CEMENTING MATERIALS	See Table No. 32-G	
CURBS AND WALLS	Suitable cant strips shall be used at all vertical intersections. Adequate attachment shall be provided for both base flashing and counterflashing on all vertical surfaces. Reglets shall be provided in wall or parapets receiving metal counterflashing.	
SURFACING	Mineral aggregate surfaced roofs shall comply with the requirements of U.B.C. Standard No. 32-5 and Table No. 32-F. Cap sheets shall be cemented to the roofing plies as set forth in Table No. 32-F.	

From the Uniform Building Code, © 1988, ICBO

Figure 12-8 (cont'd) *Built-up roofing*

TABLE NO. 32-F—BUILT-UP ROOFING
CEMENTING ADHESIVE AND SURFACING APPLICATION RATES

MATERIAL TO BE ADHERED	MINIMUM APPLICATION RATE, MATERIAL/100 FT.[2] ROOF AREA		
	HOT ASPHALT (Lbs.)	HOT COAL-TAR (Lbs.)	COLD-PROCESS CEMENT (Gal.)
Base Ply or Vapor Retarder			
1. Spot mopping	15	15	1
2. Solid cementing	20	20	1½
Insulation			
1. Solid cementing	20	20	1½
Roofing Plies (and between layers of vapor retarder)			
1. Felts	20	20	not permitted
2. Coated felts	20	20	1½
Cap Sheets			
1. Solid cementing	20	not permitted	1½
Mineral Aggregate[1] [2]			
1. Fire-retardant roof coverings			
(a) Gravel, 400 lb./sq.	50	60	not permitted
(b) Slag, 300 lb./sq.	50	60	not permitted
2. Nonrated roof coverings			
(a) Gravel, 300 lb./sq.	40	50	not permitted
(b) Slag, 250 lb./sq.	40	50	not permitted

[1]Mineral aggregate shall not be used for built-up roofing membranes at roof slopes greater than 3 inches in 12 inches.
[2]A minimum of 50 percent of the required aggregate shall be embedded in the pour coat.

From the Uniform Building Code, © 1988 ICBO

Figure 12-8 (cont'd) *Built-up roofing*

TABLE NO. 32-G—APPLICATION OF CEMENTING MATERIALS

APPLICATION	MAXIMUM SLOPE, INCHES PER 12 INCHES				
	ASPHALT TYPE				COAL-TAR PITCH
	TYPE I	TYPE II	TYPE III	TYPE IV	
Insulation to deck	—	—	All	All	—
Felt or vapor retarder to deck	—	1/2 or less	3 or less	All	1/2 or less
Felt to felt	—	1/2 or less	1/2-3	All	1/2 or less
Cap sheet to felt	—	—	3 or less	All	—
Gravel to felts	1/2 or less	1/2 or less	1/2-3	N.P.	1/2 or less
Heating of Cementing Mat'l,[1] °F:					
Temperature at kettle[2] (maximum)	475	525	525	525	425
Application temperature,[3] °F.	375-425	375-425	375-425	400-450	350-400

N.P. = Not permitted

[1]Bulk tanker temperatures shall be reduced to 320-350°F. at night or during periods when no roofing will occur.

[2]Cementing material shall not be heated above a temperature which is 25°F. below its flash point.

[3]Asphalt which is identified with the equiviscous temperature (EVT) shall be applied at the EVT ± 25°F.

From the Uniform Building Code, © 1988, ICBO

Figure 12-8 (cont'd)   *Built-up roofing*

The formula for venting area is simple: Vent area should be 1/150 of the horizontal roof area. If your attic area is 1,200 square feet, for example, you need 8 square feet of attic ventilation (1,200 divided by 150 is 8). At least 50 percent of this must come from the highest point of your attic — along the ridge, for instance. The rest can come from screened "bird holes" along the eaves.

There's an exception, as usual. If you locate all of the attic ventilators at least 3 feet above the eaves or cornice area, you can reduce the free ventilating area to 1/300. So that 1,200 square foot attic would only need 4 square feet of vent area. Cover all openings with corrosion-resistant metal mesh with 1/4-inch openings.

In some occupancies, you also have to provide smoke and heat ventilation. These occupancies are single-story Group B, Division 2 and 4 occupancies (mercantile group) with more than 50,000 square feet of undivided area, and Group H occupancies (hotels and apartments) with over 15,000 square feet on a single floor.

You can vent these occupancies with open or openable skylights or windows that open directly to the exterior. Because this ventilation is so important, the code goes into considerable detail about how many vents are required and where they should go. Still, it's a good idea to contact your local inspector and fire marshal for advice before beginning construction.

Roof Drainage

If a roof isn't designed to support accumulated water, it has to be sloped for drainage. Here are a few guidelines:

Figure 12-9   *Roof drain on built-up roof*

- Install roof drains at the lowest point on the roof.

- Roof drains must be capable of handling the water flowing to them.

- In most areas, a roof drain may not drain into the sanitary sewer.

- In many areas, roof drainage water can't flow over public property or into adjacent property.

- Concealed roof drainage must conform to the plumbing code.

Figure 12-9 shows a roof drain on a built-up roof. The grated cover is a leaf strainer. Place the drains so that they drain the water from the roof as quickly as possible.

Chimneys and Fireplaces

Not every house needs a chimney, of course. But if there is a chimney, it has to meet code requirements. Chapter 37 of the UBC lists four classes of chimneys:

Residential Appliance-type, a factory built or masonry chimney suitable for removing products of combustion from residential-type appliances producing combustion gases not in excess of 1000 degrees F measured at the appliance flue outlet.

Low-heat Industrial Appliance-type, is a factory built, masonry or metal chimney suitable for removing the products of combustion from fuel burning low-heat appliances producing combustion gases not in excess of 1000 degrees under normal operating conditions but capable of producing combustion gases of 1400 degrees F during intermittent forced firing for periods up to one hour. All temperatures are measured at the appliance flue outlet.

Medium-heat Industrial Appliance-type, is a factory-built, masonry or metal chimney suitable for removing the products of combustion from fuel-burning medium-heat appliances producing combustion gases not in excess of 2000 degrees F measured at the appliance flue outlet.

High-heat Industrial Appliance-type, is a factory-built masonry or metal chimney suitable for removing the products of combustion from fuel-burning high-heat appliances producing combustion gases in excess of 2000 degrees F measured at the appliance flue outlet.

Residential and low-heat chimneys are about the same. The only important difference is that residential chimneys may have walls 4 inches thick and a flue liner, while low-heat chimneys require 8-inch-thick walls and a flue liner. The liner in both cases must extend from a point 8 inches below the lowest inlet to a point above the enclosing walls. UBC Tables

TABLE NO. 37-A—MINIMUM PASSAGEWAY AREAS FOR MASONRY CHIMNEYS[1]			
	MINIMUM CROSS-SECTIONAL AREA		
TYPE OF MASONRY CHIMNEY	TILE LINED		LINED WITH FIREBRICK OR UNLINED
	ROUND	SQUARE OR RECTANGLE	
1. Residential	50 sq. in.	50 sq. in.	85 sq. in.
2. Fireplace[2]	$1/12$ of opening Minimum 50 sq. in.	$1/10$ of opening Minimum 64 sq. in.	$1/8$ of opening Minimum 100 sq. in.
3. Low heat	50 sq. in.	57 sq. in.	135 sq. in.
4. Incinerator Apartment type 1 opening 2 to 6 openings 7 to 14 openings 15 or more openings	196 sq. in. 324 sq. in. 484 sq. in. 484 sq. in. plus 10 sq. in. for each additional opening		Not applicable

[1]Areas for medium- and high-heat chimneys shall be determined using accepted engineering methods and as approved by the building official.

[2]Where fireplaces open on more than one side, the fireplace opening shall be measured along the greatest dimension.

Note: For altitudes over 2000 feet above sea level, the building official shall be consulted in determining the area of the passageway.

From the Uniform Building Code, © 1988, ICBO

Figure 12-10 *Passageway areas for masonry chimneys*

37-A and 37-B (Figures 12-10 and 12-11) give dimensions and construction details for most chimneys.

Every chimney must rise from its own foundation, which must be on solid ground, to a point at least 2 feet higher than any point of a building within 10 feet horizontally. Bracket flues are not permitted. A chimney can't support any portion of the building unless it was specifically designed as a supporting member.

TABLE NO. 37-B—CONSTRUCTION, CLEARANCE AND TERMINATION REQUIREMENTS FOR MASONRY AND CONCRETE CHIMNEYS

Chimneys Serving	Thickness (Min. Inches)		Height Above Roof Opening (Feet)	Height Above any Part of Building within (Feet)			Clearance to Combustible Construction (Inches)	
	Walls	Lining		10	25	50	Int. Inst.	Ext. Inst.
1. RESIDENTIAL-TYPE APPLIANCES[1] [2] (Low Btu Input)								
Clay, Shale or Concrete Brick	4[3]	5/8 fire-clay tile or 2 fire-brick	2	2			2	1 or ½ gypsum[4]
Reinforced Concrete	4[3]							
Hollow Masonry Units	4[8]							
Stone	12							
Unburned Clay Units	8	4½ fire-brick						
2. BUILDING HEATING AND INDUSTRIAL-TYPE LOW-HEAT APPLIANCES[1] [2] (1000°F. operating temp.—1400°F. Maximum)								
Clay, Shale or Concrete Brick	8	5/8 fire-clay tile or 2 fire-brick	3	2			2	2
Hollow Masonry Units	8[8]							
Reinforced Concrete	8							
Stone	12							

From the Uniform Building Code, © 1988, ICBO

Figure 12-11 *Requirements for masonry and concrete chimneys*

No.	Type	Wall thickness (in.)	Lining				
3.	MEDIUM–HEAT INDUSTRIAL–TYPE APPLIANCES[1] [5] (2000°F. Maximum) Clay, Shale or Concrete Brick — 8 Hollow Masonry Units (Grouted Solid) — 8 Reinforced Concrete — 8 Stone — 12		4½ Medium duty fire-brick	10	10	4	4
4.	HIGH–HEAT INDUSTRIAL–TYPE APPLIANCES[1] [2] (Over 2000°F.) Clay, Shale or Concrete Brick — 16[6] Hollow Masonry Units (Grouted Solid) — 16[6] Reinforced Concrete — 16[6]		4½ High duty fire-brick	20	20	7	7
5.	RESIDENTIAL TYPE INCINERATORS		Same as for Residential-Type Appliances as shown above				
6.	CHUTE-FED AND FLUE-FED INCINERATORS WITH COMBINED HEARTH AND GRATE AREA 7 SQ. FT. OR LESS Clay, Shale or Concrete Brick or Hollow Units Portion extending to 10 ft. above combustion chamber roof — 4 Portion more than 10 ft. above combustion chamber roof — 8		4½ Medium duty fire-brick 5/8 fire-clay tile liner	3	2	2	2

From the Uniform Building Code, © 1988, ICBO

Figure 12-11 (cont'd) *Requirements for masonry and concrete chimneys*

TABLE NO. 37-B—CONSTRUCTION, CLEARANCE AND TERMINATION REQUIREMENTS FOR MASONRY AND CONCRETE CHIMNEYS—(Continued)

Chimneys Serving	Thickness (Min. Inches)		Height Above Roof Opening (Feet)	Height Above any Part of Building within (Feet)			Clearance to Combustible Construction (Inches)	
	Walls	Lining		10	25	50	Int. Inst.	Ext. Inst.
7. CHUTE-FED AND FLUE-FED INCINERATORS — COMBINED HEARTH AND GRATE AREAS LARGER THAN 7 SQ. FT. Clay, Shale or Concrete Brick or Hollow Units Grouted Solid or Reinforced Concrete Portion extending to 40 ft. above combustion chamber roof Portion more than 40 ft. above combustion chamber roof Reinforced Concrete	4 8 8	4½ Medium duty fire-brick 5/8 fire-clay tile liner 4½ Medium duty fire-brick 4½ Medium duty fire-brick laid in medium duty refract mortar		10			2	2
8. COMMERCIAL OR INDUSTRIAL-TYPE INCINERATORS[2] Clay or Shale Solid Brick Reinforced Concrete	8 8	4½ Medium duty fire-brick laid in medium duty refract mortar		10			4	4

From the Uniform Building Code, © 1988, ICBO

Figure 12-11 (cont'd) *Requirements for masonry and concrete chimneys*

[1]See Table No. 9-A of the Mechanical Code for types of appliances to be used with each type of chimney.

[2]Lining shall extend from bottom to top of chimney.

[3]Chimneys having walls 8 inches or more in thickness may be unlined.

[4]Chimneys for residential-type appliances installed entirely on the exterior of the building. For fireplace and barbecue chimneys, see Section 3707 (h).

[5]Lining to extend from 24 inches below connector to 25 feet above.

[6]Two 8-inch walls with 2-inch air space between walls. Outer and inner walls may be of solid masonry units or reinforced concrete or any combination thereof.

[7]Clearance shall be approved by the building official and shall be such that the temperature of combustible materials will not exceed 160°F.

[8]Equivalent thickness including grouted cells when grouted solid. The equivalent thickness may also include the grout thickness between the liner and masonry unit.

From the Uniform Building Code, © 1988, ICBO

Figure 12-11 (cont'd) *Requirements for masonry and concrete chimneys*

Construction Standards

The area of the chimney passageway must be at least as large as the vent connection. Figure 12-11 shows the minimum passageway areas. Note that these are cross-section dimensions made after the flue liner is installed.

You can omit the liner on residential chimneys that have at least 8-inch solid masonry walls. Does that mean you can use any old concrete block? No, you can't. You still have to follow UBC Table 37-B (Figure 12-11), which shows the wall thickness you need for each type of masonry unit.

Smoke doesn't go straight up a chimney, it spirals up. This is why a round chimney is the ideal shape. A square flue is also good, since only the corners are dead space. A long, narrow, rectangular flue needs more area to get the same results. It's a good idea to consider Section 3703(b) when designing a chimney:

> *(b) Construction. Each chimney shall be so constructed as to safely convey flue gases not exceeding the maximum temperatures for the type of construction as set forth in UBC Table No. 37-B and shall be capable of producing a draft at the appliance not less than that required for safe operation.*

That's what it all boils down to. If it doesn't work, you've wasted a lot of time.

Fireplaces

Many "zero clearance" factory-built metal fireplace inserts are now available. These are pre-fabricated fireplaces and can be set directly in wood framing. They must have the ICBO stamp of approval and must be installed exactly as the manufacturer specifies. It's too early to say if they'll prove to be as durable as masonry fireplaces, but they should last a long time. And they have the advantage of being much cheaper to install than a standard masonry fireplace.

If you're installing a masonry fireplace, there are a number of things to consider. First, the depth of the firebox may not be less than 20 inches. The width of the opening isn't too important, but don't make the height of the opening higher than the size of the fire contemplated. A small fire in a large, high firebox is usually a smokey fire.

The shape of the back and sides of the firebox determines how well it will reflect heat into a room. The shapes of the smoke chamber, throat and smoke shelf are also important. The damper, when fully opened, can't restrict the flue beyond the dimensions shown in UBC Table 37-A (Figure 12-10). The damper blade, when fully opened, can't extend past the line of the inside of the flue.

Hearths— The hearth of a masonry fireplace must be at least 4-inch thick brick, concrete, stone or other approved noncombustible slab. It has to be supported by noncombustible materials or reinforced to carry its own weight and whatever loads it will carry. Make sure the hearth extends at least 16 inches in the front and at least 8 inches beyond the sides of the opening. If your hearth opening exceeds 6 square feet, the hearth has to be bigger. Then the hearth needs to extend 20 inches in the front and 12 inches on the sides.

Hearth extensions for factory-built fireplaces or fireplace stoves are a little different. These must conform to the manufacturer's installation instructions.

Metal damper hoods— Most masonry fireplaces have metal damper hoods. These hoods usually come complete with smoke shelf, damper, and a properly-sized flue outlet. According to the code, they must be made of 19-gauge corrosion-resistant metal (copper, galvanized steel or other equivalent ferrous metal). All seams must be smokeproof and unsoldered.

Hoods must be sloped 45 degrees or less and extend horizontally at least 6 inches beyond the front of the firebox. Don't install the hood closer than 18 inches to any combustible material unless its design is approved for that.

Line the top side of the hood with several inches of fiberglass to keep from losing heat into the chimney cavity. And always mortar the hood in place. This wasn't always done in the past. It was common practice to just stuff the space with fiberglass. But fiberglass, although noncombustible, can melt, leaving room for flame to enter the chimney cavity. Since that's a fire danger, all hoods must now be mortared in.

You can't place combustible material within 2 inches of a firebox, smoke chamber or chimney wall, or within 12 inches of the fireplace opening.

I'll talk more about fireplaces in Chapter 16, Combustion Air.

Fireplaces Are for Friendly Fires

Fireplaces have been warming humans for thousands of years. And they've been causing accidental fires for at least as long. Most of these fires are preventable. Building inspectors don't have much control over the way fireplaces are used. The best I can do is make sure that a fireplace used correctly will give safe, reliable service for many years. That's what I try to do.

Before building codes were written, fireplaces were built of nearly every kind of material imaginable. That doesn't happen any more. But even so, it takes real skill and craftsmanship to build a fireplace out of masonry, mortar and reinforcing alone. Not every mason can build a good fireplace. Even fewer designers can draw plans for a good fireplace. Most don't even try any more. Modern fireplace materials have greatly simplified fireplace construction. The first major improvement was the metal hood that contained the smoke shelf, damper and beginning of the flue. These hoods made it unnecessary to construct a smoke shelf. The second major improvement was the "zero clearance" all-metal fireplace. The third was the double-walled metal flue.

Modern materials make it easy to inspect a fireplace. I have to make sure that all masonry was either separated from wood framing or that the masonry was thick enough so that the wood framing won't ignite when the fireplace gets as hot as it's going to get. Metal hoods have to be properly sealed into the masonry. That isn't always easy to determine after a fireplace is built.

The area where the hood and the front of the fireplace meet always seems to cause trouble. All too often I found this area filled with fiberglass. Now we all know that fiberglass is fire-proof, right? True, fiberglass won't burn, but it can melt, letting fire and smoke escape. It took a long time to educate some builders about this. Filler between the hood and the front of the fireplace *has to be masonry.*

But even when filled correctly, modern fireplaces aren't foolproof. For example, one day I went to inspect a fireplace on a small job. It looked great. I even complimented the mason on the design. Then out of the corner of my eye I saw a slight movement in the corner of the firebox. I looked again. Sure enough, it moved. In fact, it winked. I've inspected a lot of fireplaces. But this is the first that ever winked at me. In a moment the eye was gone. I stuck my pencil through the hole. Someone grabbed my pencil and pulled it through!

There was actually a hole through the back of the fireplace into the adjoining garage. I wondered if a winking fireplace would be safe. Probably not. The mason had some more work to do.

13

Fire Safety

Despite the heroic efforts of fire fighters, people are going to die in fires. No building is entirely fire safe; some can even be called fire traps. And even in safe buildings, the occupants can make the building dangerous by misusing flammable materials. It's impossible to prevent all fires.

The best the code can do is reduce the risk to life and property from fires that do break out. It does that by requiring contractors and designers to build fire safety into every construction project. Of course, fire safety comes at a price. Fire safe buildings always cost more. But they shouldn't cost too much more. At least, that's the goal of the code.

Fire Detection and Control Systems

Many types of fire detection and control systems are available. They include simple residential smoke detectors, multiple interconnected smoke detectors placed throughout a building, automatic sprinklers, and wet and dry standpipes. Some businesses even have their own fire suppression teams.

Of course, no system is 100 percent effective. Smoke detectors or alarms detect smoke and signal the occupants. But unless they also signal a fire station, these devices can't put out a fire. They're almost useless where the occupants are severely disabled or incapacitated.

Automatic sprinklers have heat sensors that trigger the system in action. To be truly effective they should be wired to a fire station. But automatic sprinklers are subject to false alarms and can cause a great deal of water damage. It may be a toss-up which costs more to repair, the fire damage or the water damage.

Standpipes provide a source of water for fighting a fire. But they can't put one out on their own. In-house fire-suppression teams, while effective if properly trained, are expensive to maintain.

These are just some of the considerations when you're thinking about a fire detection and control system. There are many others. If your smoke detectors are electrically operated, what will happen if the power source is cut off? Will the battery back-up operate the system? What would happen to your automatic sprinklers if a fire broke out while the city had shut off the water to repair a line? Are back-up systems available?

Automatic Sprinkler Systems

The code doesn't require fire sprinklers in Group R-3 (single-family residential) and Group M (miscellaneous and agricultural) occupancies. But other occupancies (with a few exceptions) must have automatic sprinklers. According to Chapter 38 of the UBC, a building of 1,500 square feet or more will need an automatic sprinkler system. First, let's take a look at the code's general requirements.

Section 3802(b) states that automatic sprinkler systems must be installed:

> *. . . in every story or basement of all buildings when the floor area exceeds 1,500 square feet and there is not provided at least 20 square feet of opening entirely above the adjoining ground level in each 50 lineal feet or fraction thereof of exterior wall in the story or basement on at least one side of the building. Openings shall have a minimum dimension of not less than 30 inches. Such openings shall be accessible to the fire department from the exterior and shall not be obstructed in a manner that fire fighting or rescue cannot be accomplished from the exterior.*

When openings in a story are provided on only one side and the opposite wall of such story is more than 75 feet from such openings, the story shall be provided with an approved automatic sprinkler system, or openings as specified above shall be provided on at least two sides of an exterior wall of the story.

If any portion of a basement is located more than 75 feet from openings required in this section, the basement shall be provided with an approved automatic sprinkler system.

It goes on to define specific areas where sprinklers are required and offer some exceptions. For instance, in buildings where temperatures can be expected to drop below zero, you need a dry fire sprinkler system. Otherwise you'll probably have frozen pipes in cold weather. A dry system doesn't have water in the distribution pipes until water is needed. Flow to the sprinkler heads is controlled by a fusible link that melts if it gets too hot. That opens a pressure-controlled switch which floods the pipes, delivering water to the head where it's needed.

Sometimes antifreeze can be used in cold areas to prime the lines, as set forth in the UBC Standards. But this always needs to be done carefully. Spraying antifreeze could do more damage than the fire it's supposed to put out.

Sprinklers are intended to knock down the fire before it gets started and give the occupants time to get out. That's why the need for sprinklers decreases as the occupancy load decreases. In most cases, automatic sprinklers are all that's needed to put out the fire. The fire's usually out before fire fighters arrive. But what about a flash fire (like an explosion) or a smoldering fire that doesn't create enough heat to set off sprinklers but fills the room with deadly fumes?

In a the flash fire, sprinklers work — but do they work in time? Refer to your type of occupancy and area separations to keep the high-danger areas remote from the areas of high human loads.

In certain occupancies smoke detectors are required in addition to the automatic sprinklers because of the possibility of smoldering fires. In some cases they must be photo-eye controlled. All Group R-3 occupancies are now required to have small detectors next to sleeping areas.

Sprinklers aren't the only fire suppression system, but they're usually the least expensive. There are also many chemical systems on the market. Requirements vary. So check with your inspector to see what's allowed in your area.

Automatic Sprinklers for
Special Circumstances

There are some areas where sprinklers can be reduced or omitted completely — like a communication center or a power house. Can you imagine what would happen if a sprinkler system went off over a bank of telephone relays? But that doesn't mean that fire alarms or controls aren't required.

Section 3804.2 defines some permissible omissions:

> *Sprinklers shall not be installed when the application of water or flame and water to the contents may constitute a serious life or fire hazard, as in the manufacture or storage of quantities of aluminum powder, calcium carbide, calcium phosphide, metallic sodium and potassium, quicklime, magnesium powder and sodium peroxide.*

The UBC has a section that covers areas where people are drinking. Section 3802(c) states:

> **Group A Occupancies.** *1. Drinking establishments. An automatic sprinkler system shall be installed in rooms used by the occupants for the consumption of alcoholic beverages and unseparated accessory uses where the total area of such unseparated rooms and assembly uses exceeds 5,000 square feet. For uses to be considered as separated, the separation shall be not less than as required for a one-hour occupancy separation. The area of other uses shall be included unless separated by at least a one-hour occupancy separation.*

Standpipes

Not many homes have standpipes for connecting fire hoses. But most large apartment and office buildings do. UBC Table 38-A (Figure 13-1) defines the types and locations of standpipes. Section 3801(c) tells you what they are and how they're used:

TABLE NO. 38-A—STANDPIPE REQUIREMENTS

OCCUPANCY	NONSPRINKLERED BUILDING[1]		SPRINKLERED BUILDING[2] [3]	
	Standpipe Class	Hose Requirement	Standpipe Class	Hose Requirement
1. Occupancies exceeding 150 ft. in height and more than one story	III	Yes	I	No
2. Occupancies 4 stories or more but less than 150 ft. in height, except Group R, Div. 3	[I and II[4]] (or III)	[5] Yes	I	No
3. Group A Occupancies with occupant load exceeding 1000[6]	II	Yes	No requirement	No
4. Group A, Div. 2.1 Occupancies over 5000 square feet in area used for exhibition	II	Yes	II	Yes
5. Groups I, H, B, Div. 1, 2 or 3 Occupancies less than 4 stories in height but greater than 20,000 square feet per floor	II[4]	Yes	No requirement	No

[1]Except as otherwise specified in Item No. 4 of this table, Class II standpipes need not be provided in basements having an automatic fire-extinguishing system throughout.

[2]Combined systems with their related water supplies may be used in sprinklered buildings.

[3]Portions of otherwise sprinklered buildings which are not protected by automatic sprinklers shall have Class II standpipes installed as required for the unsprinklered portions.

[4]In open structures where Class II standpipes may be damaged by freezing, the building official may authorize the use of Class I standpipes which are located as required for Class II standpipes.

[5]Hose is required for Class II standpipes only.

[6]Class II standpipes need not be provided in assembly areas used solely for worship.

From the Uniform Building Code, © *1988, ICBO*

Figure 13-1 *Standpipe requirements*

Standpipe System is a wet or dry system of piping, valves, outlets, and related equipment designed to provide water at specified pressures and installed exclusively for the fighting of fires including the following:

Class I is a standpipe system equipped with 2-1/2-inch outlets.

Class II is a wet standpipe system directly connected to a water supply and equipped with 1-1/2-inch outlets and hose.

Figure 13-2 *Typical standpipe location*

> *Class III is a standpipe system directly connected to a water supply and equipped with 2-1/2-inch outlets or 2-1/2-inch and 1-1/2-inch outlets when a 1-1/2-inch hose is required. Hose connections for Class III systems may be made through 2-1/2-inch hose valves with easily removable 2-1/2-inch by 1-1/2-inch reducers.*

It's one thing to know what standpipes are — and another to know how to place them. UBC Table 38-A will help you with that. Figure 13-2 shows a typical standpipe location.

According to the UBC, every building with six stories or more must have at least one Class I standpipe for use during construction. This standpipe must be in place before the building is more than 50 feet above grade. If the standpipe isn't connected to a water main, there must be accessible locations for fire department inlet connections.

There's one problem with standpipes. Occupants sometimes try to use them to extinguish a fire before calling the fire department. That's foolish. The first few moments of a fire are critical. In any fire, the best thing to do is call the fire department — then do as much as you can.

Of course it's different if your building or company is organized to fight fire — and many industrial plants are. In that case, it makes sense to call the local department only if they're really needed.

Fire Safety Includes Construction and Exits

The primary goal of any fire control or fire safety system is to save lives. The secondary goal is to reduce property damage. Almost all structural materials and building components will either burn or melt. A fire-resistive structure can delay progress of the fire long enough for the occupants to get out and for the fire crews and equipment to arrive.

That's why the building code covers construction *and* exits. All exits must be designed to get people outdoors to safety by the quickest and most direct route. The code doesn't assume that all occupants know where exits are or that they know what to do in an emergency. Buildings should be designed so people can get out easily and quickly. Chapter 11 covers exits in detail.

Exit Size

According to Chapter 33 of the UBC, a required exit must be at least 3'0" by 6'8". That figures out to be 20 square feet for a standard exit doorway.

It's not always simple to find the "minimum dimension" of other openings above ground level, however. Section 3802(b) states that *Such openings shall have a minimum dimension of not less than 30 inches.* However, going back to Section 1204 we find that:

> *All escape or rescue windows from sleeping rooms shall have a minimum net clear opening of 5.7 square feet. The minimum net clear opening height dimension shall be 24 inches. The minimum net clear opening width dimension shall be 20 inches. When windows are provided as a means of escape or rescue they shall have a finished sill height not more than 44 inches above the floor.*

Why the difference? Maybe we're comparing apples and oranges. Section 1204 refers to sleeping rooms in any kind of structure, whether sprinklered or not. Section 3802(b) applies to all openings in all types of buildings with automatic sprinklers.

Will the Opening Be Large Enough?

When a fireman puts a ladder up to a window, the ladder must fit into the window far enough so it can't slip sideways. The average fire ladder is between 16 and 20 inches wide, so it'll fit easily into the 30-inch opening.

Let's say that the window is 44 inches above the floor, the maximum allowable distance. A healthy, able-bodied person shouldn't have too much trouble getting out the window and onto the ladder. But suppose there are four people in the room. One is the fire fighter with a bulky air pack on his back. The others are a pregnant woman, a woman who's obese and in poor health, and an elderly man riddled with arthritis. Will they all be able to escape? It makes you wonder, doesn't it? Maybe you should make those windows a little larger and lower.

What Should Be Done?

Here's how one wag defined a really safe building: It's made of reinforced concrete, has no doors or windows, is completely sprinklered, has smoke detectors, has nothing stored in it, and has no occupants. Now of course that would be a safe building, but it sure wouldn't be very economical or practical. We have to balance economy, practicality, and fire safety.

City officials, primarily the fire marshal and the building official, must take a good look at their city and ask themselves some questions:

- Does the city have enough water to make fire sprinklers effective in case of a major catastrophe?

- Does the city have a fire and police communication system that can handle all the calls likely if there's a real emergency.

- Has the city experienced many fires over the years?

- How many lives have been lost in the last three years due to fire? How many lives is that per 100,000 residents?

- Will more stringent rules reduce this figure?

- Will savings in lives and property be worth the cost?

- Are most of the buildings in town relatively new? If so, they may be fairly fire resistant.

Fire extinguishing systems are expensive. To be effective they must be installed properly. And there's another big problem. If you're building anything except a residential building, you can't be sure of what it will be used for a few years from now. The system installed today may be inadequate in ten years.

Let's say your building is a borderline size, according to the code, with a low-hazard occupancy. Should you install sprinklers now or wait until the occupancy needs of the building require it?

Automatic sprinkler systems usually pay for themselves in from 5 to 10 years. Insurance rates are much lower on sprinklered buildings. In fact, savings on insurance during the first *seven* years will usually pay for most fire protection systems. Still, many owners don't want to install fire sprinklers. Spec builders trying to make as much as possible on the smallest possible investment will usually try to avoid installing sprinklers. But someone is going to use those buildings and the code is written to protect those that do.

There's a limit to what the building code can do. The best fire suppression system isn't nearly as good as fire prevention. Good construction, clean working areas, reduced fire hazards and informed occupants are your best bet to control fire danger.

Treehouses Are Buildings, Too

Most building codes require a permit for nearly any type of structure. The Uniform Building Code defines *structure* as any two or more parts designed to act as a whole. That means nearly anything you can throw a hammer at needs a permit.

I live in a part of Washington where nearly every kid needs (and probably has) at least one treehouse. Construction of treehouses in Kennewick is a pretty serious business. And it isn't just the kids that get involved. Moms and Dads usually help with design and purchase of materials, and sometimes with construction.

Some of these tree houses are works of art, something to be proud of. But some considered them eyesores and wanted them removed. I'll admit that in the winter, when many trees are bare, they were very noticeable. But in the summer they were usually hidden within the leaves of the host tree.

Well, eventually the city got enough complaints about tree houses that the city fathers had to take official notice. They asked me to research the code and come up with a proposal. I took the police chief and the fire chief into my confidence. We began a tour of the town treehouses, talking to kids and parents and their neighbors.

We found not one tree house that was built with a permit. Some had electrical power from extension cords run up from the house below. Several even had small heaters in them.

After making our survey, the three of us drafted an exception to the code. Treehouses would be legal as long as they didn't exceed 36 square feet of floor, had no artificial lights except flashlights, and were built in trees behind the setback line of the house. That kept them out of the front yards.

The city council took our suggested ordinance, held the necessary public hearings (at which no one showed up) and duly enacted our draft into law. It didn't cause much of a stir in the town but it did make the national press. I heard from places all around the country about my "treehouse ordinance."

And to think it all started in Kennewick.

14

Skylights, Glass and Miscellaneous Components

E very building has at least a few small construction items that make it unique. Some buildings have major custom-designed items that add substantially to the cost. This chapter is a catch-all. We'll look at some of these miscellaneous components, and begin with skylights.

Skylights

Skylights are covered in two different chapters of the UBC. Chapter 34 covers glass skylights; Chapter 52 looks at plastic skylights.

Glass Skylights

UBC Chapter 34 covers glass skylights and was completely rewritten for the 1988 edition. In the first edition of this book, I said "Any discussion of glass in skylights is probably wasted because I haven't seen anything but plastic used in skylights for a long time." Readers let me know that glass skylights were alive and well — so here we go.

The code says all glass in skylights must be wired, laminated or tempered glass at least 7/32 inch thick. If you use heat-strengthened and fully-tempered glass in a single-layer glazing system, you have to include protective screens below the glazing and within 4 inches of it. The screens must be of noncombustible material with a mesh not larger than 1 inch by 1 inch. But watch the exceptions.

Plastic Skylights

Preformed skylights are almost entirely Plexiglass or similar plastic. But how would you classify the corrugated plastic panels used in most modern metal buildings? Would you consider those translucent panels a form of skylight? The code does. It covers them in Section 5206.

In all buildings except Types III, IV and V, you have to build all skylight frames of noncombustible materials. All skylights have to be able to carry any roof load that's channeled to it. Skylights set at an angle of less than 45 degrees must be mounted at least 4 inches above the plane of the roof on a suitable curb. Figure 14-1 shows a 4-inch curb. Even where it's not required, curbing is a good idea on any skylight. It's neater and more leak-resistant. But if your roof pitch is 3 in 12 or greater, a curbing isn't required if you use a self-flashing skylight.

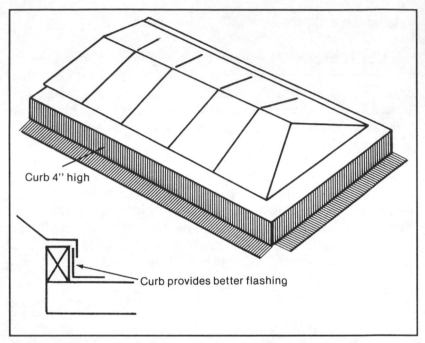

Curb 4" high

Curb provides better flashing

Figure 14-1   *Construction of a glass skylight*

There's one more item to consider: You can't install plastic roof material in any area of the roof where openings in exterior walls are prohibited as shown in Table 5-A of the UBC.

Other Glass Applications

Greenhouses

Chapter 34 also governs the construction of greenhouses. But the code says surprisingly little about greenhouses, probably because the normal occupant load is so low. A height of

20 feet above the grade at the ridge is the dividing line for several regulations. Up to 20 feet, you can use ordinary glass and a wood framework. For higher greenhouses, you need metal frames and sash bars, and screening below the glass.

Notice that I said the greenhouse can be 20 feet *above* grade. That's not the first time we've run into the word *grade* in the code. It has a specific definition:

Grade (Adjacent Ground Elevation) is the lowest point of elevation of the finished surface of the ground, paving or sidewalk within the area between the building and the property line or, when the property line is more than 5 feet from the building, between the building and a line 5 feet from the building.

Sidewalk Light Ports

Once it was common to place glass panels in sidewalks to let light into the basements below. I haven't seen any glass sidewalk light ports lately, but the ones I remember were tinted green and usually chipped. At night the light from underneath would make the glass sparkle like emeralds. The code still permits them if they're in a metal frame and at least 1/2 inch thick. If the area of the glass is over 16 square inches, it must be wire reinforced.

Floor lights or sidewalk lights must be able to carry the floor or sidewalk load unless protected by a railing at least 42 inches high. With the required railing, the design load need be no more than the roof design load.

On private property, you can build basements under sidewalks. But you might want to build a basement under a public sidewalk so a freight elevator can take deliveries directly to the basement. That usually requires an easement and a relaxation of the zoning ordinance.

Other Plastic Applications

The word plastic is a broad term that covers many materials. Chapter 52 of the UBC at one time covered only *plastic glazing material*. Now it uses the term *light transmitting plastics*. That's to differentiate it from the other definition of "plastic" that just means capable of being molded. Even concrete in its liquid state is referred to as being plastic.

Rapid changes in plastics in the last several decades have kept the code-writing people on their toes. Chapter 52 of the UBC includes exterior wall panels, roof panels, skylights, light diffusing systems, diffusers in electrical systems, partitions, awnings, patio covers, greenhouses and canopies.

Installation requirements for plastics aren't clearly defined in the code. The main requirement is that it must have enough strength and durability to withstand the mandatory design loads. The code isn't too specific on fastenings, either. They must be able to withstand design load and include space for expansion and contraction of the materials. Your job is to satisfy the inspector with the quality of your material. If you're using one of the many popular brands on the market, this shouldn't be a problem. The inspector is probably already familiar with them.

Plastic Glazing Material

In a Type V-N building, doors, sash and framed openings that don't have to be fire protected may be glazed with any approved plastic material. But the use of plastics is more regulated in other building types. For instance, the plastic glazing can't cover more than 25 percent of any wall surface on any story. No single pane of glazing material above the first story can be higher than 4 feet or have an area larger than 16 square feet. You can increase this area by 50 percent in a sprinklered building.

You can't go above 65 feet from grade with any plastic glazing. And there's one unusual requirement for plastic glazing: You have to install an approved flame barrier extending 30 inches beyond the exterior wall in the plane of the floor or vertical panel located in adjacent stories. This is to deflect heat from any fire below so the plastic won't melt.

Theaters and Stages

Chapter 39 of the UBC, which was completely rewritten in 1985, covers theaters and stages. The revisions affect legitimate stages more than movie houses. They require one-hour fire protection in more areas than ever before. In fact, nearly all accessory rooms must now have that protection.

Section 3903 requires that dressing room sections, workshops, and storerooms be separated from each other and from the stage by a one-hour fire-resistive separation. Section 3903(f) requires one well-marked exit at least 32 inches wide from each side of the stage directly (or through an exit passageway) to a street or exit court.

We covered fly galleries and proscenium walls in Chapter 2, so we won't repeat it here. But there is one more important subject: ventilation.

Proper ventilation is one of the first and most important considerations in designing a stage. Lights and human activity on the stage generate a great deal of heat. And most stages have a lot of flammable material. The two together create a very volatile situation. For that reason most permanent items on a stage must be as fire resistive as possible.

The ventilators in a theater serve two purposes. The first is obvious — drawing off excess hot air. Modern air conditioning has greatly reduced the need for ventilation alone. The second purpose is fire venting. The code requires special vents to release heat and smoke in case of a fire. Skylights serve this purpose. They must be readily opened, either by spring action or force of gravity sufficient to overcome the effects of neglect, rust, dirt, frost, snow, or expansion and warping of the framework. They must be controlled by a fusible link so they open automatically in case of fire.

Projection Rooms

Originally, theaters were for stage productions. When movies became popular, they started building theaters primarily for movies, but they still included facilities for stage productions. Gradually, the stages disappeared from new movie houses.

UBC Chapter 40 covers projection rooms. Projection rooms have separate rules even if they're in a theater with a stage. The section on projection rooms also applies to school projection rooms and drive-in theaters. Every projection room must have this sign with 1-inch block letters: Safety Film Only Permitted In This Room.

Motion picture projection rooms must have at least 80 square feet of floor area for one projection machine and 40 square feet for each additional machine. The minimum ceiling height is 7'6". The ceiling must be of the same construction required for the rest of the building. Exits must conform to Chapter 33 of the UBC, but don't have to be surfaced with fire-rated materials.

Openings in the wall between the projection room and the auditorium can't exceed 25 percent of the wall area. The openings must be framed with fire-rated materials.

In a drive-in theater, many inspectors will waive this 25 percent maximum. And ventilation isn't as important because most projection rooms are now air conditioned. But the code requires each projection room to have a lavatory and a water closet. Check the exit and fire requirements for the snack bar and its connection with the projection room. Between shows these places get quite crowded.

Use of Public Property

Permanent use of public property is restricted by the building code and zoning ordinances. Permanent use, of course, is any structure that's going to stay where it's built. The fences, barricades and shelters used during construction or demolition are temporary structures. Your jurisdiction may require special permits to use public property, but the code doesn't. Structures built for fairs, exhibitions and carnivals are also temporary.

Most temporary structures used during the construction or demolition of a building are for the protection of the public. You can use part of the sidewalk area in front of a job site if you leave pedestrians a walkway 4 feet wide. If you need to use the entire walkway, you can detour pedestrians into the street — *if* you provide a 4-foot walkway with a railing on the traffic side and a fence on the construction side. Lights are required during darkness. UBC Table 44-A (Figure 14-2) shows the protection needed for pedestrians.

Install signs and railings to direct pedestrians. Railings must be at least 42 inches high, built of new 2 x 4s or larger

HEIGHT OF CONSTRUCTION	DISTANCE FROM CONSTRUCTION	PROTECTION REQUIRED
8 feet or less	Less than 6 feet	Railing
	6 feet or more	None
More than 8 feet	Less than 6 feet	Fence and canopy
	6 feet or more but not more than one-fourth the height of construction	Fence and canopy
	6 feet or more, but between one-fourth to one-half the height of construction	Fence
	6 feet or more but exceeding one-half the construction height	None

TABLE NO. 44-A—TYPE OF PROTECTION REQUIRED FOR PEDESTRIANS

From the Uniform Building Code, © 1988, ICBO

Figure 14-2   *Protection required for pedestrians*

lumber. Railings adjacent to excavations must have a mid-rail.

The fence between the walkway and the site must be solid, substantial and at least 8 feet high. It has to extend the full length of the site. Plywood fences must be made of exterior grade plywood. Support plywood 1/4 to 5/16 inch thick with studs at least 2 feet on center unless you add a horizontal stiffener at mid-height. Plywood thicker than 5/8 inch can span 8 feet.

Sidewalk canopies (to protect pedestrians from overhead work) must have a clear height of 8 feet, a tightly sheathed roof of 2-inch nominal wood plankings, and must be lighted during hours of darkness.

Be careful when mixing or handling mortar, concrete, or other material on public property. The code say this work can't deface public property or create a nuisance. All utility lines and their frames, standards, and catch basins must be protected against interference. Incidentally, you have to protect any opening in a fence or shield with a door that will latch or lock.

Permanent Use of Public Property

The permanent use of public property is usually restricted to projections over the property line. Cornices, architectural features, eave overhangs and exterior private balconies that project beyond the floor area are governed by Section 1710 of the UBC. Projections in Type I or II buildings must be of noncombustible material. Projections in other buildings can be either noncombustible or combustible. But if you use combustible materials where protected openings are required, they must be one-hour fire-resistive, or heavy timber.

Chapter 45, Section 4504 discusses some of these projections:

> **Section 4504.** *Oriel windows, balconies, unroofed porches, cornices, belt courses and appendages such as water tables, sills, capitals, bases and architectural projections may project over the public property of the building site a distance as determined by the clearance of the lowest point of the projection above the grade immediately below, as follows:*
>
> *Clearance above grade less than 8 feet — no projection is permitted.*
>
> *Clearance above grade over 8 feet — 1 inch of projection is permitted for each additional inch of clearance, provided that no such projections shall exceed a distance of 4 feet.*

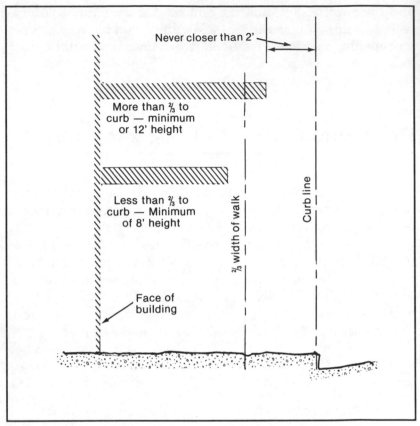

Figure 14-3 *Marquee construction measurements*

That almost sounds too easy, doesn't it? Well, near the end of Section 1710 of the UBC is this little-known item:

> *Projections shall not extend more than 12 inches into the areas where openings are prohibited.*

This is one of those things that you may have forgotten about. What is a protected opening? Where are openings in walls prohibited? Chapter 5 of this book will help you find out if the wall you're looking at will permit an opening. Carefully consider the street width. And check the local zoning ordinance. Even if the code lets you build that balcony, your local zoning regulations may not.

Awnings and Marquees

Remember the old-fashioned striped canvas awnings that used to grace main street? For many years they were in disrepute. The UBC didn't even recognize them because they were considered a fire hazard. Now they're back in vogue. But they can't encroach on public property further than 7 feet from the face of the building or within 2 feet of the face of the curb. The main awning must be at least 8 feet high. The frames, but not the covers, must be noncombustible.

Marquees are a little different. They must be solid construction and attached to the building. They can't be more than 3 feet thick when the marquee extends more than two-thirds the distance to the curb. If they're less than two-thirds of that distance, they can go to 9 feet thick.

Figure 14-3 shows the marquee requirements. Notice that no marquee can project within 2 feet of the curb. That's to prevent damage from tall trucks parking at curbside. The minimum height is 8 feet if it extends less than two-thirds the way to the curb. If it's wider, it can't be less than 12 feet high.

Doors, when fully open, can't project more than 1 foot beyond the property line. In alleys no projection is allowed.

Rolling Out the Rock

I don't think any building inspector likes to shut a job down. I know I don't. It's heavy handed — sort of a last resort after everything else has failed. Negotiation is always better than confrontation. And stopping all work is the worst type of confrontation. But I've had to order work stopped a few times. Once I did it as a favor to the contractor. There wasn't even a code violation. Here's the story.

A few years ago I had an out-of-town developer apply for a permit on a 22-home tract. I hadn't heard of this developer before, so I mentioned his name at a regional conference of building inspectors. No one had anything good to say about him. Some predicted trouble right from the start. I decided to keep an eye on him, visiting his tract daily.

Most of the time I couldn't find anything wrong. When I noticed something that needed attention, I'd note it on a piece of paper and give it to the foreman. He would either fix the problem right away or explain that the work was scheduled and suggest when it would be finished. I was having no trouble at all with this builder. He seemed very professional in every way.

Then a funny thing happened. I was making a routine inspection on one of the homes. The sheetrock hangers had been working since morning. As I walked through, I had a feeling that something was wrong. But I couldn't put my finger on it. I went through the place item by item and found nothing unusual. Still, my intuition said to keep looking. I counted the nails in each sheet of drywall, checked the blocking on joints, and everything else I could think of. Still nothing.

I started to leave through the kitchen into an attached garage. As I went through the opening, I ran my hand along the wall where the trim would go. "Here's where the light switch will probably be," I told myself. But, surprise, *there was no opening in the wallboard for the switch.* I couldn't believe it! There were no electrical openings anywhere in the wallboard. I checked some rooms that hadn't been rocked yet. The house hadn't been wired! There was no electrical wiring in the walls and the sheetrock hangers were covering up the framing! My intuition hadn't let me down.

How did that happen? Was the foreman making a horrible mistake? Or was the developer hoping to find a buyer who wanted electrical wiring run on the wall surface? That's ridiculous. No one wants a home that's wired like a barn. It had to be a mistake.

But what should I do? I had no right to stop work. There was no code violation. Neither the UBC nor the NEC require that wiring be run inside walls. But everyone does it. I've never seen a new home with exposed wiring. Someone had to tell the sheetrock crew to stop work immediately. Should I do it?

I decided to take the heat. I shut the job down. That brought the foreman to me with fire in his eyes. I had no authority to shut down his job, he screamed. And he was right. He'd been told to "rock" that house, and that's what he was going to do.

I suggested to the foreman that we take a break, consider the situation, and make a few calls. He cooled down after a while, and admitted that I was right. The wiring *should* go in first. It was nice of him to admit that — but he still had a house to wire.

15

Finish Materials and Installation Procedures

U BC Chapter 47 is called *Installation of Wall and Ceiling Coverings*. It covers plaster, lath, softwood, plywood paneling, exposed aggregate plaster (stucco) and pneumatically placed cement plaster (gunite).

Before we begin, let me clarify something. A vertical assembly is any assembly of building materials rising vertically — commonly called a wall. A horizontal assembly is any assembly of building materials laid and used in a horizontal position — in other words, floors and ceilings. We'll start at the top, with ceilings.

Suspended Ceilings

Ceiling members aren't always attached. Sometimes they're simply laid in place and held there by gravity. A suspended ceiling is a good example. The panels are laid in runners suspended from the structural framing above. The panels may be light diffusers or solid panels.

Some buildings use the space between the suspended ceiling and the structural framing above for an *extended plenum* or *plenum chamber* to circulate either heated or cooled air. That lets you install air diffusers wherever you want them. The air is forced under pressure into the space between the two ceilings and then forced out through the diffusers.

The hangers must be saddle-tied around the main runner to develop their full strength. UBC Table 47-A (Figure 15-1) gives specifications for suspended ceilings weighing less than 10 pounds per square foot.

Lath

The UBC no longer recognizes wood lath. Look at the types of lath listed in UBC Table 47-B (Figure 15-2); wood is not among them. This signals the end of an era. There was a time when wood lath was the material of choice under plaster walls and ceilings.

We'll look at metal lath first, since it's listed first in the UBC. If you're using metal lath or wire fabric lath, attach it with at least 18-gauge wire ties spaced not more than 6 inches apart or with an approved fastener.

Apply metal lath with the long dimension of the sheets perpendicular to the supports. Lap joints at least one mesh at

TABLE NO. 47-A—SUSPENDED AND FURRED CEILINGS[1]
(For Support of Ceilings Weighing Not More than 10 Pounds per Square Foot)

Minimum Sizes for Wire and Rigid Hangers

SIZE AND TYPE		MAXIMUM AREA SUPPORTED (In Square Feet)	SIZE
Hangers for Suspended Ceilings		12.5	No. 9 gauge wire
		16	No. 8 gauge wire
		18	3/16" diameter, mild steel rod[2]
		20	7/32" diameter, mild steel rod[2]
		22.5	1/4" diameter, mild steel rod[2]
		25.0	1" x 3/16" mild steel flats[3]
For Supporting Runners	Single Hangers Between Beams[4]	8	No. 12 gauge wire
		12	No. 10 gauge wire
		16	No. 8 gauge wire
	Double Wire Loops at Beams or Joists[3]	8	No. 14 gauge wire
		12	No. 12 gauge wire
		16	No. 11 gauge wire
Hangers for Attaching Runners and Furring Directly to Beams and Joists	For Supporting Furring without Runners[4] (Wire Loops at Supports) — Type of Support: Concrete	8	No. 14 gauge wire
	Steel		No. 16 gauge wire (2 loops)[5]
	Wood		No. 16 gauge wire (2 loops)[5]

From the Uniform Building Code, © 1988, ICBO

Figure 15-1   Suspended and furred ceiling

Minimum Sizes and Maximum Spans for Main Runners[6][7]

SIZE AND TYPE	MAXIMUM SPACING OF HANGERS OR SUPPORTS (ALONG RUNNERS)	MAXIMUM SPACING OF RUNNERS (TRANSVERSE)
3/4" — .3 pound per foot, cold- or hot-rolled channel	2'0"	3'0"
1 1/2" — .475 pound per foot, cold-rolled channel	3'0"	4'0"
1 1/2" — .475 pound per foot, cold-rolled channel	3'6"	3'6"
1 1/2" — .475 pound per foot, cold-rolled channel	4'0"	3'0"
1 1/2" — 1.12 pounds per foot, hot-rolled channel	4'0"	5'0"
2 — 1.26 pounds per foot, hot-rolled channel	5'0"	5'0"
2 — .59 pound per foot, cold-rolled channel	5'0"	3'6"
1 1/2" x 1 1/2" x 3/16" angle		3'6"

Minimum Sizes and Maximum Spans for Cross Furring[6][7]

SIZE AND TYPE OF CROSS FURRING	MAXIMUM SPACING OF RUNNERS OR SUPPORTS	MAXIMUM SPACING OF CROSS FURRING MEMBERS (TRANSVERSE)
1/4" diameter pencil rods	2'0"	12"
3/8" diameter pencil rods	2'0"	19"
3/8" diameter pencil rods	2'6"	12"
3/4" — .3 pound per foot, cold- or hot-rolled channel	3'0"	24"
	3'6"	16"
	4'0"	12"
1" — .410 pound per foot, hot-rolled channel	4'0"	24"
	4'6"	19"
	5'0"	12"

[1]Metal suspension systems for acoustical tile and lay-in panel ceiling systems weighing not more than 4 pounds per square foot, including light fixtures and all ceiling-supported equipment and conforming to U.B.C. Standard No. 47-18, are exempt from Table No. 47-A.

For furred and suspended ceilings with metal lath construction, see U.B.C. Standard No. 47-4.

[2]All rod hangers shall be protected with a zinc or cadmium coating or with a rust-inhibitive paint.

[3]All flat hangers shall be protected with a zinc or cadmium coating or with a rust-inhibitive paint.

[4]Inserts, special clips or other devices of equal strength may be substituted for those specified.

[5]Two loops of No. 18 gauge wire may be substituted for each loop of No. 16 gauge wire for attaching steel furring to steel or wood joists.

[6]Spans are based on webs of channels being erected vertically.

[7]Other sections of hot- or cold-rolled members of equivalent strength may be substituted for those specified.

From the Uniform Building Code, © 1988, ICBO

Figure 15-1 (cont'd) *Suspended and furred ceiling*

the sides and ends, but not less than 1 inch. You can lap metal rib lath with edge ribs wider than 1/8 inch by nesting the outside ribs. If the edge ribs are less than 1/8 inch, lap it 1/2 inch at the sides or nest the outside ribs. If the laps don't fall over supports, tie them with 18-gauge wire.

UBC Tables 47-B (Figure 15-2) and 47-C (Figure 15-3) give the type and weight of metal lath, the gauge and spacing of wire in welded or woven lath, the spacing of supports and how to attach it to wood supports.

When you're lathing exterior stud walls with metal or gypsum lath, you need a "weep screed" at or below the foundation line. Place the screed at least 4 inches above grade. It allows water to drain to the exterior of the building.

You can't use all types of gypsum lath for exterior lathing. And remember not to install interior lath until there's complete weather protection. Apply gypsum lath with the long dimension perpendicular to the supports. Stagger end joints in successive courses. If adjacent panels have end joints on the same support, apply joint stripping to the full length of the joint. If the lath joints don't touch or if the space between them is greater than 3/8 inch, you have to strip the joint.

Weather-Resistive Barriers

Section 4706(d) requires that you install a weather-resistant barrier in exterior walls. Section 1707(a) explains the requirement. You'll need to hang two layers of Grade D paper over wood base sheathing. Here's what 1707(a) says:

Section 1707(a) Weather-Resistive Barriers. All weather-exposed surfaces shall have a weather-resistive barrier to protect the interior wall covering. Such barrier shall be equal to that provided for in UBC Standard No. 17-1 for kraft waterproof building paper or UBC Stan-

TABLE NO. 47-B[1]—TYPES OF LATH—MAXIMUM SPACING OF SUPPORTS

| TYPE OF LATH[2] | MINIMUM WEIGHT (Per Square Yard) GAUGE AND MESH SIZE | VERTICAL (In Inches) | | | HORIZONTAL (In Inches) | |
		Wood	Metal – Solid Plaster Partitions	Metal – Other	Wood or Concrete	Metal
1. Expanded Metal Lath (Diamond Mesh)	2.5 3.4	16[3] 16[3]	16[3] 16[3]	12 16	12 16	12 16
2. Flat Rib Expanded Metal Lath	2.75 3.4	16 19	16 24	16 19	16 19	16 19
3. Stucco Mesh Expanded Metal Lath	1.8 and 3.6	16[4]	—	—	—	—
4. 3/8" Rib Expanded Metal Lath	3.4 4.0	24 24	24[5] 24[5]	24 24	24 24	24 24
5. Sheet Lath	4.5	24	[5]	24	24	24
6. Wire Fabric Lath — Welded	1.95 pounds, No. 11 gauge, 2" × 2" 1.16 pounds, No. 16 gauge, 2" × 2" 1.4 pounds, No. 18 gauge, 1" × 1"[6]	24 16 16[4]	24 16 —	24 16 —	24 16 —	24 16 —
6. Wire Fabric Lath — Woven[4]	1.1 pounds, No. 18 gauge, 1 1/2" Hexagonal[6] 1.4 pounds, No. 17 gauge, 1 1/2" Hexagonal[6] 1.4 pounds, No. 18 gauge, 1" Hexagonal[6]	24 24 24	16 16 16	16 16 16	24 24 24	16 16 16
7. 3/8" Gypsum Lath (plain)		16	—	16[7]	16	16
8. 1/2" Gypsum Lath (plain)		24	—	24	24	24

From the *Uniform Building Code*, © 1988, ICBO

Figure 15-2 *Maximum spacing of supports for lath*

377

[1]For fire-resistive construction, see Tables No. 43-A, No. 43-B and No. 43-C. For shear-resisting elements, see Table No. 47-I. Metal lath, wire lath, wire fabric lath and metal accessories shall conform with the provisions of U.B.C. Standard No. 47-4. Gypsum lath shall conform with the provisions of U.B.C. Standard No. 47-8.

[2]Metal lath and wire fabric lath used as reinforcement for portland cement plaster shall be furred out away from vertical supports at least 1/4 inch. Self-furring lath meets furring requirements. Exception: Furring of expanded metal lath is not required on supports having a bearing surface width of 1-5/8 inches or less.

[3]Span may be increased to 24 inches with self-furred metal lath over solid sheathing assemblies approved for this use.

[4]Wire backing required on open vertical frame construction except under expanded metal lath and paperbacked wire fabric lath.

[5]May be used for studless solid partitions.

[6]Woven wire or welded wire fabric lath, not to be used as base for gypsum plaster without absorbent paperbacking or slot-perforated separator.

[7]Span may be increased to 24 inches on vertical screw or approved nailable assemblies.

From the Uniform Building Code, © 1988, ICBO

TABLE NO. 47-C—TYPES OF LATH—ATTACHMENT TO WOOD AND METAL[1] SUPPORTS

TYPE OF LATH	NAILS[2,3]			SCREWS[3,6]		STAPLES[3,4] Round or Flattened Wire				
	TYPE AND SIZE	MAXIMUM SPACING[5]		MAX. SPACING[5]		Wire Gauge No.	Crown	Leg[7]	MAX. SPACING[5,6]	
		Vertical (In Inches)	Horizontal (In Inches)	Vertical (In Inches)	Horizontal (In Inches)		(In Inches)	(In Inches)	Vertical (In Inches)	Horizontal (In Inches)
1. Diamond Mesh Expanded Metal Lath and Flat Rib Metal Lath	4d blued smooth box 1 1/2″[11] No. 14 gauge 7/32″ head (clinched)[8] 1″ No. 11 gauge 7/16″ head, barbed 1 1/2″ No. 11 gauge 7/16″ head, barbed	6 6 6	— — 6	6	6	16	3/4	7/8	6	6
2. 3/8″ Rib Metal Lath and Sheet Lath	1 1/2″ No. 11 gauge 7/16″ head, barbed	6	6	6	6	16	3/4	1 1/4	At Ribs	At Ribs
3. 3/4″ Rib Metal Lath	4d common 1 1/2″ No. 12 1/2 gauge 1/4″ head 2″ No. 11 gauge 7/16″ head, barbed	At Ribs	— At Ribs	At Ribs	At Ribs	16	3/4	1 5/8	At Ribs	At Ribs

From the Uniform Building Code, © 1988, ICBO

Figure 15-3 ***Attaching lath to wood and metal supports***

Type of lath										
4. Wire Fabric Lath[9]	**4d blued smooth box (clinched)[8]** **1" No. 11 gauge** **7/16" head, barbed**	6 6						6 6	— —	6 6
	1 1/2" No. 11 gauge 7/16" head, barbed 1 1/4" No. 12 gauge 3/8" head, furring 1" No. 12 gauge 3/8" head	6 6 6						6 6	6 6	
5. 3/8" Gypsum Lath	1 1/8" No. 13 gauge 19/64" head, blued	8[10]	8[10]	8[10]	16	3/4	7/8	8[10]	8[10]	6
6. 1/2" Gypsum Lath	1 1/4" No. 13 gauge 19/64" head, blued	8	8[10] 6[11]	8[10] 6[11]	16	3/4	1 1/8	8[10]	8[10] 6[11]	6

[1]Metal lath, wire lath, wire fabric lath and metal accessories shall conform with the provisions of U.B.C. Standard No. 47-4.

[2]For nailable nonload-bearing metal supports, use annular threaded nails or approved staples.

[3]For fire-resistive construction, see Tables No. 43-B and No. 43-C. For shear-resisting elements, see Table No. 47-I. Approved wire and sheet metal attachment clips may be used.

[4]With chisel or divergent points.

[5]Maximum spacing of attachments from longitudinal edges shall not exceed 2 inches.

[6]Screws shall be an approved type long enough to penetrate into wood framing not less than 5/8 inch and through metal supports adaptable for screw attachment not less than 1/4 inch.

[7]When lath and stripping are stapled simultaneously, increase leg length of staple 1/8 inch.

[8]For interiors only.

[9]Attach self-furring wire fabric lath to supports at furring device.

[10]Three attachments per 16-inch-wide lath per bearing. Four attachments per 24-inch-wide lath per bearing.

[11]Supports spaced 24 inches o.c. Four attachments per 16-inch-wide lath per bearing. Five attachments per 24-inch-wide lath per bearing.

From the Uniform Building Code, © 1988, ICBO

Figure 15-3 (cont'd) *Attaching lath to wood and metal supports*

dard No. 32-1 for asphalt-saturated rag felt. Building paper and felt shall be free from holes and breaks other than those created by fasteners and construction system due to attaching of the building paper, and shall be applied over studs or sheathing of all exterior walls. Such felt or paper shall be applied weatherboard fashion, lapped not less than 2 inches at horizontal joints and not less than 6 inches at vertical joints.

You can omit the weather-protective barriers when:

• The exterior covering is approved weatherproof panels

• The construction is back-plastered

• There's no human occupancy

• The panel sheathing is water-repellent

• There's approved paper-backed metal or wire fabric lath

• There's lath and portland cement plaster on the underside of roof and eave projections

Plaster

There are generally two types of plaster used in construction today. You can use portland cement plaster for both outdoor and indoor work. Use gypsum plaster only on interior work. Both require three coats when applied over metal lath or wire fabric lath. You must apply at least two coats over any other material allowed by the code. Remember this, though: You can never apply plaster directly to fiber insulation board. The plaster thickness is measured from the face of the base it's applied over.

TABLE NO. 47-D—THICKNESS OF PLASTER[1]

PLASTER BASE	FINISHED THICKNESS OF PLASTER FROM FACE OF LATH, MASONRY, CONCRETE	
	Gypsum Plaster	Portland Cement Plaster
1. Expanded Metal Lath	5/8" minimum[2]	5/8" minimum[2]
2. Wire Fabric Lath	5/8" minimum[2]	3/4" minimum (interior)[3]
		7/8" minimum (exterior)[3]
3. Gypsum Lath	1/2" minimum	1/2" minimum
4. Masonry Walls[4]	1/2" minimum	1/2" minimum
5. Monolithic Concrete Walls[4] [5]	5/8" maximum[8]	7/8" maximum[8]
6. Monolithic Concrete Ceilings[4] [5]	3/8" maximum[6] [7] [8]	1/2" maximum[7] [8]

[1]For fire-resistive construction, see Tables Nos. 43-A, 43-B and 43-C.

[2]When measured from back plane of expanded metal lath, exclusive of ribs, or self-furring lath, plaster thickness shall be 3/4-inch minimum.

[3]When measured from face of support or backing.

[4]Because masonry and concrete surfaces may vary in plane, thickness of plaster need not be uniform.

[5]When applied over a liquid bonding agent, finish coat may be applied directly to concrete surface.

[6]Approved acoustical plaster may be applied directly to concrete, or over base coat plaster, beyond the maximum plaster thickness shown.

[7]On concrete ceilings, where the base coat plaster thickness exceeds the maximum thickness shown, metal lath or wire fabric lath shall be attached to the concrete.

[8]An approved skim-coat plaster 1/16 inch thick may be applied directly to concrete.

From the Uniform Building Code, © 1988, ICBO

Four tables set the requirement for plaster. UBC Table 47-D (Figure 15-4) gives the minimum thickness of both kinds of plaster over plaster bases. Table 47-E (Figure 15-5) shows the proportions of aggregate to cementitious materials in gypsum plaster. Table 47-F (Figure 15-6) does the same thing for portland cement plaster and portland cement-lime plaster. Curing times for portland cement or cement-lime plaster are shown in this figure.

To ensure proper bonding, concrete or masonry surfaces must be clean and free from efflorescence, sufficiently damp, and rough. If the surface isn't rough, apply bonding agents or a portland cement dash bond coat. Mix the dash bond coat in the proportions of 1-1/2 cubic feet of sand to 1 cubic foot of portland cement.

You can't apply portland cement plaster to frozen surfaces or use any frozen ingredients. Protect all work from freezing for 24 hours. If you have to work in cold weather, I recommend that you follow the procedures in Chapter 9 for laying concrete block during cold weather.

Exposed Aggregate Plaster

You probably know this material as stucco. It's used almost the same way as standard interior plaster except that more sand aggregate is added to a bedding coat. For exterior work, this bedding coat consists of one part portland cement, one part Type S lime and a maximum three parts of graded white or natural sand by volume. It must have a minimum compressive strength of 1,000 pounds per square inch. The composition of the interior bedding coat is 100 pounds of neat gypsum plaster and a maximum 200 pounds of graded white sand.

TABLE NO. 47-E—GYPSUM PLASTER PROPORTIONS[1]

NUMBER	COAT	PLASTER BASE OR LATH	MAXIMUM VOLUME AGGREGATE PER 100 POUNDS NEAT PLASTER[2][3] (Cubic Feet)	
			Damp Loose Sand[4]	Perlite or Vermiculite[4]
1. Two-coat Work	Base Coat	Gypsum Lath	2½	2
	Base Coat	Masonry	3	3
2. Three-coat Work	First Coat	Lath	2[5]	2
	Second Coat	Lath	3[5]	2[6]
	First and Second Coats	Masonry	3	3

[1]Wood-fibered gypsum plaster may be mixed in the proportions of 100 pounds of gypsum to not more than 1 cubic foot of sand where applied on masonry or concrete.

Gypsum plasters shall conform with the provisions of U.B.C. Standard No. 47-9.

[2]For fire-resistive construction, see Tables No. 43-A, No. 43-B and No. 43-C.

[3]When determining the amount of aggregate in set plaster, a tolerance of 10 percent shall be allowed.

[4]Combinations of sand and lightweight aggregate may be used, provided the volume and weight relationship of the combined aggregate to gypsum plaster is maintained. Sand and lightweight aggregate shall conform with U.B.C. Standard No. 47-3.

[5]If used for both first and second coats, the volume of aggregate may be 2½ cubic feet.

[6]Where plaster is 1 inch or more in total thickness, the proportions for the second coat may be increased to 3 cubic feet.

From the Uniform Building Code, © 1988, ICBO

TABLE NO. 47-F—PORTLAND CEMENT PLASTERS[1]

PORTLAND CEMENT PLASTER

COAT	VOLUME CEMENT	MAXIMUM WEIGHT (OR VOLUME) LIME PER VOLUME CEMENT[2]	MAXIMUM VOLUME SAND PER VOLUME CEMENT[3]	APPROXIMATE MINIMUM THICKNESS[4]	MINIMUM PERIOD MOIST CURING	MINIMUM INTERVAL BETWEEN COATS
First	1	20 lbs.	4	3/8"[5]	48[6] Hours	48[7] Hours
Second	1	20 lbs.	5	1st and 2nd Coats total 3/4"	48 hours	7 Days[8]
Finish	1	1[9]	3	1st, 2nd and Finish Coats 7/8"	—	[8]

PORTLAND CEMENT-LIME PLASTER[10]

COAT	VOLUME CEMENT[11]	MAXIMUM VOLUME LIME PER VOLUME CEMENT	MAXIMUM VOLUME SAND PER COMBINED VOLUMES CEMENT AND LIME	APPROXIMATE MINIMUM THICKNESS[4]	MINIMUM PERIOD MOIST CURING	MINIMUM INTERVAL BETWEEN COATS
First	1	1	4	3/8"[5]	48[6] Hours	48[7] Hours
Second	1	1	4½	1st and 2nd Coats total 3/4"	48 hours	7 Days[8]
Finish	1	1[9]	3	1st, 2nd and Finish Coats 7/8"	—	[8]

[1]Exposed aggregate plaster shall be applied in accordance with Section 4709. Minimum overall thickness shall be ¾ inch.

[2]Up to 20 pounds of dry hydrated lime (or an equivalent amount of lime putty) may be used as a plasticizing agent in proportion to each sack (cubic foot) of Type I and Type II standard portland cement in first and second coats of plaster. See Section 4708 (a) for use of plastic cement.

[3]When determining the amount of sand in set plaster, a tolerance of 10 percent may be allowed.

[4]See Table No. 47-D.

[5]Measured from face of support or backing to crest of scored plaster.

[6]See Section 4707 (c) 2.

[7]Twenty-four hours minimum interval between coats of interior portland cement plaster. For alternate method of application, see Section 4708 (e).

[8]Finish coat plaster may be applied to interior portland cement base coats after a 48-hour period.

[9]For finish coat plaster, up to an equal part of dry hydrated lime by weight (or an equivalent volume of lime putty) may be added to Types I, II and III standard portland cement.

[10]No additions of plasticizing agents shall be made.

[11]Type I, II or III standard portland cement. See Section 4708 (a) for use of plastic cement.

From the Uniform Building Code, © 1988, ICBO

Figure 15-6 Portland cement plasters

Section 4709 covers exposed aggregate plaster:

(a) General. Exposed natural or integrally colored aggregate may be partially embedded in a natural or colored bedding coat of portland cement or gypsum plaster, subject to the provisions of this section.

(b) Aggregate. The aggregate may be applied manually or mechanically and shall consist of marble chips, pebbles, or similar durable, nonreactive materials, moderately hard (three or more on the MOH scale.)

Pneumatically Placed Plaster

Section 4710 describes pneumatically placed plaster, usually known as gunite.

Pneumatically placed portland cement plaster shall be a mixture of portland cement and sand, mixed dry, conveyed by air through a pipe or flexible tube, hydrated at the nozzle at the end of the conveyor and deposited by air pressure in its final position.

"Hydrated at the nozzle" means that the water is added to the dry gunite mixture as it leaves the tube.

You always have to apply at least two coats of gunite. Together, the two coats must be at least 7/8 inch thick. Curing time between coats is specified in UBC Table No. 47-F (Figure 15-6).

There's one refinement that doesn't apply to other types of plaster. You can screen and reuse the rebound material as long as it doesn't exceed 25 percent of the total sand used in any batch.

Gypsum Wallboard

I've seen sheetrock put up almost every way possible. Some installers would probably sew it on if they could. I think the main reason for sloppy installation is that most installers are paid by the unit rather than by the hour. If they can take shortcuts or omit a few nails here and there, they can put up more material and make more money.

That may be why the code regulates wallboard. It must be inspected, as outlined in Section 305:

> *4. Lath and/or Gypsum Board Inspection:* To be made after all lathing and gypsum board, interior and exterior, is in place but before any plastering is applied or before gypsum board joints and fasteners are taped and finished.

Fastening Gypsum Wallboard

There are three common ways to hang wallboard. The most common is nailing, second is attaching with screws, and third is using adhesives. About the only difference between using nails and screws is that you can space screws 12 inches apart, but nails must have 7- or 8-inch spacing. Screws are commonly used in commercial areas for Type I construction with steel studding. And the wallboard is usually thicker to get the required fire rating.

There are two ways to install sheetrock where a fire rating is required: single-ply and two-ply application. Specifications are given in UBC Table 47-G (Figure 15-7) for single-ply and Table 47-H (Figure 15-8) for two-ply application.

The Gypsum Institute, which wrote most of the section on wallboard application, lists twelve step for proper application. Although this pertains mostly to nailing, many of the same rules also apply to screws.

Nailing— The footnotes on UBC Table 47-G mention two methods of nailing. The first is outlined in the table itself where it indicates that spacing of single nails will be generally

TABLE NO. 47-G—APPLICATION OF SINGLE-PLY GYPSUM WALLBOARD

THICKNESS OF GYPSUM WALLBOARD (Inch)	PLANE OF FRAMING SURFACE	LONG DIMENSION OF GYPSUM WALLBOARD SHEETS IN RELATION TO DIRECTION OF FRAMING MEMBERS	MAXIMUM SPACING OF FRAMING MEMBER[1] (Center to Center) (In Inches)	MAXIMUM SPACING OF FASTENERS[1] (Center to Center) (In Inches) Nails[3]	Screws[4]	NAILS[2]—TO WOOD
1/2	Vertical	Either direction	16	8	16	No. 13 gauge, 1 3/8" long, 19/64" head; 0.098" diameter, 1 1/4" long, annular ringed; 5d, cooler or wallboard[5] nail (0.086" dia., 1 5/8" long, 15/64" head).
	Horizontal	Either direction	16	7	12	
	Horizontal	Perpendicular	24	7	12	
	Vertical	Either direction	24	8	12	
5/8	Vertical	Either direction	16	8	16	No. 13 gauge, 1 5/8" long, 19/64" head; 0.098" diameter, 1 3/8" long, annular ringed; 6d, cooler or wallboard[5] nail (0.092" dia., 1 7/8" long, 1/4" head).
	Horizontal	Either direction	16	7	12	
	Horizontal	Perpendicular	24	7	12	
	Vertical	Either direction	24	8	12	

Nail or Screw Fastenings With Adhesives (Maximum Center to Center in Inches)

	(Column headings as above)			End	Edges	Field	NAILS[2]—TO WOOD
1/2 or 5/8	Horizontal	Either direction	16	16	16	24	As required for 1/2" and 5/8" gypsum wallboard, see above.
	Horizontal	Perpendicular	24	16	24	24	
	Vertical	Either direction	24	16	24	6	

[1]For fire-resistive construction, see Tables Nos. 43-B and 43-C. For shear-resisting elements, see Table No. 47-I.

[2]Where the metal framing has a clinching design formed to receive the nails by two edges of metal, the nails shall be not less than 5/8 inch longer than the wallboard thickness, and shall have ringed shanks. Where the metal framing has a nailing groove formed to receive the nails, the nails shall have barbed shanks or be 5d, No. 13 1/2 gauge, 1 5/8 inch long, 15/64-inch head for 1/2-inch gypsum wallboard; 6d, No. 13 gauge, 1 7/8-inch long, 15/64-inch head for 5/8-inch gypsum wallboard

[3]Two nails spaced 2 inches to 2 1/2 inches apart may be used where the pairs are spaced 12 inches on center except around the perimeter of the sheets.

[4]Screws shall conform with U.B.C. Standard No. 47-5 and be long enough to penetrate into wood framing not less than 5/8 inch and through metal framing not less than 1/4 inch.

[5]For properties of cooler or wallboard nails, see U.B.C. Standard No. 25-17, Table No. 25-17-I.

[6]Not required.

From the Uniform Building Code, © 1988, ICBO

Figure 15-7   Application of single-ply gypsum wallboard

TABLE NO. 47-H—APPLICATION OF TWO-PLY GYPSUM WALLBOARD[1]

FASTENERS ONLY

THICKNESS OF GYPSUM WALLBOARD (Each Ply) (Inch)	PLANE OF FRAMING SURFACE		LONG DIMENSION OF GYPSUM WALLBOARD SHEETS	MAXIMUM SPACING OF FRAMING MEMBERS (Center to Center) (In Inches)	MAXIMUM SPACING OF FASTENERS (Center to Center) (In Inches)				
					Base Ply			Face Ply	
					Nails[2]	Screws[3]	Staples[4]	Nails[2]	Screws[3]
3/8	Horizontal		Perpendicular only	16	16	24	16	7	12
	Vertical		Either Direction	16				8	
1/2	Horizontal		Perpendicular only	24				7	
	Vertical		Either Direction	24				8	
5/8	Horizontal		Perpendicular only	24				7	
	Vertical		Either Direction	24				8	

Fasteners and Adhesives

THICKNESS	PLANE OF FRAMING SURFACE		LONG DIMENSION OF GYPSUM WALLBOARD SHEETS	MAXIMUM SPACING OF FRAMING MEMBERS	Base Nails[2]	Base Screws[3]	Base Staples[4]	Face Ply
3/8 Base Ply	Horizontal		Perpendicular only	16	7	12	5	Temporary Nailing or Shoring to Comply with Section 4711 (d)
	Vertical		Either Direction	24	8		7	
1/2 Base Ply	Horizontal		Perpendicular only	24	7		5	
	Vertical		Either Direction	24	8		7	
5/8 Base Ply	Horizontal		Perpendicular only	24	7		5	
	Vertical		Either Direction	24	8		7	

[1]For fire-resistive construction, see Tables Nos. 43-B and 43-C. For shear-resisting elements, see Table No. 47-I.

[2]Nails for wood framing shall be long enough to penetrate into wood members not less than 3/4 inch and the sizes shall conform with the provisions of Table No. 47-G. For nails not included in Table No. 47-G, use the appropriate size cooler or wallboard nails as set forth in Table No. 25-17-I of U.B.C. Standard No. 25-17. Nails for metal framing shall conform with the provisions of Table No. 47-G.

[3]Screws shall conform with the provisions of Table No. 47-G.

[4]Staples shall be not less than No. 16 gauge by 3/4-inch crown width with leg length of 7/8 inch, 1 1/8 inch and 1 3/8 inch for gypsum wallboard thicknesses of 3/8 inch, 1/2 inch and 5/8 inch, respectively.

From the Uniform Building Code, © 1988, ICBO

Figure 15-8 Application of two ply gypsum wallboard

7 inches both on the edge or in the field. Footnote 3 mentions the "double-nailing" pattern:

> *Two nails spaced 2 inches to 2-1/4 inches apart may be used where the pairs are spaced 12 inches on center except around the perimeter of the sheets.*

You can find the Gypsum Institute's nailing recommendations in their handbook. Although the code doesn't quote them directly, most of them have made their way into the code. If you follow the Gypsum Institute recommendations, you won't have any trouble with the inspector.

The Institute says this about nailing:

1) Drive nails at least 3/8 inch from ends and edges of the wallboard.

2) Position nails on adjacent ends or edges opposite each other.

3). Begin nailing from the center of the wallboard and proceed toward edges or outer ends.

4) When nailing, apply pressure on wallboard adjacent to the nail you're driving to ensure that the wallboard is secured tightly on the framing member.

5) Drive nails with the shank perpendicular to the face of the board.

6) Use a crown-head hammer.

7) With the last blow of the hammer, seat the nail so the head is in a slight uniform dimple formed by the last blow of the hammer.

8) Don't break the paper at the nail head or around the circumference of the dimple by over-driving it. And don't use a nail set. The dimple shouldn't be over 1/32 inch deep.

9) If you tear the face paper, set an additional nail or fastener not more than 2 inches from the tear.

10) Follow the nailing schedule even when you're using adhesives.

11) You can use screws if they're approved sizes. Spacing may be altered if screws are used. Check with your building inspector.

12) Gypsum wallboard may be applied parallel or perpendicular to the studs.

Screws— Both UBC Tables 47-G and 47-H give the spacing required for fastening gypsum wallboard with screws. Footnote 4 in Table No. 47-G says that screws "shall conform with UBC Standard 47-5 and be long enough to penetrate into wood framing not less than 5/8 inch and through metal framing not less than 1/4 inch." There aren't too many surprises in UBC Standards about screws. Here are some of the main requirements:

- The head of the screw must be at least 0.315 inch in diameter.

- The driving recess must be a No. 2 Phillips design with a minimum depth of 0.105 inch.

- Screws must be self drilling and drive into the stud in less than five seconds.

- Screw threads must be capable of pulling the head of the screw below the surface of the wallboard through four layers of 0.010-inch-thick kraft paper over 5/8-inch Type X gypsum wallboard.

Adhesives— As a building inspector I made a few people unhappy by not allowing them to use adhesives on wallboard unless a full-time inspector was there to check each step of the job. To do a good job, you must apply the adhesive according to the manufacturer's recommendations. The code says you must put down a bead of adhesive that will spread to at least 1 inch wide and 1/16 inch thick. This calls for a continuous bead at least 1/4 inch to 3/8 inch for all studs and cross members.

I found that some installers were only putting down spots or thin beads of adhesive, especially when the tube was about to run out (after all, adhesives cost money, and if you don't have another tube on hand, getting one wastes time). Once the wallboard's in place, there's no easy way of telling how wide, thick or continuous the adhesive is. That's why I wanted constant supervision.

It really wasn't a very big deal. The installers found they didn't save a lot of time, anyway. For practical reasons, they had to apply the adhesive on the reverse side of the panel. That meant marking the panel for the stud locations. Then the panel had to be held in place while the adhesive dried. Back then the code didn't require nailing. But as you can see in UBC Table No. 47-G, the code now requires a certain amount of nailing on single-ply applications.

Two-ply installation— Two-ply is usually used where extra thickness is required for fire-resistiveness. Sheetrock is heavy. It's much easier to lay up two pieces of 3/8-inch wallboard than one piece that's 3/4 inch thick. If you need 1 or 1-1/2 inches of wallboard thickness, two-ply installation is the only way to go.

Another advantage of two-ply installation is that you get a smoother wall. You lay up the first layer just like a single layer, then put up the second coat with adhesives. You don't need to nail the second layer. You'll have to hold this layer in place until the adhesive sets up, but that usually doesn't take long. The amount of taping is reduced, and the overall finish is neater. To get the required fire-resistiveness, the second layer must be applied perpendicular to the base layer.

How Is Sheetrock Fire Resistive?

At first it's difficult to understand how a white powder encased in two layers of paper could be fire resistive. But it's just a simple chemical reaction. As fire burns through the paper and reaches the gypsum, the heat causes a thin layer of water vapor to form over the surface. This repels the fire and cools the surface. But the effect doesn't last long. That's why you need additional thickness to get longer fire-resistiveness. The water vapor will finally evaporate, but before it does it slows down the fire.

Glass and Glazing

You and I might call it glass and glazing, but architects and engineers call it fenestration. The word is derived from the Latin *fenestra*, which means window. So, of course, to fenestrate is to install windows. When I was a builder, I can't remember ever fenestrating. I put in a lot of windows though.

The code started covering glass and glazing as a separate item in 1967. Now Chapter 54 of the UBC regulates the use of glass by area and type. Look at UBC Graph 54-1 (Figure 15-9), which defines the allowable area of glass in relation to the thickness of the glass and the wind load. Use UBC Table 23-G (Figure 6-4, Chapter 6) to determine wind load. Pay particular attention to the height above grade in determining this load.

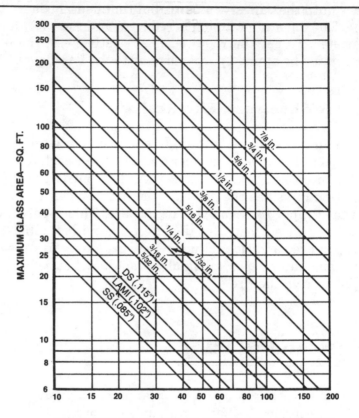

DESIGN WIND PRESSURE FROM SECTION 2311—POUNDS PER SQUARE FOOT

GRAPH NO. 54-1—MAXIMUM ALLOWABLE AREA OF GLASS[1]

[1]Applicable for ratios of width-to-length of 1:1 to 5:1. Design Factor = 2.5

From the Uniform Building Code, © 1988, ICBO

Figure 15-9 *Maximum allowable area of glass*

| TABLE NO. 54-A—ADJUSTMENT FACTORS—RELATIVE RESISTANCE TO WIND LOADS ||
Glass Type	Adjustment Factor[1]
Laminated[2]	0.75
Fully Tempered	4.00
Heat Strengthened	2.00
Wired	0.50
Insulating Glass[3] - 2 panes	1.70
- 3 panes	2.55
Patterned[4]	1.00
Regular (annealed)	1.00
Sandblasted	0.40[5]

[1]Loads determined from Section 2311 shall be divided by this adjustment factor for use with Graph No. 54-1.
[2]Applies when two plies are identical in thickness and type; use total glass thickness, not thickness of one ply
[3]Applies when each glass panel is the same thickness and type; use thickness on one panel.
[4]Use minimum glass thickness, i.e., measured at the thinnest part of the pattern; if necessary, interpolation of curves in Graph No. 54-1 may be required.
[5]Factor varies depending upon depth and severity of sand blasting; value shown is minimum.

From the Uniform Building Code, © 1988, ICBO

Figure 15-10 *Relative resistance to wind load*

UBC Table 54-A (Figure 15-10) gives you the adjustment factors for the wind load. Be sure to read the footnotes. They explain how to apply this factor to your particular situation.

Glass firmly supported on all four edges must be glazed with minimum laps and edge clearances from UBC Table 54-B (Figure 15-11). The inspector must approve any design for glass not firmly supported on all four edges. Glass supports are considered firm when support deflections at design load don't exceed 1/175 of the span. Determining deflection in the field may be difficult. Here's the rule of thumb I use. Lean on the support. If you feel any give, it won't pass inspection.

TABLE NO. 54-B—MINIMUM GLAZING REQUIREMENTS

Fixed Windows and Openable Windows Other Than Horizontal Sliding					
GLASS AREA	UP TO 6 SQ. FT.	6 TO 14 SQ. FT.	14 TO 32 SQ. FT.	32 TO 50 SQ. FT.	OVER 50 SQ. FT.
1. Minimum Frame Lap ..	$\frac{1}{4}$ "	$\frac{1}{4}$ "	$\frac{5}{16}$ "	$\frac{3}{8}$ "	$\frac{1}{2}$ "
2. Minimum Glass Edge Clearance	$\frac{1}{8}$ " 1 2	$\frac{1}{8}$ " 1 2	$\frac{3}{16}$ " 1	$\frac{1}{4}$ "	$\frac{1}{4}$ " 1
3. Continuous Glazing Rabbet and Glass Retainer[3].	Required				
4. Resilient Setting Material[4].	Not Required	Required			

Sliding Doors and Horizontal Sliding Windows				
GLASS AREA	UP TO 14 SQ. FT.	14 TO 32 SQ. FT.	32 TO 50 SQ. FT.	OVER 50 SQ. FT.
5. Minimum Glass Frame Lap	$\frac{1}{4}$ "	$\frac{5}{16}$ "	$\frac{3}{8}$ "	$\frac{1}{2}$ "
6. Minimum Glass Edge Clearance .	$\frac{1}{8}$ " 2	$\frac{3}{16}$ "	$\frac{1}{4}$ "	$\frac{1}{4}$ "
7. Continuous Glazing Rabbet and Glass Retainer[3]	Required above third story	Required		
8. Resilient Setting Material[4].	Not Required	Required		

[1]Glass edge clearance in fixed openings shall be not less than required to provide for wind and earthquake drift.

[2]Glass edge clearance at all sides of pane shall be a minimum of $\frac{3}{16}$ inch where height of glass exceeds 3 feet.

[3]Glass retainers such as metal, wood or vinyl face stops, glazing beads, gaskets, glazing clips and glazing channels shall be of sufficient strength and fixation to serve this purpose.

[4]Resilient setting material shall include preformed rubber or vinyl plastic gaskets or other materials which are proved to the satisfaction of the building official to remain resilient.

From the Uniform Building Code, © 1988, ICBO

Figure 15-11 *Minimum glazing requirements*

Glazing Subject to Human Impact

Section 5406 is one of the most important sections in Chapter 54. It covers the type of glazing you can use for areas subject to *human impact*. This means the glazing next to glass doors, the glass doors themselves, the glazing near any walking surfaces, sliding glass doors, shower doors, tub enclosures and storm doors. The code also lists certain exceptions. Instead of listing areas where protection from human impact is essential, the code excludes areas where there's little danger of human impact:

> *Exceptions:* 1. *Openings in doors through which a 3-inch sphere is unable to pass.*
>
> 2. *Assemblies of leaded glass or faceted glass and items of carved glass when used for decorative purposes indoors or in locations described in Section 5406(d), Item No. 6 or 7.*
>
> 3. *Glazing materials used as curved glazed panels in revolving doors.*
>
> 4. *Commercial refrigerated cabinet glazed doors.*

Glass for bathtub and shower enclosures must be laminated safety glass or approved plastic. How do you know if a piece of glass has been tempered? The manufacturer's brand name must be on the corner of each piece. On other than single- or double-strength glass, look for that brand name if you're thinking about cutting any glass. It might save you the embarrassment and cost of shattering a perfectly good piece of tempered glass. You don't cut tempered glass, you buy it in stock sizes.

Patio Covers

Patio covers come in so many different colors and materials that the 1970 edition of UBC gave them a separate chapter — Chapter 49 in the Appendix.

Section 4901 defines patio covers:

> *Patio covers are one-story structures not exceeding 12 feet in height. Enclosure walls may have any configuration, provided the open area of the longer wall and one additional wall is equal to at least 65 percent of the area below a minimum of 6 feet 8 inches of each wall, measured from the floor. Openings may be enclosed with insect screening or plastic.*

In the next paragraph it states what they can and can't be used for:

> *Patio covers shall be used only for recreational, outdoor living purposes and not as carports, garages, storage rooms or habitable rooms.*

This is very important. Many manufacturers claim you can use their patio covers for carports, but the code doesn't allow it. To find out if the unit is a patio cover or a carport (especially when you're facing a fast-talking salesman), get the make and model number, the manufacturer's name, and any product specs. Then call the inspector. It will only take him a minute or two to check his Evaluation Reports and find out if the cover is approved for any application. If it's a common national brand, he'll have the information on hand. You'll need his blessing anyway when you apply for a permit, so you might as well start off on the right foot.

Patio covers and carports are exposed to many stresses and strains that aren't common with other structures. They must be designed to withstand the stress limits of the code, all dead loads, and a minimum vertical live load of 10 pounds per square inch — plus one other very critical load: the uplift load. Because of their construction, patio covers and carports are more susceptible to this load than most structures. They must be designed to support a minimum wind uplift load equal to the horizontal wind load pushing upward against the roof surface. But if your patio is less than 10 feet above grade, the uplift load may be only three-fourths the horizontal wind load.

Agricultural Buildings

Recognizing that the code would eventually be used in most rural and agricultural areas, the ICBO added Chapter 15, *Agricultural Buildings*, to the code in 1973. In the 1979 edition it became Chapter 11 of the Appendix. Here's what Section 1107 says:

> *The provisions of this chapter shall apply exclusively to agricultural buildings. Such buildings shall be classified as a Group M, Division 3 Occupancy and shall include the following uses:*
>
> *1. Storage, livestock and poultry.*
>
> *2. Milking barns.*
>
> *3. Shade structures.*
>
> *4. Horticultural structures (greenhouses and crop protection).*

The allowable height and area of agricultural buildings are greatly increased and exit requirements are generally relaxed compared to other building types. UBC Table A-11-A (Figure 3-10 in Chapter 3) shows basic allowable areas. Because of their lower occupancy rate, the setbacks, occupancy separations and most other restrictions are vastly different from other types of buildings. But this chapter doesn't cover any residences, private garages, or commercial or quasi-commercial buildings; the main code sections apply to them.

Sound Transmission Control

Standards for sound transmission control appear in Chapter 35 of the Appendix. Group R occupancies now have some protection from noisy neighbors.

After reading through that chapter and the standards that go with it, I'm afraid it's still going to be difficult to enforce compliance, especially in apartment buildings. To do so you'd need a sound engineer with a battery of equipment. To make sure you're meeting the code requirements, check to see if your city has adopted Chapter 35. If it has, ask the building inspector what you have to do.

Prefabricated Buildings

These can include everything from small metal tool sheds to barns and equipment storage facilities. Most of the smaller structures are exempt from permit requirements. Section 301(b) of the UBC exempts detached accessory buildings under 120 square feet.

Prefab buildings larger than that are covered in Chapter 50 of the UBC:

> **Section 5001(a) Purpose.** *The purpose of this chapter is to regulate materials and establish methods of safe construction where any structure or portion thereof is wholly or partially prefabricated.*

> **(c) Definition.** *Prefabricated Assembly is a structural unit, the integral parts of which have been built up or assembled prior to incorporation in the building.*

Most standard prefab steel and aluminum structures meet the code requirements. Other than the interior improvements in these structures, (sanitation, insulation, interior finish), there's nothing to inspect except the footings and foundations.

That raises the question of whether you could prefab a building in your back yard that you might use later as a house. It might work except for some sneaky little provisions in Chapter 50. It says a certificate of approval must be obtained from an approved agency for each structure.

What's Your Category?

I've been inspecting buildings since 1965. I try not to, but I can't avoid putting the contractors I deal with into one of five categories. Normally I don't talk about this. But I want to share it with you. There's a reason. I suspect most building inspectors do something similar. You should know enough to stay out of the wrong categories:

Category A Contractors could get a permit from me on their say-so alone. I've even looked the other way when one of these guys had to start a job in a hurry, before the plans were drawn or permit issued. You get to be a Category A Contractor by knowing as much or more about building and the code as anyone in the community. You do nothing but quality work that meets the highest professional standards, no matter what the situation and no matter who's watching. Category A Contractors usually get the best jobs from owners with the deepest pockets. They're nearly always busy. Though this is a small group, they set a good example for everyone in the industry.

Category B Contractors probably know as much about construction as Category A Contractors. But they have to buy most jobs with low bids or by hustling a little harder. If nothing bad happens, Category B Contractors turn out good jobs at bargain prices. But when the fat hits the fire, Category B guys will cut corners. They'll compromise on quality to save their margin. They'll let a few things slide by if no one is going to notice. That's why I have to notice. This is a large group.

Category C Contractors don't know as much about construction as either Category A or Category B Contractors. Most would like to be as skilled as their more experienced brethren. But they don't know how. Very few would try to cheat the owner or confuse the inspector. But inexperience and carelessness show in their work. Not all Category C Contractors are new at building. Some have been at it for many years. They just haven't learned very fast. That's why I'm very patient with these builders. I'll explain anything as often as necessary. And I keep my eyes open. Again, this is a large group.

Category D Contractors just don't seem to care. They usually know what they should be doing. But they aren't going to do it until someone makes them. That someone is usually me. I won't use the word lazy for these guys. Maybe the word sluggish is better.

Category F Contractors stand alone. I sometimes wonder what makes this guy tick. You could camp in the middle of the project and Category F contractors would still try to cheat all around you. It's almost like a game: get away with everything you can.

A couple of years ago I gave a talk to our local home builder's association. I explained my five construction categories. That was a mistake. I was too candid. My little talk hurt the pride of some good builders and good friends who don't happen to rate at the top of my list. So I don't say much about categories any more. In fact, I wish I'd never said anything. But you should know that everyone in the construction industry is earning a reputation every day — either for craftsmanship and professionalism or for the lack of it. My advice is simple. Guard your professional reputation like you protect your favorite skill saw. Nothing you're likely to own is more valuable.

16

Combustion Air

As a building inspector I was constantly running into problems over "combustion air." How much was enough? Here's what Section 601 of the Uniform Mechanical Code has to say about it:

> **Section 601(a) Air Supply.** *Fuel-burning equipment shall be assured a sufficient supply of combustion air. The methods of providing combustion air in this chapter do not apply to direct vent appliances, appliances listed as having separated combustion systems, enclosed furnaces, listed cooking appliances, refrigerators and domestic clothes dryers.*
>
> *In buildings of unusually tight construction, combustion air shall be obtained from outside. With prior approval, in buildings of ordinary tightness insofar as infiltration is concerned, all or a portion of the combustion air for fuel-burning appliances may be obtained from*

infiltration when the requirement for 50 cubic feet per 1000 Btu/h input is met.

*(b) **Existing buildings**. When fuel-burning appliances are installed in an existing building containing other fuel-burning appliances, the room or space shall be provided with combustion air as required by this chapter for all fuel-burning appliances contained therein.*

This whole chapter in the UMC is vague. I can foresee more than a few disputes with building inspectors who haven't thought it out.

Most new or recently-remodeled buildings have combustion air inlets for fuel-burning appliances. But older buildings may not have combustion air inlets, or the inlets may be blocked. For instance, louvered vents that provide air can be blocked by dampers or by items stored in front of them. Combustion air inlets may be obstructed when rooms are remodeled.

Did you notice the term "ordinary tightness" in Section 601(a)? How would you define it? Let's look at some definitions from Chapter 4 of the UMC to help us:

Confined Space *is a room or space having a volume less than 50 cubic feet per 1000 Btu/h of the aggregate input rating of all fuel-burning appliances installed in that space.*

Unconfined Space *is a room or space having a volume equal to at least 50 cubic feet per 1000 Btu/h of the aggregate input rating of all fuel-burning appliances installed in that space. Rooms communicating directly with the space in which the appliances are installed, through openings not furnished with doors, are considered a part of the unconfined space.*

> **Unusually Tight Construction** *is construction where:*
>
> *(a) Walls and ceiling exposed to the outside atmosphere have a continuous water vapor retarder with a rating of one perm or less with any openings gasketed and sealed, and*
>
> *(b) Weatherstripping on openable windows and doors, and*
>
> *(c) Caulking or sealants are applied to areas such as joints around window and door frames, between sole plates and floors, between wall-ceiling joints, between wall panels and at penetrations for plumbing, electrical and gas lines and at other openings.*

I guess we can assume that a building is of "ordinary tightness" if it doesn't meet the definition of "unusually tight construction."

Computing Combustion Air Requirements

If you've used the previous edition of this manual, take time to read this next section very carefully. There's been a big change in the way you compute combustion air requirements.

This is what Section 603(d) of the UMC offers:

> *(d) **Interior Spaces.** In buildings of ordinary tightness, combustion air provided by infiltration may be obtained from freely communicating interior spaces, provided the combined volume in cubic feet complies with the following conditions:*
>
> *1. **Adequate volume—gas and liquid.** If the volume of the room or space in which fuel-burning appliances are installed is equal to or greater than 50 cubic feet per 1000 Btu/h of aggregate input rating of appliances, infiltration may be regarded as adequate to provide combus-*

tion air. Exclude from the calculation the input ratings of listed direct vent appliances, enclosed furnaces, cooking appliances, refrigerators and domestic clothes dryers.

2. Insufficient volume—gas and liquid. Rooms or spaces containing gas- or liquid-fuel-burning appliances which do not have the volume as specified above shall be provided with minimum unobstructed combustion air openings as specified in Section 607 and arranged as specified in Section 602.

You'll hear a lot about Btu's whenever you get involved with heat-producing appliances such as furnaces, water heaters, ovens or hot plates. A *British thermal unit* is the amount of heat required to raise the temperature of 1 pound of water 1 degree Fahrenheit at or near its point of maximum density.

Consider the Size of the Enclosure

Let's look at a common example. Your home measures 24 feet by 36 feet and you have the usual 8-foot ceilings. You've got about 7,000 cubic feet of space. Let's say your furnace is in an unfinished basement with the same dimensions as the house, so it's also in a space of about 7,000 cubic feet.

Let's further assume that your fuel needs are 150,000 Btu's per hour. Using the figures from Section 603(d), you need 50 cubic feet for each 1,000 Btu's. Multiply 150 by 50. That's 7,000 cubic feet of combustion air — just what you have. But this is with no partitions in your basement.

You may have a problem, though. An unfinished basement simply screams for the family handyman to finish it. When he does, the furnace usually ends up in a furnace room or a corner of the utility room. But that furnace, squeezed into a smaller area, still needs to have an adequate supply of air. So how much is "adequate?"

Air Required

Here again we've got to start with the size of the area where your fuel-burning appliance is located. UMC Table 6-A and Section 607(b) of the UMC have this to say on the subject:

> *(b)* ***Appliances Located in Unconfined Spaces.***
>
> *1. If the unconfined space is within a building of unusually tight construction, combustion air shall be obtained from outdoors or from spaces freely communicating with the outdoors. Under such conditions, permanent openings having a total free air of at least 1 square inch per 5000 Btu / h of total input rating of all appliances shall be provided. Ducts admitting outdoor air may be connected to the cold-air return of the heating system and shall comply with Section 604.*
>
> *2. If the unconfined space is within a building of ordinary tightness so that infiltration may be considered as contributing combustion air, Section 603(d) may be applied.*

Remember, that's for unconfined spaces. For appliances in confined spaces with all combustion air coming from inside the building, you need at least 1 square inch for each 1,000 Btu's input rating. That's five times as much. Each of the combustion air openings has to be at least 100 square inches — only 10 inches by 10 inches, probably the smallest size made.

When we have to bring in all the air from outdoors, the vertical ducts must have a free area of 1 square inch for each 4,000 Btu per hour of input (Section 607(c)2). Horizontal ducts, on the other hand, require 1 square inch of free area for each 2,000 Btu per hour of input, or twice as much. Ducts combining outdoor air and indoor air need only 1 square inch of free area for each 5,000 Btu per hour. Where ducts are admitting outdoor air, they may be connected to the cold-air return of the heating system.

Supplying the Air

According to Section 602 of the UMC, half of the required air must come from an opening located within the upper 12 inches of the room or enclosure. The other half must come from an opening not more than 12 inches above the base of the lowest appliance. That's usually two louvered openings, one at the top and one at the bottom of the door.

Does it have to be a door? No, the code doesn't *require* the louvers to be placed in a door, but it makes sense to do it that way. After all, it's cheaper to cut a door than to cut grillwork into the wall. Also, according to the heating contractors, it's safer. If the openings are placed in the door, there's little likelihood they'll ever be blocked.

Of course, there are other ways to supply combustion air. Section 602(a) of the UMC says that if the enclosure is not less than 50 square feet, all the air may come from a supply opening within the upper 12 inches of the enclosure. But there must be an equivalent supply opening extending directly to the firebox. That means you have to keep the firebox door clear, since that's usually where the combustion air enters.

Sources of Air

The source *and* condition of the air are important. Not long ago, a hospital near me converted its furnaces and boilers from oil to natural gas. Because of other remodeling, they closed the combustion air duct and opened another hole in the wall of the furnace room directly to the outside. This was properly fitted with a louvered vent electrically interlocked with the gas burner. When the thermostat called for heat, the louvers were electrically opened at the same time ignition took place.

It had been designed by a heating engineer who did a beautiful job. When the boiler fired, I was on hand to check the system and the louvers responded perfectly. The job was approved.

About the middle of January I received calls from both the contractor and the hospital. Everything in the boiler room was frozen. Why? Several steam lines and a main water line passed in front of the combustion air vent. With below-freezing weather outside and the boiler calling for heat, the icy wind blowing through the vent had frozen all the pipes in front of it. The problem was solved by placing heaters in the passageway where the cold wind entered. But it took a freeze-up to point out the problem. I couldn't find anything about it in the code except a warning that exposed pipes should be protected. But who would anticipate that pipes would need to be protected from freezing inside a room with two boilers?

Section 603(c) of the UMC specifies where you *can't* get your combustion air:

> **Prohibited Sources.** *Openings and ducts shall not connect appliance enclosures with space in which the operation of a fan may adversely affect the flow of combustion air. Combustion air shall not be obtained from a hazardous location or from any area in which objectionable quantities of flammable vapor, lint or dust are released. Combustion air shall not be taken from a refrigeration machinery room.*

You can't use combustion air openings or ducts where fire dampers are required. And you can't install volume dampers in combustion air openings or ducts.

That leaves you with three primary sources of combustion air:

1) Outside of the building

2) The underfloor area, provided there's sufficient ventilation

3) Inside the building or conditioned space

Outside— Size your duct to the volume of air needed because you can't install dampers. To use outside air, you must screen your entry duct with a corrosion-resistant screen of not more than 1/2-inch mesh. For both outside and underfloor vents, make sure the screens are kept clean. All screened openings must be kept free of dust, leaves, and other debris that will restrict the opening.

For some reason attic space is included under "outside air" instead of in a category of its own. But you can only use attic air if there are sufficient openings to the outside. You must have a minimum clear space of 30 inches at the maximum height of the attic.

Underfloor— You can use underfloor space if there's sufficient ventilation either through special vents or openings through the foundation vents.

Inside— Using air from inside a building opens up another can of worms. Section 601 of the UMC gives specifications for using combustion air solely from this source. The main consideration is that the Btu rating must not exceed 1/20 the gross cubic feet of the structure. But I prefer to go by *available space*. That's the area that can't be closed off by doors. In most homes you'll probably have enough space, even if you don't count the bedrooms that can be closed off.

Now that we have you spooked, there's a ray of sunshine. The code gives you an out. You don't have to comply with the combustion air requirements if the installation has been designed by a qualified engineer.

Consider Other Air Users

There are many other air users in your house — common household items such as fireplaces, kitchen fans and bathroom vents. Each removes air from a confined space. I doubt seriously if many people are aware of how great this air loss is. Recirculating kitchen fans draw air across a charcoal filter to remove cooking odors and grease, then put the air back into the room. *They're* not a problem. But if your fan discharges to the exterior of the building, then it's *reducing* the amount of available combustion air.

While we're at it, here's a little advice. Check the attic to make sure the kitchen fan isn't dumping kitchen grease into the attic. The same caution applies to bath vents. Make sure these vents discharge outside.

Section 606 of the UMC states:

> *Operation of exhaust fans, kitchen ventilation systems, clothes dryers, or fireplaces shall be considered in determining combustion air requirements to avoid unsatisfactory operation of installed gas appliances.*

Fireplaces

As an inspector I was often called out to investigate smoking fireplaces, especially in new homes. There are many reasons for a smoky fireplace, but fireplace construction is seldom the culprit. Houses today are more airtight than they used to be. Single-wall construction with plywood sheathing or siding doesn't admit as much exterior air as diagonal sheathing or shiplap siding. Storm windows, weatherstripping and plastic vapor barriers further reduce air leakage.

In a tight home, furnaces, kitchen and bath fans and fireplaces compete for whatever air is trapped inside the house. During the day, when windows are open and doors are being opened and closed, this isn't a problem. There's a lot of air coming into the house. But it can be a problem at night when all windows and doors are shut. I usually found that a fireplace was smoking because it was starved for oxygen. The flames were licking out for any available air.

Many fireplaces are now designed with vents and tubes to provide combustion air from the outside.

Commercial Air Users

Commercial establishments such as restaurants also have combustion air problems. The vent hoods (and many are required) take a lot of air out of most kitchens. And there are gas-flame grills, water heaters and other items gobbling up air.

In winter, the problem usually gets worse. Windows are kept shut and air conditioning units are plugged. But venting of kitchen vapor and steam continues. The kitchen becomes an airless box until someone opens a door and momentarily relieves the condition.

The same thing can happen in your home. If, on some windless night, you open a door or window and a gust of air blows in, you've got a problem. You're living in a vacuum created by your fireplace, furnace and other air-consuming devices. A properly-designed house, and one that doesn't draw cold air, is one with a slightly positive pressure.

Combustion air is probably the least considered of all of a house's ills. But, with the many devices competing for air, it's something that can't be ignored.

In the next chapter, we'll take a look at the Uniform Mechanical Code requirements for heating and cooling homes and small commercial buildings.

The Day I Got Spooked

In most cities and counties an inspection is required when new gas, water or electric lines are installed or re-opened. One day I got a call from a young lady who had just moved into an older home. A new gas line had been installed and she needed an inspection before the gas company would begin service. Would I please come out and do whatever was required?

After I'd checked the gas line, she asked me to take a look in the basement. She didn't use it, she told me, but there must be something wrong down there. She heard strange noises coming from under the house at night. She seemed completely serious. My guess was that neighborhood kids were playing down there. "No problem," I told her.

She pointed to a place in the hall where the freezer stood. The basement door was behind it and was both locked and nailed shut. I borrowed a hammer and pried the door open. I tried the light switch just inside the door, but it didn't work.

Dim light coming from across the basement showed the outline of furnace duct and an old furnace. The basement must have been a coal bin and furnace room when the home was first built. Judging by the damp, mouldy smell, the furnace hadn't been used in many years. Most likely, no one had gone down those stairs into the basement in years.

I stood just inside the basement door for a minute while my eyes became accustomed to the dim light. The door I came through opened onto a small landing at the top of a flight of stairs. Squatting down, I could see two small windows at the far end of the basement. They must have been obscured by bushes on the outside, as very little light was coming through. From where I stood, I couldn't see any way in or out except the stairway I was standing on and the two small windows.

I put my weight on the first step down the flight of stairs. It felt solid. I tested the next. The stairs seemed safe enough. But the further I got from the door at the top of the stairs, the more uncomfortable I felt. The hair on the back of my neck was standing straight up. I remember wondering, "Do I get paid for exploring haunted houses?" No doubt about it, I was scared.

I turned to look back up the stairs. The lady was still there, watching from the basement door. If she hadn't been there, I would have been up the stairs and gone, quick as a wink. Instead, I gave her a weak smile, then turned to take another cautious step down. A dozen more steps and I was on the basement floor. I went straight to one window, checked the latch, then did the same on the second window. Both window latches were stuck in the locked position. The cobwebs around the window frames showed the windows hadn't been opened in years. I turned briskly and went back up the stairs, climbing just slowly enough so I didn't look like I was running.

"Nothing to worry about," I said reassuringly. "Looks fine to me. I'll tell the gas company it's OK to start service."

Then I walked, not ran, to my car and drove away.

Several weeks later I was telling the story to some friends who live just down the street from that house. They both laughed. "Didn't you know?" they asked. "That house is haunted. You should hear some of the ghost stories the tenants tell. One couple even moved out. They couldn't sleep at night. But the lady there now says she had someone from the city come out to check the basement. She says it's fine now."

17

Heating, Ventilation and Air Conditioning

Every building code is complex. They have to be. Construction is a complex subject. And codes try to cover it all. To do that, many sections refer to other sections which refer to still more sections. To answer a specific question, you may have to understand what each of the referenced sections requires. That's no problem if you've spent a lifetime working with the code — as many inspectors have. They take pride in having mastered the complexity and subtleties in the code. Builders who haven't had a lifetime to do that, and don't want to, are at a big disadvantage. That's the reason why I wrote this book — to level the playing field a little so you can anticipate problems before they become expensive mistakes.

Heating, ventilating and air conditioning (HVAC) proves my point. The Uniform Building Code doesn't even cover HVAC work. You have to refer to the Uniform Mechanical Code. That's a separate book published by the International Conference of Building Officials, the same people who put out the UBC. Since nearly every building has heating, cooling or ventilating equipment, you can have UMC problems on nearly any job. After reading this chapter, you should be able to avoid the most common types of code problems on residential and light commercial HVAC work.

We learned in the last chapter how to be sure a furnace has enough combustion air. The next step is installing HVAC equipment so it will pass inspection under the Uniform Mechanical Code.

The UMC is another complex code. It would take another book this size to explain it completely. You don't need that. So I'll focus on what you *do* need, installing fuel-using appliances excluding electrical appliances.

Let's start with a very important section of the UMC:

> **Section 501.** *Equipment shall conform to the requirements of this code.*
>
> *Equipment shall not be installed or altered in violation of this code nor shall fuel input to equipment be increased in excess of the approved Btu/h rating at the altitude where it is being used.*
>
> *Defective material or parts shall be replaced in such a manner as not to invalidate any approval.*

In simpler terms — don't mess up good equipment with a bad installation job.

Heating equipment gets hot. That's unavoidable. It can also be deadly. An installer who tries to get a little more than the designed heat output, or a little better than the designed air circulation, may be creating work for your local firemen. Don't do it. There are good reasons for following the code and the manufacturer's design limits.

Every appliance you install or service has a data plate showing the intended function and capacity. Take the manufacturer's word on what they know best: their appliance. If the tag is missing, return the equipment. Don't install it.

> *Section 503(a). General. Each appliance shall be designed for use with the type of fuel to which it will be connected . . .*

There's more to that section, but that's the meat of it. If you have natural gas, don't try to hook up a butane or propane appliance. It won't work. If it lights at all, it'll just sputter along at a fraction of the design capacity. You might not burn the house down, but you won't heat it either. Using natural gas on an appliance intended for butane or propane can be deadly. The gas orifice is the wrong size. A natural gas appliance running on butane is a blowtorch.

In any event, you're required to install two approved shut-off valves: one within 3 feet of the appliance and another at the service meter. In each case, provide a union connection between the appliance and the valve. This makes it easier to exchange appliances.

Here's a note about safety: In California and wherever earthquakes are common, authorities recommend keeping a tool near the service entrance for closing the gas shut-off valve. After a severe earthquake, gas should be shut off until the gas system has been checked.

> *Section 503(b) Oil-burning appliances. The tank, piping and valves for appliances burning oil shall be installed in accordance with the requirements of standards referenced in Appendix C.*

I'm not going to reproduce those standards here because they just list a lot of ANSI (American National Standards Institute) standards by section number. That wouldn't be of much help. So I'll just repeat the obvious: always install the appliance according to the manufacturer's specifications. Of course, that's always good advice.

> ***503(c) Gas-burning appliances.*** *Appliances designed to burn gas shall be rigidly connected to the gas-supply outlet in an approved manner and with approved materials.*

Section 503(c) then goes on to list a number of exceptions for semi-rigid or flexible metal tubing connectors. They can't exceed 3 feet in length, except range connectors can go to 6 feet. Provide a shutoff valve between the supply and the connector. You can't conceal the connectors in walls, floors or partitions. Finally, the connectors must be at least as large as the inlet connection.

If you plan to connect more than one appliance to the same gas line, you may have to increase the size of that line. I heartily recommend checking with either the building inspector or the local gas supplier before beginning work. You might save yourself a lot of money.

One final reminder: You can't use galvanized pipe — it must be black iron or a similar approved material. The zinc coating will waste away on galvanized pipe and clog jets and orifices in the appliance.

Gas piping is covered in both the Uniform Plumbing Code and the Uniform Mechanical Code. That's because the UPC has been around a lot longer than the UMC.

Installing HVAC Equipment

I'll say this again because it's so important: When installing any appliance, always do what the manufacturer recommends. Every appliance is tested the way it's intended to be used. Using it any other way may be dangerous. If your appliance was installed by a dealer, chances are it was done correctly. Just check it over and make sure the installer left a copy of the installation and operating instructions attached to the appliance.

But if you're doing the job yourself, where are you going to install this equipment? That information is in Section 504(b): unless the equipment was designed for a closet or alcove, it must be installed in a room with a volume at least 12 times the total volume of the furnace. If you're installing a central heating boiler, the room must be at least 16 times the volume of the boiler. And there's another thing: Even if the room or space is higher than 8 feet, you still have to calculate the volume *as if* it had an 8-foot ceiling.

If you have to install an unlisted appliance, use the standard clearances from combustible construction specified in UMC Table 5-A (Figure 17-1). Figure 17-2 is the clearances with specified forms of protection.

If the appliance is designed to be permanently mounted, it must be fastened in place with supports designed to resist loads specified in the UBC. And if you're in Seismic Zones 3 and 4, even a water heater that's over 4 feet high must be anchored to resist horizontal movement — just in case the world starts to shake.

Last but not least, appliances must be accessible for inspection, service, repair and replacement. If you have an underfloor installation, remember that the access hole must be large enough to remove the appliance under the floor. If the access

TABLE NO. 5-A—STANDARD INSTALLATION CLEARANCES IN INCHES FOR UNLISTED HEAT-PRODUCING APPLIANCES
SEE SECTION 504

RESIDENTIAL-TYPE APPLIANCES	FUEL	APPLIANCE				
		ABOVE TOP OF CASING OR APPLIANCE	FROM TOP AND SIDES OF WARM-AIR BONNET OR PLENUM	FROM FRONT[1]	FROM BACK	FROM SIDES
BOILERS AND WATER HEATERS Steam Boilers—15 psi Water Boilers—250°F. Water Heaters—200°F. All Water Walled or Jacketed	Automatic Oil or Comb. Gas-Oil	6		24	6	6
	Automatic Gas	6		18	6	6
	Solid	6		48	6	6
FURNACES—CENTRAL; OR HEATERS—ELECTRIC CENTRAL WARM-AIR FURNACES Gravity, Upflow, Downflow, Horizontal and Duct Warm-air—250°F. Max.	Automatic Oil or Comb. Gas-Oil	6[2]	6[2]	24	6	6
	Automatic Gas	6[2]	6[2]	18	6	6
	Solid	18[3]	18[3]	48	18	18
	Electric	6[2]	6[2]	18	6	6
FURNACES—FLOOR For Mounting in Combustible Floors	Automatic Oil or Comb. Gas-Oil	36		12	12	12
	Automatic Gas	36		12	12	12
HEAT EXCHANGER Steam—15 psi Max. Hot Water—250°F. Max.		1	1	1	1	1
ROOM HEATERS[4] Circulating Type—Vented or Unvented	Oil or Solid	36		24	12	12
	Gas	36		24	12	12
Radiant or Other Type Vented or Unvented	Oil or Solid	36		36	36	36
	Gas	36		36	18	18
	Gas with double metal or ceramic back	36		36	12	18
Fireplace Stove	Solid	48[5]		54	48[5]	48[5]

From the Uniform Mechanical Code, © 1983, ICBO

Figure 17-1 Standard installation clearances

TABLE NO. 5-A—STANDARD INSTALLATION CLEARANCES IN INCHES FOR UNLISTED HEAT-PRODUCING APPLIANCES SEE SECTION 504—(Continued)

RESIDENTIAL-TYPE APPLIANCES	FUEL	APPLIANCE					
		ABOVE TOP OF CASING OR APPLIANCE	FROM TOP AND SIDES OF WARM-AIR BONNET OR PLENUM	FROM FRONT[1]	FROM BACK	FROM SIDES	
						Firing Side	Opp. Side
RADIATORS Steam or Hot Water[6]		36		6	6	6	
RANGES—COOKING STOVES Vented or Unvented	Oil	30[7]			9	24	18
	Gas	30[7]			6	6	6
	Solid Clay-lined Firepot	30[7]			24	24	18
	Solid Unlined Firepot	30[7]			36	36	18
	Electric	30[7]			6	6	
INCINERATORS Domestic Types		36[8]		48	36	36	

COMMERCIAL-INDUSTRIAL-TYPE LOW-HEAT APPLIANCES ANY AND ALL PHYSICAL SIZES EXCEPT AS NOTED	FUEL	APPLIANCE				
		ABOVE TOP OF CASING OR APPLIANCE[9]	FROM TOP AND SIDES OF WARM-AIR BONNET OR PLENUM	FROM FRONT[1]	FROM BACK[9]	FROM SIDES[9]
BOILERS AND WATER HEATERS 100 cu. ft. or less Any psi Steam	All Fuels	18		48	18	18
50 psi or less Any Size	All Fuels	18		48	18	18

From the Uniform Mechanical Code, © 1988, ICBO

Figure 17-1 (cont'd) Standard installation clearances

COMMERCIAL INDUSTRIAL-TYPE LOW-HEAT APPLIANCES ANY AND ALL PHYSICAL SIZES EXCEPT AS NOTED	FUEL	APPLIANCE				
		ABOVE TOP OF CASING OR APPLIANCE	FROM TOP AND SIDES OF WARM-AIR BONNET OR PLENUM	FROM FRONT[1]	FROM BACK	FROM SIDES
UNIT HEATERS Floor Mounted or Suspended—Any Size	Steam or Hot Water	1			1	1
Suspended—100 cu. ft. or less	Oil or Comb. Gas-Oil	6		24	18	18
Suspended—100 cu. ft. or less	Gas	6		18	18	18
Suspended—Over 100 cu. ft.	All Fuels	18		48	18	18
Floor Mounted—Any Size	All Fuels	18		48	18	18
RANGES—RESTAURANT-TYPE Floor Mounted	All Fuels	48		48	18	18
OTHER LOW-HEAT INDUSTRIAL APPLIANCES Floor Mounted or Suspended	All Fuels	18	18	48	18	18

(Continued)

From the Uniform Mechanical Code, © 1988, ICBO

Figure 17-1 (cont'd) *Standard installation clearances*

TABLE NO. 5-A—STANDARD INSTALLATION CLEARANCES IN INCHES FOR UNLISTED HEAT-PRODUCING APPLIANCES
SEE SECTION 504—(Continued)

COMMERCIAL INDUSTRIAL-TYPE MEDIUM-HEAT APPLIANCES	FUEL	APPLIANCE					
		ABOVE TOP OF CASING OR APPLIANCE[10]	FROM TOP AND SIDES OF WARM-AIR BONNET OR PLENUM	FROM FRONT[1]	FROM BACK[10]	FROM SIDES[10]
BOILERS AND WATER HEATERS Over 50 psi Over 100 cu. ft.	All Fuels	48		96	36	36
OTHER MEDIUM-HEAT INDUSTRIAL APPLIANCES All Sizes	All Fuels	48	36	96	36	36
INCINERATORS All Sizes		48		96	36	36
INDUSTRIAL-TYPE HIGH-HEAT APPLIANCES						
HIGH-HEAT INDUSTRIAL APPLIANCES All Sizes	All Fuels	180		360	120	120

From the Uniform Mechanical Code, © *1988, ICBO*

Figure 17-1 (cont'd) *Standard installation clearances*

FOOTNOTES FOR TABLE NO. 5-A

[1]The minimum dimension shall be that necessary for servicing the appliance, including access for cleaning and normal care, tube removal, etc.

[2]For a listed oil, combination gas-oil, gas or electric furnace this dimension may be 2 inches if the furnace limit control cannot be set higher than 250°F., or this dimension may be 1 inch if the limit control cannot be set higher than 200°F., or the appliance shall be marked to indicate that the outlet air temperature cannot exceed 200°F.

[3]The dimension may be 6 inches for an automatically stoker-fired forced-warm-air furnace equipped with 250°F. limit control and with barometric draft control operated by draft intensity and permanently set to limit draft to a maximum intensity of 0.13-inch water gage.

[4]Approved appliances shall be installed on non-combustible floors and may be installed on protected combustible floors. Heating appliances approved for installation on protected combustible flooring shall be so constructed that flame and hot gases do not come in contact with the appliance base. Protection for combustible floors shall consist of 4-inch hollow masonry covered with sheet metal at least 0.021 inch thick (No. 24 manufacturer's standard gage). Masonry shall be permanently fastened in place in an approved manner with the ends unsealed and joints matched so as to provide free circulation of air through the masonry. Floor protection shall extend 12 inches at the sides and rear of the appliance, except that at least 18 inches shall be required on the appliance-opening side or sides measured horizontally from the edges of the opening.

[5]The 48-inch clearance may be reduced to 36 inches when protection equivalent to that provided by Items (a) through (g) of Table No. 5-B is applied to the combustible construction.

[6]Steampipes and hot-water heating pipes shall be installed with a clearance of at least 1 inch to all combustible construction or material, except that at the points where pipes carrying steam or hot water at not over 15 pounds gage pressure emerge from a floor, wall or ceiling, the clearance at the opening through the finish floorboards or wall-ceiling boards may be reduced to not less than 1/2 inch. Each such opening shall be covered with a plate of noncombustible material.

Such pipes passing through stock shelving shall be covered with not less than 1 inch of approved insulation.

Wood boxes or casings enclosing uninsulated steam or hot-water heating pipes or wooden covers to recesses in walls in which such uninsulated pipes are placed shall be lined with metal or insulating millboard.

Where the temperature of the boiler piping does not exceed 160°F., the provisions of this table shall not apply.

Coverings or insulation used on steam or hot-water pipes shall be of material suitable for the operating temperature of the system. The insulation or jackets shall be of noncombustible materials, or the insulation or jackets and lap-seal adhesives shall be tested as a composite product. Such composite product shall have a flame-spread rating of not more than 25 and a smoke-developed rating not to exceed 50 when tested in accordance with U.B.C. Standard No. 42-1.

[7]To combustible material or metal cabinets. If the underside of such combustible material or metal cabinet is protected with insulating millboard at least 1/4 inch thick covered with sheet metal of not less than 0.013 inch (No. 28 gage), the distance may be not less than 24 inches.

[8]Clearance above charging door shall be not less than 48 inches.

[9]If the appliance is encased in brick, the 18-inch clearance above and at sides and rear may be reduced to not less than 12 inches.

[10]If the appliance is encased in brick, the clearance above may be not less than 36 inches and at sides and rear may be not less than 18 inches.

From the Uniform Mechanical Code, © *1988, ICBO*

Figure 17-1 (cont'd)   *Standard installation clearances*

TABLE NO. 5-B—CLEARANCES, INCHES, WITH SPECIFIED FORMS OF PROTECTION[1,2]

TYPE OF PROTECTION Applied to the Combustible Material Unless Otherwise Specified and Covering All Surfaces Within the Distance Specified as the Required Clearance With No Protection (Thicknesses are Minimum)	WHERE THE STANDARD CLEARANCE IN TABLE NO. 5-A WITH NO PROTECTION IS:														
	36 Inches			18 Inches			12 Inches			9 Inches			6 Inches		
	Above	Sides and Rear	Chimney or Vent Connector	Above	Sides and Rear	Chimney or Vent Connector	Above	Sides and Rear	Chimney or Vent Connector	Above	Sides and Rear	Chimney or Vent Connector	Above	Sides and Rear	Chimney or Vent Connector
(a) 1/4" in insulating millboard spaced out 1"[3]	30	18	30	15	9	12	9	6	9	3	6	6	3	2	3
(b) 0.013" (No. 28 manufacturer's standard gage) steel sheet on 1/4" insulating millboard	24	18	24	12	9	12	9	6	9	3	6	4	3	2	2
(c) 0.013" (No. 28 manufacturer's standard gage) steel sheet spaced out 1"[3]	18	12	18	9	6	9	6	4	6	2	4	4	2	2	2
(d) 0.013" (No. 28 manufacturer's standard gage) steel sheet on 1/8" insulating millboard spaced out 1"[3]	18	12	18	9	6	9	6	4	6	2	4	4	2	2	2
(e) 1 1/2" insulating cement covering on heating appliance	18	12	36	9	6	18	6	4	9	2	4	9	2	1	6
(f) 1/4" insulating millboard on 1" mineral fiber batts reinforced with wire mesh or equivalent	18	12	18	6	6	6	4	4	6	2	4	4	2	2	2
(g) 0.027" (No. 22 manufacturer's standard gage) steel sheet on 1" mineral fiber batts reinforced with wire or equivalent	18	12	12	4	3	3	2	2	2	2	2	2	2	2	2
(h) 1/4" insulating millboard	36	36	36	18	18	18	12	12	9	4	12	9	4	4	4

[1] For appliances complying with Sections 504 (b) and (c)

[2] Except for the protection described in (e), all clearances shall be measured from the outer surface of the appliance to the combustible material, disregarding any intervening protection applied to the combustible material.

[3] Spacers shall be of noncombustible material.

Note: Insulating millboard is a factory made product formed of noncombustible materials, normally fibers, and having a thermal conductivity of 1 Btu-inch per square foot per degree F. or less.

From the Uniform Mechanical Code, © 1988, ICBO

Figure 17-2 Clearances with specified forms of protection

hole is within the building, it can't be covered with carpeting or hidden in a closet. "Readily accessible" means just that.

The inspector probably wouldn't let you put an LPG appliance down there anyway. They can't be placed in pits where heavier-than-air gases might be trapped. If the underfloor space is above grade, you'd have no problem.

Automatic Control Devices

All heating appliances must be equipped with a listed device which will shut off the fuel supply to the main burner in the case of a pilot or ignition failure. Nearly all heaters come with a device that meets code requirements. It's best to check, though, to be sure. This rule doesn't apply to ranges, log lighters, or similar devices.

If your heater is located in a remote area or isn't readily accessible, install a remote control shut-off valve.

All furnaces, whether forced air or gravity type, must have an air outlet temperature control set for a maximum of 250 degrees. These are usually installed in the outlet plenum within 2 feet of the heating element. For electric furnaces, set the limit at not more than 200 degrees and install a fusible link or manual reset control that keeps the outlet air temperature below 250 degrees.

The data plate on gas, oil and electric heaters and heat pumps has to show serial and model numbers as well as rated capacities.

Indirect Waste Connections

Now we come to a sticky wicket. Section 510(a) says this:

Condensate Disposal. Condensate from air-cooling, fuel-burning condensing appliances and the overflow from evaporative coolers and similar water-supplied

Equipment Capacity	Minimum Condensate Drain Diameter
Up to 20 tons of refrigeration	3/4 inch
21 to 40 tons of refrigeration	1 inch
41 to 90 tons of refrigeration	1 1/4 inch
91 to 125 tons of refrigeration	1 1/2 inch
126 to 250 tons of refrigeration	2 inch

Size of condensate drains may be for one unit or a combination of units, or as recommended by the manufacturer. Drain capacity is based on 1/8 inch per foot slope, drains running three-quarters full:

Outside Air—20%		Room Air—80%	
DB	WB	DB	WB
90°F.	73°F.	75°F.	62.5°F.

Condensate drain sizing for other slopes or other conditions shall be approved by the building official.

(c) **Fuel-burning Appliance Condensate Drains.** Condensate drain lines from individual fuel-burning condensing appliances shall be sized according to the manufacturers' recommendations. Condensate drain lines serving more than one appliance shall be approved by the building official prior to installation.

From the Uniform Mechanical Code, © 1988, ICBO

Figure 17-3   *Condensate drain sizing*

equipment shall be collected and discharged to an approved plumbing fixture or disposal area. The drain shall have a slope of not less than 1/8 inch per foot and shall be of approved corrosion-resistant pipe not smaller than the drain outlet size as required in either Subsection (b) or (c) below for air cooling coils or condensing fuel-burning appliances, respectively. Condensate or waste water shall not drain over a public way.

Subsections (b) and (c) go on to list the various pipe sizes as shown in Figure 17-3.

This can get you in a lot of trouble. In humid climates air-conditioning units give off a lot of condensate. You've got to get rid of it — legally. If your unit is above grade, the disposal problem is easier than if it's in a basement. To handle condensate in a basement with no floor drain, you can locate the underfloor sewer and connect it to that, or you can install a sump and a pump. Figure 17-3 shows how much condensate to plan for, based on the size of the cooling system.

If you stop to think about it, every clothes washer, water heater, and toilet is going to fail some day. And when that happens, the first thing you have to do is get rid of the water. That's why my city and many others require a floor drain or floor sink wherever plumbing fixtures are installed below grade. A lot of plumbers resisted at first, but it didn't take them long to get the point. It's no picnic replacing an appliance if you have to begin by bailing water out the window.

Two final words of warning: Place your air-conditioning unit where condensate dripping out of the unit won't run down into the furnace heat exchanger. Wet heat exchangers rust out very quickly. And if your heater is in a garage at floor level, protect it from car bumpers and fenders with a curb to stop the front wheels, or with steel posts in the floor.

Warm-Air Heating Systems

Most single-family homes are heated with forced or gravity air systems. Chapter 7 of the UMC covers them. The requirements in Chapter 7 of the UMC are in addition to what we've already covered. Before getting into Chapter 7, I'll mention Chapters 9 and 10 of the UMC. Chapter 9 controls vents for fuel-burning warm air furnaces. Chapter 10 specifies the air ducts and plenums you have to use. We'll look at

Chapters 9 and 10 later in this chapter. But first let's consider access in Chapter 7.

Access

> **Section 703.** *A furnace room shall have an opening or door and passageway thereto not less than 2 feet in width and large enough to permit removal of the largest furnace in such room. The furnace shall be installed so as to permit removal without disturbing piping, conduits, appurtenant valves and junction boxes.*

It then goes on to give several exceptions:

> *1) If the furnace room is large enough to permit dismantling of the furnace, the exit just needs to be as large as the largest piece. But this doesn't waive any minimum requirements.*

> *2) Access to furnaces in underfloor areas must conform to Section 709. Section 708 applies to furnaces in attics, while Section 710 regulates roof-mounted furnaces. You can install furnaces upright in an attic as long as the attic is at least 5 feet high.*

All of these sections address the same problem: Anything you install will probably have to be replaced some day. Another thing to remember: unless a furnace is designed for outdoor use, it must be protected from the elements. That means that an underfloor furnace must rest on a concrete pad, not on the ground.

Section 707(a) restricts the duct size. A duct for a forced air furnace must have an unobstructed area on the supply side of not less than 2 square inches per 1000 Btu/h of furnace output. If your furnace is a gravity type, you must have 7 square inches of duct area per 1000 Btu/h output. Dampers, grilles and registers aren't considered obstructions. If you're using a heat pump, provide 6 square inches per 1000 Btu/h of output.

Miscellaneous Heating Devices

These include vented decorative appliances, floor furnaces, vented wall furnaces, unit heaters and room heaters. Most are approved for use in any house or small commercial building. You can't use them in surgical operating rooms, hazardous locations, Group H, Division 1, 2, or 3 (hazardous) occupancies, or any room where open flame is prohibited. Overhead heaters installed in aircraft hangars must be at least 10 feet above the ground.

Always follow the manufacturer's installation instructions, unless the building inspector has more stringent regulations.

Venting Appliances

Venting is important for all gas-fired appliances. Although natural gas, by itself, isn't toxic, it can replace all the oxygen in a room. That can lead to asphyxiation. Following the manufacturer's recommendation will nearly eliminate that risk.

Section 901. Venting systems shall consist of approved chimneys, Type B vents, Type BW vents, Type L vents, plastic pipe recommended by the manufacturer of listed condensing appliances for use with specified models, or a venting assembly which is an integral part of a listed appliance.

You can't put manually-operated dampers in chimneys, although automatically-operated ones are acceptable. And make sure all unused openings in a vent are sealed. All vents have to be generally vertical, but you can use offsets not over 45 degrees from the vertical. Support all offset vents. An angle that exceeds 45 degrees is considered a horizontal vent, which can't exceed 75 percent of the vertical height of the vent.

The type of vent you're using determines how far it has to extend above the roof surface.

- *Gravity-type vents:* Except for Type BW gas venting systems, the vent has to extend at least 5 feet above the highest vent collar they serve.

- *Wall furnaces:* A Type BW vent serving a vented wall furnace has to terminate at least 12 vertical feet above the bottom of the furnace.

- *Type B or BW gas vents:* Terminate them at least 1 foot above the roof and 4 feet from any portion of the roof that extends at an angle of more than 45 degrees from the vertical.

- *Type L gas vents:* The requirement is the same as Type B vents, except they must terminate at least 2 feet above the roof.

- *Vent terminals:* The required distance is at least 1 foot above, 4 feet below, or 4 feet horizontally from any door, window, or gravity air inlet into the building.

- *Wall furnaces:* Vents for these heaters are usually placed within the wall cavity. UMC Section 907 lists nine requirements that must be met:

    1) Attach Type BW gas vents to a solid header, using the attachment furnished with the equipment.

2) The stud space must be free of obstructions, except required fire stops in multi-story buildings, and all ceiling and floor places must be cut flush.

3) The vent clearance provided by the base plate must be maintained after all wall coverings are in place.

4) If the vent is listed only for single-story use, you can't use it in a multi-story building. But a multiple-story vent can go in either single- *or* multi-story structures.

5) The stud space in the top floor of a multi-story structure has to be open to an attic space or to a ventilated roof flashing equipped with a storm collar. There's one exception: Instead of a ventilated roof flashing, you can vent the stud space by an opening into the room heated by the wall heater. The opening must be within 12 inches of the top of the space.

6) If you're installing a vented recessed wall furnace in a stud space, ventilate it at the first ceiling plate above the furnace with the spacer furnished with the vent. Use the fire stop space at each floor or ceiling.

7) Install a suitable metal guard at the floor line of each floor to assure required clearance from combustible material.

8) The wall covering must be removed from the stud space for installation and inspection purposes when a Type BW gas vent is installed in an existing building.

9) Type BW gas vents must extend from the header plate of the vented wall furnace to the highest ceiling plate through which the vent passes, including any offsets or crossovers. From that point, you can complete the vent with a Type B gas vent.

You can put multiple appliances on the same vent *if* they all use the same fuel and they're offset from each other. Every appliance that burns a different fuel must have its own flue. If you have an oil furnace, a gas water heater, and a wood fireplace, you need three vent stacks or chimneys. They could share a single brick chimney as long as it contained three different flues.

And let me repeat this for emphasis: Install all appliances according to the manufacturer's instructions. This applies to all fuel-burning appliances, controls, vents and accessories. As a builder, I know it's tempting to make some economies. But as a building inspector, I know building inspectors look hard at appliance installations. A non-approved economy here can cost you a bundle.

Selecting the Chimney

Check UMC Table 9-A (Figure 17-4) to find the right chimney. Table 9-B (Figure 17-5) covers vents. Construction clearances for unlisted metal chimneys are shown in UMC Table 9-C (Figure 17-6).

Ductwork

Chapter 10 of the Uniform Mechanical Code covers ductwork:

> **Section 1002(a) General.** *Supply air, return air and outside air for heating, cooling or evaporative cooling systems shall be conducted through duct systems constructed of metal as set forth in Tables 10-A, 10-B and 10-C; metal ducts complying with UMC Standard 10-2 with prior approval; or factory-made air ducts complying with UMC Standard 10-1. Ducts, plenums and fittings may be constructed of asbestos cement, concrete, clay or*

TABLE NO. 9-A—CHIMNEY SELECTION CHART

CHIMNEYS FOR RESIDENTIAL APPLIANCES	CHIMNEYS FOR LOW-HEAT APPLIANCES		CHIMNEYS FOR MEDIUM-HEAT APPLIANCES	CHIMNEYS FOR HIGH-HEAT APPLIANCES
	BUILDING-HEATING APPLIANCES	INDUSTRIAL-TYPE LOW-HEAT APPLIANCES		
1. Factory-built (Residential) 2. Masonry (Residential) 3. Metal (Residential)	1. Factory-built (low-heat) 2. Masonry (low-heat type) 3. Metal (smokestack)	1. Factory-built (industrial low-heat type) 2. Masonry (low-heat type) 3. Metal (smokestack)	1. Factory-built (medium-heat type) 2. Masonry (medium-heat type) 3. Metal (smokestack)	1. Masonry (high-heat type) 2. Metal (smokestack)

TYPES OF APPLIANCES TO BE USED WITH EACH TYPE CHIMNEY

COLUMN I	COLUMN II	COLUMN III	COLUMN IV	COLUMN V
A. Residential-type appliances, such as: 1. Ranges 2. Warm-air furnaces 3. Water heaters 4. Hot water heating boilers 5. Low-pressure steam-heating boilers (not over 15 psig) 6. Domestic incinerators 7. Floor furnaces 8. Wall furnaces 9. Room heaters 10. Fireplace stoves	A. All appliances shown in Column I B. Nonresidential-type building-heating appliances for heating a total volume of space exceeding 25,000 cubic feet C. Steam boilers operating at not over 1000°F. flue gas temperature; pressing machine boilers	All appliances shown in Columns I and II, and appliances such as: 1. Annealing baths for hard glass (fats, paraffin, salts, or metals) 2. Bake ovens (in bakeries) 3. Boiling vats, for wood fibre, straw, lignin, etc. 4. Candy furnaces 5. Coffee roasting ovens 6. Core ovens 7. Cruller furnaces 8. Feed drying ovens 9. Fertilizer drying ovens 10. Fireplaces, other than residential type 11. Forge furnaces (solid fuel)	All appliances shown in Columns I, II and III, and appliances such as: 1. Alabaster gypsum kilns 2. Annealing furnaces (glass or metal) 3. Charcoal furnaces 4. Cold stirring furnaces 5. Feed driers (direct fire heated) 6. Fertilizer driers (direct-fire-heated) 7. Galvanizing furnaces 8. Gas producers 9. Hardening furnaces (cherry to pale red) 10. Incinerators, commercial and industrial-type 11. Lehrs and glory holes 12. Lime kilns	All appliances shown in Columns I, II, III, and IV and appliances such as: 1. Bessemer retorts 2. Billet and bloom furnaces 3. Blast furnaces 4. Bone calcining furnaces 5. Brass furnaces 6. Carbon point furnaces 7. Cement brick and tile kilns 8. Ceramic kilns 9. Coal and water gas retorts 10. Cupolas 11. Earthenware kilns 12. Glass blow furnaces

From the Uniform Mechanical Code, © 1988, ICBO

Figure 17-4 Chimney selection chart

TABLE NO. 9-A—CHIMNEY SELECTION CHART—(Continued)

CHIMNEYS FOR RESIDENTIAL APPLIANCES	CHIMNEYS FOR LOW-HEAT APPLIANCES		CHIMNEYS FOR MEDIUM-HEAT APPLIANCES	CHIMNEYS FOR HIGH-HEAT APPLIANCES
	BUILDING-HEATING APPLIANCES	INDUSTRIAL-TYPE LOW-HEAT APPLIANCES		
B. Fireplaces		12. Gypsum kilns 13. Hardening furnaces (below dark red) 14. Hot-air engine furnaces 15. Ladle-drying furnaces 16. Lead-melting furnaces 17. Nickel plate (drying) furnaces 18. Paraffin furnaces 19. Recuperative furnaces (spent materials) 20. Rendering furnaces 21. Restaurant-type cooking appliances using solid or liquid fuel 22. Rosin-melting furnaces 23. Stereotype furnaces 24. Sulphur furnaces 25. Tripoli kilns (clay, coke and gypsum) 26. Type foundry furnaces 27. Wood-drying furnaces 28. Wood-impregnating furnaces 29. Zinc-amalgamating furnaces	13. Linseed-oil-boiling furnaces 14. Porcelain biscuit kilns 15. Pulp driers (direct-fire-heated) 16. Steam boilers operating at over 1000°F. flue gas temperature 17. Water-glass kiln 18. Wood-distilling furnaces 19. Wood-gas retorts	13. Glass furnaces (smelting) 14. Glass kilns 15. Open hearth furnaces 16. Ore-roasting furnaces 17. Porcelain-baking and glazing kilns 18. Pot-arches 19. Puddling furnaces 20. Regenerative furnaces 21. Reverberatory furnaces 22. Stacks, carburetor or superheating furnaces (in water-gas works) 23. Vitreous enameling ovens (ferrous metals) 24. Wood-carbonizing furnaces

From the Uniform Mechanical Code, © 1988, ICBO

Figure 17-4 (cont'd)   *Chimney selection chart*

TABLE NO. 9-B—VENT SELECTION CHART			
COLUMN I **TYPE B, GAS** **Round or Oval**	**COLUMN II** **TYPE BW GAS**	**COLUMN III** **TYPE L**	**COLUMN IV** **PLASTIC PIPE**
All listed gas appliances with draft hoods such as: 1. Central furnaces 2. Floor furnaces 3. Heating boilers 4. Ranges and ovens 5. Recessed wall furnaces (above wall section) 6. Room and unit heaters 7. Water heaters	1. Gas-burning wall heaters listed for use with Type BW vents	1. Oil-burning appliances listed for use with Type L vents 2. Gas appliances as shown in first column	1. Condensing appliances listed for use with a specific plastic pipe recommended and identified in the manufacturer's installation instructions.

From the Uniform Mechanical Code, © 1988, ICBO

Figure 17-5 *Vent selection chart*

ceramics when installed in the ground or in a concrete slab, provided the joints are tightly sealed.

Section 1002 goes on to say that you can use the concealed building space or independent construction within a building. Tables 10-A through 10-C are shown in Figures 17-7 through 17-9. When gypsum wallboard is exposed in ducts or plenums, the air temperature can range only between 50 degrees and 125 degrees. Both temperature and moisture content must be controlled to keep the gypsum dry. That's why you can't use it to enclose evaporative cooler ductwork.

The flame-spread rating of material exposed within ductwork is limited to 25, and the smoke-developed rate can't exceed 50. And finally, venting systems can't extend into or through ducts or plenums.

TABLE NO. 9-C—CONSTRUCTION, CLEARANCE AND TERMINATION REQUIREMENTS FOR UNLISTED SINGLE-WALL METAL CHIMNEYS

CHIMNEYS SERVING	MINIMUM THICKNESS		TERMINATION				CLEARANCE			
	WALL	LINING	ABOVE ROOF OPENING	ABOVE ANY PART OF BUILDING WITHIN 10' 25' 50'			COMBUSTIBLE CONSTRUCTION		NONCOMBUSTIBLE CONSTRUCTION	
				10'	25'	50'	INTERIOR INST.	EXTERIOR INST.	INTERIOR INST.	EXTERIOR INST.
Building-heating and industrial-type low-heat appliances (1000°F. operating-1400°F. temp. maximum)[1]	0.127" (Mfrs. Std. 10 ga.)	None	3'	2'			18"	6"	Up to 18" diameter, 2" Over 18" diameter, 4"	
Medium-heat industrial-type appliances (2000°F. maximum)[1] [3]	0.127" (Mfrs. Std. 10 ga.)	Up to 18" dia.—2½" Over 18" 4½" on 4½" bed	10'	10'			36"	24"		

From the Uniform Mechanical Code, © 1988, ICBO

Figure 17-6   Requirements for unlisted single-wall metal chimneys

					See Footnote 4		
High-heat industrial-type appliances (Over 2000°F;)[1][2]	0.127" (Mfrs. Std. 10 ga.)	4½" laid on 4½" bed	20'	20'			4"
Residential-type incinerator[5]	0.127" (Mfrs. Std. 10 ga.)	None	3'	2'	Not permitted	18"	Not permitted
Chute-fed, flue-fed commercial or industrial-type incinerators[2][5]	0.127" (Mfrs. Std. 10 ga.)	4½" laid on 4½" bed	3' above sloping roof or 8' above flat roof	10'	36"	24"	Up to 18" diameter, 2"; Over 18" diameter, 4"

[1] See Table No. 9-A for types of appliances to be used with each type of chimney.

[2] Lining shall extend from bottom to top of chimney.

[3] Lining shall extend from 24 inches below connector to 24 feet above.

[4] Clearance shall be as specified by the design engineer and shall have sufficient clearance from buildings and structures to avoid overheating combustible materials (maximum 160°F.).

[5] Spark arrestors shall be provided in accordance with Subsection 914 (f).

From the Uniform Mechanical Code, © 1988, ICBO

Figure 17-6 (cont'd) *Requirements for unlisted single-wall metal chimneys*

TABLE NO. 10-A—CONSTRUCTION DETAILS FOR RECTANGULAR SHEET METAL DUCTS FOR LOW-PRESSURE SYSTEMS WHERE VELOCITIES DO NOT EXCEED 2000 FEET PER MINUTE

For Pressures in Excess of 2-inch Water Column, Duct Wall Thickness Shall be Two Gages Heavier Than Set Forth in This Table.

Duct specifications shown here are applicable when ducts larger than 18 inches are cross broken. Where cross breaking is not used, duct wall thickness shall be two gages heavier on ducts 19 inches through 60 inches wide unless longitudinal standing seams are used.

| MINIMUM METAL GAGES | | | | |
Steel—U.S. Standard Inches (Gage)	Aluminum B. & S. Inches (Gage)	Copper Cold Rolled	Duct Dimension (In Inches)	PERMISSIBLE GIRTH JOINTS AND LONGITUDINAL SEAMS
0.019 (26)	0.020 (24)	16 oz.	Up through 12	Drive Slip, Plain "S" Slip, or 1" Pocket Lock
			13 through 18	Drive Slip, Plain "S" Slip, or 1" Pocket Lock
0.024 (24)	0.025 (22)	24 oz.	19 through 30	Hemmed "S" Slip, 1" Bar Slip, or 1" Pocket Lock on 5' centers Hemmed "S" Slip, 1" Bar Slip, or 1" Pocket Lock on 10' Centers with 1" x 1" x 1/8" angles on center line between Hemmed "S" Slip, 1" Bar Slip, or 1" Pocket Lock on 10' centers with Cross Break 1" Standing Seam on 5' centers
			31 through 42	1" Bar Slip, Reinforced Bar Slip, or Pocket Lock, on 5' centers 1" Bar Slip, Reinforced Bar Slip, or Pocket Lock on 10' centers with 1" x 1" x 1/8" angles on center line between 1" Standing Seam on 5' centers Inside Longitudinal Standing Seams with 1" x 1" x 1/8" angles on 5' center on exterior
0.030 (22)	0.032 (20)	32 oz.	43 through 54	1 1/2" Bar Slip, Reinforced Bar Slip, or Pocket Lock on 4' centers 1 1/2" Bar Slip, Reinforced Bar Slip, or Pocket Lock on 8' centers with 1 1/2" x 1 1/2" x 1/8" angles on center line between 1 1/2" Bar Slip, Reinforced Bar Slip, or Pocket Lock on 4' centers with Cross Break 1 1/2" Standing Seam on 3' centers
0.036 (20)	0.040 (18)	36 oz.	55 through 60	Inside Longitudinal Standing Seam with 1 1/2" x 1 1/2" x 1/8" angles on 4' centers on exterior

From the Uniform Mechanical Code, © 1988, ICBO

Figure 17-7 *Construction details for rectangular sheet metal ducts*

				Construction details
0.036 (20)	0.040 (18)	36 oz.	61 through 84	Reinforced Bar Slip, Angle Slip, Alternate Bar Slip, or Angle Reinforced Pocket Lock on 4' centers using 1½" x 1½" x ⅛" reinforcing angles and with 1½" x 1½" x ⅛" angles on center line between Reinforced Bar Slip, Angle Slip, Alternate Bar Slip, or Angle Reinforced Pocket Lock on 8' centers using 1½" x 1½" x ⅛" reinforcing angles and with 1½" x 1½" x ⅛" angles 2' on centers in between 1½" Angle Reinforced Standing Seam on 2' centers using 1½" x 1½" x ⅛" reinforcing angles Inside Longitudinal Standing Seams with 1½" x 1½" x ⅛" angles on 2' centers on exterior
0.047 (18)	0.050 (16)	48 oz.	85 through 96	Companion Angles, Angle Slip, or Angle Reinforced Pocket Lock using 1½" x 1½" x ³⁄₁₆" companion or reinforcing angles on 4' centers with 1½" x 1½" x ³⁄₁₆" angles on center line between Companion Angles, Angle Slip, or Angle Reinforced Pocket Lock using 1½" x 1½" x ³⁄₁₆" companion or reinforcing angles on 8' centers with 1½" x 1½" x ³⁄₁₆" angles on 2' centers in between 1½" Angle Reinforced Standing Seam on 2' centers using 1½" x 1½" x ³⁄₁₆" reinforcing angles Inside Longitudinal Standing Seams with 1½" x 1½" x ³⁄₁₆" angles on 2' centers on exterior

(Continued)

From the Uniform Mechanical Code, © 1988, ICBO

Figure 17-7 (cont'd)   *Construction details for rectangular sheet metal ducts*

TABLE NO. 10-A—CONSTRUCTION DETAILS FOR RECTANGULAR SHEET METAL DUCTS FOR LOW-PRESSURE SYSTEMS WHERE VELOCITIES DO NOT EXCEED 2000 FEET PER MINUTE—(Continued)

For Pressures in Excess of 2-inch Water Column, Duct Wall Thickness Shall be Two Gages Heavier Than Set Forth in This Table.

Duct specifications shown here are applicable when ducts larger than 18 inches are cross broken. Where cross breaking is not used, duct wall thickness shall be two gages heavier on ducts 19 inches through 60 inches wide unless longitudinal standing seams are used.

Steel—U.S. Standard Inches (Gage)	Aluminum B. & S. Inches (Gage)	Copper Cold Rolled	Duct Dimension (In Inches)	PERMISSIBLE GIRTH JOINTS AND LONGITUDINAL SEAMS
		MINIMUM METAL GAGES		
0.047 (18)	0.050 (16)	48 oz.	Over 96	Companion Angles, Angle Slip, or Angle Reinforced Pocket Lock using 2" x 2" x ¼" companion or reinforcing angles on 4' centers with 2" x 2" x ¼" angles on center line between. Companion Angles, Angle Slip, or Angle Reinforced Pocket Lock using 2" x 2" x ¼" companion or reinforcing angles on 8' centers with 2" x 2" x ¼" angles 2' on center line between. 1½" Angle Reinforced Standing Seam on 2' centers using 2" x 2" x ¼" reinforcing angles. Inside Longitudinal Standing Seams with 2" x 2" x ¼" angles on 2' centers on exterior

From the Uniform Mechanical Code, © 1988, ICBO

Figure 17-7 (cont'd) *Construction details for rectangular sheet metal ducts*

TABLE NO. 10-B—CONSTRUCTION DETAILS FOR ROUND AND FLAT-OVAL DUCTS (LOW, MEDIUM AND HIGH PRESSURE)

DUCT DIAMETER MAXIMUM WIDTH (In Inches)	Aluminum B. & S. Gage — Low Pressure — Round	STEEL—THICKNESS IN INCHES (STEEL—GALVANIZED SHEET GAGE) Low Pressure[2] — Round	Flat-Oval	Medium and High Pressure — Spiral Seam	Longitudinal Seam	Welded Fittings	GIRTH JOINTS[1] — Medium and High Pressure	Minimum Girth Reinforcing, Maximum Spacing and Angle Size
Up to 9	24	0.019 (26)	0.024 (24)	0.019 (26)	0.024 (24)	0.030 (22)	2" Slip	None
9 to 14	24	0.019 (26)	0.024 (24)	0.024 (24)	0.030 (22)	0.036 (20)	4" Slip	None
14 to 23	22	0.024 (24)	0.030 (22)	0.024 (24)	0.030 (22)	0.036 (20)	4" Slip	None
23 to 37	20	0.030 (22)	0.036 (20)	0.030 (22)	0.036 (20)	0.036 (20)	4" Slip	None
37 to 51	18	0.036 (20)	0.047 (18)	0.036 (20)	0.036 (20)	0.047 (18)	1¼" x 1¼" x ⅛" Flange	1¼" x 1¼" x ⅛" on 72"
51 to 61	16	0.047 (18)	0.058 (16)	X	0.047 (18)	0.047 (18)	1¼" x 1¼" x ⅛" Flange	1¼" x 1¼" x ⅛" on 72"
61 to 84	14	0.058 (16)	0.070 (14)	X	0.058 (16)	0.058 (16)	1½" x 1½" x ⅛" Flange	1½" x 1½" x ⅛" on 48"

[1]For low-pressure systems any of the following joints are acceptable: butt slip; pipe slip; pipe lock; roll slip; snap slip; plenum lock and companion flange.

[2]Acceptable longitudinal seams for low-pressure systems: Acme (grooved); snap lock; standing and spiral.

From the Uniform Mechanical Code, © 1988, ICBO

Figure 17-8 Construction details for round and flat-oval ducts

TABLE NO. 10-C—THICKNESS OF METAL DUCTS AND PLENUMS USED FOR HEATING OR COOLING FOR A SINGLE DWELLING UNIT

	GALVANIZED STEEL		Approximate Aluminum B. & S. Gage
	Minimum Thickness (in inches)	Equivalent Galvanized Sheet Gage No.	
Round ducts and enclosed rectangular ducts			
14" or less	0.013	30	26
Over 14"	0.016	28	24
Exposed rectangular ducts			
14" or less	0.016	28	24
Over 14"	0.019	26	22

From the Uniform Mechanical Code, © 1988, ICBO

Figure 17-9   *Thickness of metal ducts*

Insulating the Ducts

Section 1005. *Every supply- and return-air duct and plenum of a heating or cooling system shall be insulated with not less than the amount of insulation set forward in Table No. 10-D, except for ducts and plenums used exclusively for evaporative cooling systems.*

Table 10-D appears here as Figure 17-10. You can use only approved materials with a mold-, humidity-, and erosion-resistant face. If your duct is handling velocities in excess of 2,000 feet per minute, all liners must be securely fastened with both adhesive and mechanical fasteners. When the insulation is installed on the exterior of the duct, the material is limited to a flame spread of 25 and a smoke density of 50.

TABLE NO. 10-D—INSULATION OF DUCTS

DUCT LOCATION	INSULATION TYPES MECHANICALLY COOLED	HEATING ZONE[1]	INSULATION TYPES HEATING ONLY
On roof on exterior of building	C, V[2] and W	I	A and W
		II	B and W
		III	C and W
Attics, garages and crawl spaces	A and V[2]	I	A
		II	A
		III	B
In walls,[3] within floor-ceiling spaces[3]	A and V[2]	I	A
		II	A
		III	B
Within the conditioned space or in basements; return ducts in air plenums	None required		None required
Cement slab or within ground	None required		None required

NOTE: Where ducts are used for both heating and cooling, the minimum insulation shall be as required for the most restrictive condition.

[1]Heating Degree Days:

    Zone I   below 4500 D.D.
    Zone II   4501 to 8000 D.D.
    Zone III   over 8001 D.D.

[2]Vapor barriers shall be installed on supply ducts in spaces vented to the outside in geographic areas where the average July, August and September mean dew point temperature exceeds 60°F.

[3]Insulation may be omitted on that portion of a duct which is located within a wall- or a floor-ceiling space where:

    a. Both sides of the space are exposed to conditioned air.
    b. The space is not ventilated.
    c. The space is not used as a return plenum.
    d. The space is not exposed to unconditioned air.
    Ceilings which form plenums need not be insulated.

INSULATION TYPES:

A. 1-inch, 0.60 lb./cu. ft. mineral fiber blankets and felt, rock, slag or glass
     1/2-inch, 1.5 to 3 lb./cu. ft. blanket duct liner, rock, slag or glass
     1/2-inch, 3 to 10 lb./cu. ft. board, mineral fiber, rock, slag or glass
     or equivalent to provide an installed conductance = 0.48

B. 2-inch, 0.60 lb./cu. ft. mineral fiber blanket
     1-inch, 1.5 to 3 lb./cu. ft. board, mineral blanket (duct liner)
     1-inch, 3 to 10 lb./cu. ft. mineral fiber board
     or equivalent to provide an installed conductance = 0.24

C. 3-inch, 0.60 lb./cu. ft. mineral fiber blanket
     1 1/2-inch, 1.5 to 3 lb./cu. ft. mineral blanket (duct liner)
     1 1/2-inch, 3 to 10 lb./cu. ft. mineral fiber board
     or equivalent to provide an installed conductance = 0.16

V. Vapor Barrier: Material with a perm rating not exceeding 0.5 perm. All joints to be sealed.

W. Approved weatherproof barrier.

From the Uniform Mechanical Code, © 1988, ICBO

Figure 17-10 *Insulation of ducts*

Underfloor Space

You can use underfloor areas as a supply plenum in residences of one or two stories if the area is free of combustible materials and tightly sealed.

Any furnace located in underfloor space must have an automatic control that starts an air-circulating fan when the bonnet temperature reaches 150 degrees. Fuel-gas lines and plumbing waste cleanouts can't be located in the area. And you have to cover the entire ground surface with a vapor barrier.

As usual, you have to provide access to the equipment. Cut an opening in the floor that's at least 24 by 24 inches. Hang noncombustible receptacles that measure 3 inches beyond each side of the opening not more than 18 inches below each floor opening. Most installers use sheet metal pans to catch refuse that falls through the opening. Finally, the registers for each opening must be easily removable for cleaning the receptacles.

Cooling

New homes in many parts of the U.S. come with cooling systems (air conditioning). There are two common cooling methods. If you live in the arid southwest, you might be quite comfortable with an evaporative cooler. In a humid climate, an evaporative cooler is nearly worthless. A refrigeration cooler is needed.

Evaporative Coolers

Even in dry climates, you'll have some hot, muggy days. When that happens, an evaporative cooler won't do much cooling. Another disadvantage of evaporative coolers is that they require a constant source of water.

Chapter 13 of the Uniform Mechanical Code describes installation requirements for evaporative coolers. The code isn't too stringent here because these coolers go on building exteriors. You can mount them on the wall to cool one or two rooms or on the roof if you're running ducts throughout the building. The requirements are simple. The unit has to be accessible for service and inspection, substantially level, well-supported and at least 6 inches above ground.

Refrigerated Coolers

Refrigeration cooling is usually done with cooling coils located on the upstream side of the furnace. These cooling coils may contain the refrigerant itself, but that's not the most common method. Normally, the cooling agent is cooled by the refrigeration unit and then piped into the furnace. The air is then blown over the coils, cooled, and transported to where it's needed. In humid climates, this can create a moisture problem. As the warm humid air passes over the coils, moisture condenses on the coils and must be collected.

Section 510(b) shows the size of condensate drains required for various sizes of air-cooling systems. Look back to Figure 17-3.

Prohibited Refrigerants

Section 1201(c) prohibits the use of Group 2 refrigerants in any air-cooling or air-conditioning system used for human comfort.

Section 1503(a) lists Group 2 refrigerants:

Refrigerant designation	Name	Chemical formula
R-40	Methyl chloride	CH_3Cl
R-610	Methyl formate	$HCOOCH$
R-717	Ammonia	NH_3
R-764	Sulphur dioxide	SO_2

Access

Leave plenty of space for servicing and inspecting the unit. The code calls for a space 2 feet wide by 6-1/2 feet high. There's one exception: If the unit is in an attic, you can reduce servicing and inspecting space to 30 inches in length and width if the unit can be replaced from some opening in the area.

All filters, fuel valves and air handlers must have an unobstructed access space not less than 24 x 30 inches.

If your unit is located under the floor or in an attic or furred space, you must provide a light and an electrical outlet at or near the equipment. But you can omit the light if the building lighting is adequate.

Return Air and Outside Air

Section 1206(b) lists the prohibited sources of outside or return air, or both. You can't take air from these sources:

1) Closer than 10 feet from any appliance vent outlet, unless each vent outlet is 3 feet above the outside air inlet.

2) Where it will pick up objectionable odors, fumes or flammable vapors.

3) Any hazardous or unsanitary location or a refrigeration machinery room.

4) Closer than 10 feet from a plumbing drainage system vent opening unless it's at least 3 feet above the outside air inlet.

5) A closet.

You can't discharge return air from one dwelling unit into another dwelling unit through the cooling system. Make sure the air velocity doesn't exceed the filter manufacturer's recommendation. And cover all required outside-air inlets with screen having 1/4-inch openings.

That's the end of our brief look at the Uniform Mechanical Code. The next chapter is our last: What you need to know about the Uniform Plumbing Code.

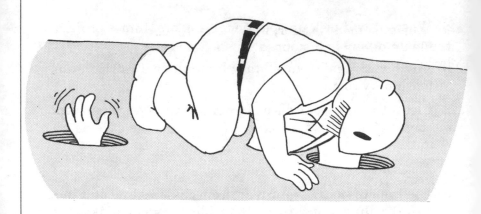

The Plugged Sewer

Once in a while something happens on a construction site that really *couldn't* happen. You've probably got a favorite story of your own. Here's mine.

A developer was building an enclosed shopping mall in Kennewick — one of the first in eastern Washington. As usual, the city ran the utilities to the property line. From there, piping to each unit was the developer's responsibility. The shopping center required hundreds of feet of mainline sewer, feeder lines, and lines to individual shops.

Sewer lines, manholes and cleanouts have to be inspected before they're covered with backfill and compacted. The best way to inspect a sewer is to shine a flashlight straight down the line. If the inspector at one end can see the beam at that other end, the line must be straight, on grade and clear of obstructions.

The work on the lines continued for several months. As each section of line was completed, I checked it carefully. This was a major project and I wanted it to be as good and trouble-free as we could make it. Finally I was able to certify that the line was constructed properly and would flow in the right direction.

Eighteen months later, with the mall nearly ready to open, the main sewer line stopped flowing, not just once but regularly. Running a Roto-Rooter through the line would get it flowing again — but only for a few days. That shouldn't happen. In fact, it couldn't happen. The line was perfect. I checked every foot of it myself.

After about a month of removing blockages, the superintendent invited me to help him recheck the grade at each manhole. We checked carefully and couldn't find anything wrong with the line pitch. It should have worked perfectly. Still, sewage would not flow through that line!

Completely by accident a workman noticed a length of 2 x 4 floating in a manhole one afternoon. It was too long to pull out, so he called the foreman, who notified the superintendent, who called me to the job. We had to cut the 2 x 4 into short lengths to get it out of the line. When the pieces were placed end to end on the sidewalk, we had assembled a 2 x 4 eighteen feet long. Solids would gather on the end of the timber and gradually build a dam. Removing the timber solved the blockage problem, but how did that 2 x 4 get into the line?

I'd certified the line as clear. There was no way the timber could have been placed in the line after my inspections. I'm afraid we'll never know the answer to that mystery. But I always double-checked for stray lumber when I inspected sewer lines after that.

When the mall was completed, the developer held an opening ceremony for everyone involved in construction. To commemorate the city's participation, the superintendent presented me with the offending 2 x 4. I thanked him and his crew, but had to decline the souvenir. Our office has a strict policy on accepting gifts from contractors.

18

Plumbing for Small Buildings

The Uniform Plumbing Code, like the Uniform Mechanical Code, isn't organized in a logical start-to-finish order. The information you need to finish any particular job is spread throughout the book. That makes it harder to use the code as a guide when planning your plumbing jobs.

I'll try to organize the material in this chapter a little better — starting with the underground utilities and ending with installing the fixtures. That's probably the order you'd follow when constructing a residential or small commercial building. Let's begin with the building sewers.

Building Sewers

UPC Section 1101 begins the subject this way:

> **Sewer Required.** *(a) Every building in which plumbing fixtures are installed and every premises having drainage piping therein, shall have a connection to a public or private sewer, except as provided in Section 320 and in subsections (b) and (d) of this section.*

Subsection (b) merely states that if there's no public sewer system available, you have to install a private disposal system. Subsection (d) tells us that a public system is considered available if it's within 200 feet of any proposed building. Section 320 is a grandfather clause. It exempts existing buildings if their system was legal at the time it was constructed *unless* the old plumbing is unsafe, insanitary, or a nuisance. There is nothing about septic tanks on these pages. Their size, depth and drainfield are nearly always controlled locally. Check with your inspector.

Let me take a minute to define *building sewer*. It starts 2 feet from the building and extends to either a public or private disposal system. The *building drainage system* is that part within a building and extending 2 feet beyond the building, where it hooks up to the building sewer.

Building Sewer Materials

All materials must be approved by the building department. Unless you're experimenting with something exotic, this approval should be pretty routine. Most common sewer items are accepted if they're marked with the manufacturer's name, the weight and quality of the product, and any other markings required by the code.

The Uniform Plumbing Code has the complete standards in the back of the book, not in a separate volume like the UBC.

Estimating Sewer Size

The size of your building sewer is based on the number of *units* on your system. Notice I said units, not fixtures. You'll have to count the units assigned to the fixtures. UPC Table 4-1 (Figure 18-1) lists the common fixtures, the size of the trap and trap arm, and the number of units assigned to it. If you have a fixture that's not listed here, the inspector would probably work from UPC Table 4-2 (Figure 18-2).

The plans examiner checking your plans will count the fixture units and check your proposed trap arm sizes. Then he'd use UPC Table 4-3 (Figure 18-3) to see if your proposed building sewer line is big enough to carry the load. Of course, you'll have figured all of this out before the inspector ever sees the plans. He just checks your numbers to make sure you did it right.

Grade, Support and Protection of Building Sewers

Section 1106 states that building sewers must run in a practical alignment toward the point of disposal and at a uniform slope of not less than 1/4 inch per foot. The code doesn't give a maximum slope, and for very good reason. What if the building sewer dropped straight down? No problem. But there are slopes that are too steep to work well. The liquids have a tendency to run away from the solids. The solids that are left behind can build up dams, causing stoppages.

I recommend using the 1/4-inch slope across the property up to the property line. Then, if the sewer is deep under the street, the line should drop at about a 45-degree angle to the sewer connection. That saves money because you don't have to dig a deep trench across the property.

TABLE 4-1

Kind of Fixture	Minimum Trap & Trap Arm Size (inches)	(mm)	Units
Bathtubs	1½	(38.1)	2
Bidets	1½	(38.1)	2
Dental units or cuspidors	1¼	(31.8)	1
Drinking fountains	1¼	(31.8)	1
Floor drains	2	(50.8)	2
*Interceptors for grease, oil, solids, etc. .	2	(50.8)	3
*Interceptors for sand, auto wash, etc. ...	3	(76.2)	6
Laundry tubs	1½	(38.1)	2
Clotheswashers	2	(50.8)	2
*Receptors (floor sinks), indirect waste receptors for refrigerators, coffee urns, water stations, etc.	1½	(38.1)	1
*Receptors, indirect waste receptors for commercial sinks, dishwashers, airwashers, etc.	2	(50.8)	3
Showers, single stalls	2	(50.8)	2
*Showers, gang, (one unit per head)	2	(50.8)	
Sinks, bar, private (1½" (38.1 mm) min. waste)	1½	(38.1)	1
Sinks, bar, commercial (2" (50.8 mm) min. waste)	1½	(38.1)	2
Sinks, commercial or industrial, schools, etc. including dishwashers, wash up sinks and wash fountains (2" (50.8 mm) min. waste)	1½	(38.1)	3
Sinks, flushing rim, clinic	3	(76.2)	6
Sinks, and/or dishwashers (residential) (2" (50.8 mm) min. waste)	1½	(38.1)	2
Sinks, service	2	(50.8)	3
Mobile home park traps (one (1) for each trailer)	3	(76.2)	6
Urinals, pedestal, trap arm only	3	(76.2)	6
Urinals, stall	2	(50.8)	2
Urinals, wall (2" (50.8 mm) min. waste) ...	1½	(38.1)	2
Wash basins (lavatories) single	1¼	(31.8)	1
Wash basins, in sets	1½	(38.1)	2
*Water closet, private installation, trap arm only	3	(76.2)	4
Water closet, public installation, trap arm only	3	(76.2)	6

*NOTE — The size and discharge rating of each indirect waste receptor and each interceptor shall be based on the total rated discharge

From the Uniform Plumbing Code, © 1988, IAPMO

Figure 18-1 *Minimum trap and trap arm size*

capacity of all fixtures, equipment or appliances discharging thereinto, in accordance with Table 4-2.

Drainage piping serving batteries of appliances capable of producing continuous flows shall be adequately sized to provide for peak loads. Clotheswashers in groups of three (3) or more shall be rated at six (6) units each for the purpose of common waste pipe sizing.

Water closets shall be computed as six (6) fixture units when determining septic tank size based on Appendix I of this Code.

Trap sizes shall not be increased to a point where the fixture discharge may be inadequate to maintain their self-scouring properties.

From the Uniform Plumbing Code, © 1988, IAPMO

Figure 18-1 (cont'd) *Minimum trap and trap arm size*

TABLE 4-2
DISCHARGE CAPACITY
(In gals. per min.) (liters per sec.)
For Intermittent Flow Only

GPM	L/s		
Up to 7½	Up to .47	Equals	1 Unit
8 to 15	.50 to .95	Equals	2 Units
16 to 30	1 to 1.89	Equals	4 Units
31 to 50	1.95 to 3.15	Equals	6 Units

Over 50 gals. per min. (3.15 L/s) shall be determined by the Administrative Authority.

For a continuous flow into a drainage system, such as from a pump, sump ejector, air conditioning equipment, or similar device, two (2) fixture units shall be allowed for each gallon per minute (0.06 L/s) of flow.

From the Uniform Plumbing Code, © 1988, IAPMO

Figure 18-2 *Discharge capacity*

TABLE 4-3
Maximum Unit Loading and Maximum Length of Drainage and Vent Piping

Sizer of Pipe (inches)	1-1/4	1-1/2	2	2-1/2	3	4	5	6	8	10	12
(mm)	31.8	38.1	50.8	63.5	76.2	101.6	127	152.4	203.2	254	304.8
Max. Units											
Drainage Piping[1]											
Vertical	1	2[2]	16[3]	32[3]	48[4]	256	600	1380	3600	5600	8400
Horizontal[5]	1	2[2]	8[3]	14[3]	35[4]	216	428	720	2640	4680	8200
Max. Length											
Drainage Piping											
Vertical (feet)	45	65	85	148	212	300	390	510	750		
(m)	13.7	19.8	25.8	45	64.5	91.2	118.6	155	228		
Horizontal (Unlimited)											
Vent Piping											
Horizontal and Vertical											
Max. Units	1	8	24	48	84	256	600	1380	3600		
Max. Lengths (feet)	45	60	120	180	212	300	390	510	750		
(m)	13.7	18.2	36.5	54.7	64.5	91.2	118.6	155	228		
(See Note)											

[1] Excluding trap arm.
[2] Except sinks, urinals and dishwashers.
[3] Except six-unit traps or water closets.
[4] Only four (4) water closets or six-unit traps allowed on any vertical pipe or stack; and not to exceed three (3) water closets or six-unit traps on any horizontal branch or drain.
[5] Based upon one-fourth (¼) inch per foot (20.9 mm/m) slope. For one-eighth (⅛) inch per foot (10.4 mm/m) slope, multiply horizontal fixture units by a factor of 0.8.
NOTE: The diameter of an individual vent shall not be less than one and one-fourth (1¼) inches (31.8 mm) nor less than one-half (½) the diameter of the drain to which it is connected. Fixture unit load values for drainage and vent piping shall be computed from Tables 4-1 and 4-2. Not to exceed one-third (⅓) of the total permitted length of any vent may be installed in a horizontal position. When vents are increased one (1) pipe size for their entire length, the maximum length limitations specified in this table do not apply.

From the Uniiform Plumbing Code, © 1988, IAPMO

Figure 18-3   Unit loading and drainage and vent piping

What if your street sewer is quite shallow, too shallow for a 1/4" per foot slope? The code allows a shallower slope if you increase the pipe size. If the street sewer is still too shallow, the only solution is to install a sewage pump.

One more requirement: Your sewer line must run at least 2 feet below any building foundation you might be passing under, or 2 feet beneath a sidewalk. But I don't recommend putting a sewer under any building but your own. Repairing a sewer line under a foundation can be a very expensive project.

Cleanouts

> *Section 1107(a) Cleanouts. Cleanouts shall be placed inside the building near the connection between the building drain and the building sewer or installed outside the building at the lower end of the building drain and extended to grade.*

If your building is a long way from the public sewer, you may have to use several cleanouts — or even install a manhole. The code limits the distance between cleanouts to 100 feet. The maximum distance between manholes is 300 feet. But remember that sewers must run in a straight line. If you need to change direction, you may be required to install a manhole. Incidentally, each cleanout must extend upward to grade level.

I never liked to see cleanouts installed in a basement unless they were at the base of a vertical stack. Cleanouts in a basement floor can be a serious problems. The code says they have to be accessible. When they're installed, there's no basement floor yet. So the inspector notes that a cleanout is installed and goes on his way. Several weeks or months later, when the basement floor is installed, the cleanout is stuck under a stairway, covered with carpet — or even covered with concrete.

Backwater Valves

There's a chance for some misunderstandings here. The code requires a backflow preventer to keep pollutants from being siphoned back into the water system if water pressure fails. But we're not talking about backflow preventers here. Backwater valves are something different.

For any house with plumbing in the basement, I heartily recommend a backwater valve. It keeps the basement from filling with sewage if the sewer line gets stopped up. The code doesn't require it, but it does describe these valves in Section 209. Many jurisdictions do require them, however. Check with your inspector about backwater valves if the job includes a basement.

Backwater valves must be near the place where your sewer leaves the building, and they must be readily accessible. Sewage flows downstream past a flapper valve as long as the main is flowing normally. If there's a stoppage downstream, the flapper valve swings shut, keeping sewage out of the basement. At least, that's the theory, and it usually works fine.

It works, that is, until the first time the pipes stop up and the homeowner calls Roto-Rooter. A powerful drain snake will usually go right through the backwater valve, ripping it to shreds. And you'll never know it until the city sewer stops up and the basement fills with sewage. Insurance may not cover the loss if a backwater valve has been destroyed. Consider having the valve checked after drains have been cleaned out.

Inspections

Each section of your plumbing must be inspected before it's concealed. Sewers are normally tested with air or water under pressure to be sure the joints don't leak. To test with water, plug all the outlets (special plugs are available at plumbing supply stores) and add a section of vent stack. This stack must be at least 10 feet higher than any portion of the system to be tested. Then fill the vent stack with water and watch for leaks. The inspector is usually satisfied if it doesn't leak after about 15 minutes.

For an air test, plug all outlets and pump the system up to 5 pounds per square inch, or enough to balance a column of mercury 10 inches in height. This pressure must be maintained for at least fifteen minutes. Whichever test you use, the inspector will want to see it done.

Vents and Venting

Section 501, Vents Required. Each plumbing fixture trap, except as otherwise provided in this Code, shall be protected against siphonage and back pressure, and air circulation shall be assured throughout all parts of the drainage system by means of vent pipes and installed in accordance with the requirements of this chapter and as otherwise required by this Code.

Yes, your system may drain if it isn't vented — eventually. But it'll work much better if it *is* vented. That's why the code requires venting. You can use vent pipe and fittings made of any material approved for the rest of the system. The sizes are listed in Figure 18-3.

Vent Pipe Grades and Connections

Vents help keep the waste system at normal air pressure so liquids drain smoothly. There are a few do's and don'ts when it comes to vent construction.

1) They have to be level or drain by gravity back into the drainage pipe. Drops and sags aren't allowed.

2) The invert of the vent should be above the centerline of a horizontal drain.

3) The vent must rise vertically to a point above the flood line of the fixture being served.

4) Vent openings from a soil or waste pipe, except for water closets and similar fixtures, can't be below the weir of the trap.

5) Vents must extend full size above the roof.

6) Vents have to extend through roof flashing and terminate at least 6 inches above the roof.

7) They can't terminate within 3 feet from or 3 feet above an openable window, door, air intake, vent shaft, or lot line.

8) On outdoor installations, vent pipes must extend 10 feet above the surrounding ground and be adequately supported.

9) In high snow load areas, vents must extend above the average snow line on the roof.

Indirect Wastes

Section 110(a), Indirect Waste Pipe— An indirect waste pipe doesn't connect directly with the drainage system. Instead it discharges liquid waste into a plumbing

> *fixture, intercepter or receptacle which is connected directly to the drainage system.*

The condensate drain from your air conditioning system is an example of an indirect waste. Water from the air conditioner may go directly into a floor drain in a basement. The bar in your local saloon probably has a sink drain that runs into a floor sink. The advantage is that you don't have to install vent lines for these indirect connections.

For indirect wastes you don't need a vent, but you do need an *air gap* between the drain and the flood line of the receptor. This air gap keeps drain water from being siphoned into the plumbing fixture. Section 102(e) defines it this way:

> **Air Gap**— *An air gap is the unobstructed vertical distance through the free atmosphere between the lowest opening from any pipe or faucet conveying water or waste to a tank, plumbing fixture, receptor or other device and the flood level rim of the receptacle.*

Many appliances have an air gap device or anti-siphonage system built in. The domestic dishwasher is one example.

You've probably noticed the faucet in your kitchen sink, tub, and lavatory are high enough above the sink so it can't siphon water back into the tap even if the sink is full. That's an air gap.

Traps and Interceptors

> *Section 701(a)— Traps Required. Each plumbing fixture, excepting those having integral traps, shall be separately trapped by an approved type waterseal. Not more than one (1) trap shall be permitted on a trap arm.*

That's the general requirement. It also says that you can't connect a sink, laundry tub or lavatory with more than three compartments to a single trap. Even then, the trap arm can't be longer than 30 inches.

The vertical distance between the fixture outlet and the trap weir must be as short as possible, never longer than 24 inches.

Every trap must have a vent pipe to protect against siphonage and back pressure. This vent assures free air circulation throughout the system. UPC Table 7-1 (Figure 18-4) shows the maximum length of the trap arm from the trap weir to the inner edge of the vent.

A trap arm can change direction as long as the change doesn't exceed 135 degrees. Last but not least, the vent pipe opening from a waste pipe must not be below the weir of the trap.

TABLE 7-1
Horizontal Distance of Trap Arms
(Except for water closets and similar fixtures)

Trap Arm Inches	Distance Trap to Vent Feet	Inches	Trap Arm mm	(Metric) Distance Trap to Vent m
1¼	2	6	31.8	.76
1½	3	6	38.1	1.07
2	5	0	50.8	1.52
3	6	0	76.2	1.83
4 and larger	10	0	101.6 and larger	3.05

Slope one-fourth (¼) inch per foot (20.9 mm/m)

*The developed length between the trap of a water closet or similar fixture (measured from the top of closet ring [closet flange] to inner edge of vent) and its vent shall not exceed six (6) feet (1.8m).

From the Uniform Plumbing Code, © 1988, IAPMO

Figure 18-4 *Horizontal distance of trap arms*

Water Distribution

> **Section 1001— Running Water Required.** *Except where not deemed necessary by the Administrative Authority, each plumbing fixture shall be provided with an adequate supply of potable running water piped thereto in an approved manner, so arranged as to flush and keep it in a clean and sanitary condition without danger of backflow or cross-connection. Water closets and urinals shall be flushed by means of an approved flush tank or flushometer valve. Faucets and diverters shall be connected to the water distribution system so that hot water corresponds to the left side of the fittings.*

Here's a little gem you have to watch out for: *cross-connection.* Suppose you have more than one type of piped water. For example, some areas have both irrigation water systems and drinking water systems. Irrigation water may be provided only during the growing season. But what if someone needs to irrigate earlier or later than the normal growing season? Can you connect your domestic water supply to your yard sprinklers?

In most communities the answer is an unqualified *"no"*. Section 1002 says that you can't install potable water supply piping in any way that makes it possible for used, unclean, polluted or contaminated water to enter any portion of the potable water system.

Maybe I should define potable water. It's *water that's intended for drinking, cooking or cleaning and meets the requirements of the local health authority.*

But how could watering a lawn with potable water contaminate the drinking water system? Your hose doesn't carry germs, does it? I've taken a drink from a hose many times. You have too.

But suppose someone runs down a fire hydrant somewhere and the valve on a water main has to be closed until repairs are made. The water's off. No pressure anywhere. In fact maybe there's a negative pressure. Open the valve anywhere and air is sucked back into the pipe. The hose you were using to spray insecticide in the garden is now sucking insecticide back into the hose and maybe all the way back to the water main. When the hydrant is fixed, that insecticide is going to be delivered through piping systems all over the neighborhood. I know that sounds far-fetched, but it's happened.

An approved vacuum breaker installed on the discharge side of the last valve will prevent this.

Size of Potable Water Piping

Unless you're installing an unusual number of fixtures in the house, you shouldn't have too much trouble with this one. UPC Table 10-1 (Figure 18-5) lists water demand units assigned to most of the fixtures you'll see in a residence or small commercial building. If you install something that isn't listed here, get the unit count from the building inspector.

Find the unit value for each fixture in your building. Total these numbers. Then use Table 10-2 (Figure 18-6) to size your house piping.

Fixtures

There isn't much I can say about fixtures except that they must be installed properly. Even if the building sewer rough-in is done correctly, careless installation of fixtures can make a mess of the job.

TABLE 10-1
Equivalent Fixture Units
(Includes Combined Hot and Cold Water Demand)

Fixture	Number of Fixture Units	
	Private Use	Public Use
Bar sink	1	2
Bathtub (with or without shower over)	2	4
Bidet	2	4
Dental unit or cuspidor	—	1
Drinking fountain (each head)	1	2
Hose bibb or sill cock (standard type)	3	5
Mobile home (each)	6	6
Laundry tub or clotheswasher (each pair of faucets)	2	4
Lavatory	1	2
Lavatory (dental)	1	1
Lawn sprinklers (standard type, each head) .	1	1
Shower (each head)	2	4
Sink (bar)	1	2
Sink or dishwasher	2	4
Sink (flushing rim, clinic)	—	10
Sink (washup, each set of faucets)	—	2
Sink (washup, circular spray)	—	4
Urinal (pedestal or similar type)	—	10
Urinal (stall)	—	5
Urinal (wall)	—	5
Urinal (flush tank)	—	3
Water closet (flush tank)	3	5
*Water closet (flushometer valve)	*	*

Water supply outlets for items not listed above shall be computed at their maximum demand, but in no case less than:

⅜ inch . (9.5 mm)	1	2
½ inch . (12.7 mm)	2	4
¾ inch . (19.1 mm)	3	6
1 inch . (25.4 mm)	6	10

*See subsection (j) of Section 1009 for method of sizing flushometer valve installations using Table 10-2.

From the Uniform Plumbing Code, © 1988, IAPMO

Figure 18-5 *Equivalent fixture units*

TABLE 10-2
FIXTURE UNIT TABLE FOR DETERMINING WATER PIPE AND METER SIZES

PRESSURE RANGE—30 to 45 psi

Meter and street service (inches)	Building supply and branches (inches)	Maximum Allowable Length in Feet (meters)														
		40 (12)	60 (18)	80 (24)	100 (30)	150 (46)	200 (61)	250 (76)	300 (91)	400 (122)	500 (152)	600 (183)	700 (213)	800 (244)	900 (274)	1000 (305)
¾	½	** 6	5	4	3*	2*	1*	1*	1*	0*	0*	0*	0*	0*	0*	0*
¾	¾	16	16	14*	12*	9*	6*	5*	5*	4*	4*	3*	2	2	2	1
¾	1	20	25	23	21	17	15	13	12	10	8	6	6	6	6	6
1	1	36	31	27	25	20	17	15	13	12	10	8	6	6	6	6
1	1¼	54	47	42	38	32	28	25	23	19	17	14	12	12	11	11
1½	1¼	78	68	57	48	38	32	28	25	21	18	15	12	12	11	11
1½	1½	150	124	105	91	70	57	49	45	36	31	26	23	21	20	20
2	1½	151	129	129	110	80	64	53	46	38	32	27	23	21	20	20
1½	2	220	205	190	176	155	138	127	120	104	85	70	61	57	54	51
2	2	370	327	292	265	217	185	164	147	124	96	70	61	57	54	51
2	2½	445	418	390	370	330	300	280	265	240	220	198	175	158	143	133

PRESSURE RANGE—46 to 60 psi

Meter and street service (inches)	Building supply and branches (inches)	Maximum Allowable Length in Feet (meters)														
		40 (12)	60 (18)	80 (24)	100 (30)	150 (46)	200 (61)	250 (76)	300 (91)	400 (122)	500 (152)	600 (183)	700 (213)	800 (244)	900 (274)	1000 (305)
¾	½	** 7	7	6	5	4	3*	2*	2*	1*	1*	0*	0*	0*	0*	0
¾	¾	20	20	19	17	14*	11*	9*	8*	6*	5*	4*	4*	3*	3*	3*
¾	1	39	39	36	33	28	23	21	19	17	14	12	10	9	8	8
1	1	39	39	39	36	30	25	23	20	18	15	12	10	9	8	8
1	1¼	78	78	76	67	52	44	39	36	30	27	24	20	19	17	16
1½	1¼	78	78	78	78	66	52	44	39	33	29	24	20	19	17	16
1½	1½	151	151	151	151	128	105	90	78	62	52	42	38	35	32	30
2	1½	151	151	151	151	150	117	98	84	67	55	42	38	35	32	30
1½	2	370	370	340	318	272	240	220	198	170	150	135	123	110	102	94
2	2	370	370	370	370	368	318	280	250	205	165	142	123	110	102	94
2	2½	654	640	610	580	535	500	470	440	400	365	335	315	285	267	250

PRESSURE RANGE—Over 60 psi

Meter and street service (inches)	Building supply and branches (inches)	Maximum Allowable Length in Feet (meters)														
		40 (12)	60 (18)	80 (24)	100 (30)	150 (46)	200 (61)	250 (76)	300 (91)	400 (122)	500 (152)	600 (183)	700 (213)	800 (244)	900 (274)	1000 (305)
¾	½	** 7	7	7	6	5	4	3*	3*	2*	1*	1*	1*	1*	1*	0*
¾	¾	20	20	20	20	17	13*	11*	10*	8*	7*	6*	6*	5*	4*	4*
¾	1	39	39	39	39	35	30	27	24	21	17	14	13	12	12	11
1	1	39	39	39	39	38	32	29	26	22	18	14	13	12	12	11
1	1¼	78	78	78	78	74	62	53	47	39	31	26	25	23	22	21
1½	1¼	78	78	78	78	78	74	65	54	43	34	26	25	23	22	21
1½	1½	151	151	151	151	151	151	130	113	88	73	51	51	46	43	40
2	1½	151	151	151	151	151	151	142	122	98	82	64	51	46	43	40
1½	2	370	370	370	370	360	335	305	282	244	212	187	172	153	141	129
2	2	370	370	370	370	370	370	370	340	288	245	204	172	153	141	129
2	2½	654	654	654	654	654	650	610	570	510	460	430	404	380	356	329

*Branch pipes up to 20 ft. (6 m) developed length (from main to outlet or fixture) may supply maximum of four fixture units for ½ in. size and maximum 16 fixture units for ¾ in. nominal size

**Building supply, ¾ in. nominal size minimum

From the Uniform Plumbing Code, © 1988, IAPMO

Figure 18-6 *Fixture unit table for determining pipe and meter sizes*

Here's the point to remember: Nearly every fixture you install will have to be repaired some day. Repair and replacement will be much easier if the original installation is done right. Make sure fixture shutoffs are readily accessible. Retaining rings and brackets should be mounted square and snug. Supply and waste lines should connect smoothly without straining either side of the joint. Threaded couplings should be turned snug without over-tightening or cross-threading.

Attention to details like these will make repairs much easier. And it's details like these that identify true professional craftsmanship.

Summary

Well, there it is — the best way to build "by the book" in 18 succinct chapters. If you learn only one significant lesson, it'll save you many times the cost of this book. And if there's one thing I'm sure of, it's that most builders are in business to do two things: the best job possible, and to make good money doing it. I hope I've helped you do both.

Appendix

Span Tables

T he following pages contain most of the wood span information you're likely to need.

Detailed instructions on how to use these tables can be found in Chapter 10 of this book.

TABLE NO. 25-A-1—ALLOWABLE UNIT STRESSES—STRUCTURAL LUMBER
Allowable Unit Stresses for Structural Lumber—VISUAL GRADING
(Normal loading. See also Section 2504)

SPECIES AND COMMERCIAL GRADE	SIZE CLASSIFICATION	EXTREME FIBER IN BENDING F_b		Tension Parallel to Grain F_t	Horizontal Shear F_v	Compression perpendicular to Grain $F_c\perp$ 21	Compression Parallel to Grain F_c	MODULUS OF ELASTICITY E 21	U.B.C. STDS. UNDER WHICH GRADED
		Single-member Uses	Repetitive-member Uses						
ASPEN (BIGTOOTH—QUAKING) (Surfaced dry or surfaced green. Used at 19% max. m.c.)									
Select Structural	2" to 4" thick 2" to 4" wide	1300	1500	775	60	265	850	1,100,000	
No. 1		1100	1300	650	60	265	675	1,100,000	
No. 2		925	1050	525	60	265	550	1,000,000	
No. 3		500	575	300	60	265	325	900,000	
Appearance		1100	1300	650	60	265	825	1,100,000	25-4
Stud		500	575	300	60	265	325	900,000	25-5
Construction	2" to 4" thick 4" wide	650	750	400	60	265	625	900,000	and 25-8
Standard		375	425	225	60	265	500	900,000	(See footnotes
Utility		175	200	100	60	265	325	900,000	2 through 8,
Select Structural	2" to 4" thick 5" and wider	1150	1300	750	60	265	750	1,100,000	13, 15 and 16)
No. 1		950	1100	650	60	265	675	1,100,000	
No. 2		775	900	425	60	265	575	1,000,000	
No. 3 and Stud		450	525	250	60	265	375	900,000	
Appearance		950	1100	650	60	265	825	1,100,000	

ALLOWABLE UNIT STRESSES IN POUNDS PER SQUARE INCH

From the Uniform Building Code, © 1988, ICBO

Allowable Unit Stresses—Structural Lumber

BALSAM FIR (Surfaced dry or surfaced green. Used at 19% max. m.c.)

Grade	Classification								
Select Structural	2" to 4" thick	1750	2000	1000	70	305	1350	1,500,000	25-5
No. 1	2" to 4" wide	1450	1700	850	70	305	1050	1,500,000	25-8
No. 2		1200	1400	700	70	305	860	1,300,000	(See footnotes
No. 3		675	775	400	70	305	525	1,200,000	1 through 9)
Appearance		1450	1700	850	70	305	1250	1,500,000	
Stud		675	775	400	70	305	525	1,200,000	
Construction	2" to 4" thick	875	1000	525	70	305	950	1,200,000	
Standard	4" wide	500	575	275	70	305	775	1,200,000	
Utility		225	275	125	70	305	525	1,200,000	
Select Structural	2" to 4" thick	1500	1700	1000	70	305	1200	1,500,000	
No. 1	5" and wider	1250	1450	850	70	305	1050	1,500,000	
No. 2		1050	1200	550	70	305	900	1,300,000	
No. 3		600	700	325	70	305	575	1,200,000	
Appearance		1250	1450	850	70	305	1250	1,500,000	
Stud		600	700	325	70	305	575	1,200,000	
Select Structural	Beams and Stringers	1350	—	900	65	305	950	1,400,000	
No. 1		1100	—	750	65	305	800	1,400,000	
Select Structural	Posts and Timbers	1250	—	825	65	305	1000	1,400,000	
No. 1		1000	—	675	65	305	875	1,400,000	
Select	Decking	—	1650	—	—	—	—	1,500,000	25-8
Commercial		—	1400	—	—	—	—	1,300,000	(See footnotes 1 through 9)

(Continued)

From the Uniform Building Code, © 1988, ICBO

Allowable Unit Stresses—Structural Lumber

TABLE NO. 25-A-1—ALLOWABLE UNIT STRESSES—STRUCTURAL LUMBER—(Continued)
Allowable Unit Stresses for Structural Lumber—VISUAL GRADING
(Normal loading. See also Section 2504)

ALLOWABLE UNIT STRESSES IN POUNDS PER SQUARE INCH

SPECIES AND COMMERCIAL GRADE	SIZE CLASSIFICATION	EXTREME FIBER IN BENDING F_b		Tension Parallel to Grain F_t	Horizontal Shear F_v	Compression perpendicular to Grain $F_c\perp$ [21]	Compression Parallel to Grain F_c	MODULUS OF ELASTICITY E [21]	U.B.C. STDS UNDER WHICH GRADED
		Single-member Uses	Repetitive-member Uses						
BLACK COTTONWOOD (Surfaced dry or surfaced green. Used at 19% max. m.c.)									
Select Structural	2" to 4" thick 2" to 4" wide	1000	1200	600	50	180	725	1,200,000	
No. 1		875	1000	500	50	180	575	1,200,000	
No. 2		725	825	425	50	180	450	1,100,000	
No. 3		400	450	225	50	180	275	900,000	
Appearance		875	1000	500	50	180	700	1,200,000	
Stud		400	450	225	50	180	275	900,000	
Construction	2" to 4" thick 4" wide	525	600	300	50	180	525	900,000	25-2 (See footnotes 2 through 9, 11, 13, 15 and 16)
Standard		300	325	175	50	180	425	900,000	
Utility		150	150	75	50	180	275	900,000	
Select Structural	2" to 4" thick 5" and wider	875	1000	600	50	180	650	1,200,000	
No. 1		750	875	500	50	180	575	1,200,000	
No. 2		625	700	325	50	180	475	1,100,000	
No. 3 and Stud		350	425	175	50	180	300	900,000	
Appearance		750	875	500	50	180	700	1,200,000	
CALIFORNIA REDWOOD (Surfaced dry or surfaced green. Used at 19% max. m.c.)									
Clear Heart Structural	4" & less thick, any width	2300	2650	1500	145	650	2150	1,400,000	25-7 (See footnotes 2 through 7 9, 13, 15 and 16)
Clear Structural		2300	2650	1500	145	650	2150	1,400,000	
Select Structural	2" to 4" thick 2" to 4" wide	2050	2350	1200	80	650	1750	1,400,000	
Select Structural, Open grain		1600	1850	950	80	425	1300	1,100,000	

From the Uniform Building Code, © 1988, ICBO
Allowable Unit Stresses, Structural Lumber

25-7
(See footnotes 2 through 7, 9, 13, 15 and 16)

No. 1	2" to 4" thick 2" to 4" wide	1700	1950	975	80	650	1400	1,400,000
No. 1, Open grain		1350	1550	775	80	425	1050	1,100,000
No. 2		1400	1600	800	80	650	1100	1,250,000
No. 2, Open grain		1100	1250	625	80	425	825	1,000,000
No. 3		800	900	475	80	650	675	1,100,000
No. 3, Open grain		625	725	375	80	425	500	900,000
Stud		625	725	375		425	500	900,000
Construction	2" to 4" thick 4" wide	825	950	475	80	425	925	900,000
Standard		450	525	250	80	425	775	900,000
Utility		225	250	125	80	425	500	900,000
Select Structural	2" to 4" thick 5" and wider	1750	2000	1150	80	650	1550	1,400,000
Select Structural, Open grain		1400	1600	925	80	425	1150	1,100,000
No. 1		1500	1700	975	80	650	1400	1,400,000
No. 1, Open grain		1150	1350	775	80	425	1050	1,100,000
No. 2		1200	1400	650	80	650	1200	1,250,000
No. 2, Open grain		950	1100	500	80	425	875	1,000,000
No. 3		700	800	375	80	650	725	1,100,000
No. 3, Open grain		550	650	350	80	425	525	900,000
Clear Heart Structural	5" by 5" and larger	1850	—	1250	135	650	1650	1,300,000
Clear Structural		1850	—	1250	135	650	1650	1,300,000
Select Structural		1400	—	950	95	650	1200	1,300,000
No. 1		1200	—	800	95	650	1050	1,300,000
No. 2		975	—	650	95	650	900	1,100,000
No. 3		550	—	375	95	650	550	1,000,000

(Continued)

From the Uniform Building Code, © 1988, ICBO
Allowable Unit Stresses—Structural Lumber

473

TABLE NO. 25-A-1—ALLOWABLE UNIT STRESSES—STRUCTURAL LUMBER—(Continued)
Allowable Unit Stresses for Structural Lumber—VISUAL GRADING
(Normal loading. See also Section 2504)

SPECIES AND COMMERCIAL GRADE	SIZE CLASSIFICATION	EXTREME FIBER IN BENDING F_b Single-member Uses	Repetitive-member Uses	Tension Parallel to Grain F_t	Horizontal Shear F_v	Compression perpendicular to Grain $F_{c\perp}$ 21	Compression Parallel to Grain F_c	MODULUS OF ELASTICITY E 21	U.B.C. STDS UNDER WHICH GRADED
Select Decking, Close grain	Decking	1850	2150	—	—	—	—	1,400,000	25-7 (See footnotes 2, 5 and 6)
Select Decking	2" thick	1450	1700	—	—	—	—	1,100,000	
Commercial Decking	6" & wider	1200	1350	—	—	—	—	1,000,000	
COAST SITKA SPRUCE (Surfaced dry or surfaced green. Used at 19% max. m.c.)									
Select Structural	2" to 4" thick	1500	1700	875	65	455	1100	1,700,000	25-2 (See footnotes 2 through 9, 11, 13, 15 and 16)
No. 1		1250	1450	750	65	455	875	1,700,000	
No. 2		1050	1200	625	65	455	700	1,500,000	
No. 3	2" to 4" wide	575	675	350	65	455	425	1,300,000	
Appearance		1250	1450	725	65	455	1050	1,700,000	
Stud		600	675	350	65	455	425	1,300,000	
Construction	2" to 4" thick	750	875	450	65	455	800	1,300,000	
Standard	4" wide	425	500	250	65	455	650	1,300,000	
Utility		200	225	125	65	455	425	1,300,000	
Select Structural	2" to 4" thick	1300	1500	850	65	455	975	1,700,000	
No. 1		1100	1250	725	65	455	875	1,700,000	
No. 2		900	1050	475	65	455	750	1,500,000	
No. 3 and Stud	5" and wider	525	575	275	65	455	475	1,300,000	
Appearance		1100	1250	725	65	455	1050	1,700,000	
Select Structural	Beams and Stringers	1150	—	675	60	455	775	1,500,000	
No. 1		950	—	475	60	455	650	1,500,000	
Select Structural	Posts and Timbers	1100	—	725	60	455	825	1,500,000	
No. 1		875	—	575	60	455	725	1,500,000	
Select	Decking	1250	1450	—	—	455	—	1,700,000	
Commercial		1050	1200	—	—	455	—	1,500,000	

From the Uniform Building Code, © 1988, ICBO

474

COAST SPECIES (Surfaced dry or surfaced green. Used at 19% max. m.c.)

Grade	Size							25-2 (See footnotes 2 through 9, 11, 13, 15 and 16)
Select Structural	2" to 4" thick 2" to 4" wide	1500	1700	850	65	370	1100	1,500,000
No. 1		1250	1450	750	65	370	875	1,500,000
No. 2		1050	1200	625	65	370	700	1,400,000
No. 3		575	675	350	65	370	425	1,200,000
Appearance		1250	1450	725	65	370	1050	1,500,000
Stud		575	675	350	65	370	425	1,200,000
Construction	2" to 4" thick 4" wide	750	875	450	65	370	800	1,200,000
Standard		425	500	250	65	370	650	1,200,000
Utility		200	225	125	65	370	425	1,200,000
Select Structural	2" to 4" thick 5" and wider	1300	1500	875	65	370	975	1,500,000
No. 1		1100	1250	725	65	370	875	1,500,000
No. 2		900	1050	475	65	370	750	1,400,000
No. 3 and Stud		525	600	275	65	370	475	1,200,000
Appearance		1100	1250	725	65	370	1050	1,500,000
Select	Decking	1250	1450	—	—	370	—	1,500,000
Commercial		1050	1200	—	—	370	—	1,400,000

COTTONWOOD (Surfaced dry or surfaced green. Used at 19% max. m.c.)

Grade	Size							25-5 (See footnotes 1 through 9)
Stud	2" to 3" thick 2" to 4" wide	525	600	300	65	320	350	1,000,000
Construction	2" to 4" thick 4" wide	675	775	400	65	320	650	1,000,000
Standard		375	425	225	65	320	525	1,000,000
Utility		175	200	100	65	320	350	1,000,000

(Continued)

From the Uniform Building Code, © 1988, ICBO

Allowable Unit Stresses—Structural Lumber

TABLE NO. 25-A-1—ALLOWABLE UNIT STRESSES—STRUCTURAL LUMBER—(Continued)
Allowable Unit Stresses for Structural Lumber—VISUAL GRADING
(Normal loading. See also Section 2504)

SPECIES AND COMMERCIAL GRADE	SIZE CLASSIFICATION	Extreme Fiber in Bending F_b Single-member Uses	Extreme Fiber in Bending F_b Repetitive-member Uses	Tension Parallel to Grain F_t	Horizontal Shear F_v	Compression perpendicular to Grain $F_{c\perp}$ 21	Compression Parallel to Grain F_c	MODULUS OF ELASTICITY E 21	U.B.C. STDS UNDER WHICH GRADED
DOUGLAS FIR – LARCH (Surfaced dry or surfaced green. Used at 19% max. m.c.) DOUGLAS FIR – LARCH (North)									
Dense Select Structural		2450	2800	1400	95	730	1850	1,900,000	
Select Structural		2100	2400	1200	95	625	1600	1,800,000	
Dense No. 1		2050	2400	1200	95	730	1450	1,900,000	
No. 1	2" to 4" thick	1750	2050	1050	95	625	1250	1,800,000	
Dense No. 2	2" to 4" wide	1700	1950	1000	95	730	1150	1,700,000	
No. 2		1450	1650	850	95	625	1000	1,700,000	
No. 3		800	925	475	95	625	600	1,500,000	25-2 25-3 and 25-4
Appearance		1750	2050	1050	95	625	1500	1,800,000	(See footnotes 2 through 9, 11, 13, 15 and 16)
Stud		800	925	475	95	625	600	1,500,000	
Construction	2" to 4" thick	1050	1200	625	95	625	1150	1,500,000	
Standard	4" wide	600	675	350	95	625	925	1,500,000	
Utility		275	325	175	95	625	600	1,500,000	
Dense Select Structural		2100	2400	1400	95	730	1650	1,900,000	
Select Structural		1800	2050	1200	95	625	1400	1,800,000	
Dense No. 1	2" to 4" thick	1800	2050	1200	95	730	1450	1,900,000	
No. 1	5" and wider	1500	1750	1000	95	625	1250	1,800,000	
Dense No. 2		1450	1700	775	95	730	1250	1,700,000	
No. 2		1250	1450	650	95	625	1050	1,700,000	
No. 3 and Stud		725	850	375	95	625	675	1,500,000	
Appearance		1500	1750	1000	95	625	1500	1,800,000	

From the Uniform Building Code, © 1988, ICBO

25-3 (See footnotes 2 through 9)

Grade	Classification							
Dense Select Structural	Beams and Stringers[12]	1900	—	1100	85	730	1300	1,700,000
Select Structural		1600	—	950	85	625	1100	1,600,000
Dense No. 1		1550	—	775	85	730	1100	1,700,000
No. 1		1300	—	675	85	625	925	1,600,000
Dense Select Structural	Posts and Timbers[12]	1750	—	1150	85	730	1350	1,700,000
Select Structural		1500	—	1000	85	625	1150	1,600,000
Dense No. 1		1400	—	950	85	730	1200	1,700,000
No. 1		1200	—	825	85	625	1000	1,600,000
Select Dex	Decking	1750	2000	—	—	625	—	1,800,000
Commercial Dex		1450	1650	—	—	625	—	1,700,000

25-4 (See footnotes 2 through 10)

Grade	Classification							
Dense Select Structural	Beams and Stringers[12]	1850	—	1100	85	730	1300	1,700,000
Select Structural		1600	—	950	85	625	1100	1,600,000
Dense No. 1		1550	—	775	85	730	1100	1,700,000
No. 1		1350	—	675	85	625	925	1,600,000
Dense No. 2		1000	—	500	85	730	700	1,400,000
No. 2		875	—	425	85	625	600	1,300,000
Dense Select Structural	Posts and Timbers[12]	1750	—	1150	85	730	1350	1,700,000
Select Structural		1500	—	1000	85	625	1150	1,600,000
Dense No. 1		1400	—	950	85	730	1200	1,700,000
No. 1		1200	—	825	85	625	1000	1,600,000
Dense No. 2		800	—	550	85	730	550	1,400,000
No. 2		700	—	475	85	625	475	1,300,000
Selected Decking	Decking	—	2000	—	—	—	—	1,800,000
Commercial Decking		—	1650	—	—	—	—	1,700,000
Selected Decking	Decking	—	2150	(Surfaced at 15% max. m.c. and used at 15% max. m.c.)				1,900,000
Commercial Decking		—	1800					1,700,000

(Continued)

From the Uniform Building Code, © 1988, ICBO

Allowable Unit Stresses—Structural Lumber

TABLE NO. 25-A-1—ALLOWABLE UNIT STRESSES—STRUCTURAL LUMBER—(Continued)
Allowable Unit Stresses for Structural Lumber—VISUAL GRADING
(Normal loading. See also Section 2504)

SPECIES AND COMMERCIAL GRADE	SIZE CLASSIFICATION	EXTREME FIBER IN BENDING F_b		Tension Parallel to Grain F_t	Horizontal Shear F_v	Compression perpendicular to Grain $F_{c\perp}$ 21	Compression Parallel to Grain F_c	MODULUS OF ELASTICITY E 21	U.B.C. STDS UNDER WHICH GRADED
		Single-member Uses	Repetitive-member Uses						
Select Structural No. 1	Beams and Stringers	1600 1300	— —	950 675	85 85	625 625	1100 925	1,600,000 1,600,000	25-2 (See footnotes 9 and 11)
Select Structural No. 1	Posts and Timbers	1500 1200	— —	1000 825	85 85	625 625	1150 1000	1,600,000 1,600,000	
Select Commercial	Decking	1750 1450	2000 1650	— —	— —	625 625	— —	1,800,000 1,700,000	
DOUGLAS FIR SOUTH (Surfaced dry or surfaced green. Used at 19% max. m.c.)									
Select Structural No. 1 & Appearance No. 2 No. 3 Stud	2" to 4" thick 2" to 4" wide	2000 1700 1400 775 775	2300 1950 1600 875 875	1150 975 825 450 450	90 90 90 90 90	520 520 520 520 520	1400 1150 900 550 550	1,400,000 1,400,000 1,300,000 1,100,000 1,100,000	25-4 (See footnotes 2 through 10, 13, 15 and 16)
Construction Standard Utility	2" to 4" thick 4" wide	1000 550 275	1150 650 300	600 325 150	90 90 90	520 520 520	1000 850 550	1,100,000 1,100,000 1,100,000	
Select Structural No. 1 & Appearance No. 2 No. 3 and Stud	2" to 4" thick 5" and wider	1700 1450 1200 700	1950 1650 1350 800	1150 975 625 350	90 90 90 90	520 520 520 520	1250 1150 950 600	1,400,000 1,400,000 1,300,000 1,100,000	

From the Uniform Building Code, © 1988, ICBO

Grade	Use / Size								Table
Select Structural	Beams and Stringers	1550	—	900	85	520	1000	1,200,000	25-4 (See footnotes 2 through 10, 13, 15 and 16)
No. 1		1300	—	625	85	520	850	1,200,000	
No. 2		825	—	425	85	520	525	1,000,000	
Select Structural	Posts and Timbers	1400	—	950	85	520	1050	1,200,000	
No. 1		1150	—	775	85	520	925	1,200,000	
No. 2		650	—	400	85	520	425	1,000,000	
Selected Decking	Decking	—	1900	—			—	1,400,000	
Commercial Decking	Decking	—	1600	—			—	1,300,000	
Selected Decking	Decking	—	2050	(Stresses for Decking apply at 15% moisture content)			—	1,500,000	
Commercial Decking	Decking	—	1750				—	1,300,000	
EASTERN HEMLOCK (Surfaced dry or surfaced green. Used at 19% max. m.c.)									25-8 (See footnotes 1 through 9)
Select Structural	2" to 4" thick, 2" to 4" wide	1750	2050	1050	85	550	1350	1,200,000	
No. 1		1500	1750	875	85	550	1050	1,200,000	
No. 2		1250	1450	725	85	550	850	1,100,000	
No. 3		675	800	400	85	550	525	1,000,000	
Appearance		1500	1750	875	85	550	1250	1,200,000	
Stud		675	800	400	85	550	525	1,000,000	
Construction	2" to 4" thick, 4" wide	900	1050	525	85	550	950	1,000,000	
Standard		500	575	300	85	550	800	1,000,000	
Utility		250	275	150	85	550	525	1,000,000	
Select Structural	2" to 4" thick, 5" and wider	1550	1750	1000	85	550	1200	1,200,000	
No. 1		1300	1500	875	85	550	1050	1,200,000	
No. 2		1050	1250	550	85	550	900	1,100,000	
No. 3		625	700	325	85	550	575	1,000,000	
Appearance		1300	1500	875	85	550	1250	1,200,000	
Stud		625	700	325	85	550	575	1,000,000	
Select Structural	Beams and Stringers	1350	—	925	80	550	950	1,200,000	
No. 1		1150	—	775	80	550	800	1,200,000	
Select Structural	Posts and Timbers	1250	—	850	80	550	1000	1,200,000	
No. 1		1050	—	700	80	550	875	1,200,000	

(Continued)

From the Uniform Building Code, © 1988, ICBO

Allowable Unit Stresses—Structural Lumber

TABLE NO. 25-A-1—ALLOWABLE UNIT STRESSES—STRUCTURAL LUMBER—(Continued)
Allowable Unit Stresses for Structural Lumber—VISUAL GRADING
(Normal loading. See also Section 2504)

SPECIES AND COMMERCIAL GRADE	SIZE CLASSIFICATION	ALLOWABLE UNIT STRESSES IN POUNDS PER SQUARE INCH							U.B.C. STDS UNDER WHICH GRADED
		EXTREME FIBER IN BENDING F_b		Tension Parallel to Grain F_t	Horizontal Shear F_v	Compression perpendicular to Grain $F_c \perp$ 21	Compression Parallel to Grain F_c	MODULUS OF ELASTICITY E 21	
		Single-member Uses	Repetitive-member Uses						
EASTERN HEMLOCK—TAMARACK (Surfaced dry or surfaced green. Used at 19% max. m.c.)									
EASTERN HEMLOCK—TAMARACK (NORTH)									
Select Structural	2" to 4" thick 2" to 4" wide	1800	2050	1050	85	555	1350	1,300,000	25-2 25-5 and 25-8 (See footnotes 2 through 9, 11, 13, 15 and 16)
No. 1		1500	1750	900	85	555	1050	1,300,000	
No. 2		1250	1450	725	85	555	850	1,100,000	
No. 3		700	800	400	85	555	525	1,000,000	
Appearance		1300	1500	875	85	555	1300	1,300,000	
Stud		700	800	400	85	555	525	1,000,000	
Construction	2" to 4" thick 4" wide	900	1050	525	85	555	975	1,000,000	
Standard		500	575	300	85	555	800	1,000,000	
Utility		250	275	150	85	555	525	1,000,000	
Select Structural	2" to 4" thick 5" and wider	1550	1750	1050	85	555	1200	1,300,000	
No. 1		1300	1500	875	85	555	1050	1,300,000	
No. 2		1050	1200	575	85	555	900	1,100,000	
No. 3 and Stud		625	725	325	85	555	575	1,000,000	
Appearance		1300	1500	875	85	555	1300	1,300,000	
Select Structural	Beams and Stringers	1400	—	925	80	555	950	1,200,000	25-2 (See footnotes 1 through 9 and 11)
No. 1		1150	—	775	80	555	800	1,200,000	
Select Structural	Posts and Timbers	1300	—	875	80	555	1000	1,200,000	
No. 1		1050	—	700	80	555	875	1,200,000	
Select	Decking	1500	1700	—	—	—	—	1,300,000	
Commercial		1250	1450	—	—	—	—	1,100,000	

From the Uniform Building Code, © 1988, ICBO

Species and grade	Size classification	Fb (single)	Fb (repetitive)	Ft	Fv	Fc⊥	Fc‖	E	Grading rules / footnotes
Select Structural	Beams and Stringers	1400	—	925	80	555	950	1,200,000	25-5
No. 1	Beams and Stringers	1150	—	775	80	555	800	1,200,000	25-8 (See footnotes 2 through 9)
Select Structural	Posts and Timbers	1300	—	875	80	555	1000	1,200,000	25-8
No. 1	Posts and Timbers	1050	—	700	80	555	875	1,200,000	(See footnotes 2 through 9)
Select	Decking	1500	1700	—	—	—	—	1,300,000	25-8
Commercial	Decking	1250	1450	—	—	—	—	1,100,000	(See footnotes 2 through 9)
Select Structural	Beams and Stringers	1450	—	850	85	555	950	1,300,000	25-2
No. 1	Beams and Stringers	1200	—	600	85	555	800	1,300,000	(See footnotes 2 through 9 and 11)
Select Structural	Posts and Timbers	1300	—	875	80	555	1000	1,200,000	
No. 1	Posts and Timbers	1050	—	700	80	555	875	1,200,000	
Select	Decking	1500	1700	—	—	555	—	1,300,000	
Commercial	Decking	1250	1450	—	—	555	—	1,100,000	
EASTERN SOFTWOODS (Surfaced dry or surfaced green, Used at 19% max. m.c.)									
Select Structural	2" to 4" thick, 2" to 4" wide	1350	1550	800	70	335	1050	1,200,000	25-5
No. 1		1150	1350	675	70	335	825	1,200,000	(See footnotes 1 through 9)
No. 2		950	1100	550	70	335	650	1,100,000	
No. 3		525	600	300	70	335	400	1,000,000	
Stud	2" to 4" thick, 2" to 4" wide	525	600	300	70	335	400	1,000,000	25-5, 25-8 (See footnotes 1 through 8)
Construction	2" to 4" thick, 4" wide	700	800	400	70	335	750	1,000,000	25-5
Standard		375	450	225	70	335	625	1,000,000	(See footnotes 1 through 9)
Utility		175	200	100	70	335	400	1,000,000	
Select Structural	2" to 4" thick, 5" and wider	1150	1350	775	70	335	925	1,200,000	25-5
No. 1		1000	1150	675	70	335	825	1,200,000	(See footnotes 1 through 9)
No. 2		825	950	425	70	335	700	1,100,000	
No. 3		475	550	250	70	335	450	1,000,000	
Appearance		1000	1150	675	70	335	1000	1,200,000	
Stud	2" to 4" thick, 5" and wider	475	550	250	70	335	450	1,000,000	25-5, 25-8 (See footnotes 1 through 9)

(Continued)

From the Uniform Building Code, © 1988, ICBO

Allowable Unit Stresses—Structural Lumber

TABLE NO. 25-A-1—ALLOWABLE UNIT STRESSES—STRUCTURAL LUMBER—(Continued)
Allowable Unit Stresses for Structural Lumber—VISUAL GRADING
(Normal loading. See also Section 2504)

ALLOWABLE UNIT STRESSES IN POUNDS PER SQUARE INCH

Species and commercial grade	Size classification	Extreme fiber in bending F_b Single-member uses	Extreme fiber in bending F_b Repetitive-member uses	Tension parallel to grain F_t	Horizontal shear F_v	Compression perpendicular to grain $F_c\perp$ 21	Compression parallel to grain F_c	Modulus of elasticity E 21	U.B.C. STDS UNDER WHICH GRADED
EASTERN SPRUCE (Surfaced dry or surfaced green. Used at 19% max. m.c.)									
Select Structural	2" to 4" thick, 2" to 4" wide	1400	1600	800	70	390	1050	1,500,000	25-5 25-8 (See footnotes 1 through 9)
No. 1		1200	1350	700	70	390	825	1,500,000	
No. 2		975	1100	575	70	390	650	1,400,000	
No. 3		550	625	325	70	390	400	1,400,000	
Appearance		1200	1350	700	70	390	1000	1,500,000	
Stud		550	625	325	70	390	400	1,200,000	
Construction	2" to 4" thick, 4" wide	700	800	400	70	390	750	1,200,000	
Standard		400	450	225	70	390	625	1,200,000	
Utility		175	225	100	70	390	400	1,200,000	
Select Structural	2" to 4" thick, 5" and wider	1200	1350	800	70	390	925	1,500,000	
No. 1		1000	1150	675	70	390	825	1,500,000	
No. 2		825	950	425	70	390	700	1,400,000	
No. 3		475	550	250	70	390	450	1,200,000	
Appearance		1000	1150	675	70	390	1000	1,500,000	
Stud		475	550	250	70	390	450	1,200,000	
Select Structural	Beams and Stringers	1050	—	725	65	390	750	1,400,000	25-8 (See footnotes 1 through 9)
No. 1		900	—	600	65	390	625	1,400,000	
Select Structural	Posts and Timbers	1000	—	675	65	390	775	1,400,000	
No. 1		800	—	550	65	390	675	1,400,000	
Select	Decking	—	1300	—	—	—	—	1,500,000	
Commercial		—	1100	—	—	—	—	1,400,000	

From the Uniform Building Code, © 1988, ICBO

Allowable Unit Stresses—Structural Lumber

EASTERN WHITE PINE (Surfaced dry or surfaced green. Used at 19% max. m.c.)
EASTERN WHITE PINE (NORTH)

Grade	Size								Grading rules / Footnotes
Select Structural	2" to 4" thick	1350	1550	800	65	350	1050	1,200,000	25-2 and 25-8 (See footnotes 2 through 9, 12 and 14)
No. 1	thick	1150	1350	675	65	350	850	1,200,000	
No. 2	2" to 4"	950	1100	550	65	350	675	1,100,000	
No. 3	wide	525	600	300	65	350	400	1,000,000	
Appearance		1150	1350	675	65	350	1000	1,200,000	
Stud	2" to 4" thick 2" to 4" wide	525	600	300	65	350	400	1,000,000	25-2, 25-5 and 25-8 (See footnotes 2 through 9, 11, 12, 13 and 14)
Construction	2" to 4" thick	700	800	400	65	350	750	1,000,000	25-2 and 25-8 (See footnotes 2 through 9, 11, 12, 13 and 14)
Standard	4" wide	375	450	225	65	350	625	1,000,000	
Utility		175	200	100	65	350	400	1,000,000	
Select Structural	2" to 4" thick	1150	1350	775	65	350	950	1,200,000	25-2 and 25-8 (See footnotes 2 through 9, 11, 12 and 14)
No. 1	thick	1000	1150	675	65	350	850	1,200,000	
No. 2	5" and	825	950	450	65	350	700	1,100,000	
No. 3 and Stud	wider	475	550	250	65	350	450	1,000,000	
Appearance		1000	1150	675	65	350	1000	1,200,000	
Select Structural	Beams and Stringers	1050	—	700	65	350	675	1,100,000	25-8 (See footnotes 2 through 9)
No. 1		875	—	600	65	350	575	1,100,000	
Select Structural	Posts and Timbers	975	—	650	65	350	725	1,100,000	25-8 (See footnotes 2 through 9)
No. 1		800	—	525	65	350	625	1,100,000	

(Continued)

From the Uniform Building Code, © 1988, ICBO

Allowable Unit Stresses—Structural Lumber

TABLE NO. 25-A-1—ALLOWABLE UNIT STRESSES—STRUCTURAL LUMBER—(Continued)
Allowable Unit Stresses for Structural Lumber—VISUAL GRADING
(Normal loading. See also Section 2504)

SPECIES AND COMMERCIAL GRADE	SIZE CLASSIFICATION	EXTREME FIBER IN BENDING F_b		Tension Parallel to Grain F_t	Horizontal Shear F_v	Compression perpendicular to Grain $F_{c\perp}$ 21	Compression Parallel to Grain F_c	MODULUS OF ELASTICITY E 21	U.B.C. STDS UNDER WHICH GRADED
		Single-member Uses	Repetitive-member Uses						
Select	Decking	900	1050	—	—	—	—	1,200,000	25-2 and 25-8 (See footnotes 2 through 9, 11 and 12)
Commercial		775	875	—	—	—	—	1,100,000	
EASTERN WOODS (Surfaced dry or surfaced green. Used at 19% max. m.c.)									
Select Structural	2" to 4" thick 2" to 4" wide	1300	1500	775	60	270	850	1,100,000	25-5 and 25-8 (See footnotes 9 2 through 9 13, 15 and 16)
No. 1		1100	1300	650	60	270	675	1,100,000	
No. 2		925	1050	525	60	270	550	1,000,000	
No. 3		500	575	300	60	270	325	900,000	
Stud		500	575	300	60	270	325	900,000	
Construction	2" to 4" thick 4" wide	650	750	400	60	270	625	900,000	
Standard		375	425	225	60	270	500	900,000	
Utility		175	200	100	60	270	325	900,000	
Appearance	2" to 4" thick 2" to 4" wide	1100	1300	650	60	270	825	1,100,000	
Select Structural	2" to 4" thick 5" and wider	1150	1300	750	60	270	750	1,100,000	25-5 (See footnotes 2 through 9, 15 and 16)
No. 1		950	1100	650	60	270	675	1,100,000	
No. 2		775	900	425	60	270	575	1,000,000	
No. 3 and Stud		450	525	250	60	270	375	900,000	
Appearance		950	1100	650	60	270	825	1,100,000	

From the Uniform Building Code, © 1988, ICBO

Allowable Unit Stresses—Structural Lumber

ENGELMANN SPRUCE—ALPINE FIR (ENGELMANN SPRUCE—LODGEPOLE PINE) (Surfaced dry or surfaced green. Used at 19% max. m.c.)

Grade	Size classification								25-4 (See footnotes 2 through 10, 13, 15 and 16)
Select Structural	2" to 4" thick	1350	1550	800	70	320	950	1,300,000	
No. 1	2" to 4" wide	1150	1350	675	70	320	750	1,300,000	
No. 2		950	1100	550	70	320	600	1,100,000	
No. 3		525	600	300	70	320	375	1,000,000	
Appearance		1150	1350	675	70	320	900	1,300,000	
Stud		525	600	300	70	320	375	1,000,000	
Construction	2" to 4" thick	700	800	400	70	320	675	1,000,000	
Standard	4" wide	375	450	225	70	320	550	1,000,000	
Utility		175	200	100	70	320	375	1,000,000	
Select Structural	2" to 4" thick	1200	1350	775	70	320	850	1,300,000	
No. 1	5" and wider	1000	1150	675	70	320	750	1,300,000	
No. 2		825	950	425	70	320	625	1,100,000	
No. 3 and Stud		475	550	250	70	320	400	1,000,000	
Appearance		1000	1150	675	70	320	900	1,300,000	
Select Structural	Beams and Stringers	1050	—	625	65	320	675	1,100,000	
No. 1		875	—	450	65	320	550	1,100,000	
No. 2		575	—	275	65	320	350	900,000	
Select Structural	Posts and Timbers	975	—	650	65	320	700	1,100,000	
No. 1		800	—	525	65	320	625	1,100,000	
No. 2		450	—	300	65	320	275	900,000	
Selected Decking	Decking	—	1300	—	—	—	—	1,300,000	
Commercial Decking		—	1100	—	—	—	—	1,100,000	
Selected Decking	Decking	—	1400	(Surfaced at 15% max. m.c. and used at 15% max. m.c.)			—	1,300,000	
Commercial Decking		—	1200				—	1,200,000	

(Continued)

From the *Uniform Building Code*, © 1988, ICBO

Allowable Unit Stresses—Structural Lumber

TABLE NO. 25-A-1—ALLOWABLE UNIT STRESSES—STRUCTURAL LUMBER—(Continued)
Allowable Unit Stresses for Structural Lumber—VISUAL GRADING
(Normal loading. See also Section 2504)

SPECIES AND COMMERCIAL GRADE	SIZE CLASSIFICATION	EXTREME FIBER IN BENDING F_b		Tension Parallel to Grain F_t	Horizontal Shear F_v	Compression perpendicular to Grain $F_{c\perp}$ 21	Compression Parallel to Grain F_c	MODULUS OF ELASTICITY E 21	U.B.C. STDS UNDER WHICH GRADED
		ALLOWABLE UNIT STRESSES IN POUNDS PER SQUARE INCH							
		Single-member Uses	Repetitive-member Uses						
HEM-FIR (Surfaced dry or surfaced green. Used at 19% max. m.c.)									
Select Structural	2" to 4" thick	1650	1900	975	75	405	1300	1,500,000	25-3 and 25-4 (See footnotes 2 through 9, 11, 12, 13 15 and 16)
No. 1	2" to 4" wide	1400	1600	825	75	405	1050	1,500,000	
No. 2		1150	1350	675	75	405	825	1,400,000	
No. 3		650	725	375	75	405	500	1,200,000	
Appearance		1400	1600	825	75	405	1250	1,500,000	
Stud		650	725	375	75	405	500	1,200,000	
Construction	2" to 4" thick	825	975	500	75	405	925	1,200,000	
Standard	4" wide	475	550	275	75	405	775	1,200,000	
Utility		225	250	125	75	405	500	1,200,000	
Select Structural	2" to 4" thick	1400	1650	950	75	405	1150	1,500,000	
No. 1	5" and wider	1200	1400	800	75	405	1050	1,500,000	
No. 2		1000	1150	525	75	405	875	1,400,000	
No. 3 and Stud		575	675	300	75	405	550	1,200,000	
Appearance		1200	1400	800	75	405	1250	1,500,000	
• Select Structural	Beams and Stringers	1300	—	750	70	405	925	1,300,000	
No. 1		1050	—	525	70	405	750	1,300,000	
Select Structural	Posts and Timbers	1200	—	800	70	405	975	1,300,000	25-3 (See footnotes 2 through 9, 15 and 16)
No. 1		975	—	650	70	405	850	1,300,000	
Select Dex	Decking	1400	1600	—	—	405	—	1,500,000	
Commercial Dex		1150	1350	—	—	405	—	1,400,000	

From the Uniform Building Code, © 1988, ICBO

Allowable Unit Stresses—Structural Lumber

Species and grade	Classification							E	Footnotes
Select Structural	Beams and Stringers	1250	—	725	70	405	925	1,300,000	25-4 (See footnotes 2 through 9, 15 and 16)
No. 1		1050	—	525	70	405	775	1,300,000	
No. 2		675	—	325	70	405	475	1,100,000	
Select Structural	Posts and Timbers	1200	—	800	70	405	975	1,300,000	
No. 1		950	—	650	70	405	850	1,300,000	
No. 2		525	—	350	70	405	375	1,100,000	
Select Structural	Beams and Stringers 12	1250	—	850	70	405	925	1,300,000	25-2 (See footnotes 2 through 12)
No. 1		1050	—	725	70	405	775	1,300,000	
Select Structural	Posts and Timbers	1200	—	800	70	405	975	1,300,000	
No. 1		950	†	650	70	405	850	1,300,000	
Selected Decking	Decking	—	1600	—	—	—	—	1,500,000	25-2 and 25-4 (See footnotes 2 through 12)
Commercial Decking		—	1350	—	—	—	—	1,400,000	
Selected Decking	Decking	—	1700	(Surfaced at 15% max. m.c. and used at 15% max. m.c.)				1,600,000	
Commercial Decking		—	1450					1,400,000	
Select	Decking	1350	1550	—	—	405	—	1,500,000	
Commercial		1150	1300	—	—	405	—	1,400,000	

(Continued)

From the Uniform Building Code, © 1988, ICBO

Allowable Unit Stresses—Structural Lumber

TABLE NO. 25-A-1—ALLOWABLE UNIT STRESSES—STRUCTURAL LUMBER—(Continued)
Allowable Unit Stresses for Structural Lumber—VISUAL GRADING
(Normal loading. See also Section 2504)

Species and commercial grade	Size classification	ALLOWABLE UNIT STRESSES IN POUNDS PER SQUARE INCH							
		Extreme fiber in bending F_b		Tension parallel to grain F_t	Horizontal shear F_v	Compression perpendicular to grain $F_{c\perp}$ 21	Compression parallel to grain F_c	Modulus of elasticity E 21	U.B.C. STDS UNDER WHICH GRADED
		Single-member uses	Repetitive-member uses						
HEM-FIR (NORTH) (Surfaced dry or surfaced green. Used at 19% max. m.c.)									
Select Structural	2" to 3" thick 2" to 4" wide	1600	1800	925	75	370	1300	1,500,000	
No. 1		1350	1550	800	75	370	1050	1,500,000	
No. 2		1100	1300	650	75	370	800	1,400,000	
No. 3		625	700	350	75	370	500	1,200,000	
Appearance		1350	1550	800	75	370	1250	1,500,000	
Stud		625	700	350	75	370	500	1,200,000	
Construction	2" to 4" thick 4" wide	800	925	475	75	370	925	1,200,000	25-2 (See footnotes 1 through 9 and 11)
Standard		450	525	275	75	370	775	1,200,000	
Utility		225	250	125	75	370	500	1,200,000	
Select Structural	2" to 4" thick 5" and wider	1350	1550	900	75	370	1150	1,500,000	
No. 1		1150	1350	775	75	370	1050	1,500,000	
No. 2		950	1100	500	75	370	850	1,400,000	
No. 3		550	650	300	75	370	550	1,200,000	
Appearance		1150	1350	775	75	370	1250	1,500,000	
Stud		550	650	300	75	370	550	1,200,000	
Select Structural	Beams and Stringers	1250	—	725	70	370	900	1,300,000	
No. 1		1000	—	500	70	370	750	1,300,000	
Select Structural	Posts and Timbers	1150	—	775	70	370	950	1,300,000	
No. 1		925	—	625	70	370	850	1,300,000	
Select	Decking	1350	1500	—	—	370	—	1,500,000	
Commercial		1100	1300	—	—	370	—	1,400,000	

From the Uniform Building Code, © 1988, ICBO

Allowable Unit Stresses—Structural Lumber

IDAHO WHITE PINE (Surfaced dry or surfaced green. Used at 19% max. m.c.)

Grade	Size							
Select structural	2" to 4" thick	1350	1550	775	70	315	1100	1,400,000
No. 1	2" to 4" wide	1150	1300	650	70	315	875	1,400,000
No. 2		925	1050	550	70	315	675	1,300,000
No. 3		525	600	300	70	315	425	1,200,000
Appearance		1150	1300	650	70	315	1050	1,400,000
Stud		525	600	300	70	315	425	1,200,000
Construction	2" to 4" thick	675	775	400	70	315	775	1,200,000
Standard	4" wide	375	425	225	70	315	650	1,200,000
Utility		175	200	100	70	315	425	1,200,000
Select Structural	2" to 4" thick	1150	1300	775	70	315	950	1,400,000
No. 1	5" and wider	975	1100	650	70	315	875	1,400,000
No. 2		800	925	425	70	315	725	1,300,000
No. 3 and Stud		475	550	250	70	315	450	1,200,000
Appearance		975	1100	650	70	315	1050	1,400,000
Select Structural	Beams and Stringers	1000	—	600	65	315	775	1,300,000
No. 1		850	—	425	65	315	650	1,300,000
No. 2		550	—	275	65	315	400	1,100,000
Select Structural	Posts and Timbers	950	—	650	65	315	800	1,300,000
No. 1		775	—	525	65	315	700	1,300,000
No. 2		450	—	300	65	315	325	1,100,000
Selected Decking	Decking	—	1300	—	—	—	—	1,400,000
Commercial Decking		—	1050	—	—	—	—	1,300,000
Selected Decking	Decking	—	1400	(Surfaced at 15% max. m.c. and used at 15% max. m.c.)				1,500,000
Commercial Decking		—	1150					1,400,000

25-4 (See footnotes 2 through 10, 13, 15 and 16)

(Continued)

From the Uniform Building Code, © 1988, ICBO

Allowable Unit Stresses—Structural Lumber

TABLE NO. 25-A-1—ALLOWABLE UNIT STRESSES—STRUCTURAL LUMBER—(Continued)
Allowable Unit Stresses for Structural Lumber—VISUAL GRADING
(Normal loading. See also Section 2504)

SPECIES AND COMMERCIAL GRADE	SIZE CLASSIFICATION	ALLOWABLE UNIT STRESSES IN POUNDS PER SQUARE INCH							U.B.C. STDS UNDER WHICH GRADED
		EXTREME FIBER IN BENDING F_b		Tension Parallel to Grain F_t	Horizontal Shear F_v	Compression perpendicular to Grain $F_{c\perp}$ 21	Compression Parallel to Grain F_c	MODULUS OF ELASTICITY E 21	
		Single-member Uses	Repetitive-member Uses						
LODGEPOLE PINE (Surfaced dry or surfaced green. Used at 19% max. m.c.)									
Select Structural	2" to 4" thick 2" to 4" wide	1500	1750	875	70	400	1150	1,300,000	25-4 (See footnotes 2 through 10, 13, 15 and 16)
No. 1		1300	1500	750	70	400	900	1,300,000	
No. 2		1050	1200	625	70	400	700	1,200,000	
No. 3		600	675	350	70	400	425	1,000,000	
Appearance		1300	1500	750	70	400	1050	1,300,000	
Stud		600	675	350	70	400	425	1,000,000	
Construction	2" thick 4" wide	775	875	450	70	400	800	1,000,000	
Standard		425	500	250	70	400	675	1,000,000	
Utility		200	225	125	70	400	425	1,000,000	
Select Structural	2" to 4" thick 5" and wider	1300	1500	875	70	400	1000	1,300,000	
No. 1		1100	1300	750	70	400	900	1,300,000	
No. 2		925	1050	475	70	400	750	1,200,000	
No. 3 and Stud		525	625	275	70	400	475	1,000,000	
Appearance		1100	1300	750	70	400	1050	1,300,000	
Select Structural	Beams and Stringers	1150	—	700	65	400	800	1,100,000	
No. 1		975	—	500	65	400	675	1,100,000	
No. 2		625	—	325	65	400	425	900,000	
Select Structural	Posts and Timbers	1100	—	725	65	400	850	1,100,000	
No. 1		875	—	600	65	400	725	1,100,000	
No. 2		500	—	350	65	400	350	900,000	

From the Uniform Building Code, © 1988, ICBO

Allowable Unit Stresses—Structural Lumber

Species and commercial grade	Size classification								Grading rules / footnotes
Selected Decking	Decking	—	1450	—	—	—	—	1,300,000	25-4 (See footnotes 2 through 10, 13, 15 and 16)
Commercial Decking	Decking	—	1200	—	—	—	—	1,200,000	
Selected Decking	Decking	—	1550	(Surfaced at 15% max. m.c. and used at 15% max. m.c.)				1,400,000	25-3 and 25-4 (See footnotes 2 through 9, 13, 15 and 16)
Commercial Decking	Decking	—	1300					1,200,000	
MOUNTAIN HEMLOCK (Surfaced dry or surfaced green. Used at 19% max. m.c.)									
Select Structural	2" to 4" thick 2" to 4" wide	1750	2000	1000	95	570	1250	1,300,000	
No. 1		1450	1700	850	95	570	1000	1,300,000	
No. 2		1200	1400	700	95	570	775	1,100,000	
No. 3		675	775	400	95	570	475	1,000,000	
Appearance		1450	1700	850	95	570	1200	1,300,000	
Stud		675	775	400	95	570	475	1,000,000	
Construction	2" to 4" thick 4" wide	875	1000	525	95	570	900	1,000,000	25-3 and 25-4 (See footnotes 2 through 9, 13, 15 and 16)
Standard		500	575	275	95	570	725	1,000,000	
Utility		225	275	125	95	570	475	1,000,000	
Select Structural	2" to 4" thick 5" and wider	1500	1700	1000	95	570	1100	1,300,000	
No. 1		1250	1450	850	95	570	1000	1,300,000	
No. 2		1050	1200	550	95	570	825	1,100,000	
No. 3 and Stud		625	700	325	95	570	525	1,000,000	
Appearance		1250	1450	850	95	570	1200	1,300,000	
Select Structural	Beams and Stringers	1350	—	775	90	570	875	1,100,000	
No. 1		1100	—	550	90	570	725	1,100,000	
Select Structural	Posts and Timbers	1250	—	825	90	570	925	1,100,000	25-3 (See footnotes 2 through 9)
No. 1		1000	—	675	90	570	800	1,100,000	
Select Dex	Decking	1450	1650	—	—	570	—	1,300,000	
Commercial Dex	Decking	1200	1400	—	—	570	—	1,100,000	

(Continued)

From the *Uniform Building Code*, © 1988, ICBO

Allowable Unit Stresses—Structural Lumber

TABLE NO. 25-A-1.—ALLOWABLE UNIT STRESSES—STRUCTURAL LUMBER—(Continued)
Allowable Unit Stresses for Structural Lumber—VISUAL GRADING
(Normal loading. See also Section 2504)

SPECIES AND COMMERCIAL GRADE	SIZE CLASSIFICATION	EXTREME FIBER IN BENDING F_b Single-member Uses	Repetitive-member Uses	Tension Parallel to Grain F_t	Horizontal Shear F_v	Compression perpendicular to Grain $F_{c\perp}$ 21	Compression Parallel to Grain F_c	MODULUS OF ELASTICITY E 21	U.B.C. STDS UNDER WHICH GRADED
Select Structural	Beams and Stringers	1350	—	775	90	570	875	1,100,000	
No. 1		1100	—	550	90	570	750	1,100,000	
No. 2		725	—	375	90	570	475	900,000	
Select Structural	Posts and Timbers	1250	—	825	90	570	925	1,100,000	25-4 (See footnotes 2 through 10)
No. 1		1000	—	675	90	570	800	1,100,000	
No. 2		575	—	375	90	570	375	900,000	
Selected Decking	Decking	—	1650	—	—	—	—	1,300,000	
Commercial Decking		—	1400	—	—	—	—	1,100,000	
Selected Decking	Decking	—	1800	(Surfaced at 15% max. m.c. and used at 15% max. m.c.)				1,300,000	
Commercial Decking		—	1500					1,200,000	

MOUNTAIN HEMLOCK—HEM-FIR (Surfaced dry or surfaced green. Used at 19% max. m.c.)

SPECIES AND COMMERCIAL GRADE	SIZE CLASSIFICATION	EXTREME FIBER IN BENDING F_b Single-member Uses	Repetitive-member Uses	Tension Parallel to Grain F_t	Horizontal Shear F_v	Compression perpendicular to Grain $F_{c\perp}$ 21	Compression Parallel to Grain F_c	MODULUS OF ELASTICITY E 21	U.B.C. STDS UNDER WHICH GRADED
Select Structural	2" to 4" thick, 2" to 4" wide	1650	1900	975	75	405	1250	1,300,000	
No. 1		1400	1600	825	75	405	1000	1,300,000	
No. 2		1150	1350	675	75	405	775	1,100,000	
No. 3		650	725	375	75	405	475	1,000,000	
Appearance		1400	1600	825	75	405	1200	1,300,000	
Stud		650	725	375	75	405	475	1,000,000	
Construction	2" to 4" thick, 4" wide	825	975	500	75	405	900	1,000,000	25-4 (See footnotes 2 through 10, 13, 15 and 16)
Standard		475	550	275	75	405	725	1,000,000	
Utility		225	250	125	75	405	475	1,000,000	
Select Structural	2" to 4" thick, 5" and wider	1400	1650	950	75	405	1100	1,300,000	
No. 1		1200	1400	800	75	405	1000	1,300,000	
No. 2		1000	1150	525	75	405	825	1,100,000	
No. 3 and Stud		575	675	300	75	405	525	1,000,000	
Appearance		1200	1400	800	75	405	1200	1,300,000	

From the Uniform Building Code. © 1988 ICBO

Grade	Size Classification							Modulus of Elasticity	Footnotes
Select Structural	Beams and Stringers	1250	—	725	70	405	875	1,100,000	
No. 1		1050	—	525	70	405	750	1,100,000	
No. 2		675	—	325	70	405	475	900,000	
Select Structural	Posts and Timbers	1200	—	800	70	405	925	1,100,000	25-4 (See footnotes 2 through 10, 13, 15 and 16)
No. 1		950	—	650	70	405	800	1,100,000	
No. 2		525	—	350	70	405	375	900,000	
Selected Decking	Decking	—	1600	—	—	—	—	1,300,000	
Commercial Decking		—	1350	—	—	—	—	1,100,000	
Selected Decking	Decking	—	1700	(Surfaced at 15% max. m.c. and used at 15% max. m.c.)				1,300,000	
Commercial Decking		—	1450					1,200,000	
NORTHERN ASPEN (Surfaced dry or surfaced green. Used at 19% max. m.c.)									
Select Structural	2" to 4" thick, 2" to 4" wide	1300	1500	750	60	320	850	1,400,000	
No. 1		1100	1250	650	60	320	675	1,400,000	
No. 2		900	1050	525	60	320	525	1,200,000	
No. 3		500	575	275	60	320	325	1,100,000	
Appearance		1100	1250	650	60	320	800	1,400,000	
Stud		500	575	275	60	320	325	1,100,000	
Construction	2" to 4" thick, 4" wide	650	750	375	60	320	600	1,100,000	25-2 (See footnotes 2 through 9, 11, 13, 15 and 16)
Standard		350	425	200	60	320	500	1,100,000	
Utility		175	200	100	60	320	325	1,100,000	
Select Structural	2" to 4" thick, 5" and wider	1100	1250	750	60	320	750	1,400,000	
No. 1		950	1100	625	60	320	675	1,400,000	
No. 2		775	900	400	60	320	575	1,200,000	
No. 3 and Stud		450	525	250	60	320	350	1,100,000	
Appearance		950	1100	625	60	320	800	1,400,000	

(Continued)

From the Uniform Building Code, © 1988, ICBO

Allowable Unit Stresses—Structural Lumber

TABLE NO. 25-A-1—ALLOWABLE UNIT STRESSES—STRUCTURAL LUMBER—(Continued)
Allowable Unit Stresses for Structural Lumber—VISUAL GRADING
(Normal loading. See also Section 2504)

SPECIES AND COMMERCIAL GRADE	SIZE CLASSIFICATION	ALLOWABLE UNIT STRESSES IN POUNDS PER SQUARE INCH							U.B.C. STDS UNDER WHICH GRADED
		EXTREME FIBER IN BENDING F_b		Tension Parallel to Grain F_t	Horizontal Shear F_v	Compression perpendicular to Grain $F_{c\perp}$ 21	Compression Parallel to Grain F_c	MODULUS OF ELASTICITY E 21	
		Single-member Uses	Repetitive-member Uses						
NORTHERN PINE (Surfaced dry or surfaced green. Used at 19% max. m.c.)									
Select Structural	2" to 4" thick 2" to 4" wide	1650	1850	950	70	435	1200	1,400,000	25-5 and 25-8 (See footnotes 2 through 9, 13, 15 and 16)
No. 1		1400	1600	825	70	435	975	1,400,000	
No. 2		1150	1300	675	70	435	775	1,300,000	
No. 3		625	725	375	70	435	475	1,100,000	
Appearance		1200	1400	800	70	435	1150	1,400,000	
Stud		625	725	375	70	435	475	1,100,000	
Construction	2" to 4" thick 4" wide	825	950	475	70	435	875	1,100,000	
Standard		450	525	275	70	435	725	1,100,000	
Utility		225	250	125	70	435	475	1,100,000	
Select Structural	2" to 4" thick 5" and wider	1400	1600	950	70	435	1100	1,400,000	
No. 1		1200	1400	800	70	435	975	1,400,000	
No. 2		950	1100	525	70	435	825	1,300,000	
No. 3 and Stud		575	650	300	70	435	525	1,100,000	
Appearance		1200	1400	800	70	435	1150	1,400,000	
Select Structural	Beams and Stringers	1250	—	850	65	435	850	1,300,000	
No. 1		1050	—	700	65	435	725	1,300,000	
Select Structural	Posts and Timbers	1150	—	800	65	435	900	1,300,000	
No. 1		950	—	650	65	435	800	1,300,000	
Select	Decking	1350	1550	—	—	—	—	1,400,000	25-8 (See footnotes 2 through 9)
Commercial		1150	1300	—	—	—	—	1,300,000	

From the Uniform Building Code, © 1988, ICBO

NORTHERN SPECIES (Surfaced dry or surfaced green. Used at 19% max. m.c.)

Grade	Size							25-2 (See footnotes 2 through 9, 11, 13, 15 and 16)
Select Structural	2" to 3" thick 2" to 4" wide	1350	1550	775	65	350	1050	1,100,000
No. 1		1150	1300	675	65	350	825	1,100,000
No. 2		925	1050	550	65	350	650	1,000,000
No. 3		525	600	300	65	350	400	900,000
Appearance		1150	1300	675	65	350	975	1,100,000
Stud		525	600	300	65	350	400	900,000
Construction	2" to 4" thick 4" wide	675	775	400	65	350	750	900,000
Standard		375	425	225	65	350	600	900,000
Utility		175	200	100	65	350	400	900,000
Select Structural	2" to 4" thick 5" and wider	1150	1300	775	65	350	900	1,100,000
No. 1		975	1150	650	65	350	825	1,100,000
No. 2		800	925	425	65	350	675	1,000,000
No. 3 and Stud		475	550	250	65	350	425	900,000
Appearance		975	1150	650	65	350	850	1,100,000
Select	Decking	900	1050	—	—	350	—	1,100,000
Commercial		775	875	—	—	350	—	1,000,000

(Continued)

From the Uniform Building Code, © 1988, ICBO

Allowable Unit Stresses—Structural Lumber

TABLE NO. 25-A-1—ALLOWABLE UNIT STRESSES—STRUCTURAL LUMBER—(Continued)
Allowable Unit Stresses for Structural Lumber—VISUAL GRADING
(Normal loading. See also Section 2504)

SPECIES AND COMMERCIAL GRADE	SIZE CLASSIFICATION	EXTREME FIBER IN BENDING F_b		Tension Parallel to Grain F_t	Horizontal Shear F_v	Compression perpendicular to Grain $F_{c\perp}$ 21	Compression Parallel to Grain F_c	MODULUS OF ELASTICITY E 21	U.B.C. STDS UNDER WHICH GRADED
		Single-member Uses	Repetitive-member Uses						
NORTHERN WHITE CEDAR (Surfaced dry or surfaced green. Used at 19% max. m.c.)									
Select Structural	2" to 4" thick 2" to 4" wide	1150	1350	700	65	370	875	800,000	
No. 1		1000	1150	600	65	370	675	800,000	
No. 2		825	950	500	65	370	550	700,000	
No. 3		450	525	275	65	370	325	600,000	
Appearance		850	1000	575	65	370	825	800,000	
Stud		450	525	275	65	370	325	600,000	
Construction	2" to 4" thick 4" wide	600	675	350	65	370	625	600,000	25-8 (See footnotes 2 through 9, 13, 15 and 16)
Standard		325	375	200	65	370	500	600,000	
Utility		150	175	100	65	370	325	600,000	
Select Structural	2" to 4" thick 5" and wider	1000	1150	675	65	370	775	800,000	
No. 1		850	1000	575	65	370	675	800,000	
No. 2		700	825	375	65	370	575	700,000	
No. 3 and Stud		425	475	225	65	370	375	600,000	
Appearance		850	1000	575	65	370	825	800,000	
Select Structural	Beams and Stringers	900	—	600	60	370	600	700,000	
No. 1		750	—	500	60	370	500	700,000	
Select Structural	Posts and Timbers	850	—	575	60	370	650	700,000	
No. 1		675	—	450	60	370	550	700,000	
Select	Decking	975	1100	—	—	—	—	800,000	
Commercial		825	950	—	—	—	—	700,000	

From the Uniform Building Code, © 1988, ICBO

PONDEROSA PINE—SUGAR PINE (PONDEROSA PINE—LODGEPOLE PINE) (Surfaced dry or surfaced green.)

Grade	Size classification						Used at 19% max. m.c.	Notes
Select Structural	2" to 4" thick 2" to 4" wide	1400	1650	825	70	375	1050	1,200,000	25-2 and 25-4 (See footnotes 2 through 13, 15 and 16)
No. 1		1200	1400	700	70	375	850	1,200,000	
No. 2		1000	1150	575	70	375	675	1,100,000	
No. 3		550	625	325	70	375	400	1,000,000	
Appearance		1200	1400	700	70	375	1000	1,200,000	
Stud		550	625	325	70	375	400	1,000,000	
Construction	2" to 4" thick 4" wide	725	825	425	70	375	775	1,000,000	
Standard		400	450	225	70	375	625	1,000,000	
Utility		200	225	100	70	375	400	1,000,000	
Select Structural	2" to 4" thick 5" and wider	1200	1400	825	70	375	950	1,200,000	
No. 1		1050	1200	700	70	375	850	1,200,000	
No. 2		850	975	450	70	375	700	1,100,000	
No. 3 and Stud		500	575	250	70	375	450	1,000,000	
Appearance		1050	1200	700	70	375	1000	1,200,000	
Select Structural	Beams and Stringers	1100	—	650	65	375	750	1,100,000	
No. 1		925	—	450	65	375	625	1,100,000	
No. 2		600	—	300	65	375	400	900,000	
Select Structural	Posts and Timbers	1000	—	675	65	375	800	1,100,000	
No. 1		825	—	550	65	375	700	1,100,000	
No. 2		475	—	325	65	375	325	900,000	
Selected Decking	Decking	—	1350	—	—	—	—	1,200,000	25-2 and 25-4 (See footnotes 2 through 13)
Commercial Decking		—	1150	—	—	—	—	1,100,000	
Selected Decking	Decking	—	1450	(Surfaced at 15% max. m.c. and used at 15% max. m.c.)			—	1,300,000	
Commercial Decking		—	1250				—	1,100,000	
Select	Decking	1200[20]	1450	—	—	375	—	1,300,000	
Commercial		1000[20]	1250	—	—	375	—	1,100,000	

(Continued)

From the *Uniform Building Code*, © 1988, ICBO

Allowable Unit Stresses—Structural Lumber

TABLE NO. 25-A-1—ALLOWABLE UNIT STRESSES—STRUCTURAL LUMBER—(Continued)
Allowable Unit Stresses for Structural Lumber—VISUAL GRADING
(Normal loading. See also Section 2504)

ALLOWABLE UNIT STRESSES IN POUNDS PER SQUARE INCH

SPECIES AND COMMERCIAL GRADE	SIZE CLASSIFICATION	EXTREME FIBER IN BENDING F_b Single-member Uses	EXTREME FIBER IN BENDING F_b Repetitive-member Uses	Tension Parallel to Grain F_t	Horizontal Shear F_v	Compression perpendicular to Grain $F_{c\perp}$ 21	Compression Parallel to Grain F_c	MODULUS OF ELASTICITY E 21	U.B.C. STDS UNDER WHICH GRADED
RED PINE (Surfaced dry or surfaced green. Used at 19% max. m.c.)									
Select Structural	2" to 3" thick 2" to 4" wide	1400	1600	800	70	440	1050	1,300,000	25-2 (See footnotes 2 through 9, 11, 13, 15 and 16)
No. 1		1200	1350	700	70	440	825	1,300,000	
No. 2		975	1100	575	70	440	650	1,200,000	
No. 3		525	625	325	70	440	400	1,000,000	
Appearance		1200	1350	700	70	440	975	1,300,000	
Stud		525	625	325	70	440	400	1,000,000	
Construction	2" to 4" thick 4" wide	700	800	400	70	440	750	1,000,000	
Standard		400	450	225	70	440	600	1,000,000	
Utility		175	225	100	70	440	400	1,000,000	
Select Structural	2" to 4" thick 5" and wider	1200	1350	775	70	440	900	1,300,000	
No. 1		1000	1150	675	70	440	825	1,300,000	
No. 2		825	950	425	70	440	675	1,200,000	
No. 3 and Stud		500	550	250	70	440	425	1,000,000	
Appearance		1000	1150	675	70	440	975	1,300,000	
Select Structural	Beams and Stringers	1050	—	625	65	440	725	1,100,000	
No. 1		875	—	450	65	440	600	1,100,000	
Select Structural	Posts and Timbers	1000	—	675	65	440	775	1,100,000	
No. 1		800	—	550	65	440	675	1,100,000	
Select	Decking	1150	1350	—	—	440	—	1,300,000	
Commercial		975	1100	—	—	440	—	1,200,000	

From the Uniform Building Code, © 1988, ICBO

Allowable Unit Stresses—Structural Lumber

SITKA SPRUCE (Surfaced dry or surfaced green. Used at 19% max. m.c.)

Grade	Size							25-3 (See footnotes 2 through 9, 13, 15 and 16)
Select Structural	2" to 4" thick 2" to 4" wide	1550	1800	925	75	435	1150	1,500,000
No. 1		1350	1550	775	75	435	925	1,500,000
No. 2		1100	1250	650	75	435	725	1,300,000
No. 3		600	700	350	75	435	450	1,200,000
Appearance		1350	1500	750	75	435	1100	1,500,000
Stud		600	700	350	75	435	450	1,200,000
Construction	2" to 4" thick 4" wide	800	925	475	75	435	825	1,200,000
Standard		450	500	250	75	435	675	1,200,000
Utility		200	250	125	75	435	450	1,200,000
Select Structural	2" to 4" thick 5" and wider	1350	1550	900	75	435	1000	1,500,000
No. 1		1150	1300	775	75	435	925	1,500,000
No. 2		925	1050	500	75	435	775	1,300,000
No. 3 and Stud		525	600	275	75	435	500	1,200,000
Appearance		1150	1300	750	75	435	1100	1,500,000
Select Structural	Beams and Stringers	1200	—	675	70	435	825	1,300,000
No. 1		1000	—	500	70	435	675	1,300,000
Select Structural	Posts and Timbers	1150	—	750	70	435	875	1,300,000
No. 1		925	—	600	70	435	750	1,300,000
Select Dex	Decking	1300	1500	—	—	435	—	1,500,000
Commercial Dex		1100	1250	—	—	435	—	1,300,000

(Continued)

From the Uniform Building Code, © 1988, ICBO

Allowable Unit Stresses—Structural Lumber

499

TABLE NO. 25-A-1—ALLOWABLE UNIT STRESSES—STRUCTURAL LUMBER—(Continued)
Allowable Unit Stresses for Structural Lumber—VISUAL GRADING
(Normal loading. See also Section 2504)

SPECIES AND COMMERCIAL GRADE	SIZE CLASSIFI-CATION	ALLOWABLE UNIT STRESSES IN POUNDS PER SQUARE INCH							U.B.C. STDS UNDER WHICH GRADED
		EXTREME FIBER IN BENDING F_b		Tension Parallel to Grain F_t	Horizontal Shear F_v	Compression perpendicular to Grain $F_{c\perp}$ 21	Compression Parallel to Grain F_c	MODULUS OF ELASTICITY E 21	
		Single-member Uses	Repetitive-member Uses						
SOUTHERN PINE (Surfaced at 15% moisture content, K.D. Used at 15% max. m.c.)									
Select Structural	2" to 4" thick, 2" to 4" wide	2150	2500	1250	105	565	1800	1,800,000	
Dense Select Structural		2500	2900	1500	105	660	2100	1,900,000	
No. 1		1850	2100	1050	105	565	1450	1,800,000	
No. 1 Dense		2150	2450	1250	105	660	1700	1,900,000	
No. 2		1550	1750	900	95	565	1150	1,600,000	
No. 2 Dense		1800	2050	1050	95	660	1350	1,700,000	
No. 3		850	975	500	95	565	675	1,500,000	25-6 (See footnotes 3, 4, 9, 13, 15, 16, 18 and 19)
No. 3 Dense		1000	1150	575	95	660	800	1,500,000	
Stud		850	975	500	95	565	675	1,500,000	
Construction	2" to 4" thick, 4" wide	1100	1250	650	105	565	1300	1,500,000	
Standard		625	725	375	95	565	1050	1,500,000	
Utility		275	300	175	95	565	675	1,500,000	
Select Structural	2" to 4" thick, 5" and wider	1850	2150	1200	95	565	1600	1,800,000	
Dense Select Structural		2200	2500	1450	95	660	1850	1,900,000	
No. 1		1600	1850	1050	95	565	1450	1,800,000	
No. 1 Dense		1850	2150	1250	95	660	1700	1,900,000	
No. 2		1300	1500	675	95	565	1200	1,600,000	
No. 2 Dense		1550	1750	800	95	660	1400	1,700,000	
No. 3		750	875	400	95	565	725	1,500,000	
No. 3 Dense		875	1000	450	95	660	850	1,500,000	
Stud		800	900	400	95	565	725	1,500,000	

From the Uniform Building Code, © 1988, ICBO

Allowable Unit Stresses—Structural Lumber

Grade	Size							Remarks
Dense Standard Decking	2" to 4" thick	2150	2450	1250	105	660	1700	1,900,000
Select Decking		1550	1750	900	95	565	1150	1,600,000
Dense Select Decking	2" and wider Decking	1800	2050	1050	95	660	1350	1,700,000
Commercial Decking		1550	1750	900	95	565	1150	1,600,000
Dense Commercial Decking		1800	2050	1050	95	660	1350	1,700,000
Dense Structural 86	2" to 4" thick	2800	3250	1900	165	660	2300	1,900,000
Dense Structural 72		2400	2750	1600	135	660	1950	1,900,000
Dense Structural 65		2150	2450	1450	125	660	1750	1,900,000
KD-15 or MC-15								
Industrial 86 KD	1" to 4" thick	2400	2750	1600	160	415	1950	1,800,000
Dense Ind. 86 KD		2800	3250	1900	160	475	2300	1,900,000
Industrial 72 KD		2050	2350	1350	135	415	1650	1,800,000
Dense Ind. 72 KD		2400	2750	1600	135	475	1950	1,900,000
Industrial 65 KD		1850	2100	1200	125	415	1500	1,800,000
Dense Ind. 65 KD		2150	2450	1400	125	475	1750	1,900,000

25-6 (See footnotes 4, 9, 15, 16, 18 and 19)

Grade	Size							Remarks
SOUTHERN PINE (Surfaced dry. Used at 19% max. m.c.)								
Select Structural	2" to 4" thick	2000	2300	1150	100	565	1550	1,700,000
Dense Select Structural		2350	2700	1350	100	660	1800	1,800,000
No. 1	2" to 4" wide	1700	1950	1000	100	565	1250	1,700,000
No. 1 Dense		2000	2300	1150	100	660	1450	1,800,000
No. 2		1400	1650	825	90	565	975	1,600,000
No. 2 Dense		1650	1900	975	90	660	1150	1,600,000
No. 3		775	900	450	90	565	575	1,400,000
No. 3 Dense		925	1050	525	90	660	675	1,500,000
Stud		775	900	450	90	565	575	1,400,000
Construction	2" to 4" thick	1000	1150	600	100	565	1100	1,400,000
Standard	4" wide	575	675	350	90	565	900	1,400,000
Utility		275	300	150	90	565	575	1,400,000
Select Structural	2" to 4" thick	1750	2000	1150	90	565	1350	1,700,000
Dense Select Structural		2050	2350	1300	90	660	1600	1,800,000
No. 1	5" and wider	1450	1700	975	90	565	1250	1,700,000
No. 1 Dense		1700	2000	1150	90	660	1450	1,800,000
No. 2		1200	1400	625	90	565	1000	1,600,000
No. 2 Dense		1400	1650	725	90	660	1200	1,600,000
No. 3		700	800	350	90	565	625	1,400,000
No. 3 Dense		825	925	425	90	660	725	1,500,000
Stud		725	850	350	90	565	625	1,400,000

25-6 (See footnotes 2, 4, 9, 13, 15, 16, 18 and 19)

(Continued)

From the Uniform Building Code, © 1988, ICBO
Allowable Unit Stresses—Structural Lumber

TABLE NO. 25-A-1—ALLOWABLE UNIT STRESSES—STRUCTURAL LUMBER—(Continued)
Allowable Unit Stresses for Structural Lumber—VISUAL GRADING
(Normal loading. See also Section 2504.)

SPECIES AND COMMERCIAL GRADE	SIZE CLASSIFICATION	ALLOWABLE UNIT STRESSES IN POUNDS PER SQUARE INCH							U.B.C. STDS. UNDER WHICH GRADED
		EXTREME FIBER IN BENDING F_b		Tension Parallel to Grain F_t	Horizontal Shear F_v	Compression Perpendicular to Grain $F_{c\perp}$ [21]	Compression Parallel to Grain F_c [21]	MODULUS OF ELASTICITY E [21]	
		Single-member Uses	Repetitive-member Uses						
Dense Standard Decking	2" to 4" thick	2000	2300	1150	100	660	1450	1,800,000	25-6 (See footnotes 3, 4, 9, 13, 15, 16, 17, 18 and 19)
Select Decking		1400	1650	825	90	565	975	1,600,000	
Dense Select Decking	2" and wider Decking	1650	1900	975	90	660	1150	1,600,000	
Commercial Decking		1400	1650	825	90	565	975	1,600,000	
Dense Commercial Decking	Decking	1650	1900	975	90	660	1150	1,600,000	
Dense Structural 86	2" to 4" thick	2600	3000	1750	155	660	2000	1,800,000	
Dense Structural 72		2200	2550	1450	130	660	1650	1,800,000	
Dense Structural 65		2000	2300	1300	115	660	1500	1,800,000	
KD-19 or S-Dry Industrial 86	1" to 4" thick	2250	2600	1500	155	415	1700	1,700,000	
Dense Ind. 86		2600	3000	1750	155	475	2000	1,800,000	
Industrial 72		1900	2200	1250	130	415	1400	1,700,000	
Dense Ind. 72		2200	2550	1450	130	475	1650	1,800,000	
Industrial 65		1700	1950	1100	115	415	1250	1,700,000	
Dense Ind. 65		2000	2300	1300	115	475	1500	1,800,000	
SOUTHERN PINE (Surfaced green. Used any condition.)									
Select Structural		1600	1850	925	95	375	1050	1,500,000	
Dense Select Structural	2½" to 4" thick	1850	2150	1100	95	440	1200	1,600,000	
No. 1		1350	1550	800	95	375	825	1,500,000	
No. 1 Dense	2½" to 4" thick	1600	1800	925	95	440	950	1,600,000	
No. 2	2½" to 4" wide	1150	1300	675	85	375	650	1,400,000	
No. 2 Dense		1350	1500	775	85	440	750	1,400,000	
No. 3		625	725	375	85	375	400	1,200,000	
No. 3 Dense		725	850	425	85	440	450	1,300,000	
Stud		625	725	375	85	375	400	1,200,000	
Construction	2½" to 4" thick	825	925	475	95	375	725	1,200,000	
Standard	4" wide	475	525	275	85	375	600	1,200,000	
Utility		200	259	125	85	375	400	1,200,000	

From the Uniform Building Code, © 1988, ICBO

Allowable Unit Stresses—Structural Lumber

Grade	Size							25-6 (See footnotes 3, 4, 9, 13, 15, 16, 17, 18 and 19)
Select Structural	2½" to 4" thick 5" and wider	1400	1600	900	85	375	900	1,500,000
Dense Select Structural		1600	1850	1050	85	440	1050	1,600,000
No. 1		1200	1350	775	85	375	825	1,500,000
No. 1 Dense		1400	1600	925	85	440	950	1,600,000
No. 2		975	1100	500	85	375	675	1,400,000
No. 2 Dense		1150	1300	600	85	440	800	1,400,000
No. 3		550	650	300	85	375	425	1,200,000
No. 3 Dense		650	750	350	85	440	475	1,300,000
Stud		575	675	300	85	375	425	1,200,000
Dense Standard Decking	2½" to 4 thick 2" and wider Decking	1600	1800	925	95	440	950	1,600,000
Select Decking		1150	1300	675	85	375	650	1,400,000
Dense Select Decking		1350	1500	775	85	440	750	1,400,000
Commercial Decking		1150	1300	675	85	375	650	1,400,000
Dense Commercial Decking		1350	1500	775	85	440	750	1,400,000
No. 1 SR	5" and thicker	1350	—	875	110	375	775	1,500,000
No. 1 Dense SR		1550	—	1050	110	440	925	1,600,000
No. 2 SR		1100	—	725	95	375	625	1,400,000
No. 2 Dense SR		1250	—	850	95	440	725	1,400,000
Dense Structural 86	2½" and thicker	2100	2400	1400	145	440	1300	1,600,000
Dense Structural 72		1750	2050	1200	120	440	1100	1,600,000
Dense Structural 65		1600	1800	1050	110	440	1000	1,600,000
MC over 19%								
Industrial 86	2½" and thicker	1800	2050	1200	140	270	1150	1,500,000
Dense Ind. 86		2100	2400	1400	140	315	1300	1,600,000
Industrial 72		1500	1750	1000	120	270	950	1,500,000
Dense Ind.72		1750	2050	1200	120	315	1100	1,600,000
Industrial 65		1350	1500	900	110	270	850	1,500,000
Dense Ind. 65		1600	1800	1050	110	315	1000	1,600,000

(Continued)

From the Uniform Building Code, © 1988, ICBO

Allowable Unit Stresses—Structural Lumber

TABLE NO. 25-A-1—ALLOWABLE UNIT STRESSES—STRUCTURAL LUMBER—(Continued)
Allowable Unit Stresses for Structural Lumber—VISUAL GRADING
(Normal loading. See also Section 2504)

SPECIES AND COMMERCIAL GRADE	SIZE CLASSIFICATION	ALLOWABLE UNIT STRESSES IN POUNDS PER SQUARE INCH							
		EXTREME FIBER IN BENDING F_b		Tension Parallel to Grain F_t	Horizontal Shear F_v	Compression perpendicular to Grain $F_{c\perp}$ 21	Compression Parallel to Grain F_c	MODULUS OF ELASTICITY E 21	U.B.C. STDS UNDER WHICH GRADED
		Single-member Uses	Repetitive-member Uses						
SPRUCE—PINE—FIR (Surfaced dry or surfaced green. Used at 19% max. m.c.)									
Select Structural	2" to 4" thick 2" to 4" wide	1450	1650	850	70	425	1100	1,500,000	
No. 1		1200	1400	725	70	425	875	1,500,000	
No. 2		1000	1150	600	70	425	675	1,300,000	
No. 3		550	650	325	70	425	425	1,200,000	
Appearance		1200	1400	700	70	425	1050	1,500,000	
Stud		550	650	325	70	425	425	1,200,000	
Construction	2" to 4" thick 4" wide	725	850	425	70	425	775	1,200,000	
Standard		400	475	225	70	425	650	1,200,000	25-2 (See footnotes 2 through 9, 11, 13, 15 and 16)
Utility		175	225	100	70	425	425	1,200,000	
Select Structural	2" to 4" thick 5" and wider	1250	1450	825	70	425	975	1,500,000	
No. 1		1050	1200	700	70	425	875	1,500,000	
No. 2		875	1000	450	70	425	725	1,300,000	
No. 3 and Stud		500	575	275	70	425	450	1,200,000	
Appearance		1050	1200	700	70	425	1050	1,500,000	
Select Structural	Beams and Stringers	1100	—	650	65	425	775	1,300,000	
No. 1		900	—	450	65	425	625	1,300,000	
Select Structural	Posts and Timbers	1050	—	700	65	425	800	1,300,000	
No. 1		850	—	550	65	425	700	1,300,000	
Select	Decking	1200	1400	—	—	425	—	1,500,000	
Commercial		1000	1150	—	—	425	—	1,300,000	

From the Uniform Building Code, © 1988, ICBO

Allowable Unit Stresses—Structural Lumber

WESTERN CEDARS (Surfaced dry or surfaced green. Used at 19% max. m.c.)
WESTERN CEDARS (NORTH)

Grade	Size								Footnotes
Select Structural	2" to 3"	1500	1750	875	75	425	1200	1,100,000	25-2, 25-3 and 25-4 (See footnotes 2 through 9, 11, 12 and 13)
No. 1	thick	1300	1500	750	75	425	950	1,100,000	
No. 2	2" to 4"	1050	1200	625	75	425	750	1,000,000	
No. 3	wide	600	675	350	75	425	450	900,000	
Appearance		1300	1500	750	75	425	1100	1,100,000	
Stud		600	675	350	75	425	450	900,000	
Construction	2" to 4"	775	875	450	75	425	850	900,000	
Standard	thick	425	500	250	75	425	700	900,000	
Utility	4" wide	200	225	125	75	425	450	900,000	
Select Structural	2" to 4"	1300	1500	825	75	425	1050	1,100,000	
No. 1	thick	1100	1300	750	75	425	950	1,100,000	
No. 2	5" and	925	1050	475	75	425	800	1,000,000	
No. 3 and Stud	wider	525	625	275	75	425	500	900,000	
Appearance		1100	1300	750	75	425	1100	1,100,000	
Select Structural	Beams and	1150	—	675	70	425	875	1,000,000	25-2 and 25-3 (See footnotes 2 through 9, 11 and 12)
No. 1	Stringers	925	—	475	70	425	725	1,000,000	
Select Structural	Posts and	1050	—	700	70	425	900	1,000,000	
No. 1	Timbers	850	—	575	70	425	800	1,000,000	
Select Dex	Decking	1200	1400	—	—	425	—	1,100,000	25-3 (See footnotes 2 through 9)
Commercial Dex		1050	1200	—	—	425	—	1,000,000	
Select	Decking	1200	1400	—	—	425	—	1,100,000	25-2 (See footnotes 2 through 9 and 11)
Commercial		1050	1200	—	—	425	—	1,000,000	

(Continued)

From the *Uniform Building Code*, © 1988, ICBO

Allowable Unit Stresses—Structural Lumber

TABLE NO. 25-A-1—ALLOWABLE UNIT STRESSES—STRUCTURAL LUMBER—(Continued)
Allowable Unit Stresses for Structural Lumber—VISUAL GRADING
(Normal loading. See also Section 2504)

SPECIES AND COMMERCIAL GRADE	SIZE CLASSIFICATION	ALLOWABLE UNIT STRESSES IN POUNDS PER SQUARE INCH							U.B.C. STDS UNDER WHICH GRADED
		EXTREME FIBER IN BENDING F_b		Tension Parallel to Grain F_t	Horizontal Shear F_v	Compression perpendicular to Grain $F_{c\perp}$ [21]	Compression Parallel to Grain F_c	MODULUS OF ELASTICITY E [21]	
		Single-member Uses	Repetitive-member Uses						
Select Structural	Beams and Stringers	1150	—	700	70	425	875	1,000,000	25-4 (See footnotes 2 through 10)
No. 1		975	—	475	70	425	725	1,000,000	
No. 2		625	—	325	70	425	475	800,000	
Select Structural	Posts and Timbers	1100	—	725	70	425	925	1,000,000	
No. 1		875	—	600	70	425	800	800,000	
No. 2		500	—	350	70	425	375	800,000	
Selected Decking	Decking	—	1450	—	—	—	—	1,100,000	
Commercial Decking		—	1200	—	—	—	—	1,000,000	
Selected Decking	Decking	—	1550	(Surfaced at 15% max. m.c. and used at 15% max. m.c.)			—	1,100,000	
Commercial Decking		—	1300				—	1,000,000	
WESTERN HEMLOCK (Surfaced dry or surfaced green. Used at 19% max. m.c.) **WESTERN HEMLOCK (NORTH)**									
Select Structural	2" to 4" thick, 2" to 4" wide	1800	2100	1050	90	410	1450	1,600,000	25-2 (See footnote 11) 25-3 and 25-4 (See footnotes 2 through 9, 13, 15 and 16)
No. 1		1550	1800	900	90	410	1150	1,600,000	
No. 2		1300	1450	750	90	410	900	1,400,000	
No. 3		700	800	425	90	410	550	1,300,000	
Appearance		1550	1800	900	90	410	1350	1,600,000	
Stud		700	800	425	90	410	550	1,300,000	
Construction	2" to 4" thick, 4" wide	925	1050	550	90	410	1050	1,300,000	
Standard		525	600	300	90	410	850	1,300,000	
Utility		250	275	150	90	410	550	1,300,000	

From the Uniform Building Code, © 1988, ICBO

Species and commercial grade	Size classification							Grading rules agency / footnotes
Select Structural	2" to 4" thick	1550	1800	1050	90	410	1300	1,600,000
No. 1	5" and wider	1350	1550	900	90	410	1150	1,600,000
No. 2		1100	1250	575	90	410	975	1,400,000
No. 3 and Stud		650	750	325	90	410	625	1,300,000
Appearance		1350	1550	900	90	410	1350	1,600,000
								25-3 and 25-4 (See footnotes 2 through 9, 13, 15 and 16)
Select Structural	Beams and Stringers	1400	—	825	85	410	1000	1,400,000
No. 1		1150	—	575	85	410	850	1,400,000
Select Structural	Posts and Timbers	1300	—	875	85	410	1100	1,400,000
No. 1		1050	—	700	85	410	950	1,400,000
								25-3 (See footnotes 2 through 9)
Select Dex	Decking	1500	1750	—	—	410	—	1,600,000
Commercial Dex		1300	1450	—	—	410	—	1,400,000
Select Structural	Beams and Stringers	1400	—	825	85	410	1000	1,400,000
No. 1		1150	—	575	85	410	850	1,400,000
No. 2		750	—	375	85	410	550	1,100,000
Select Structural	Posts and Timbers	1300	—	875	85	410	1100	1,400,000
No. 1		1050	—	700	85	410	950	1,400,000
No. 2		600	—	400	85	410	425	1,100,000
								25-4 (See footnotes 2 through 10)
Selected Decking	Decking		1750	(Surfaced at 15% max. m.c.				1,600,000
Commercial Decking			1450	and used at 15% max. m.c.)				1,400,000
Selected Decking	Decking		1900					1,700,000
Commercial Decking			1600					1,500,000

(Continued)

From the Uniform Building Code, © 1988, ICBO

Allowable Unit Stresses—Structural Lumber

TABLE NO. 25-A-1—ALLOWABLE UNIT STRESSES—STRUCTURAL LUMBER—(Continued)
Allowable Unit Stresses for Structural Lumber—VISUAL GRADING
(Normal loading. See also Section 2504)

WESTERN WHITE PINE (Surfaced dry or surfaced green. Used at 19% max. m.c.)

SPECIES AND COMMERCIAL GRADE	SIZE CLASSIFICATION	EXTREME FIBER IN BENDING F_b		Tension Parallel to Grain F_t	Horizontal Shear F_v	Compression perpendicular to Grain $F_{c\perp}$ 21	Compression Parallel to Grain F_c	MODULUS OF ELASTICITY E 21	U.B.C. STDS UNDER WHICH GRADED
		Single-member Uses	Repetitive-member Uses						
Select Structural	2" to 4" thick 2" to 4" wide	1350	1550	775	65	375	1100	1,400,000	25-2 (See footnotes 2 through 9, 11, 13, 15 and 16)
No. 1		1150	1300	675	65	375	875	1,400,000	
No. 2		925	1050	550	65	375	675	1,300,000	
No. 3		525	600	300	65	375	425	1,200,000	
Appearance		1150	1300	650	65	375	1050	1,400,000	
Stud		525	600	300	65	375	425	1,200,000	
Construction	2" to 4" thick 4" wide	675	775	400	65	375	775	1,200,000	
Standard		375	425	225	65	375	650	1,200,000	
Utility		175	200	100	65	375	425	1,200,000	
Select Structural	2" to 4" thick 5" and wider	1150	1300	775	65	375	975	1,400,000	
No. 1		975	1150	650	65	375	875	1,400,000	
No. 2		800	925	425	65	375	725	1,300,000	
No. 3 and Stud		475	550	250	65	375	450	1,200,000	
Appearance		975	1150	650	65	375	1050	1,400,000	
Select Structural	Beams and Stringers	1050	—	600	60	375	775	1,300,000	
No. 1		850	—	425	60	375	625	1,300,000	
Select Structural	Posts and Timbers	975	—	650	60	375	800	1,300,000	
No. 1		775	—	525	60	375	700	1,300,000	
Select	Decking	1100	1300	—	—	375	—	1,400,000	
Commercial		925	1050	—	—	375	—	1,300,000	

From the Uniform Building Code, © 1988, ICBO

WHITE WOODS (WESTERN WOODS) (Surfaced dry or surfaced green. Used at 19% max. m.c.)
(MIXED SPECIES) (WEST COAST WOODS)

25-4
(See footnotes 2 through 10, 13, 15 and 16)

Grade	Size							E
Select Structural	2" to 4" thick, 2" to 4" wide	1350	1550	775	70	315	950	1,100,000
No. 1		1150	1300	650	70	315	750	1,100,000
No. 2		925	1050	550	70	315	600	1,000,000
No. 3		525	600	300	70	315	375	900,000
Appearance		1150	1300	650	70	315	900	1,100,000
Stud		525	600	300	70	315	375	900,000
Construction	2" to 4" thick, 4" wide	675	775	400	70	315	675	900,000
Standard		375	425	225	70	315	550	900,000
Utility		175	200	100	70	315	375	900,000
Select Structural	2" to 4" thick, 5" and wider	1150	1300	775	70	315	850	1,100,000
No. 1		975	1100	650	70	315	750	1,100,000
No. 2		800	925	425	70	315	625	1,000,000
No. 3 and Stud		475	550	250	70	315	400	900,000
Appearance		975	1100	650	70	315	900	1,100,000
Select Structural	Beams and Stringers	1000	—	600	65	315	675	1,000,000
No. 1		850	—	425	65	315	550	1,000,000
No. 2		550	—	275	65	315	350	800,000
Select Structural	Posts and Timbers	950	—	650	65	315	700	1,000,000
No. 1		775	—	525	65	315	625	1,000,000
No. 2		450	—	300	65	315	275	800,000
Selected Decking	Decking	—	1300	—	—	—	—	1,100,000
Commercial Decking		—	1050	—	—	—	—	1,000,000
Selected Decking	Decking	—	1400	(Surfaced at 15% max. m.c. and used at 15% max. m.c.)				1,100,000
Commercial Decking		—	1150					1,000,000

(Continued)

From the Uniform Building Code, © 1988, ICBO

Allowable Unit Stresses—Structural Lumber

TABLE NO. 25-A-1—ALLOWABLE UNIT STRESSES—STRUCTURAL LUMBER—(Continued)
Allowable Unit Stresses for Structural Lumber—VISUAL GRADING
(Normal loading. See also Section 2504.)

SPECIES AND COMMERCIAL GRADE	SIZE CLASSIFICATION	ALLOWABLE UNIT STRESSES IN POUNDS PER SQUARE INCH							U.B.C. STDS. UNDER WHICH GRADED
		EXTREME FIBER IN BENDING F_b		Tension Parallel to Grain F_t	Horizontal Shear F_v	Compression Perpendicular to Grain $F_{c\perp}$ [21]	Compression Parallel to Grain F_c	MODULUS OF ELASTICITY E [21]	
		Single-member Uses	Repetitive-member Uses						
YELLOW-POPLAR (Surfaced dry or surfaced green. Used at 19% max. m.c.)									
Select Structural	2" to 3" thick 2" to 4" wide	1500	1700	875	80	420	1050	1,500,000	
No. 1		1250	1450	750	80	420	825	1,500,000	
No. 2		1050	1200	625	75	420	650	1,300,000	
No. 3		575	675	350	75	420	400	1,200,000	
Stud		575	675	350	75	420	400	1,200,000	
Construction	2" to 4" thick 4" wide	750	875	450	80	420	750	1,200,000	25-5 (See footnotes 1 through 9
Standard		425	500	250	75	420	625	1,200,000	
Utility		200	225	125	75	420	400	1,200,000	
Select Structural	2" to 4" thick 5" and wider	1300	1500	850	75	420	925	1,500,000	
No. 1		1100	1250	725	75	420	825	1,500,000	
No. 2		900	1050	475	75	420	700	1,300,000	
No. 3		525	600	275	75	420	425	1,200,000	
Appearance		1100	1250	725	75	420	1000	1,500,000	
Stud		525	600	275	75	420	425	1,200,000	

[1]Where eastern spruce and balsam fir are shipped in a combination, the tabulated values for balsam fir shall apply.

[2]The design values shown in Table No. 25-A-1 are applicable to lumber that will be used under dry conditions such as in most covered structures. For 2-inch- to 4-inch-thick lumber the DRY surfaced size shall be used. In calculating design values, the natural gain in strength and stiffness that occurs as lumber dries has been taken into consideration as well as the reduction in size that occurs when unseasoned lumber shrinks. The gain in load-carrying capacity due to increased strength and stiffness resulting from drying more than offsets the design effect of size reductions due to shrinkage. For 5-inch and thicker lumber, the surfaced sizes also may be used because design values have been adjusted to compensate for any loss in size by shrinkage which may occur.

From the Uniform Building Code, © 1988, ICBO

[3]Values for F_b, F, and F_c for the grades of Construction, Standard and Utility apply only to 4-inch widths.

[4]The values in Table No. 25-A-1 for dimension 2 inches to 4 inches are based on edgewise use. Where such lumber is used flatwise, the recommended design values for extreme fiber stress in bending may be multiplied by following factors:

WIDTH	THICKNESS		
	2"	3"	4"
2 inches to 4 inches	1.10	1.04	1.00
5 inches and wider	1.22	1.16	1.11

Values for decking may be increased by 10 percent for 2-inch decking and 4 percent for 3-inch decking.

[5]When 2-inch- to 4-inch-thick lumber is manufactured at a maximum moisture content of 15 percent and used in a condition where the moisture content does not exceed 15 percent, the design values shown in Table No. 25-A-1 for surfaced dry and surfaced green may be multiplied by the following factors:

EXTREME FIBER IN BENDING F_b	TENSION PARALLEL TO GRAIN F_t	HORIZONTAL SHEAR F_v	COMPRESSION PERPENDICULAR TO GRAIN $F_c\perp$	COMPRESSION PARALLEL TO GRAIN F_c	MODULUS OF ELASTICITY E
1.08	1.08	1.05	1.00	1.17*	1.05*

*For redwood use 1.15 for F_c and 1.04 for E.

[6]When 2-inch- to 4-inch-thick lumber is designed for use where the moisture content will exceed 19 percent for an extended period of time, the values shown in Table No. 25-A-1 shall be multiplied by the following factors:

EXTREME FIBER IN BENDING F_b	TENSION PARALLEL TO GRAIN F_t	HORIZONTAL SHEAR F_v	COMPRESSION PERPENDICULAR TO GRAIN $F_c\perp$	COMPRESSION PARALLEL TO GRAIN F_c	MODULUS OF ELASTICITY E
0.86	0.84	0.97	0.67	0.70	0.97

(Continued)

From the Uniform Building Code, © 1988, ICBO
Allowable Unit Stresses—Structural Lumber

FOOTNOTES FOR TABLE NO. 25-A-1

[7]When lumber 5 inches and thicker is designed for use where the moisture content will exceed 19 percent for an extended period of time, the values shown in Table No. 25-A-1 shall be multiplied by the following factors:

EXTREME FIBER IN BENDING F_b	TENSION PARALLEL TO GRAIN F_t	HORIZONTAL SHEAR F_v	COMPRESSION PERPENDICULAR TO GRAIN $F_c\perp$	COMPRESSION PARALLEL TO GRAIN F_c	MODULUS OF ELASTICITY E
1.00	1.00	1.00	0.67	0.91	1.00

[8]Specific horizontal shear values may be established by using the following tables when the length of split or check is known:

WHEN LENGTH OF SPLIT ON WIDE FACE IS:	MULTIPLY TABULATED F_v VALUE BY: (NOMINAL 2-INCH) LUMBER)
No split.	2.00
1/2 x wide face	1.67
3/4 x wide face	1.50
1 x wide face	1.33
1 1/2 x wide face or more.	1.00

WHEN LENGTH OF SPLIT ON WIDE FACE IS:	MULTIPLY TABULATED F_v VALUE BY: (3-INCH AND THICKER LUMBER)
No split.	2.00
1/2 x narrow face.	1.67
1 x narrow face	1.33
1 1/2 x narrow face or more	1.00

[9]Stress-rated boards of nominal 1-inch, 1 1/4-inch and 1 1/2-inch thickness, 2 inches and wider, are permitted the recommended design values shown for Select Structural, No. 1, No. 2, No. 3, Construction, Standard, Utility, Appearance, Clear Heart Structural and Clear Structural grades as shown in the 2-inch- to 4-inch-thick categories herein, where graded in accordance with the stress-rated board provisions in the applicable grading rules.

From the Uniform Building Code © 1988 ICBO

[10] When decking is used where the moisture content will exceed 15 percent for an extended period of time, the tabulated design values shall be multiplied by the following factors: Extreme Fiber in Bending F_b – 0.79; Modulus of Elasticity E – 0.92.

[11] Where lumber is graded under U.B.C. Standard No. 25-2 values shown for Select Structural, No. 1, No. 2, No. 3, and Stud grades are not applicable to 3-inch x 4-inch and 4-inch x 4-inch sizes.

[12] Lumber in the beam and stringer or post and timber size classification may be assigned different working stresses for the same grade name and species based upon the grading rules of the specific agency involved. It is therefore necessary that the grading rule agency be identified to properly correlate permitted design stresses with the grade mark.

[13] Utility grades of all species may be used only under conditions specifically approved by the building official.

[14] A horizontal shear F_v of 70 may be used for eastern white pine graded under U.B.C. Standards No. 25-5 and No. 25-8 (grading rules of Northern Hardwood and Pine Manufacturers, Inc. and Northeastern Lumber Manufacturers Association, Inc.).

[15] Tabulated tension parallel to grain values for species 5 inches and wider, 2 inches to 4 inches thick (and 2½ inches to 4 inches thick) size classifications apply to 5-inch and 6-inch widths only, for grades of Select Structural, No. 1, No. 2, No. 3, Appearance and Stud (including dense grades). For lumber wider than 6 inches in these grades, the tabulated F_t values shall be multiplied by the following factors:

GRADE (2 inches to 4 inches thick, 5 inches and wider) (2½ inches to 4 inches thick, 5 inches and wider) (Includes "Dense" grades)	Multiply tabulated F_t values by		
	5 inches and 6 inches wide	8 inches wide	10 inches and wider
Select Structural	1.00	0.90	0.80
No. 1, No. 2, No. 3 and Appearance	1.00	0.80	0.60
Stud	1.00		

[16] Design values for all species of Stud grade in 5-inch and wider size classifications apply to 5-inch and 6-inch widths only.

[17] Repetitive member design values for extreme fiber in bending for southern pine grades of Dense Structural 86, 72 and 65 apply to 2-inch to 4-inch thicknesses only.

[18] When 2-inch- to 4-inch-thick southern pine lumber is surfaced dry or at 15 percent maximum moisture content (KD) and is designed for use where the moisture content will exceed 19 percent for an extended period of time, the design values in Table No. 25-A-1 for the corresponding grades of 2½-inch- to 4-inch-thick surfaced green southern pine lumber shall be used. The net green size may be used in such designs.

[19] When 2-inch- to 4-inch-thick southern pine lumber is surfaced dry or at 15 percent maximum moisture content (KD) and is designed for use under dry conditions, such as in most covered structures, the net DRY size shall be used in design. For other sizes and conditions of use, the net green size may be used in design.

[20] Values apply only to ponderosa pine graded under U.B.C. Standard No. 25-2.

[21] The duration of load modification factors given in Section 2504 (c) 4 shall not apply.

From the Uniform Building Code, © 1988, ICBO

Allowable Unit Stresses—Structural Lumber

TABLE NO. 25-U-J-6—ALLOWABLE SPANS FOR CEILING JOISTS—10 LBS. PER SQ. FT. LIVE LOAD
(Drywall Ceiling)

DESIGN CRITERIA: Deflection—For 10 lbs. per sq. ft. live load. Limited to span in inches divided by 240. Strength—Live load of 10 lbs. per sq. ft. plus dead load of 5 lbs. per sq. ft. determines the required fiber stress value.

JOIST SIZE (IN)	SPACING (IN)	Modulus of Elasticity, E, in 1,000,000 psi													
		0.8	0.9	1.0	1.1	1.2	1.3	1.4	1.5	1.6	1.7	1.8	1.9	2.0	2.2
2x4	12.0	9-10 / 710	10-3 / 770	10-7 / 830	10-11 / 880	11-3 / 930	11-7 / 980	11-10 / 1030	12-2 / 1080	12-5 / 1130	12-8 / 1180	12-11 / 1220	13-2 / 1270	13-4 / 1310	13-9 / 1400
	16.0	8-11 / 780	9-4 / 850	9-8 / 910	9-11 / 970	10-3 / 1030	10-6 / 1080	10-9 / 1140	11-0 / 1190	11-3 / 1240	11-6 / 1290	11-9 / 1340	11-11 / 1390	12-2 / 1440	12-6 / 1540
	24.0	7-10 / 900	8-1 / 970	8-5 / 1040	8-8 / 1110	8-11 / 1170	9-2 / 1240	9-5 / 1300	9-8 / 1360	9-10 / 1420	10-0 / 1480	10-3 / 1540	10-5 / 1600	10-7 / 1650	10-11 / 1760
2x6	12.0	15-6 / 710	16-1 / 770	16-8 / 830	17-2 / 880	17-8 / 930	18-2 / 980	18-8 / 1030	19-1 / 1080	19-6 / 1130	19-11 / 1180	20-3 / 1220	20-8 / 1270	21-0 / 1310	21-8 / 1400
	16.0	14-1 / 780	14-7 / 850	15-2 / 910	15-7 / 970	16-1 / 1030	16-6 / 1080	16-11 / 1140	17-4 / 1190	17-8 / 1240	18-1 / 1290	18-5 / 1340	18-9 / 1390	19-1 / 1440	19-8 / 1540
	24.0	12-3 / 900	12-9 / 970	13-3 / 1040	13-8 / 1110	14-1 / 1170	14-5 / 1240	14-9 / 1300	15-2 / 1360	15-6 / 1420	15-9 / 1480	16-1 / 1540	16-4 / 1600	16-8 / 1650	17-2 / 1760
2x8	12.0	20-5 / 710	21-2 / 770	21-11 / 830	22-8 / 880	23-4 / 930	24-0 / 980	24-7 / 1030	25-2 / 1080	25-8 / 1130	26-2 / 1180	26-9 / 1220	27-2 / 1270	27-8 / 1310	28-7 / 1400
	16.0	18-6 / 780	19-3 / 850	19-11 / 910	20-7 / 970	21-2 / 1030	21-9 / 1080	22-4 / 1140	22-10 / 1190	23-4 / 1240	23-10 / 1290	24-3 / 1340	24-8 / 1390	25-2 / 1440	25-11 / 1540
	24.0	16-2 / 900	16-10 / 970	17-5 / 1040	18-0 / 1110	18-6 / 1170	19-0 / 1240	19-6 / 1300	19-11 / 1360	20-5 / 1420	20-10 / 1480	21-2 / 1540	21-7 / 1600	21-11 / 1650	22-8 / 1760
2x10	12.0	26-0 / 710	27-1 / 770	28-0 / 830	28-11 / 880	29-9 / 930	30-7 / 980	31-4 / 1030	32-1 / 1080	32-9 / 1130	33-5 / 1180	34-1 / 1220	34-8 / 1270	35-4 / 1310	36-5 / 1400
	16.0	23-8 / 780	24-7 / 850	25-5 / 910	26-3 / 970	27-1 / 1030	27-9 / 1080	28-6 / 1140	29-2 / 1190	29-9 / 1240	30-5 / 1290	31-0 / 1340	31-6 / 1390	32-1 / 1440	33-1 / 1540
	24.0	20-8 / 900	21-6 / 970	22-3 / 1040	22-11 / 1110	23-8 / 1170	24-3 / 1240	24-10 / 1300	25-5 / 1360	26-0 / 1420	26-6 / 1480	27-1 / 1540	27-6 / 1600	28-0 / 1650	28-11 / 1760

NOTES:

(1) The required extreme fiber stress in bending (F_b) in pounds per square inch is shown below each span.

(2) Use single or repetitive member bending stress values (F_b) and modulus of elasticity values (E) from Tables Nos. 25-A-1 and 25-A-2.

(3) For more comprehensive tables covering a broader range of bending stress values (F_b) and modulus of elasticity values (E), other spacing of members and other conditions of loading, see U.B.C. Standard No. 25-21.

(4) The spans in these tables are intended for use in covered structures or where moisture content in use does not exceed 19 percent.

From the Uniform Building Code, © 1988, ICBO

TABLE NO. 25-U-R-1—ALLOWABLE SPANS FOR LOW- OR HIGH-SLOPE RAFTERS
20 LBS. PER SQ. FT. LIVE LOAD (Supporting Drywall Ceiling)

DESIGN CRITERIA: Strength—15 lbs. per sq. ft. dead load plus 20 lbs. per sq. ft. live load determines required fiber stress. **Deflection**—For 20 lbs. per sq. ft. live load. Limited to span in inches divided by 240. **RAFTERS:** Spans are measured along the horizontal projection and loads are considered as applied on the horizontal projection.

RAFTER SIZE	SPACING (IN)	Allowable Extreme Fiber Stress in Bending F_b (psi).														
		500	600	700	800	900	1000	1100	1200	1300	1400	1500	1600	1700	1800	1900
2x6	12.0	8-6 / 0.26	9-4 / 0.35	10-0 / 0.44	10-9 / 0.54	11-5 / 0.64	12-0 / 0.75	12-7 / 0.86	13-2 / 0.98	13-8 / 1.11	14-2 / 1.24	14-8 / 1.37	15-2 / 1.51	15-8 / 1.66	16-1 / 1.81	16-7 / 1.96
	16.0	7-4 / 0.23	8-1 / 0.30	8-8 / 0.38	9-4 / 0.46	9-10 / 0.55	10-5 / 0.65	10-11 / 0.75	11-5 / 0.85	11-10 / 0.97	12-4 / 1.07	12-9 / 1.19	13-2 / 1.31	13-7 / 1.44	13-11 / 1.56	14-4 / 1.70
	24.0	6-0 / 0.19	6-7 / 0.25	7-1 / 0.31	7-7 / 0.38	8-1 / 0.45	8-6 / 0.53	8-11 / 0.61	9-4 / 0.70	9-8 / 0.78	10-0 / 0.88	10-5 / 0.97	10-9 / 1.07	11-1 / 1.17	11-5 / 1.28	11-8 / 1.39
2x8	12.0	11-2 / 0.26	12-3 / 0.35	13-3 / 0.44	14-2 / 0.54	15-0 / 0.64	15-10 / 0.75	16-7 / 0.86	17-4 / 0.98	18-0 / 1.11	18-9 / 1.24	19-5 / 1.37	20-0 / 1.51	20-8 / 1.66	21-3 / 1.81	21-10 / 1.96
	16.0	9-8 / 0.23	10-7 / 0.30	11-6 / 0.38	12-3 / 0.46	13-0 / 0.55	13-8 / 0.65	14-4 / 0.75	15-0 / 0.85	15-7 / 0.96	16-3 / 1.07	16-9 / 1.19	17-4 / 1.31	17-10 / 1.44	18-5 / 1.56	18-11 / 1.70
	24.0	7-11 / 0.19	8-8 / 0.25	9-4 / 0.31	10-0 / 0.38	10-7 / 0.45	11-2 / 0.53	11-9 / 0.61	12-3 / 0.70	12-9 / 0.78	13-3 / 0.88	13-8 / 0.97	14-2 / 1.07	14-7 / 1.17	15-0 / 1.28	15-5 / 1.39
2x10	12.0	14-3 / 0.26	15-8 / 0.35	16-11 / 0.44	18-1 / 0.54	19-2 / 0.64	20-2 / 0.75	21-2 / 0.86	22-1 / 0.98	23-0 / 1.11	23-11 / 1.24	24-9 / 1.37	25-6 / 1.51	26-4 / 1.66	27-1 / 1.81	27-10 / 1.96
	16.0	12-4 / 0.23	13-6 / 0.30	14-8 / 0.38	15-8 / 0.46	16-7 / 0.55	17-6 / 0.65	18-4 / 0.75	19-2 / 0.85	19-11 / 0.96	20-8 / 1.07	21-5 / 1.19	22-1 / 1.31	22-10 / 1.44	23-5 / 1.56	24-1 / 1.70
	24.0	10-1 / 0.19	11-1 / 0.25	11-11 / 0.31	12-9 / 0.38	13-6 / 0.45	14-3 / 0.53	15-0 / 0.61	15-8 / 0.70	16-3 / 0.78	16-11 / 0.88	17-6 / 0.97	18-1 / 1.07	18-7 / 1.17	19-2 / 1.28	19-8 / 1.39
2x12	12.0	17-4 / 0.26	19-0 / 0.35	20-6 / 0.44	21-11 / 0.54	23-3 / 0.64	24-7 / 0.75	25-9 / 0.86	26-11 / 0.98	28-0 / 1.11	29-1 / 1.24	30-1 / 1.37	31-1 / 1.51	32-0 / 1.66	32-11 / 1.81	33-10 / 1.96
	16.0	15-0 / 0.23	16-6 / 0.30	17-9 / 0.38	19-0 / 0.46	20-2 / 0.55	21-3 / 0.65	22-4 / 0.75	23-3 / 0.85	24-3 / 0.97	25-2 / 1.07	26-0 / 1.19	26-11 / 1.31	27-9 / 1.44	28-6 / 1.56	29-4 / 1.70
	24.0	12-3 / 0.19	13-5 / 0.25	14-6 / 0.31	15-6 / 0.38	16-6 / 0.45	17-4 / 0.53	18-2 / 0.61	19-0 / 0.70	19-10 / 0.78	20-6 / 0.88	21-3 / 0.97	21-11 / 1.07	22-8 / 1.17	23-3 / 1.28	23-11 / 1.39

NOTES:

(1) The required modulus of elasticity (E) in 1,000,000 pounds per square inch is shown below each span.

(2) Use single or repetitive member bending stress values (F_b) and modulus of elasticity values (E) from Tables Nos. 25-A-1 and 25-A-2. For duration of load stress increases, see Section 2504 (c) 4.

(3) For more comprehensive tables covering a broader range of bending stress values (F_b) and modulus of elasticity values (E), other spacing of members and other conditions of loading, see U.B.C. Standard No. 25-21.

(4) The spans in these tables are intended for use in covered structures or where moisture content in use does not exceed 19 percent.

From the Uniform Building Code, © *1988, ICBO*

Allowable Spans for Low - or High Slope Rafters

TABLE NO. 25-U-R-2—ALLOWABLE SPANS FOR LOW- OR HIGH-SLOPE RAFTERS
30 LBS. PER SQ. FT. LIVE LOAD (Supporting Drywall Ceiling)

DESIGN CRITERIA: Strength—15 lbs. per sq. ft. dead load plus 30 lbs. per sq. ft. live load determines required fiber stress. Deflection—For 30 lbs. per sq. ft. live load. Limited to span in inches divided by 240. RAFTERS: Spans are measured along the horizontal projection and loads are considered as applied on the horizontal projection.

Each cell shows allowable span (ft-in) over required modulus of elasticity E (in 1,000,000 psi).

RAFTER SIZE (IN)	SPACING (IN)	Allowable Extreme Fiber Stress in Bending F_b (psi)														
		500	600	700	800	900	1000	1100	1200	1300	1400	1500	1600	1700	1800	1900
2x6	12.0	7-6 / 0.27	8-2 / 0.36	8-10 / 0.45	9-6 / 0.55	10-0 / 0.66	10-7 / 0.77	11-1 / 0.89	11-7 / 1.01	12-1 / 1.14	12-6 / 1.28	13-0 / 1.41	13-5 / 1.56	13-10 / 1.71	14-2 / 1.86	14-7 / 2.02
2x6	16.0	6-6 / 0.24	7-1 / 0.31	7-8 / 0.39	8-2 / 0.48	8-8 / 0.57	9-2 / 0.67	9-7 / 0.77	10-0 / 0.88	10-5 / 0.99	10-10 / 1.10	11-3 / 1.22	11-7 / 1.35	11-11 / 1.48	12-4 / 1.61	12-8 / 1.75
2x6	24.0	5-4 / 0.19	5-10 / 0.25	6-3 / 0.32	6-8 / 0.39	7-1 / 0.46	7-6 / 0.54	7-10 / 0.63	8-2 / 0.72	8-6 / 0.81	8-10 / 0.90	9-2 / 1.00	9-6 / 1.10	9-9 / 1.21	10-0 / 1.31	10-4 / 1.43
2x8	12.0	9-10 / 0.27	10-10 / 0.36	11-8 / 0.45	12-6 / 0.55	13-3 / 0.66	13-11 / 0.77	14-8 / 0.89	15-3 / 1.01	15-11 / 1.14	16-6 / 1.28	17-1 / 1.41	17-8 / 1.56	18-2 / 1.71	18-9 / 1.86	19-3 / 2.02
2x8	16.0	8-7 / 0.24	9-4 / 0.31	10-1 / 0.39	10-10 / 0.48	11-6 / 0.57	12-1 / 0.67	12-8 / 0.77	13-3 / 0.88	13-9 / 0.99	14-4 / 1.10	14-10 / 1.22	15-3 / 1.35	15-9 / 1.48	16-3 / 1.61	16-8 / 1.75
2x8	24.0	7-0 / 0.19	7-8 / 0.25	8-3 / 0.32	8-10 / 0.39	9-4 / 0.46	9-10 / 0.54	10-4 / 0.63	10-10 / 0.72	11-3 / 0.81	11-8 / 0.90	12-1 / 1.00	12-6 / 1.10	12-10 / 1.21	13-3 / 1.31	13-7 / 1.43
2x10	12.0	12-7 / 0.27	13-9 / 0.36	14-11 / 0.45	15-11 / 0.55	16-11 / 0.66	17-10 / 0.77	18-8 / 0.89	19-6 / 1.01	20-4 / 1.14	21-1 / 1.28	21-10 / 1.41	22-6 / 1.56	23-3 / 1.71	23-11 / 1.86	24-6 / 2.02
2x10	16.0	10-11 / 0.24	11-11 / 0.31	12-11 / 0.39	13-9 / 0.48	14-8 / 0.57	15-5 / 0.67	16-2 / 0.77	16-11 / 0.88	17-7 / 0.99	18-3 / 1.10	18-11 / 1.22	19-6 / 1.35	20-1 / 1.48	20-8 / 1.61	21-3 / 1.75
2x10	24.0	8-11 / 0.19	9-9 / 0.25	10-6 / 0.32	11-3 / 0.39	11-11 / 0.46	12-7 / 0.54	13-2 / 0.63	13-9 / 0.72	14-4 / 0.81	14-11 / 0.90	15-5 / 1.00	15-11 / 1.10	16-5 / 1.21	16-11 / 1.31	17-4 / 1.43
2x12	12.0	15-4 / 0.27	16-9 / 0.36	18-1 / 0.45	19-4 / 0.55	20-6 / 0.66	21-8 / 0.77	22-8 / 0.89	23-9 / 1.01	24-8 / 1.14	25-7 / 1.28	26-6 / 1.41	27-5 / 1.56	28-3 / 1.71	29-1 / 1.86	29-10 / 2.02
2x12	16.0	13-3 / 0.24	14-6 / 0.31	15-8 / 0.39	16-9 / 0.48	17-9 / 0.57	18-9 / 0.67	19-8 / 0.77	20-6 / 0.88	21-5 / 0.99	22-2 / 1.10	23-0 / 1.22	23-9 / 1.35	24-5 / 1.48	25-2 / 1.61	25-10 / 1.75
2x12	24.0	10-10 / 0.19	11-10 / 0.25	12-10 / 0.32	13-8 / 0.39	14-6 / 0.46	15-4 / 0.54	16-1 / 0.63	16-9 / 0.72	17-5 / 0.81	18-1 / 0.90	18-9 / 1.00	19-4 / 1.10	20-0 / 1.21	20-6 / 1.31	21-1 / 1.43

NOTES: (1) The required modulus of elasticity (E) in 1,000,000 pounds per square inch is shown below each span.

(2) Use single or repetitive member bending stress values (F_b) and modulus of elasticity values (E) from Tables Nos. 25-A-1 and 25-A-2. For duration of load stress increases, see Section 2504 (c) 4.

(3) For more comprehensive tables covering a broader range of bending stress values (F_b) and modulus of elasticity values (E), other spacing of members and other conditions of loading, see U.B.C. Standard No. 25-21.

(4) The spans in these tables are intended for use in covered structures or where moisture content in use does not exceed 19 percent.

From the Uniform Building Code, © 1988, ICBO

Allowable Spans for Low - or High Slope Rafters

TABLE NO. 25-U-R-7—ALLOWABLE SPANS FOR LOW-SLOPE RAFTERS, SLOPE 3 IN 12 OR LESS
20 LBS. PER SQ. FT. LIVE LOAD (No Ceiling Load)

DESIGN CRITERIA: Strength—10 lbs. per sq. ft. dead load plus 20 lbs. per sq. ft. live load determines required fiber stress. **Deflection**—For 20 lbs. per sq. ft. live load. Limited to span in inches divided by 240. **RAFTERS:** Spans are measured along the horizontal projection and loads are considered as applied on the horizontal projection.

Allowable Extreme Fiber Stress in Bending F_b (psi).

RAFTER SIZE (IN)	SPACING (IN)	500	600	700	800	900	1000	1100	1200	1300	1400	1500	1600	1700	1800	1900
2x6	12.0	9-2 / 0.33	10-0 / 0.44	10-10 / 0.55	11-7 / 0.67	12-4 / 0.80	13-0 / 0.94	13-7 / 1.09	14-2 / 1.24	14-9 / 1.40	15-4 / 1.56	15-11 / 1.73	16-5 / 1.91	16-11 / 2.09	17-5 / 2.28	17-10 / 2.47
	16.0	7-11 / 0.29	8-8 / 0.38	9-5 / 0.48	10-0 / 0.58	10-8 / 0.70	11-3 / 0.82	11-9 / 0.94	12-4 / 1.07	12-10 / 1.21	13-3 / 1.35	13-9 / 1.50	14-2 / 1.65	14-8 / 1.81	15-1 / 1.97	15-6 / 2.14
	24.0	6-6 / 0.24	7-1 / 0.31	7-8 / 0.39	8-2 / 0.48	8-8 / 0.57	9-2 / 0.67	9-7 / 0.77	10-0 / 0.88	10-5 / 0.99	10-10 / 1.10	11-3 / 1.22	11-7 / 1.35	11-11 / 1.48	12-4 / 1.61	12-8 / 1.75
2x8	12.0	12-1 / 0.33	13-3 / 0.44	14-4 / 0.55	15-3 / 0.67	16-3 / 0.80	17-1 / 0.94	17-11 / 1.09	18-9 / 1.24	19-6 / 1.40	20-3 / 1.56	20-11 / 1.73	21-7 / 1.91	22-3 / 2.09	22-11 / 2.28	23-7 / 2.47
	16.0	10-6 / 0.29	11-6 / 0.38	12-5 / 0.48	13-3 / 0.58	14-0 / 0.70	14-10 / 0.82	15-6 / 0.94	16-3 / 1.07	16-10 / 1.21	17-6 / 1.35	18-2 / 1.50	18-9 / 1.65	19-4 / 1.81	19-10 / 1.97	20-5 / 2.14
	24.0	8-7 / 0.24	9-4 / 0.31	10-1 / 0.39	10-10 / 0.48	11-6 / 0.57	12-1 / 0.67	12-8 / 0.77	13-3 / 0.88	13-9 / 0.99	14-4 / 1.10	14-10 / 1.22	15-3 / 1.35	15-9 / 1.48	16-3 / 1.61	16-8 / 1.75
2x10	12.0	15-5 / 0.33	16-11 / 0.44	18-3 / 0.55	19-6 / 0.67	20-8 / 0.80	21-10 / 0.94	22-10 / 1.09	23-11 / 1.24	24-10 / 1.40	25-10 / 1.56	26-8 / 1.73	27-7 / 1.91	28-5 / 2.09	29-3 / 2.28	30-1 / 2.47
	16.0	13-4 / 0.29	14-8 / 0.38	15-10 / 0.48	16-11 / 0.58	17-11 / 0.70	18-11 / 0.82	19-10 / 0.94	20-8 / 1.07	21-6 / 1.21	22-4 / 1.35	23-2 / 1.50	23-11 / 1.65	24-7 / 1.81	25-4 / 1.97	26-0 / 2.14
	24.0	10-11 / 0.24	11-11 / 0.31	12-11 / 0.39	13-9 / 0.48	14-8 / 0.57	15-5 / 0.67	16-2 / 0.77	16-11 / 0.88	17-7 / 0.99	18-3 / 1.10	18-11 / 1.22	19-6 / 1.35	20-1 / 1.48	20-8 / 1.61	21-3 / 1.75
2x12	12.0	18-9 / 0.33	20-6 / 0.44	22-2 / 0.55	23-9 / 0.67	25-2 / 0.80	26-6 / 0.94	27-10 / 1.09	29-1 / 1.24	30-3 / 1.40	31-4 / 1.56	32-6 / 1.73	33-6 / 1.91	34-7 / 2.09	35-7 / 2.28	36-7 / 2.47
	16.0	16-3 / 0.29	17-9 / 0.38	19-3 / 0.48	20-6 / 0.58	21-9 / 0.70	23-0 / 0.82	24-1 / 0.94	25-2 / 1.07	26-2 / 1.21	27-2 / 1.35	28-2 / 1.50	29-1 / 1.65	29-11 / 1.81	30-10 / 1.97	31-8 / 2.14
	24.0	13-3 / 0.24	14-6 / 0.31	15-8 / 0.39	16-9 / 0.48	17-9 / 0.57	18-9 / 0.67	19-8 / 0.77	20-6 / 0.88	21-5 / 0.99	22-2 / 1.10	23-0 / 1.22	23-9 / 1.35	24-5 / 1.48	25-2 / 1.61	25-10 / 1.75

NOTES: (1)The required modulus of elasticity (E) in 1,000,000 pounds per square inch is shown below each span.
(2)Use single or repetitive member bending stress values (F_b) and modulus of elasticity values (E) from Tables Nos. 25-A-1 and 25-A-2. For duration of load stress increases, see Section 2504 (c) 4.
(3)For more comprehensive tables covering a broader range of bending stress values (F_b) and modulus of elasticity values (E), other spacing of members and other conditions of loading, see U.B.C. Standard No. 25-21.
(4)The spans in these tables are intended for use in covered structures or where moisture content in use does not exceed 19 percent.

From the Uniform Building Code, © 1988, ICBO
Allowable Spans for Low Slope Rafters

TABLE NO. 25-U-R-8—ALLOWABLE SPANS FOR LOW-SLOPE, RAFTERS SLOPE 3 IN 12 OR LESS 30 LBS. PER SQ. FT. LIVE LOAD (No Ceiling Load)

DESIGN CRITERIA: Strength—10 lbs. per sq. ft. dead load plus 30 lbs. per sq. ft. live load determines required fiber stress. **Deflection**—For 30 lbs. per sq. ft. live load. Limited to span in inches divided by 240. RAFTERS: Spans are measured along the horizontal projection and loads are considered as applied on the horizontal projection.

Allowable Extreme Fiber Stress in Bending F_b (psi).

RAFTER SIZE (IN)	SPACING (IN)	500	600	700	800	900	1000	1100	1200	1300	1400	1500	1600	1700	1800	1900
2x6	12.0	7-11 / 0.32	8-8 / 0.43	9-5 / 0.54	10-0 / 0.66	10-8 / 0.78	11-3 / 0.92	11-9 / 1.06	12-4 / 1.21	12-10 / 1.36	13-3 / 1.52	13-9 / 1.69	14-2 / 1.86	14-8 / 2.04	15-1 / 2.22	15-6 / 2.41
2x6	16.0	6-11 / 0.28	7-6 / 0.37	8-2 / 0.47	8-8 / 0.57	9-3 / 0.68	9-9 / 0.80	10-2 / 0.92	10-8 / 1.05	11-1 / 1.18	11-6 / 1.32	11-11 / 1.46	12-4 / 1.61	12-8 / 1.76	13-1 / 1.92	13-5 / 2.08
2x6	24.0	5-7 / 0.23	6-2 / 0.30	6-8 / 0.38	7-1 / 0.46	7-6 / 0.55	7-11 / 0.65	8-4 / 0.75	8-8 / 0.85	9-1 / 0.96	9-5 / 1.08	9-9 / 1.19	10-0 / 1.31	10-4 / 1.44	10-8 / 1.57	10-11 / 1.70
2x8	12.0	10-6 / 0.32	11-6 / 0.43	12-5 / 0.54	13-3 / 0.66	14-0 / 0.78	14-10 / 0.92	15-6 / 1.06	16-3 / 1.21	16-10 / 1.36	17-6 / 1.52	18-2 / 1.69	18-9 / 1.86	19-4 / 2.04	19-10 / 2.22	20-5 / 2.41
2x8	16.0	9-1 / 0.28	9-11 / 0.37	10-9 / 0.47	11-6 / 0.57	12-2 / 0.68	12-10 / 0.80	13-5 / 0.92	14-0 / 1.05	14-7 / 1.18	15-2 / 1.32	15-8 / 1.46	16-3 / 1.61	16-9 / 1.76	17-2 / 1.92	17-8 / 2.08
2x8	24.0	7-5 / 0.23	8-1 / 0.30	8-9 / 0.38	9-4 / 0.46	9-11 / 0.55	10-6 / 0.65	11-0 / 0.75	11-6 / 0.85	11-11 / 0.96	12-5 / 1.08	12-10 / 1.19	13-3 / 1.31	13-8 / 1.44	14-0 / 1.57	14-5 / 1.70
2x10	12.0	13-4 / 0.32	14-8 / 0.43	15-10 / 0.54	16-11 / 0.66	17-11 / 0.78	18-11 / 0.92	19-10 / 1.06	20-8 / 1.21	21-6 / 1.36	22-4 / 1.52	23-2 / 1.69	23-11 / 1.86	24-7 / 2.04	25-4 / 2.22	26-0 / 2.41
2x10	16.0	11-7 / 0.28	12-8 / 0.37	13-8 / 0.47	14-8 / 0.57	15-6 / 0.68	16-4 / 0.80	17-2 / 0.92	17-11 / 1.05	18-8 / 1.18	19-4 / 1.32	20-0 / 1.46	20-8 / 1.61	21-4 / 1.76	21-11 / 1.92	22-6 / 2.08
2x10	24.0	9-5 / 0.23	10-4 / 0.30	11-2 / 0.38	11-11 / 0.46	12-8 / 0.55	13-4 / 0.65	14-0 / 0.75	14-8 / 0.85	15-3 / 0.96	15-10 / 1.08	16-4 / 1.19	16-11 / 1.31	17-5 / 1.44	17-11 / 1.57	18-5 / 1.70
2x12	12.0	16-3 / 0.32	17-9 / 0.43	19-3 / 0.54	20-6 / 0.66	21-9 / 0.78	23-0 / 0.92	24-1 / 1.06	25-2 / 1.21	26-2 / 1.36	27-2 / 1.52	28-2 / 1.69	29-1 / 1.86	29-11 / 2.04	30-10 / 2.22	31-8 / 2.41
2x12	16.0	14-1 / 0.28	15-5 / 0.37	16-8 / 0.47	17-9 / 0.57	18-10 / 0.68	19-11 / 0.80	20-10 / 0.92	21-9 / 1.05	22-8 / 1.18	23-6 / 1.32	24-4 / 1.46	25-2 / 1.61	25-11 / 1.76	26-8 / 1.92	27-5 / 2.08
2x12	24.0	11-6 / 0.23	12-7 / 0.30	13-7 / 0.38	14-6 / 0.46	15-5 / 0.55	16-3 / 0.65	17-0 / 0.75	17-9 / 0.85	18-6 / 0.96	19-3 / 1.08	19-11 / 1.19	20-6 / 1.31	21-2 / 1.44	21-9 / 1.57	22-5 / 1.70

NOTES: (1)The required modulus of elasticity (E) in 1,000,000 pounds per square inch is shown below each span.

(2)Use single or repetitive member bending stress values (F_b) and modulus of elasticity values (E) from Tables Nos. 25-A-1 and 25-A-2. For duration of load stress increases, see Section 2504 (c) 4.

(3)For more comprehensive tables covering a broader range of bending stress values (F_b) and modulus of elasticity values (E), other spacing of members and other conditions of loading, see U.B.C. Standard No. 25-21.

(4)The spans in these tables are intended for use in covered structures or where moisture content in use does not exceed 19 percent.

From the Uniform Building Code, © 1988, ICBO

Allowable Spans for Low Slope Rafters

TABLE NO. 25-U-R-10—ALLOWABLE SPANS FOR HIGH-SLOPE RAFTERS, SLOPE OVER 3 IN 12
20 LBS. PER SQ. FT. LIVE LOAD (Heavy Roof Covering)

DESIGN CRITERIA: Strength—15 lbs. per sq. ft. dead load plus 20 lbs. per sq. ft. live load determines required fiber stress. **Deflection**—For 20 lbs. per sq. ft. live load. Limited to span in inches divided by 180. RAFTERS: Spans are measured along the horizontal projection and loads are considered as applied on the horizontal projection.

RAFTER SIZE (IN)	SPACING (IN)	Allowable Extreme Fiber Stress in Bending F_b (psi).														
		500	600	700	800	900	1000	1100	1200	1300	1400	1500	1600	1700	1800	1900
2x4	12.0	5-5 / 0.20	5-11 / 0.26	6-5 / 0.33	6-10 / 0.40	7-3 / 0.48	7-8 / 0.56	8-0 / 0.65	8-4 / 0.74	8-8 / 0.83	9-0 / 0.93	9-4 / 1.03	9-8 / 1.14	9-11 / 1.24	10-3 / 1.36	10-6 / 1.47
	16.0	4-8 / 0.17	5-1 / 0.23	5-6 / 0.28	5-11 / 0.35	6-3 / 0.41	6-7 / 0.49	6-11 / 0.56	7-3 / 0.64	7-6 / 0.72	7-10 / 0.80	8-1 / 0.89	8-4 / 0.98	8-7 / 1.08	8-10 / 1.17	9-1 / 1.27
	24.0	3-10 / 0.14	4-2 / 0.18	4-6 / 0.23	4-10 / 0.28	5-1 / 0.34	5-5 / 0.40	5-8 / 0.46	5-11 / 0.52	6-2 / 0.59	6-5 / 0.66	6-7 / 0.73	6-10 / 0.80	7-0 / 0.88	7-3 / 0.96	7-5 / 1.04
2x6	12.0	8-6 / 0.20	9-4 / 0.26	10-0 / 0.33	10-9 / 0.40	11-5 / 0.48	12-0 / 0.56	12-7 / 0.65	13-2 / 0.74	13-8 / 0.83	14-2 / 0.93	14-8 / 1.03	15-2 / 1.14	15-8 / 1.24	16-1 / 1.36	16-7 / 1.47
	16.0	7-4 / 0.17	8-1 / 0.23	8-8 / 0.28	9-4 / 0.35	9-10 / 0.41	10-5 / 0.49	10-11 / 0.56	11-5 / 0.64	11-10 / 0.72	12-4 / 0.80	12-9 / 0.89	13-2 / 0.98	13-7 / 1.08	13-11 / 1.17	14-4 / 1.27
	24.0	6-0 / 0.14	6-7 / 0.18	7-1 / 0.23	7-7 / 0.28	8-1 / 0.34	8-6 / 0.40	8-11 / 0.46	9-4 / 0.52	9-8 / 0.59	10-0 / 0.66	10-5 / 0.73	10-9 / 0.80	11-1 / 0.88	11-5 / 0.96	11-8 / 1.04
2x8	12.0	11-2 / 0.20	12-3 / 0.26	13-3 / 0.33	14-2 / 0.40	15-0 / 0.48	15-10 / 0.56	16-7 / 0.65	17-4 / 0.74	18-0 / 0.83	18-9 / 0.93	19-5 / 1.03	20-0 / 1.14	20-8 / 1.24	21-3 / 1.36	21-10 / 1.47
	16.0	9-8 / 0.17	10-7 / 0.23	11-6 / 0.28	12-3 / 0.35	13-0 / 0.41	13-8 / 0.49	14-4 / 0.56	15-0 / 0.64	15-7 / 0.72	16-3 / 0.80	16-9 / 0.89	17-4 / 0.98	17-10 / 1.08	18-5 / 1.17	18-11 / 1.27
	24.0	7-11 / 0.14	8-8 / 0.18	9-4 / 0.23	10-0 / 0.28	10-7 / 0.34	11-2 / 0.40	11-9 / 0.46	12-3 / 0.52	12-9 / 0.59	13-3 / 0.66	13-8 / 0.73	14-2 / 0.80	14-7 / 0.88	15-0 / 0.96	15-5 / 1.04
2x10	12.0	14-3 / 0.20	15-8 / 0.26	16-11 / 0.33	18-1 / 0.40	19-2 / 0.48	20-2 / 0.56	21-2 / 0.65	22-1 / 0.74	23-0 / 0.83	23-11 / 0.93	24-9 / 1.03	25-6 / 1.14	26-4 / 1.24	27-1 / 1.36	27-10 / 1.47
	16.0	12-4 / 0.17	13-6 / 0.23	14-8 / 0.28	15-8 / 0.35	16-7 / 0.41	17-6 / 0.49	18-4 / 0.56	19-2 / 0.64	19-11 / 0.72	20-8 / 0.80	21-5 / 0.89	22-1 / 0.98	22-10 / 1.08	23-5 / 1.17	24-1 / 1.27
	24.0	10-1 / 0.14	11-1 / 0.18	11-11 / 0.23	12-9 / 0.28	13-6 / 0.34	14-3 / 0.40	15-0 / 0.46	15-8 / 0.52	16-3 / 0.59	16-11 / 0.66	17-6 / 0.73	18-1 / 0.80	18-7 / 0.88	19-2 / 0.96	19-8 / 1.04

NOTES: (1)The required modulus of elasticity (E) in 1,000,000 pounds per square inch is shown below each span.

(2)Use single or repetitive member bending stress values (F_b) and modulus of elasticity values (E) from Tables Nos. 25-A-1 and 25-A-2. For duration of load stress increases, see Section 2504 (c) 4.

(3)For more comprehensive tables covering a broader range of bending stress values (F_b) and modulus of elasticity values (E), other spacing of members and other conditions of loading, see U.B.C. Standard No. 25-21.

(4)The spans in these tables are intended for use in covered structures or where moisture content in use does not exceed 19 percent.

From the Uniform Building Code, © 1988, ICBO

Allowable Spans for High Slope Rafters

TABLE NO. 25-U-R-11—ALLOWABLE SPANS FOR HIGH-SLOPE RAFTERS, SLOPE OVER 3 IN 12
30 LBS. PER SQ. FT. LIVE LOAD (Heavy Roof Covering)

DESIGN CRITERIA: Strength—15 lbs. per sq. ft. dead load plus 30 lbs. per sq. ft. live load determines required fiber stress. Deflection—For 30 lbs. per sq. ft. live load. Limited to span in inches divided by 180. RAFTERS: Spans are measured along the horizontal projection and loads are considered as applied on the horizontal projection.

RAFTER SIZE (IN)	SPACING (IN)	Allowable Extreme Fiber Stress in Bending F_b (psi).														
		500	600	700	800	900	1000	1100	1200	1300	1400	1500	1600	1700	1800	1900
2x4	12.0	4-9	5-3	5-8	6-0	6-5	6-9	7-1	7-5	7-8	8-0	8-3	8-6	8-9	9-0	9-3
		0.20	0.27	0.34	0.41	0.49	0.58	0.67	0.76	0.86	0.96	1.06	1.17	1.28	1.39	1.51
	16.0	4-1	4-6	4-11	5-3	5-6	5-10	6-1	6-5	6-8	6-11	7-2	7-5	7-7	7-10	8-0
		0.18	0.23	0.29	0.36	0.43	0.50	0.58	0.66	0.74	0.83	0.92	1.01	1.11	1.21	1.31
	24.0	3-4	3-8	4-0	4-3	4-6	4-9	5-0	5-3	5-5	5-8	5-10	6-0	6-3	6-5	6-7
		0.14	0.19	0.24	0.29	0.35	0.41	0.47	0.54	0.61	0.68	0.75	0.83	0.90	0.99	1.07
2x6	12.0	7-6	8-2	8-10	9-6	10-0	10-7	11-1	11-7	12-1	12-6	13-0	13-5	13-10	14-2	14-7
		0.20	0.27	0.34	0.41	0.49	0.58	0.67	0.76	0.86	0.96	1.06	1.17	1.28	1.39	1.51
	16.0	6-6	7-1	7-8	8-2	8-8	9-2	9-7	10-0	10-5	10-10	11-3	11-7	11-11	12-4	12-8
		0.18	0.23	0.29	0.36	0.43	0.50	0.58	0.66	0.74	0.83	0.92	1.01	1.11	1.21	1.31
	24.0	5-4	5-10	6-3	6-8	7-1	7-6	7-10	8-2	8-6	8-10	9-2	9-6	9-9	10-0	10-4
		0.14	0.19	0.24	0.29	0.35	0.41	0.47	0.54	0.61	0.68	0.75	0.83	0.90	0.99	1.07
2x8	12.0	9-10	10-10	11-8	12-6	13-3	13-11	14-8	15-3	15-11	16-6	17-1	17-8	18-2	18-9	19-3
		0.20	0.27	0.34	0.41	0.49	0.58	0.67	0.76	0.86	0.96	1.06	1.17	1.28	1.39	1.51
	16.0	8-7	9-4	10-1	10-10	11-6	12-1	12-8	13-3	13-9	14-4	14-10	15-3	15-9	16-3	16-8
		0.18	0.23	0.29	0.36	0.43	0.50	0.58	0.66	0.74	0.83	0.92	1.01	1.11	1.21	1.31
	24.0	7-0	7-8	8-3	8-10	9-4	9-10	10-4	10-10	11-3	11-8	12-1	12-6	12-10	13-3	13-7
		0.14	0.19	0.24	0.29	0.35	0.41	0.47	0.54	0.61	0.68	0.75	0.83	0.90	0.99	1.07
2x10	12.0	12-7	13-9	14-11	15-11	16-11	17-10	18-8	19-6	20-4	21-1	21-10	22-6	23-3	23-11	24-6
		0.20	0.27	0.34	0.41	0.49	0.58	0.67	0.76	0.86	0.96	1.06	1.17	1.28	1.39	1.51
	16.0	10-11	11-11	12-11	13-9	14-8	15-5	16-2	16-11	17-7	18-3	18-11	19-6	20-1	20-8	21-3
		0.18	0.23	0.29	0.36	0.43	0.50	0.58	0.66	0.74	0.83	0.92	1.01	1.11	1.21	1.31
	24.0	8-11	9-9	10-6	11-3	11-11	12-7	13-2	13-9	14-4	14-11	15-5	15-11	16-5	16-11	17-4
		0.14	0.19	0.24	0.29	0.35	0.41	0.47	0.54	0.61	0.68	0.75	0.83	0.90	0.99	1.07

NOTES: (1)The required modulus of elasticity (E) in 1,000,000 pounds per square inch is shown below each span.

(2)Use single or repetitive member bending stress values (F_b) and modulus of elasticity values (E) from Tables Nos. 25-A-1 and 25-A-2. For duration of load stress increases, see Section 2504 (c) 4.

(3)For more comprehensive tables covering a broader range of bending stress values (F_b) and modulus of elasticity values (E), other spacing of members and other conditions of loading, see U.B.C. Standard No. 25-21.

(4)The spans in these tables are intended for use in covered structures or where moisture content in use does not exceed 19 percent.

From the Uniform Building Code, © 1988, ICBO

TABLE NO. 25-U-R-13—ALLOWABLE SPANS FOR HIGH-SLOPE RAFTERS, SLOPE OVER 3 IN 12
20 LBS. PER SQ. FT. LIVE LOAD (Light Roof Covering)

DESIGN CRITERIA: Strength—7 lbs. per sq. ft. dead load plus 20 lbs. per sq. ft. live load determines required fiber stress. **Deflection**—For 20 lbs. per sq. ft. live load. Limited to span in inches divided by 180. **RAFTERS:** Spans are measured along the horizontal projection and loads are considered as applied on the horizontal projection.

RAFTER SIZE	SPACING (IN)	Allowable Extreme Fiber Stress in Bending F_b (psi).														
		500	600	700	800	900	1000	1100	1200	1300	1400	1500	1600	1700	1800	1900
2x4	12.0	6-2 / 0.29	6-9 / 0.38	7-3 / 0.49	7-9 / 0.59	8-3 / 0.71	8-8 / 0.83	9-1 / 0.96	9-6 / 1.09	9-11 / 1.23	10-3 / 1.37	10-8 / 1.52	11-0 / 1.68	11-4 / 1.84	11-8 / 2.00	12-0 / 2.17
	16.0	5-4 / 0.25	5-10 / 0.33	6-4 / 0.42	6-9 / 0.51	7-2 / 0.61	7-6 / 0.72	7-11 / 0.83	8-3 / 0.94	8-7 / 1.06	8-11 / 1.19	9-3 / 1.32	9-6 / 1.45	9-10 / 1.59	10-1 / 1.73	10-5 / 1.88
	24.0	4-4 / 0.21	4-9 / 0.27	5-2 / 0.34	5-6 / 0.42	5-10 / 0.50	6-2 / 0.59	6-5 / 0.68	6-9 / 0.77	7-0 / 0.87	7-3 / 0.97	7-6 / 1.08	7-9 / 1.19	8-0 / 1.30	8-3 / 1.41	8-6 / 1.53
2x6	12.0	9-8 / 0.29	10-7 / 0.38	11-5 / 0.49	12-3 / 0.59	13-0 / 0.71	13-8 / 0.83	14-4 / 0.96	15-0 / 1.09	15-7 / 1.23	16-2 / 1.37	16-9 / 1.52	17-3 / 1.68	17-10 / 1.84	18-4 / 2.00	18-10 / 2.17
	16.0	8-4 / 0.25	9-2 / 0.33	9-11 / 0.42	10-7 / 0.51	11-3 / 0.61	11-10 / 0.72	12-5 / 0.83	13-0 / 0.94	13-6 / 1.06	14-0 / 1.19	14-6 / 1.32	15-0 / 1.45	15-5 / 1.59	15-11 / 1.73	16-4 / 1.88
	24.0	6-10 / 0.21	7-6 / 0.27	8-1 / 0.34	8-8 / 0.42	9-2 / 0.50	9-8 / 0.59	10-2 / 0.68	10-7 / 0.77	11-0 / 0.87	11-5 / 0.97	11-10 / 1.08	12-3 / 1.19	12-7 / 1.30	13-0 / 1.41	13-4 / 1.53
2x8	12.0	12-9 / 0.29	13-11 / 0.38	15-1 / 0.49	16-1 / 0.59	17-1 / 0.71	18-0 / 0.83	18-11 / 0.96	19-9 / 1.09	20-6 / 1.23	21-4 / 1.37	22-1 / 1.52	22-9 / 1.68	23-6 / 1.84	24-2 / 2.00	24-10 / 2.17
	16.0	11-0 / 0.25	12-1 / 0.33	13-1 / 0.42	13-11 / 0.51	14-10 / 0.61	15-7 / 0.72	16-4 / 0.83	17-1 / 0.94	17-9 / 1.06	18-5 / 1.19	19-1 / 1.32	19-9 / 1.45	20-4 / 1.59	20-11 / 1.73	21-6 / 1.88
	24.0	9-0 / 0.21	9-10 / 0.27	10-8 / 0.34	11-5 / 0.42	12-1 / 0.50	12-9 / 0.59	13-4 / 0.68	13-11 / 0.77	14-6 / 0.87	15-1 / 0.97	15-7 / 1.08	16-1 / 1.19	16-7 / 1.30	17-1 / 1.41	17-7 / 1.53
2x10	12.0	16-3 / 0.29	17-10 / 0.38	19-3 / 0.49	20-7 / 0.59	21-10 / 0.71	23-0 / 0.83	24-1 / 0.96	25-2 / 1.09	26-2 / 1.23	27-2 / 1.37	28-2 / 1.52	29-1 / 1.68	30-0 / 1.84	30-10 / 2.00	31-8 / 2.17
	16.0	14-1 / 0.25	15-5 / 0.33	16-8 / 0.42	17-10 / 0.51	18-11 / 0.61	19-11 / 0.72	20-10 / 0.83	21-10 / 0.94	22-8 / 1.06	23-7 / 1.19	24-5 / 1.32	25-2 / 1.45	25-11 / 1.59	26-8 / 1.73	27-5 / 1.88
	24.0	11-6 / 0.21	12-7 / 0.27	13-7 / 0.34	14-6 / 0.42	15-5 / 0.50	16-3 / 0.59	17-1 / 0.68	17-10 / 0.77	18-6 / 0.87	19-3 / 0.97	19-11 / 1.08	20-7 / 1.19	21-2 / 1.30	21-10 / 1.41	22-5 / 1.53

NOTES: (1) The required modulus of elasticity (E) in 1,000,000 pounds per square inch is shown below each span.

(2) Use single or repetitive member bending stress values (F_b) and modulus of elasticity values (E) from Tables Nos. 25-A-1 and 25-A-2. For duration of load stress increases, see Section 2504 (c) 4.

(3) For more comprehensive tables covering a broader range of bending stress values (F_b) and modulus of elasticity values (E), other spacing of members and other conditions of loading, see U.B.C. Standard No. 25-21.

(4) The spans in these tables are intended for use in covered structures or where moisture content in use does not exceed 19 percent.

From the Uniform Building Code, © 1988, ICBO

Allowable Spans for High Slope Rafters

TABLE NO. 25-U-R-14—ALLOWABLE SPANS FOR HIGH-SLOPE RAFTERS, SLOPE OVER 3 IN 12
30 LBS. PER SQ. FT. LIVE LOAD (Light Roof Covering)

DESIGN CRITERIA: Strength—7 lbs. per sq. ft. dead load plus 30 lbs. per sq. ft. live load determines required fiber stress. **Deflection**—For 30 lbs. per sq. ft. live load. Limited to span in inches divided by 180. RAFTERS: Spans are measured along the horizontal projection and loads are considered as applied on the horizontal projection.

Allowable Extreme Fiber Stress in Bending F_b (psi). Each cell shows allowable span (ft-in) over required modulus of elasticity E (×1,000,000 psi).

RAFTER SIZE	SPACING (IN)	500	600	700	800	900	1000	1100	1200	1300	1400	1500	1600	1700	1800	1900
2x4	12.0	5-3 / 0.27	5-9 / 0.36	6-3 / 0.45	6-8 / 0.55	7-1 / 0.66	7-5 / 0.77	7-9 / 0.89	8-2 / 1.02	8-6 / 1.15	8-9 / 1.28	9-1 / 1.42	9-5 / 1.57	9-8 / 1.72	10-0 / 1.87	10-3 / 2.03
2x4	16.0	4-7 / 0.24	5-0 / 0.31	5-5 / 0.39	5-9 / 0.48	6-1 / 0.57	6-5 / 0.67	6-9 / 0.77	7-1 / 0.88	7-4 / 0.99	7-7 / 1.11	7-11 / 1.23	8-2 / 1.36	8-5 / 1.49	8-8 / 1.62	8-10 / 1.76
2x4	24.0	3-9 / 0.19	4-1 / 0.25	4-5 / 0.32	4-8 / 0.39	5-0 / 0.47	5-3 / 0.55	5-6 / 0.63	5-9 / 0.72	6-0 / 0.81	6-3 / 0.91	6-5 / 1.01	6-8 / 1.11	6-10 / 1.21	7-1 / 1.32	7-3 / 1.43
2x6	12.0	8-3 / 0.27	9-1 / 0.36	9-9 / 0.45	10-5 / 0.55	11-1 / 0.66	11-8 / 0.77	12-3 / 0.89	12-9 / 1.02	13-4 / 1.15	13-10 / 1.28	14-4 / 1.42	14-9 / 1.57	15-3 / 1.72	15-8 / 1.87	16-1 / 2.03
2x6	16.0	7-2 / 0.24	7-10 / 0.31	8-5 / 0.39	9-1 / 0.48	9-7 / 0.57	10-1 / 0.67	10-7 / 0.77	11-1 / 0.88	11-6 / 0.99	12-0 / 1.11	12-5 / 1.23	12-9 / 1.36	13-2 / 1.49	13-7 / 1.62	13-11 / 1.76
2x6	24.0	5-10 / 0.19	6-5 / 0.25	6-11 / 0.32	7-5 / 0.39	7-10 / 0.47	8-3 / 0.55	8-8 / 0.63	9-1 / 0.72	9-5 / 0.81	9-9 / 0.91	10-1 / 1.01	10-5 / 1.11	10-9 / 1.21	11-1 / 1.32	11-5 / 1.43
2x8	12.0	10-11 / 0.27	11-11 / 0.36	12-10 / 0.45	13-9 / 0.55	14-7 / 0.66	15-5 / 0.77	16-2 / 0.89	16-10 / 1.02	17-7 / 1.15	18-2 / 1.28	18-10 / 1.42	19-6 / 1.57	20-1 / 1.72	20-8 / 1.87	21-3 / 2.03
2x8	16.0	9-5 / 0.24	10-4 / 0.31	11-2 / 0.39	11-11 / 0.48	12-8 / 0.57	13-4 / 0.67	14-0 / 0.77	14-7 / 0.88	15-2 / 0.99	15-9 / 1.11	16-4 / 1.23	16-10 / 1.36	17-4 / 1.49	17-11 / 1.62	18-4 / 1.76
2x8	24.0	7-8 / 0.19	8-5 / 0.25	9-1 / 0.32	9-9 / 0.39	10-4 / 0.47	10-11 / 0.55	11-5 / 0.63	11-11 / 0.72	12-5 / 0.81	12-10 / 0.91	13-4 / 1.01	13-9 / 1.11	14-2 / 1.21	14-7 / 1.32	15-0 / 1.43
2x10	12.0	13-11 / 0.27	15-2 / 0.36	16-5 / 0.45	17-7 / 0.55	18-7 / 0.66	19-8 / 0.77	20-7 / 0.89	21-6 / 1.02	22-5 / 1.15	23-3 / 1.28	24-1 / 1.42	24-10 / 1.57	25-7 / 1.72	26-4 / 1.87	27-1 / 2.03
2x10	16.0	12-0 / 0.26	13-2 / 0.34	14-3 / 0.43	15-2 / 0.53	16-2 / 0.63	17-0 / 0.74	17-10 / 0.85	18-7 / 0.97	19-5 / 1.09	20-1 / 1.22	20-10 / 1.35	21-6 / 1.49	22-2 / 1.63	22-10 / 1.78	23-5 / 1.93
2x10	24.0	9-10 / 0.19	10-9 / 0.25	11-7 / 0.32	12-5 / 0.39	13-2 / 0.47	13-11 / 0.55	14-7 / 0.63	15-2 / 0.72	15-10 / 0.81	16-5 / 0.91	17-0 / 1.01	17-7 / 1.11	18-1 / 1.21	18-7 / 1.32	19-2 / 1.43

NOTES: (1) The required modulus of elasticity (E) in 1,000,000 pounds per square inch is shown below each span.
(2) Use single or repetitive member bending stress values (F_b) and modulus of elasticity values (E) from Tables Nos. 25-A-1 and 25-A-2. For duration of load stress increases, see Section 2504 (c) 4.
(3) For more comprehensive tables covering a broader range of bending stress values (F_b) and modulus of elasticity values (E), other spacing of members and other conditions of loading, see U.B.C. Standard No. 25-21.
(4) The spans in these tables are intended for use in covered structures or where moisture content in use does not exceed 19 percent.

From the Uniform Building Code, © 1988, ICBO

Allowable Spans for High Slope Rafters

TABLE NO. 25-V—WALL BRACING

SEISMIC ZONE	CONDITION	TYPE OF BRACE[1]								AMOUNT OF BRACING
		A	B	C	D	E	F	G	H	
0, 1 and 2	One Story Top of Two or Three Story	X	X	X	X	X	X	X	X	Each end and each 25' of wall.
	First Story of Two Story or Second Story of Three Story	X	X	X	X	X	X	X	X	
	First Story of Three Story		X	X	X	X[3]	X	X	X	
3 and 4	One Story Top of Two or Three Story	X	X	X	X	X	X	X	X	Each end and each 25' of wall.
	First Story of Two Story or Second Story of Three Story		X	X	X	X[3]	X	X	X	Each end. 25% of wall length to be sheathed.
	First Story of Three Story		X	X	X	X[3]	X	X	X	Each end. 40% of wall length to be sheathed.

[1]See Section 2517 (g) 3 for full description.

[2]Bracing at ends shall be near thereto as possible. Braces shall be installed so that there is no unbraced section along the wall exceeding 25 feet.

[3]Gypsum wallboard applied to supports at 16 inches on center.

From the Uniform Building Code, © 1988, ICBO

Wall Bracing

Index

Practical References For Builders

National Construction Estimator

Current building costs in dollars and cents for residential, commercial and industrial construction. Prices for every commonly used building material, and the proper labor cost associated with installation of the material. Everything figured out to give you the "in place" cost in seconds. Many time-saving rules of thumb, waste and coverage factors and estimating tables are included. **544 pages, 8-1/2 x 11, $19.50. Revised annually**

Rough Carpentry

All rough carpentry is covered in detail: sills, girders, columns, joists, sheathing, ceiling, roof and wall framing, roof trusses, dormers, bay windows, furring and grounds, stairs and insulation. Many of the 24 chapters explain practical code approved methods for saving lumber and time without sacrificing quality. Chapters on columns, headers, rafters, joists and girders show how to use simple engineering principles to select the right lumber dimension for whatever species and grade you are using. **288 page, 8-1/2 x 11, $17.00**

Builder's Guide to Accounting Revised

Step-by-step, easy to follow guidelines for setting up and maintaining an efficient record keeping system for your building business. Not a book of theory, this practical, newly-revised guide to all accounting methods shows how to meet state and federal accounting requirements, including new depreciation rules, and explains what the tax reform act of 1986 can mean to your business. Full of charts, diagrams, blank forms, simple directions and examples. **304 pages, 8-1/2 x 11, $20.00**

Planning Drain, Waste, and Vent Systems

Anyone who has designed plumbing systems knows from experience how important it is to follow the code exactly. Even a small oversight can keep a plan from being approved and cause expensive delays. Unfortunately, the plumbing code isn't easy to understand, so it's easy to make mistakes. In this new book. Howard Massey, a recognized expert on the plumbing codes and author of several plumbing manuals, shows you how to design drainage, waste and vent systems so you never lose time and money by having your plans rejected by the examiner or engineer. **192 pages, 8-1/2 x 11, $19.25**

Video: Stair Framing

Shows how to use a calculator to figure the rise and run of each step, the height of each riser, the number of treads, and the tread depths. Then watch how to take these measurements to construct an actual set of stairs. You'll see how to mark and cut your carriages, treads, and risers, and install a stairway that fits your calculations for the perfect set of stairs. **60 minutes, VHS, $24.75**

Blueprint Reading for the Building Trades

How to read and understand construction documents, blueprints, and schedules. Includes layouts of structural, mechanical and electrical drawings, how to interpret sectional views, how to follow diagrams; plumbing, HVAC and schematics, and common problems experienced interpreting construction specifications. This book is your course for understanding and following construction documents. **192 pages, 5-1/2 x 8-1/2, $11.25**

Wood-Frame House Construction

From the layout of the outer walls, excavation and formwork, to finish carpentry and painting, every step of construction is covered in detail, with clear illustrations and explanations. Everything the builder needs to know about framing, roofing, siding, insulation and vapor barrier, interior finishing, floor coverings, and stairs — complete step by step "how to" information on what goes into building a frame house. **240 pages, 8-1/2 x 11, $14.25. Revised edition**

Estimating Painting Costs

Here is an accurate step-by-step estimating system, based on a set of easy-to-use manhour tables that anyone can use for estimating painting costs: from simple residential repaints to complicated commercial jobs — even heavy industrial and government work. Explains taking field measurements, doing take-offs from plans and specs, predicting productivity, figuring labor, material costs, overhead and profit. Includes manhour and material tables, plus samples, forms, and checklists for your use. **448 pages, 8-1/2 x 11, $28.00**

Painter's Handbook

Loaded with "how-to" information you'll use every day to get professional results on any job: the best way to prepare a surface for painting or repainting; selecting and using the right materials and tools (including airless spray); tips for repainting kitchens, bathrooms, cabinets, eaves and porches; how to match and blend colors; why coatings fail and what to do about it. Thirty profitable specialties that could be your gravy train in the painting business. Every professional painter needs this practical handbook. **320 pages, 8-1/2 x 11, $21.25**

Roof Framing

Frame any type of roof in common use today, even if you've never framed a roof before. Shows how to use a pocket calculator to figure any common, hip, valley, and jack rafter length in seconds. Over 400 illustrations take you through every measurement and every cut on each type of roof: gable, hip, Dutch, Tudor, gambrel, shed, gazebo and more. **480 pages, 5-1/2 x 8-1/2, $22.00**

Stair Builders Handbook

If you know the floor to floor rise, this handbook will give you everything else: the number and dimension of treads and risers, the total run, the correct well hole opening, the angle of incline, the quantity of materials and settings for your framing square for over 3,500 code approved rise and run combination — several for every 1/8 inch interval from a 3 foot to a 12 foot floor to floor rise. **416 pages. 5-1/2 x 8-1/2, $15.50**

Audio: Estimating Remodeling

Listen to the "hands-on" estimating instruction in this popular remodeling seminar. Make your own unit price estimate based on the prints enclosed. Then check your completed estimate with those prepared in the actual seminar. After listening to these tapes you will know how to establish an operating budget for your business, determine indirect costs and profit, and estimate remodeling with the unit cost method. **Includes seminar workbook, project survey and unit price estimating form, and six 20-minute cassettes, $65.00**

Plumbers Handbook Revised

This new edition shows what will and what will not pass inspection in drainage, vent, and waste piping, septic tanks, water supply, fire protection, and gas piping systems. All tables, standards, and specifications are completely up-to-date with recent changes in the plumbing code. Covers common layouts for residential work, how to size piping, selecting and hanging fixtures, practical recommendations and trade tips. This book is the approved reference for the plumbing contractors exam in many states. **240 pages, 8-1/2 x 11, $18.00**

Fences & Retaining Walls

Everything you need to know to run a profitable business in fence and retaining wall contracting. Takes you through layout and design, construction techniques for wood, masonry and chain link fences, gates and entries, including finishing and electrical details. How to build retaining walls and rock walls. Also includes chapters on how to get your business off to the right start, keep the books, stay within the law and estimate accurately. If your state requires a contractor's exam, you'll appreciate the chapter on contractor's math. **400 pages, 8-1/2 x 11, $23.25**

Easy-To-Use 10 Day Examination Cards

Craftsman Mail This No Risk Card Today

☐ Please send me the books checked for 10 days free examination. At the end of that time I will pay in full plus postage (& 6% tax in Calif.) or return the books postpaid and owe nothing.

☐ Enclosed is my full payment or Visa/MasterCard/American Express number. Please rush me the books without charging for postage.

☐ 11.25 Blueprint Reading for Building Trades
☐ 20.00 Builder's Guide to Accounting Revised
☐ 23.25 Fences and Retaining Walls
☐ 19.50 National Construction Estimator
☐ 19.25 Planning Drain, Waste and Vent Systems
☐ 18.00 Plumber's Handbook Revised
☐ 17.00 Rough Carpentry
☐ 24.75 Video: Stair Framing
☐ 24.25 Contractor's Guide to the Building Code Rev.
☐ Free Construction Book Catalog

In a hurry?
We accept phone orders charged
to your MasterCard, Visa or
American Express.
Call 1-800-829-8123

Name (Please print clearly)

Company

Address

City   **State**   **Zip**

☐ Visa ☐ MasterCard
☐ American Express

Expiration date _____

Card # _____
                                    cod card

Craftsman Mail This No Risk Card Today

☐ Please send me the books checked for 10 days free examination. At the end of that time I will pay in full plus postage (& 6% tax in Calif.) or return the books postpaid and owe nothing.

☐ Enclosed is my full payment or Visa/MasterCard/American Express number. Please rush me the books without charging for postage.

☐ 11.25 Blueprint Reading for Building Trades
☐ 20.00 Builder's Guide to Accounting Revised
☐ 23.25 Fences and Retaining Walls
☐ 19.50 National Construction Estimator
☐ 19.25 Planning Drain, Waste and Vent Systems
☐ 18.00 Plumber's Handbook Revised
☐ 17.00 Rough Carpentry
☐ 24.75 Video: Stair Framing
☐ 24.25 Contractor's Guide to the Building Code Rev.
☐ Free Construction Book Catalog

In a hurry?
We accept phone orders charged
to your MasterCard, Visa or
American Express.
Call 1-800-829-8123

Name (Please print clearly)

Company

Address

City   **State**   **Zip**

☐ Visa ☐ MasterCard
☐ American Express

Expiration date _____

Card # _____
                                    cod card

BUSINESS REPLY MAIL

FIRST CLASS MAIL   PERMIT NO.271   CARLSBAD, CA

POSTAGE WILL BE PAID BY ADDRESSEE

Craftsman Book Company
6058 Corte Del Cedro
P. O. Box 6500
Carlsbad, CA 92008—0992

ΙΙ.Ι....Ι.ΙΙΙ...ΙΙ...Ι.Ι.Ι.Ι.Ι.Ι.Ι..Ι.Ι.Ι.;Ι.ΙΙ

BUSINESS REPLY MAIL

FIRST CLASS MAIL   PERMIT NO.271   CARLSBAD, CA

POSTAGE WILL BE PAID BY ADDRESSEE

Craftsman Book Company
6058 Corte Del Cedro
P. O. Box 6500
Carlsbad, CA 92008—0992

ΙΙ.Ι....Ι.ΙΙΙ...ΙΙ...Ι.Ι.Ι.Ι.Ι.Ι.Ι..Ι.Ι.Ι.Ι.ΙΙ